Social Services

Ma

The N
has b
espec
but ca
be us
an aic
Howe
the re
step b
clearl
throu
has b
exper
takin
mode
to en
effect
acqui

on, N.21 Cat. No. 1207   DG 02242/71

Social Services

Made Simple

Tony Byrne, BA, BSc(Econ)
and Colin F. Padfield, LLB, DPA(Lond)

Fourth edition

MADE SIMPLE
BOOKS

361
BYR

Made Simple Books
An imprint of Heinemann Professional Publishing Ltd
Halley Court, Jordan Hill, Oxford OX2 8EJ

OXFORD LONDON MELBOURNE AUCKLAND SINGAPORE
IBADAN NAIROBI GABORONE KINGSTON

First published 1978
Second edition 1983
Third edition 1985
Reprinted 1985
Reprinted 1987
Fourth edition 1990

© A. Byrne and Mrs G. Padfield 1978, 1983, 1985, 1990

British Library Cataloguing in Publication Data
Byrne, A. (Anthony)
    Social services: made simple. – 4th ed. – (Made simple books).
    1.   Great Britain. Social services
    I. Title   II. Padfield, Colin F. (Colin Frank)   III. series
    361'.941

ISBN 0 434 90076 1

Typeset by Key Graphics, Aldermaston, Berks
Printed in Great Britain by Richard Clay Ltd, Bungay, Suffolk

(12 . 9 . 96)

Contents

Preface to the second edition

This book provides an introduction to the social services in Britain. It will be of particular interest to students preparing for examinations such as those approved by the Business and Technician Education Council (BTEC), the Institute of Chartered Secretaries and Administrators (ICSA), the Institute of Health Service Management, the Institute of Housing and similar professional and examining bodies.

Many universities and polytechnics have Departments of Social Administration or Departments of Social Work, and most run courses where a knowledge of the social services is essential (such as the Diploma in Social Studies or in Social Administration). Many universities and polytechnics run courses for the Certificate of Qualification in Social Work (CQSW), the Certificate in Social Services (CSS) and the In-service Certificate in Social Care (ICSC). This book will provide much useful information for such trainee social workers.

The impact of the Welfare State today is such that some knowledge of social policy is now an established part of courses in politics, economics, sociology, law and home economics, as well as the more obvious professional and pre-professional social work training courses. Thus, many schools and colleges will find that this book covers sections of the GCSE syllabus for Welfare and Society, Public and Social Administration, Sociology, Government and Politics, and Home Economics. Colleges running courses in Home and Family Care, Social Care and Residential Care courses will also find the book useful. But the book should be of equal interest and use to the ordinary citizen who may have need of the social services at any time and who is financing these services through taxation. A brief outline of the legal and governmental systems is included for those with only a rudimentary knowledge of these institutions and processes.

Since this book was first written, in 1977, there have been many important changes in social policy. This has been due to a general tightening of economic resources and to a change of government in 1979 when Margaret Thatcher's Conservative government replaced that of Labour. The new government has adopted a 'monetarist' approach to economic policy which aims to reduce the scale of public

(State) spending. But the Conservatives also have a preference for greater individual private and voluntary group effort in society at large. Consequently, State social services have been squeezed in relation to needs or cut from earlier growth targets.

However, it has by no means all been 'doom and gloom', and many people applaud developments which have occurred in the fields of housing, education, training, planning or the treatment of offenders. These changes are detailed in the chapters which follow, and consequently, the book has been substantially revised and re-written.

Sadly this work of revision has not benefited from the energy, dedication and breadth of vision of Colin Padfield, who died tragically in 1978.

I am grateful to readers and teachers who have written or otherwise contacted me with various points which I have sought to incorporate into the new text. I hope they will find an improvement in the book, and that it will continue to meet the needs of students and those engaged in, or about to enter, public administration and the caring professions.

In the preparation of this revision I am grateful for the expert advice, help and opinions which I have received directly or indirectly from John Chant, Director of Social Services, Somerset County Council; Mike Clark, Housing Officer, Taunton Deane Borough Council; Barrie Taylor, Chief Education Officer, Somerset County Council; Brian Bailey, Chairman of the SW Regional Health Authority and Somerset County Councillor; Reuben Buchanan, Regional Inspector for the NSPCC; Mike Hansen of the DHSS; and Peter Bates, Somerset Planning Department. To counter fears that I have been unduly influenced by 'establishment' views, I should also like to acknowledge my debt to friends and colleagues teaching and writing in this field, especially those in the Social Administration Association. And I should like to thank my students at the Somerset College of Arts and Technology for keeping me alert (I hope) to ideas, issues and events. I am also grateful for the help I have received from Bryan McEnroe of Taunton Library and Stuart Macwilliam of Exeter University library.

Finally, I must thank my wife Sari for her help and support throughout.

Tony Byrne, Taunton, December 1982

Preface to the fourth edition

There is never a 'right' time for revising a book: it is always too soon or too late. This is particularly the case with books (such as this one) which deal with social life, for society is always changing – habits, beliefs, patterns of behaviour alter; new problems arise or old ones persist; different ideas or solutions are proposed, and a mixture of politics, personalities and finance shape the necessary policy decisions. But even these policies are not final – they are subject to review, criticism and amendment. Consequently, the new edition of this book is only a snapshot of our Welfare State.

This revision aims to take account of a number of important changes in our social services since 1984 and to generally up-date the whole text. It was substantially completed towards the end of 1988, with some updating, where possible, in Summer/Autumn 1989. Although this was before the final details of some important legislation (the Children Bill and the Employment Bill) and government plans for the NHS and for community social services, I have attempted to indicate their main elements (but have not been tempted into anticipating rumoured proposals for further changes in housing and social security or local government).

I am grateful to those readers who have contacted me about certain aspects of the third edition and have attempted to incorporate their suggestions as far as possible in this new edition.

Tony Byrne, Taunton, September 1989

The Welfare State:
Twentieth century milestones

1902   *Education Act*
1905   *Unemployed Workmen's Act*
1906   *Education (Meals) Act*
1907   *Education (Medical) Act*
1907   *Probation of Offenders Act*
1908   *Children's Act*
1908   *Old Age Pensions Act*
1909   *Labour Exchanges Act*
1909   *Town Planning Act*
1909   *Trade Boards Act*
1909   *The People's Budget*
1910   *Education (Choice of Employment) Act*
1911   *National Insurance Act*
1913   *Mental Deficiency Act*
1918   *Education Act*
1919   *Maternity and Child Welfare Act*
1919   *Housing, Town Planning Act*
1920   Unemployed insurance extended to most workers
1925   Contributory pensions – for old age, widows and orphans
1929   *Local Government Act* abolished Boards of Guardians
1930   *Mental Health Act*
1934   Unemployment Assistance Board
1934   Milk in schools scheme
1944   *Education Act*
1944   *Disabled Persons (Employment) Act*
1945   *Family Allowances Act*
1946   *National Health Service Act*
1946   *National Insurance Act*
1947   *Town and Country Planning Act*
1948   *Children's Act*
1948   *National Assistance Act*
1957   *Rent Act*
1959   *Mental Health Act*
1963   *Children Act*
1968   *Health Services and Public Health Act*
1969   *Children and Young Persons Act*
1970   *Chronically Sick and Disabled Persons Act*
1970   *Local Authority Social Services Act*
1972   *Housing Finance Act*
1972   *Town and Country Planning Act*
1973   *National Health Service (Reorganisation) Act*
1975   *Children Act*
1975   *Social Security Pensions Act*

1977 *Housing (Homeless Persons) Act*
1980 *Housing Act*
1981 *Education Act*
1982 *Criminal Justice Act*
1983 *Mental Health Act*
1984 *Rates Act*
1985 *Social Security Act*
1988 *Education Reform Act*
1988 *Housing Act*
1988 *Local Government Finance Act* (poll tax)
1989 *Children Act*

1
Background to the modern social services

General and introductory

All societies make arrangements for the welfare of their people, but there are great variations in the way this is done. Some societies depend on informal provision – by the family, clan or tribe. Others make formal, legal arrangements such as public hospitals, State schools, tax systems, etc. Most modern societies have a mixture of the formal and informal forms of social provision.

This is certainly true of Britain. Our lives depend very much on the help and support of our friends, neighbours, **family** and relations. Many of us have also come to rely on the material and emotional support given by **voluntary organisations** (including trade unions and the church). Then there is the important role of **employers** who not only provide vital employment and wages, but many also have elaborate schemes for pensions, sickness benefit, housing and recreation. (It could be further suggested that work itself provides companionship and even a meaning to many people's lives.) Finally, there is the **State**. Over the course of the past 200 years, the State has come to assume a bigger place in everyone's life. Whilst it has always been responsible for defence and for law and order (both in themselves vital, indirectly, to welfare), it has also acquired responsibility for such things as the regulation of employment and the management of the economy, with all that this implies for people's incomes, taxation and mortgage payments etc. However, in this century, the State has become responsible for the direct and immediate welfare of its citizens, and it does this through institutions we call '**Social Services**'.

Clearly, it is difficult to calculate the welfare benefits derived from health services or housing in comparison to the benefits we derive from, say, defence or transport or trade policy. But we can say that, in general, the aim of social service provision, or social policy, is to reduce the differences in people's life chances, i.e. to help equalise opportunities and so enhance welfare (or wellbeing). Thus if people are ill, the health services seek to restore them to average health; if people lose their jobs the social security system at least provides an income; similarly state schools provide everyone with at least an average education. In other words, no one needs to feel deprived or feel like an 'outsider' from the rest of society.

Whether, in practice, the social services live up to this idea is another matter. Equally it is an open question as to *how far* the State should make such provision: how much can it *afford to make*? How much should be left to private initiative – be it individual, the family, commercial enterprise or voluntary bodies?

These questions raise fundamental issues of resource allocation, freedom, efficiency, political values and social justice, to which there are no simple answers.

The domain of the social services

We may spend much time trying to define what is meant by 'social services'. Obviously it is important to know the boundaries of the area we are to study. Otherwise we waste time on irrelevant material or, conversely, important areas will be omitted. For example, when discussing social security (which provides cash benefits to those in need) should we take account of the tax system (income tax, VAT, land tax, etc.)? Is industrial training and re-training a social service or an economic service? To what extent should we include the legal service (lawyers, police, court officials) in the scheme of social services? Is transport or the mail a social service? These are important questions if only to show that the boundaries of what is a 'social service' are by no means clear and precise.

Generally we may say that a social service 'is a social institution which has been developed to meet the personal needs of individual members of society not adequately or effectively met by either the individual from his own or his family's resources or by commercial or industrial concerns' (J. Eyden, *An Introduction to Social Administration*).

More specifically, we take the social services to be:

1   **Social security.** This includes sickness and unemployment benefits and contributions; disablement payments; pensions of various kinds; Income Support; Housing Benefit; Family Credit; some aspects of taxation, such as tax allowances.
2   **Health.** This includes environmental health as well as personal, medical and mental health.
3   **Welfare.** This includes the care of the old, disabled and children.
4   **Education.** This includes the education of those of pre-school age and all those up to adults who pursue higher education.
5   **Housing.** This includes town and country planning and the preser-

vation of amenities, as well as the provision and control of accommodation.

6 **Treatment of offenders.** This includes those sent to prisons, borstals and those immediately released from court who are subject to probation orders and the like.

7 **Employment services.** This includes finding work for the unemployed, easing transfers of persons from one job to another, as well as training and retraining.

8 **Services for special groups.** In these we include, for example, immigrants, gypsies, drug addicts.

While accepting that much, indeed most, social provision is made by the family, neighbours, voluntary groups etc., in this book we are essentially concerned with the welfare provisions made by the State. We therefore concentrate on *public sector* social services and social policy.

For a rough guide to the relative importance of the main State social services, see Table 15 on page 420.

Administration of the social services

The provision of these services is invariably the responsibility of the State *and* various voluntary organisations. The voluntary organisations play a relatively minor role, but they are nevertheless important for certain services, e.g. personal welfare. It is important to be clear what is meant by 'voluntary'. It does not necessarily mean doing 'voluntary work' since many workers in, say, the NSPCC or Shelter are salaried; and, conversely, some people do voluntary and free work for the official or 'statutory' social services departments – for example, at youth clubs, primary school mums, etc. A **voluntary organisation** is an association or society which has come into existence of its own accord; it has been created by its members rather than being called into existence or created by the State. Briefly, therefore, a voluntary organisation (or 'vol orgs') is non-official or non-statutory in its formation and operation, though obviously it is subject to the general law of the land. Voluntary organisations abound in the British social services, but for illustration we may mention the British Red Cross, Age Concern, Workers' Educational Association, Multiple Sclerosis Society, Society for Mentally Handicapped Children, Cruse, Mind, Shelter, League of Friends (of local hospitals), the Howard League for Penal Reform. You may notice that some of these act more as 'pressure groups' on the Government than actual providers of a service.

The **statutory or official social services** derive from legislation and are the responsibility of a Secretary of State or Minister (for Home

Affairs, or Education, or Social Services, etc.). Here there are a number of different forms of administration. It may be:

1 Direct through a Government department and its local offices, e.g. Social Security.
2 Indirect, being administered by *ad hoc* semi-public bodies, e.g. the Housing Corporation or Manpower Services Commission.
3 A local government responsibility, as with education and housing to a large extent, and the various personal welfare services now known as the Local Authority Social Services (LASS) or Personal Social Services (PSS), or (in Scotland) Social Work Departments.

This variety in administrative form is the result of various factors, including politics, tradition and the quest for efficiency. A study of the development of the social services should elucidate this point.

Main features in the development of the social services

A glance at the past often helps to explain the present. If we look at the way the social services have developed we can use the past to explain the current situation, including not only the institutions but also the policies.

The social services in Britain are impressive in their coverage – so impressive in fact that the name 'Welfare State' is given to this comprehensive system. The services started growing slowly but accelerated at particular points in our history until they are now so extensive that there are very few points at which they do not touch us during our lives – from 'the cradle to the grave'.

But it is misleading to say that the Welfare State has emerged as the fruit of a plant which has grown steadily. In the first place it is unlikely that the Welfare State will ever be finally realised since it is continuously confronted with new problems or by old ones seen in a different light and needing methods of 'solution'. As Professor Titmuss has said, a social service is a 'dynamic process' rather than a finished article. Second, the Welfare State has now evolved neatly or regularly from a master-plan or blueprint. The emergence of the social services has been piecemeal in response to various pressures, revelations, changing philosophies and changes in the state of the economy.

The main features of the development of the social services can be summarised as follows:

1 The wide range of social services from basic subsistence and institutional care to many specialised services, e.g. education, housing, mental health, etc., which gives the social services a **'comprehensive' aspect**.

2 Responsibility for social services transferred from voluntary bodies to **provision by the State** and its organs.
3 The change of emphasis to a more **positive and personal** service from the nineteenth century where emphasis was environmental, e.g. Public Health Acts, Factory Acts, etc.
4 The **piecemeal nature** of the development.
5 Social services grew to cover a wider population, rather than just certain groups or sections. This is their **'universalist'** aspect.
6 The acceptance of the services as **a right** to be claimed, rather than a gift to be haphazardly bestowed and often carrying an element of shame and stigma.
7 The problem of **depersonalisation** as the scope and units of administration increase, and the attempts to meet this with the social work (case-work) approach, specialisation and training.
8 The growth of **knowledge** through the collection of statistics and the development of the technique of social inquiry.
9 The growing realisation that many problems are not merely the result of material difficulties, such as poverty and homelessness, but arise from **social and psychological maladjustment**, e.g. the problems of new housing estates (see page 273).

These features will become clearer as we examine the historical development of particular social services and the Welfare State.

The Poor Law

Much time could be spent on examining the origins and early development of charity and the relief of suffering. From medieval times relief was to be sought from the Church, the manor, the parish, guilds, the family and individuals.

The Poor Law legislation of the fourteenth century penalised able-bodied beggars and required the infirm to remain in their home districts (parishes). The basic purpose was that each parish should look after its own poor. Tudor legislation, especially that of 1598 and 1601, during the reign of Elizabeth I, sought to give uniformity to local practices. Under this legislation the Justices of the Peace were required to supervise the work of parish officers called 'Overseers of the Poor'. These were appointed for one year at a time and their task was to relieve the poor by collecting alms or voluntary contributions from inhabitants. In time this practice became compulsory and formed a local tax, later to be called 'the rates'.

Relieving the poor took two main forms:

1 **Outdoor relief**, where paupers received money or food or clothing.

2   **Indoor relief**, where paupers were brought into the almshouse of the parish.

The able-bodied poor were expected to do some kind of work in return for their succour. This would help to offset the cost of poor relief. Another reason for the requirement of work was the general prejudice against poor people who were able-bodied, because it suggested idleness and scrounging. Many parishes established Houses of Correction to provide a mixture of work, correction and punishment for 'rogues, vagabonds, sturdy beggars and vagrants'. For those who did not cooperate by working satisfactorily there were the stocks or even whipping.

Over the years there were a number of developments in the scope and form of poor relief:

(a)   Some parishes combined to provide poor relief, some establishing a common workhouse.

(b)   Many parishes 'apprenticed' pauper children to industry, ostensibly for training, in reality to reduce their costs (paid for by the local rates).

(c)   The 'Speenhamland' System provided, from 1795 onwards, a new system of outdoor relief in the form of cash payments varying with the cost of living.

(d)   The Roundsman System pushed responsibility for poor relief on to local farmers by requiring them at regular intervals to employ and take care of groups of able-bodied poor.

The most important development, however, was the growth in numbers and the increase in the cost of the poor to the country as a whole. Between 1784 and 1818 parish poor relief rose from £2 million to £8 million and many people feared the old system could no longer cope. This was not surprising for in the early nineteenth century Britain was experiencing:

(i)   A massive growth in population (in 1750 it was 7.5 million; in 1800, 10.5 million and in 1850, 21 million people).

(ii)   The Industrial Revolution, which disrupted centuries-old modes of living and working, and concentrated people into urban environments.

(iii) War with France (1793–1815) which disrupted the economy and caused inflation.

The 1830s was a period of reform – in factories, education, local government and Parliament. The arrangements for poor relief came under the scrutiny of a **Royal Commission on the Poor Laws** (1832–34) set up to inquire into the problem. The Commission was much influenced by the complaints of ratepayers, but more fundamentally by ideas of the Rev. T. Malthus, who preached of the danger of overpopulation, and Jeremy Bentham (1748–1832) who advocated the principles of efficiency and utility and reform. The over-riding influence of the period was that of Adam Smith (1723–90), the Scottish philosopher and economist who advocated new principles of economics, the market mechanism and *laissez faire*, i.e. free enterprise.

The existing poor law system was:

1 Increasingly costly for ratepayers.
2 Administratively untidy.
3 In the opinion of some, boosting the birthrate, which was already dangerously high.
4 Condemned for reducing the mobility of labour.
5 Inadequate to deal with the increasing poverty in town and country resulting from the Agricultural and Industrial Revolutions.

Many of these views were reflected in the Report of the Royal Commission, which called for a thorough revision of the provisions for the poor. Above all, the Report concentrated attention on the able-bodied poor. In general, it said their destitution was the result of a weakness of character, and, in particular, the Speenhamland system of relief tended to demoralise those who received it by undermining their independence, as those who were earning wages had to seek additional relief to avoid starvation.

The Royal Commission Report of 1832 recommended:

1 'The appointment of a *Central Board* (i.e. a central Government body) to control the administration of the Poor Law, with such assistant Commissioners as may be found requisite; and that the Commissioners be empowered and directed to frame and enforce regulations for the government of workhouses; and as to the nature and amount of relief to be given and the labour to be exacted from them; and that such regulations shall, as far as may be practical, be uniform throughout the country.
2 'That the Central Board be empowered to cause any *number of parishes* which they may think convenient to be incorporated for the purpose of workhouse management, and for providing new workhouses where necessary. To settle the general qualifications which shall be necessary to candidates for paid offices connected with the relief of the poor . . . and to remove any paid officers whom they may think unfit for their situations.
3 'That, except as to medical attendance, all relief whatever to *able-bodied persons* or to their families, otherwise than in well-

regulated workhouses, shall be declared unlawful, and shall cease.

4 'Every penny bestowed, that tends to render the condition of the pauper *more eligible* than that of the independent labourer is a bounty on indolence and vice. But once the condition of the pauper is made *more uncomfortable* than that of the independent labourer then new life, new energy is infused into the constitution of the pauper: he is aroused like one from sleep, his relation with all his neighbours, high and low, is changed; he surveys his former employers with new eyes. He begs a job – he will not take a denial, he discovers that everyone wants something to be done.'

Legislation quickly followed in the shape of the ***Poor Law Amendment Act, 1834***. This Act implemented the recommendations of the Royal Commission's Report, and introduced what was called the 'New Poor Law'. In many ways its provisions were not new, but, in reinstating and reinforcing a number of previous ideas and practices, the 1834 Act sought to introduce a measure of uniformity and control over the 15,000 poor law authorities. The Act:

1 Created a central department of three Commissioners to supervise the arrangements for poor relief over the country.
2 Grouped parishes into bigger units called 'unions'.
3 Made provision for the election of Boards of Guardians in each Poor Law Union.
4 Restricted outdoor relief to the aged, sick or disabled.
5 Laid down that the able-bodied (and their families) would only be supported within the workhouse.
6 Ensured that 'well-regulated' workhouses were to operate in conditions of 'lesser eligibility', i.e. lower physical standards, than could be found outside. Coupled with a strict and demeaning work schedule this produced the deterrent many people advocated to induce the loafers to find work. Only the desperately needy would seek relief: only they would pass the 'workhouse test', a test of desperation. The parish intended to prove itself the hardest taskmaster and the worst paymaster.

Underlying the Act was the notion of independence, self-reliance and the inherent value of work. This reflected the prevailing philosophy of *laissez faire*, which after all was producing the goods and enabling Great Britain to become the 'workshop of the world'. On the other hand, the 1834 Act also catered for those who were not able-bodied. They could continue to receive relief outside the workhouse, and if they chose indoor relief instead, conditions for them were not required to be 'less eligible'. Yet in practice many of the 700 new unions created from the 15,000 parishes failed to make separate and superior provision for the non able-bodied: it was easier and cheaper to run a single mixed workhouse, and here something approaching 'lesser eligibility' was applied to all inmates. Some Boards of Guardians began to apply the Workhouse Test to the non able-bodied on the ground that better provision would weaken the resolve of workers to make their own provision for old age and early death. Hence the universal fear and loathing of the workhouse, or 'Bastille', as it was often called.

The Poor Law was despised because it divided families physically, in the workhouse, and emotionally, in the family means test. It humiliated and degraded the recipient, who was denied the franchise (the right to vote) between 1867 and 1918. Above all, the whole Poor Law machinery was based on the idea of culpability or blame; that idleness and improvidence were the prime causes of poverty, so that the poor did not really deserve better treatment. In the prosperous mid-nineteenth century to be poor was unfortunate, but to be poor *and* able-bodied was careless, even criminal.

However, the Poor Law was not all bad. Many Boards of Guardians were hostile to the new system, partly because they were outraged at the prospect of interference by the new central authority and partly because they felt that the system was impracticable in their industrial parishes: in times of good trade there would be few entrants to the workhouse while in times of depression the workhouse would be too small. Besides it was impossible to apply 'lesser eligibility' where the 'situation of the independent labourer of the lowest class' varied with the fluctuating fortunes of trade, employment and wages. Consequently the Poor Law Commission, acknowledging the situation, allowed many of the Guardians to exercise their own discretion. (In 1844 and 1852 Labour Test Orders were issued which, under certain circumstances, allowed outdoor relief to be paid in return for some kind of work, usually nominal. In some areas this even amounted to giving outdoor relief in supplementation of wages – see Chapter 2.)

The legacy of the new Poor Law

The *Poor Law Amendment Act, 1834*, was important not only for what it did for people physically but also for what it did for them psychologically. The underlying message got across that poverty was a blameworthy condition to be in; that 'lesser eligibility' was necessary to deter potential applicants; that poverty was to be relieved rather than prevented. The result was that large sections of the community regarded the Poor Law with fear and loathing: 'In the eyes of working people, anything controlled by the Poor Law authorities was automatically tainted with the shameful stigma of pauperism' (M. Rose). In 1948 Aneurin Bevan said that the body of the

Elizabethan Poor Law was finally buried, but even today its spirit lives on – for example, some old people resist entry to homes which were former workhouses.

Other developments in the nineteenth century

It would be misleading to imply that the 'new' Poor Law was the only or even the main contribution of the nineteenth century to the development of social welfare. Indeed, in spite of being popularly characterised as the age of *laissez faire*, this period of British history saw the growth of substantial **intervention by the State** – see, for example, the legislation mentioned below.

There was, admittedly, a great deal of **voluntary** concern and action over social problems, viz. the founding of the 'ragged schools', Dr Barnardo's orphanages, prison reform through the efforts of John Howard (1726–90) and later Elizabeth Fry (1780–1845), housing provision through the efforts of Octavia Hill (1838–1912), the protection of children by such bodies as the National Society for the Prevention of Cruelty to Children (NSPCC) which survives today, etc. Samuel Smiles (1812–1904), a medical practitioner, achieved wide popularity by his book *Self Help*, which had an enormous sale. This attitude of **self help** also manifested itself in collective provision through the formation of friendly societies, trade unions, the Co-operative Movement, savings banks and building societies.

But, as one writer has put it, 'the origins of British collectivism run back to the Victorian era', implying not only legislative provision but also the establishment of administrative machinery and staff to deal with it in the form of reformed local and central government and the Civil Service. The following legislation, though to a large extent environmental, speaks for itself:

Factory legislation
1802   *Health and Morals of Apprentices Act*
1833 ⎫
1842 ⎪ *Factories Acts* and *Mines Acts* to improve health and safety
1844 ⎬   conditions and to regulate hours
1847 ⎭
1891   *Factory and Workshops Act*
1897   *Workmen's Compensation Act*

Health
1848   *Public Health Act*
1875   *Public Health Act*

1867   *Metropolitan Poor Act* ⎫   to set up public hospitals and dis-
1883   *Metropolitan Poor Act* ⎭   pensaries by Boards of Guardians
1890   *Lunacy Act*

Housing
1851   *Lodging Houses Act*
1864   *Metropolitan Houseless Poor Act* authorising casual wards
        for vagrants
1868, 1875   *Artisans and Labourers' Dwellings Act*
1890   *Housing Act*

Education
1833   Government grants
1870   *Education Act* authorised State elementary (primary) educa-
        tion
1880   *Education Act* required school attendance up to age 10 (11 in
        1893, 12 in 1899)
1891   *Education Act* authorising *free* education

Reasons for nineteenth-century developments

The reasons are numerous and varied: some apply to a particular
service; others apply generally.

1   There were urgent problems caused by the Industrial Revolution
    and rapid urbanisation, e.g. concentrated unemployment, slums
    and epidemics.
2   Action was needed to avert social unrest, perhaps revolution.
3   Conscience, religious duty, philanthropy, humanitarian refor-
    mers.
4   International competition, both economic and military.
5   Foreign example.
6   Economic depressions.
7   Pressures from voters, political parties, groups, media and pro-
    fessions.
8   Surveys and Royal Commission reports.
9   Population growth.
10 Changing philosophy and theories of the State's role.
11 Growing national wealth.

As we observed at the beginning of this chapter, the provision of a
social service is a **dynamic process**, not a finished article. It could be
argued that the nineteenth-century contribution to the provision of
social services was generally small. There was a general tendency to
rely upon economic growth and improved environment. Within that
context people should fend for themselves, either through commer-

cial provision or via **self-help**. Failing this, people could resort to **charity** and voluntary provision. In the last resort the **State** would provide, but only with minimum standards of service, be it of health, education or housing.

Developments in the twentieth century

Towards the end of the nineteenth century a number of assumptions underlying the provision of social services were being questioned: e.g. that economic growth by itself is no solution without a *redistribution* of wealth; that encouraging people to be *thrifty* is a long-term process (and impossible for those on low incomes); that *charity* can only touch the fringe of the problem of the needy and deprived. Besides, why should children suffer while their parents are being chastened by the Poor Law? Increasingly, it was felt that the only really effective way to cope with the social situation was for the State to really commit itself to dealing with the problems and where possible to try to prevent them. As these and other ideas gained ascendancy, so we observe the development of the Welfare State of the twentieth century.

The development (see page xiv) occurred broadly in two stages:

1 The era of the 'Liberal reforms' between 1906 and 1919, when new services were established in the fields of **social security** (old age pensions, and cash benefits for sickness and unemployment), **health** (the free doctor or 'panel' system, and mother and baby clinics), **education** (meals, medicals and a raised school-leaving age), **housing** (rent controls and subsidies), **employment** (labour exchanges and youth employment services) and the **treatment of offenders** (probation and juvenile courts). These were important foundations, financed from increased and new forms of taxation, and from State insurance contributions (1911). In the 1920s and 1930s, there was a certain amount of retrenchment in Government expenditure which hit some services – housing subsidies and unemployment benefits were cut; so were certain planned educational developments. However, progress was made in these and other new fields (e.g. mental health, school milk and voluntary welfare services) and the Boards of Guardians were disbanded (1929).

2 The second stage occurred under the Labour Government 1945–50, though much had been planned or committed earlier by the war coalition Government (e.g. *Education Act, 1944*). The importance of this period lay partly in the creation of new services such as family allowances, the employment of the handicapped and a national system of personal (or 'welfare') services provision.

But the main significance of the post-war legislation lay in its widening of the State's welfare net: education up to 15 became free and available to all; the National Health Service became a free and universal service; local authority (council) housing was no longer to be confined to the working class as in the past; and social security was transformed into a comprehensive service, applicable to the nation as a whole. In the past 20 years we have seen these founding services augmented, altered and refined, but not fundamentally changed – though recently some have been drastically cut (e.g. council housing provision). The following chapters trace the details of these developments.

The provision of social services is described as 'a dynamic process'. It is never finished; developments and improvements are made and some mistakes occur. For example, it was considered that high-rise buildings were the post-war answer to the housing shortage. However, they have brought many problems, and they are not the blessing they were thought to be. We have made mistakes in planning. The clearing of inner-city slums and low-class housing is a desirable and worthy object, but the actual eradication and clearance have produced inner areas of desolation. They are bleak and arid, and the former community spirit is not created simply by moving the folk to New Towns. You will readily grasp, therefore, that what was considered in one era to be a solution and remedy may in a succeeding era be a blight and a problem for those whose task it is to provide the services to make life in society more enjoyable and tolerable for the ordinary person.

Questions

1 Distinguish between (a) 'statutory' and 'voluntary' (b) 'comprehensive' and 'universal' in the provision of social services.
2 Name three voluntary social services.
3 What are the three forms of administration of the statutory social services?
4 Explain the two phases in the development of the Welfare State.
5 What were the 'workhouse test' and 'lesser eligibility' under the Poor Law?
6 State the main features of the *Poor Law Amendment Act, 1834*.
7 Apart from the help provided by the State, what other forms of help were there in the nineteenth century?
8 Give four reasons for the development of the social services 1800–1900.

2
An outline of government

Newcomers to the study of the social services may find a short description of the political structure and institutions (i.e. 'the Government' in broad terms) will be helpful in understanding how the social services are brought into being and administered.

The British Constitution

The British Constitution is somewhat different from other nations' constitutions. A number of labels – monarchical, parliamentary, unitary and democratic – indicate its main features. It is *monarchical* in that the Queen is Head of State, although she now plays only a formal part in the conduct of government, acting always on the advice of her ministers. It is *parliamentary* in the sense that Parliament is the sovereign law-making body and that the Government is formed out of Parliament and dependent on its continuing support. It is *unitary* in the sense that Parliament is ultimately responsible for the whole of the United Kingdom, although it may delegate some of its powers to other institutions such as local authorities. It is *democratic* in the sense that the House of Commons (the more important and effective of the two Houses) is elected on the basis of universal adult suffrage, all persons over eighteen having the right to vote at Parliamentary elections.

The main organs of government

There are three main organs of government:

1 The **legislature** (Parliament).
2 The **executive** (the Cabinet and other ministers in charge of Government departments, staffed by civil servants; local authorities; and a number of statutory boards such as British Coal and British Rail).
3 The **judiciary** (the judges and the law courts).

The separation of powers

This is a doctrine that the three functions of government (legislative, executive and judicial) should be discharged by separate bodies. To prevent misgovernment no two of these functions should be entrusted to the same hands. For example, if the power of making laws were exercised by the same persons who execute or interpret them (i.e. the judiciary) the result could be tyranny. We have always feared absolute power concentrated in one person or body of persons, and have sought to separate the three institutions to enable each part or body to act as a check on the other or others. In theory, each body should be staffed by its own personnel, and no one person should be a member of any of the other two powers or institutions. We have, therefore, mutual checks on governmental power.

In the British Constitution there is no complete separation of powers – for example, the Cabinet and Ministers (forming the executive) are also members of Parliament (the legislature), and some of the judges, e.g. the Lords of Appeal in Ordinary (the judiciary), are members of the House of Lords (the legislature). And, of course, the Queen, as well as Head of the State, is an integral part of all three inasmuch as she is head of the administration, head of the judiciary and an integral part of the legislature.

However, our Constitution does possess various **checks** and **balances** to prevent despotism and to ensure that liberty, within the law, and effective government can be simultaneously achieved.

The rule of law

This is still one of the fundamental characteristics of the British Constitution. Broadly, the rule of law is the principle that the process of government is bound up with the law and that the law is supreme. A government or ministry must act *according to law*, i.e. within the law. Thus a Home Secretary cannot forcibly enter my house or imprison me unless he has legal power to do so. The rule of law may, therefore, be said to prevail when the exercise of all forms of public authority (i.e. central government authorities, local authorities, police or other bodies) is subject to review by the ordinary courts of law to which all citizens have equal access.

The rule of law is perhaps best grasped by contrasting its opposite, i.e. the arbitrary use of authority against any person or property, unchecked by any other power or body. That state of affairs leads straight to despotism or anarchy. Most reasonable people prefer order and peace to the confusion and misery of anarchy. So we may say the rule of law includes two important main rules:

1   Absence of arbitrary (uncontrolled) power.
2   Equality before the law.

Equality before the law means that in the courts of law all persons are equal, or there is equal subjection of all classes to the ordinary law of the land which is administered by the *ordinary* law courts. There are some exceptions to this rule, e.g. the Queen cannot be compelled to appear before her own courts. However, lest it be thought that position and wealth excuse or exclude a person from the due process of law a reading of ordinary newspapers will show that some important figures have been sued or prosecuted. So too local authorities may be sued and prosecuted. The rule is that the courts are open to every citizen in the realm to pursue his or her remedies, and that justice according to law will be administered by holding the scales of justice evenly. That task is left to an impartial judiciary.

Parliament

Parliament consists of the Queen, the House of Lords and the House of Commons. Collectively these form the legislature. The Queen only remains a part of the legislature in a formal sense. The House of Commons is the more important of the two Houses in that it is popularly elected.

The maximum life of a parliament is five years, but on the advice of a prime minister, the Queen may dissolve parliament and issue a Proclamation calling for the election of a new parliament. Parliament is adjourned from day to day while in session. At the end of a session (usually 12 months in length) it is prorogued. At the expiry of its life it is dissolved.

Political parties

The party system is essential to the operation of Parliament. At the moment we have two main political parties: Conservative and Labour.

Parties are highly organised and disciplined. Once elected, the party which obtains the majority of seats has the right to have its leaders form the Government. The other party forms Her Majesty's Opposition.

The party forming the Government seeks to sustain itself in power. The minority party accepts that position and, because of the rigidity of the party system, the Opposition sees its role as one of criticising Government policy and setting forth an alternative programme which it hopes will win the support of the electorate at the next election. For generations now we have worked on a two-party system with Government alternating at one time between Conservative and Liberal, and more recently between Conservative and Labour. The Liberal Democratic party is a new development.

There is not the space here to enter into a discussion of the political nature of our state, but we may note that an effective official Opposition is essential to our form of Government. There have been many restraints upon the exercise of parliamentary 'dictatorship', but great vigilance is needed to ensure that the freedoms we have are not eroded – usually for the best of all possible reasons, according to the party in power. How those freedoms should be protected is a matter for thought. Is a written constitution needed with entrenched provisions in a Bill of Rights, irrevocable by any Government except subject to stringent provisions?

The House of Lords

This is the older of the two Chambers. It is composed of about 1,100 Spiritual and Temporal Lords. Some peers of the realm are hereditary, and some are life peers created under the *Life Peerages Act, 1958*. Life peerages are awarded to distinguished persons in public life on the nomination of the Prime Minister of the day. They number about 350. The hereditary element numbering some 800 is still important but declining.

The House of Lords is unrepresentative in that it is not democratically elected. It may therefore be considered to be of limited usefulness. Its main function is to ease the burden of the Commons by examining some Bills in detail and initiating bills of a non-controversial character. It may also debate important public issues more effectively than the Commons since in modern times the Commons has too many Bills to pass with consequent loss of time for debate in the Chamber.

The *Parliament Acts, 1911 and 1949*, have limited the effect of the House of Lords, especially in regard to Money Bills, but in other respects it still has an important role to play, particularly in that it is a forum where men and women distinguished in all fields of national life may discuss and vote on issues of importance free from the reins of party discipline.

The House of Commons

The House of Commons is a representative assembly and consists (since 1983) of 650 MPs elected by simple majority on the basis of single-member constituencies.

We have referred to the vital part played by the party system in the Constitution. Parliament has an important function as an assembly to which the Government (i.e. the Cabinet and Ministers) is ultimately responsible; in making legislation; in voting money; and in acting as a body in which complaints can be raised and aired.

Legislation

The law of England is made up of common law and statute law. When, therefore, a government assumes power it will begin to alter existing laws or introduce entirely new Bills which will in time become Statutes (laws).

The actual process of bringing in Bills and debating and amending them is a technical and sometimes long process. The Bills have a First, Second and Third Reading, and in between, a Committee Stage and Report Stage during which time they are subjected to criticism and examination to ensure they are clear and achieve the object in view. The House of Commons votes on a Bill, which if it passes through all stages is sent to the House of Lords where a similar procedure is followed, being debated and criticised in that Chamber.

The Lords cannot require the Commons to agree to amendments; nor can they delay a Bill indefinitely. They have no power in respect of Money Bills, and since the passing of the *Parliament Act, 1949*, any other public Bill which has been passed in the Commons in two successive sessions may be presented for Royal Assent without the consent of the Lords provided that a year has elapsed between the date of the Second Reading of the Bill in the Commons and the date on which it was finally passed in that House.

Once the Bill has passed both Houses it is sent to the Queen for Royal Assent, a formality which is in practice never refused.

The Bill emerges as a Statute or Act or Parliament and is then enforced by the Civil Service or local authorities, and in the event of a dispute arising over a Statute the courts of law adjudicate and apply the rule of law referred to above.

Money functions of the Commons

The second important function of the Commons is to provide the State (i.e. Ministries) with money. The Government cannot raise money by taxation or spend money without the authority of Parliament; and this authority belongs exclusively to the Commons.

First, the House can vote money only on the demand and on the responsibility of a Minister of the Crown. This is done annually, and the procedure of the House centres around the annual 'voting of Supply' which is based on the Estimates provided by the Government.

Now a Government can only provide itself with money (through Parliament) if it obtains revenue. Accordingly, money will be raised by taxation and other means. The Chancellor of the Exchequer's Budget Statement, announced in the House usually in March or April, is the highlight of the financial year, for it is then that the Chancellor reveals how he proposes to raise the money (e.g. in taxation on persons or property, etc.). He introduces a Finance Bill. This Bill has to be enacted (i.e. must be made law) before the end of the summer recess.

So the House of Commons maintains a strong control both over the raising of money and on the spending of money and there is usually an important debate on this highly significant subject. Many issues can be raised and the Government of the day can be criticised publicly so that everyone in the realm can understand how the finances of the country are arranged and managed.

Again, once the legal authority of the Commons has been obtained, Government can proceed to carry out its plans, e.g. by enlarging public services or by cutting them down. The procedure of checking of expenditure by Government is a technical one involving several committees, the most important being the Public Accounts Committee.

Just as an ordinary household has to balance its books so, too, the Government as a whole has to balance its books, and if there has been waste or mismanagement the Opposition exposes it to ensure that wiser courses be followed. A glance at the main subjects of defence, housing, health, transport, nationalised industries, social services and education will show the difficulties. How much do we spend or should we spend on each of these subjects? Therein lies the difficulty and therein lies the area for deep political debate.

Critical functions of the Commons

The third function of the Commons is to criticise Government policy. Ministers can be criticised on the floor of the House, and MPs have the opportunity of questioning them and asking supplementary questions to any reply offered. The Opposition can table motions for debate which may help to mould public opinion. A reading of newspapers will reveal the subjects debated, the questions asked and the replies given by the Government Ministers. All the proceedings are on view, and they are reported in 'Hansard', the official record of proceedings, published daily.

Ultimately the position is based on the ability of the Commons to withdraw its support from the Government by voting a motion of 'no confidence', which would entail its resignation (as happened with Mr Callaghan's Labour Government in 1979). If a Government resigns a general election will be held and the political parties will make their appeal for support to the electorate either on the particular issue over which it resigned or over general policies which they stand for.

This critical function is basic to our idea of democracy, for were it not so there would be abuses and no check on Governmental power. It must not be imagined that Government and Opposition are in perpetual conflict; there are many matters about which both parties are agreed. Compromises are made and frequently the parties work in concert. Where there is difference is in policy, though both parties would contend that the ultimate aim is a humane and civilised society. That aim is best achieved through the established institutions of Parliament, Cabinet Government, the executive and the judiciary.

The judiciary

The judiciary is responsible for the interpretation of statutes and the determination of the common law.

Under the doctrine of Separation of Powers already referred to, the judicial functions are exercised quite separately from legislative or executive functions. However, there are some links in personnel.

Judges are appointed by the Queen acting on the advice of Ministers. To safeguard their independence all senior judges can only be removed by the Sovereign on an Address presented by both Houses of Parliament.

The Lord Chancellor, the head of the judiciary, is the only *political* appointment. He, as a member of the Cabinet, resigns his position with a change of Government. The Lord Chancellor also serves as Speaker to the House of Lords.

The Lords of Appeal are members of the House of Lords, which is the final court of appeal on all legal matters in the UK. The judges of the Court are the Lord Chancellor, ex-Lords Chancellor and the Lords of Appeal in Ordinary, and other persons who have held high judicial office.

The executive

This is a general term and includes the Prime Minister and the Cabinet, together with Ministers. It includes the Civil Service, local authorities, the nationalised corporations and the Police.

Central government

It will be useful at this stage to examine the main functions of those government departments of special importance to those with an interest in social care. These are:

1 The Department of Health
2 The Department of Employment
3 The Home Office
4 The Department of the Environment
5 The Department of Education and Science
6 The Department of Trade and Industry
7 The Treasury
8 The Department of Social Security

Scotland and Northern Ireland have different administrative systems from those in force in England. The Scottish Office has its own Home, Agriculture, Health and Education Departments. Wales has important offices situated in Cardiff.

Notwithstanding these peculiarities we may mention that the Department of Social Security functions for the whole of the United Kingdom.

Government departments

We shall now examine the responsibilities of those Government departments responsible for some aspects of the field of social services.

At the head of each Ministry stands the Minister, who may be designated Secretary of State (the more dignified title) or Minister. He may be assisted by junior Ministers who are also MPs. Under the Minister or Secretary of State are the various grades of civil servants who advise the Minister and carry out his commands.

Where a Statute lays down that certain functions be carried out by local authorities, the Minister maintains control by means of directives or circulars advising the local authorities. The relationship is characterised as a 'partnership'. We must remember that local authorities are composed of councillors who are there to make decisions for their own localities and wish to make decisions for themselves. Democratically elected to office, the councillors do not want to be dictated to, and they are not servants of the central Government.

We may now look at the Government departments to describe their main functions.

Department of Social Security (DOSS)

Formerly the main part of the Department of Health and Social Security (DHSS), this became a separate Department (again) in 1988. It is responsible for the national administration of the scheme of social security which includes National Insurance, War Pensions, Child Benefit, Attendance Allowance, Industrial Injuries, Mobility Allowance, Care Allowance, Family Credit, Housing Benefit and Income Support (see Chapter 3). The DSS has regional and local offices. It is advised at national level by the Social Security Advisory Committee.

Department of Health (DOH)

The Secretary of State for Health is responsible for the broad policy and central administration of the health and personal social (welfare) services. Local provision of the health services is the responsibility of regional and district health authorities of the National Health Service (see Chapter 4), and welfare services are provided through the Personal Social Services (or social work) departments of local authorities.

Department of Employment (DE)

The Department is responsible for Government policies on the working of the labour (or manpower) market, and the needs and conditions of people at work. These policies include the encouragement of employment and of effective training, the provision of special measures to deal with unemployment, the promotion of good industrial relations and healthy and safe working conditions. Many of the Department's executive functions are exercised by separate public agencies, including the Health and Safety Commission, the Advisory, Conciliation and Arbitration Service (ACAS), the Careers Service, the Race Relations Employment Advisory Service and (until 1988) the Manpower Services Commission (MSC).

The Department is also responsible (as an agent of the DSS) for the payment of unemployment benefit, repayment of income tax to unemployed workers, the collection and publication of statistics on labour and industrial matters, the relations of the British Government with the International Labour Office and for providing representation on employment and related matters at sessions of other international bodies.

Home Office

The main responsibilities of the Home Office, which is headed by one of the most senior of the Government Ministers, are: the police service; the prison service; the treatment of offenders, including juveniles; the probation and after-care service; the Criminal Injuries Compensation scheme; immigration control and naturalisation; cases relating to British nationality and citizenship of the UK and colonies; racial integration problems; and the coordination of the Government's Urban Programme for aid to areas of special social need and coordination of Government interest in relation to voluntary social service.

Department of the Environment (DOE)

This Department is responsible in England for a whole range of functions which affect people's environment: e.g. urban and regional planning; inner city matters; main roads; New Towns; sport and recreation; conservation of the countryside and of historic buildings and towns, pollution control; water and sewerage; the housing programme, and the structure and functions of local government. The Property Services Agency is responsible for meeting the needs of Government departments for land, accommodation, supplies and transport services.

Department of Education and Science (DES)

The main responsibility of this Department is the promotion of education in England. It is responsible for the Government's relations with the universities in England, Wales and Scotland, and it fosters the progress of civil science both in England and in collaboration with other nations.

The Department is concerned with the development of primary, secondary and further education; the supply, training and superannuation of teachers; the capital programmes for the building of new schools and other institutions. In all these matters the Department works in cooperation with local education authorities whose duty it is to secure adequate facilities for all forms of education in their areas. The Department's relations with the higher education institutions are conducted through the funding councils for universities (the UFC) and the polytechnics and colleges (the PCFC).

Its activities concerning civil science are discharged through five research councils: Medical, Agricultural, Natural Environment, Economic and Social Science and Science Research Councils. Advisory Boards of the research councils advise the Secretary of State who heads the Department.

Wales has its own Secretary of State who is responsible for primary and secondary education. In Scotland and Northern Ireland these come under the Scottish Education Department and the Ministry of Education respectively.

Department of Trade and Industry (DTI)

The Department is responsible for home and overseas trade policy (import controls, monopolies regulation, consumer protection, etc.), and for industrial policy, including regional policy and financial assistance to industry under the *Industry Act* (except for certain aspects administered by the Welsh and Scottish Offices).

The Department sponsors individual manufacturing industries, both in the private and public sectors, including textiles, steel, aircraft and ship-building. The Department is also responsible for technical services to industry and for industrial research and development, including civil aerospace research and the supervision of industrial research establishments (including the National Research Development Council and the Design Council) and the promotion of information technology. It also acts as the sponsoring Department for the Post Office.

The Treasury

As the name implies, this Government Department is primarily responsible for handling the finances of the State (taxes and spending) and also (in this century) for the development of an overall strategy for the economy generally.

The main body of its work is carried out by four large sections: (i) the Public Services Sector, which is responsible for controlling aggregate public expenditure and for most of the individual expenditure programmes, (ii) the Public Finance Sector which is concerned with fiscal (i.e. tax), monetary and with counter-inflation policies, (iii) Overseas Finance Sector, which is responsible for balance of payments policies, the management of UK foreign currency reserves, international financial relations and the aid programme, and (iv) the Chief Economic Adviser's Sector, which is responsible for the preparation of short-term and medium-term forecasts and for specialist advice on broad economic policies. The Treasury also has responsibilities for the management and effectiveness of the Civil Service.

Scotland, Northern Ireland and Wales

The administrative system differs in Scotland and Northern Ireland. The Scottish Office has its own Home, Agriculture, Health and Education Departments. Considerable functions have been devolved on to the Welsh Office and to Government offices in Cardiff. (See HMSO handbook *Britain* for further details.)

Local government

Loal government in the UK is the creation of Parliament. Its structure is laid down by Parliament and local authorities may only exercise those powers which Parliament either commands or permits them to exercise. Their functions include responsibility for education services (except most higher education), housing, personal social services, planning and transport, in each case subject to some central Government control.

Structure and areas in England

Up to 1986 England had a two-tier system of local government (excluding the small parish and community councils) comprising county and district councils, covering metropolitan and non-metropolitan (or 'shire') counties and districts (see Figures 1 and 2). For Scotland, Wales and Northern Ireland, see pages 29–30.

Thus in England there were six **metropolitan counties** each with a council. These counties cover the main conurbations outside Greater London: Tyne and Wear, West Midlands, Merseyside, Greater Manchester, West Yorkshire and South Yorkshire. They range in population from 1,200,000 (Tyne and Wear) to 2,800,000 (West Midlands). Each metropolitan county extends to the edge of the general continuously build-up area of the conurbation.

Similarly, the Greater London area had a council, the GLC, with a number of local government responsibilities.

In 1986 all of these top-tier councils were abolished (although the boundaries and areas remain).

The six metropolitan county areas are divided into 36 **metropolitan districts**, each with a borough or city council. These range in population from 173,000 (South Tyneside) to 1,100,000 (Birmingham). Most of them have a population over 200,000. They took over a number of the functions of the metropolitan county councils when these were abolished in 1986. Similarly the 32 London Borough councils assumed responsibility for many of the former GLC services.

In England there are 39 **non-metropolitan counties**, ranging in population from 110,000 (Isle of Wight) and 283,000 (Northumberland) to 1,400,000 (Kent).

Each of the non-metropolitan counties is divided into **non-metropolitan districts**, of which there are 296. These districts cover areas with populations broadly between 60,000 and 100,000, though some have bigger populations because of the need to avoid dividing large towns. Some districts, mainly in sparsely populated areas, have populations below 60,000 although only 14 have populations below 40,000.

Permanent Local Government Boundary Commissions for England and Wales have been set up to keep the areas and electoral arrangements of the new local authorities under review.

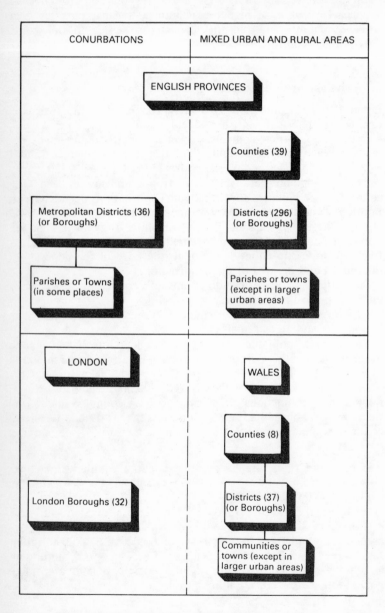

Figure 1   *Structure of local authorities since 1986*

Figure 2 *County and regional local authority areas*

Constitution and elections

The county and district councils consist of directly elected councillors. County councils usually comprise 60–100 members; metropolitan district councils 50–80 members; non-metropolitan district councils 30–60 members. All councillors are elected for a term of four years and they annually elect one of their number as chairman.

County Councils are elected as a whole in 1981, 1985, etc. London Boroughs and Scottish Regions are similarly elected in 1982, 1986, etc. While most district councils are elected as a whole in 1983, 1987, etc., some have one third of their council elected every year for 3 years in succession.

All British subjects or citizens of the Republic of Ireland of eighteen or over, resident on the qualifying date in the area for which the election is being held, are entitled to vote at local government elections. A register of electors is prepared and published annually by local electoral registration officers.

A returning officer has the overall responsibility for an election. Voting takes place at polling stations, arranged by the local authority and under the supervision of a presiding officer specially appointed for the purpose. Candidates, who are subject to various statutory qualifications and disqualifications designed to secure that they are suitable persons to hold office, must be nominated by electors for the electoral area concerned.

Functions of the authorities

Allocation of Main Functions between County and District Councils

County Councils	District Councils
Education	Passenger transport
Personal social services	Planning (local plans and control)
Libraries	Road maintenance (urban unclassified)
Planning:	Housing (including clearance and improvement)
Structure plans	Building regulations
Development control (strategic and reserve decisions)	Environmental health (clean air, food safety, nuisance, slaughterhouses, shops and offices legislation, port health, refuse collection and sewers)
Acquisition and disposal of land for planning purposes, development and re-development	
Highway authorities, traffic and transport coordination	
Housing (certain reserve powers, e.g. for overspill)	Museums and galleries*

Allocation of Main Functions between County and District Councils

County Councils	District Councils
Consumer protection: 　Weights and measures 　Food and drugs Refuse disposal Museums and art galleries* Parks and open spaces* Playing fields and swimming 　baths* Police† Fire†	Parks and open spaces* Playing fields and swimming 　baths* Cemeteries and crematoria *Metropolitan District Councils* As for district councils, *plus* education, libraries and personal social services

---

*Concurrent powers exercisable by county councils and district councils.
†Some counties are amalgamated for fire or police purposes (e.g. Somerset and Avon). In London and metropolitan areas separate boards exist for certain services, including transport, waste disposal and civil defence.

Internal organisation and local government services in England

The council is the final decision-making body within any authority. The councils are free to a large extent to make their own internal organisational arrangements. Questions of major policy are normally settled by the full council; while the administration of the various services is the responsibility of committees of members. Day-to-day decisions are delegated to the council's officers who act within the policies laid down by the members.

Many councils have set up 'corporate management' teams of the chief executive and chief officers. Such teams consider the operations of their authority as a whole, rather than dealing with each service separately, as was often the case in the past, especially before 1974.

Wales

As we have shown in Figure 1, there are eight counties and 37 districts in Wales, which has a total population of 2.8 million (1981 census).

The division of functions between Welsh county and district authorities is broadly the same as that which operates outside the metropolitan counties in England. The main exceptions are that: (1) Welsh district councils are responsible for refuse disposal as well as refuse collection; (2) district councils may be designated to exercise library, weights and measures, trade descriptions, and food and drugs functions; (3) county councils will have no reserve powers over housing.

Communities. At a more local level than the districts, 'communities' are created throughout Wales, many of which have councils with powers broadly equivalent to those of former parish councils. Community councils also have concurrent powers with the districts relating to allotments, cemeteries and crematoria, public baths, swimming baths and washhouses. They also have powers relating to museums and art galleries, parks and playing fields.

The main differences between England and Wales are in the allocation of functions; and that whereas England has parishes and parish councils, Wales has communities and community councils, though the functions of these bodies are very similar.

Northern Ireland

In Northern Ireland (Ulster), with a population of 1.56 million, there is a single-tier structure of local government comprising 26 district authorities. At the same time, responsibility for administering many of the more important services (planning, roads, education, personal social services) rests with central government departments. Thus their administration is carried out either through local offices of the ministries concerned or through area boards responsible to them, each working closely with the district councils. A Housing Executive responsible for the Department of the Environment for Northern Ireland, administers public sector housing.

Scotland

Scotland has a population of 5,150,000 (1981 census). Under the *Local Government (Scotland) Act, 1973*, which came into effect on May 16, 1975, Scotland is for local government purposes divided into nine regions and three island areas covering respectively Orkney, Shetland and the Western Isles. Within the regions there is a second independent tier of 53 districts.

Functions. Regions and districts have separate responsibility for specific functions. In addition, they share responsibility for certain concurrent functions. Islands' area councils are all-purpose authorities responsible in these areas for the functions (except police and fire services) which are the separate or concurrent responsibility of regions and districts.

Regional Functions. Regional authorities are directly responsible for overall planning strategy and highly technical or expensive services, e.g. the provision of major infrastructure services such as transportation, roads and passenger transport, airports, water, sewerage, river purification, flood prevention, as well as education, social work, police and fire services.

District Functions. District authorities deal with more local matters, e.g. local planning; development control; building control; housing; environmental health, including cleansing, refuse collection and disposal, food hygiene, inspection of shops, offices and factories, clean air, markets and slaughterhouses, burial and cremation; regulation and licensing, including cinemas and theatres, betting and gaming, taxis, house-to-house collections; libraries.

Concurrent Functions. These include countryside and tourism, industrial development, recreation parks, art galleries and museums.

Community Councils. Schemes for the creation of these were submitted to the Secretary of State in 1976. Such councils are not local authorities but have a statutory base, and will be expected to take such action in the community interest as appears to their members to be desirable and practicable.

Powers of local authorities

Statutes may (i) impose a **duty** on a local authority or (ii) give it a **permissive power**. The essential difference between these is that in (i) a local authority *must comply* with the law imposed by statute, whereas in (ii) a local authority *may* use its discretion whether to adopt the power or provide the service which the particular Act permits.

Under the *Education Act, 1944*, the Secretary of State for Education and Science is required by law 'to promote the education of the people of England and Wales, and to secure the effective execution by local authorities under his control and direction, of the national policy for providing a varied and comprehensive educational service in every area'. A county council *must* set up a local education authority and education committee, and the authority *must* provide schools and teachers.

Where a statute is permissive, the local authority *may* decide whether or not to provide a particular service or facility for the people within its area of control. Thus a local authority has power to provide parks, swimming pools and playing fields. Whether provision is made or not depends on the decision of the local authority, which is composed of councillors who reflect the wishes of the electorate. The law would not compel the authority to take action, and the remedy in this type of case is in the hands of the electorate to try to alter the minds of their representatives or to replace them at an election with new members who will provide the service which the public may want.

The *Local Authority Social Services Act, 1970*, came into force in 1971. It integrated the administration of personal social services and placed *a duty* on county councils, for example, to appoint a Social

Services Committee and to appoint a director to administer the Statute and ensure that the services be available to the public.

Control of local authorities by law

Local authorities are controlled by law, so that if they act outside the powers laid down by statute, they may be deemed to have acted *ultra vires*. If a local authority does not provide a service when it is under a duty to do so it may be compelled by action in the courts of law to do what it is legally bound to do. Thus the rule of law is maintained.

Furthermore, a local authority may sue and be sued; it may also prosecute others and it may itself be prosecuted. A local authority may, for example, sue *B* for debt, or arrears of rent. And where, let us say, a child *X* is injured as a result of an unsafe children's home he, *X*, may sue the local authority for damages. Where, for example, a local authority uses a vehicle which has defective brakes, steering or does not comply with the Road Traffic Construction and Use Regulations it may be prosecuted by the police (or even a private person if he so desires). The rule of law is thus maintained.

Control of local authorities by central government

'The interests of the local areas must be subservient to the nation as a whole, and so there must be control from the centre to achieve the dominance of this interest' (Jeremy Bentham). Central control by the Government over local authorities is justified on the following grounds:

1 **Minimum Standards.** Certain services are so important that they should not be allowed to fall below a certain minimum, e.g. health, education, police.
2 **Finance.** Government provides grants and financial aid to local authorities so it expects a satisfactory service for the aid given.
3 **Prevention of Corruption.** Central control assists in preventing fraud, whether by councillors or officers, so an audit of accounts may be ordered, and HM Inspectors are appointed to inspect certain services, e.g. police and education.
4 **Provision of Expertise.** The central government has greater technical resources, knowledge and data, and a greater number of specialists. Local authorities are encouraged to take advantage of these resources.

Complaints of maladministration

One of the features of our modern society is the vast amount of legislation (statutes and statutory instruments, plus numerous bylaws) enacted by Parliament and local authorities. Much of the legislation and the subordinate legislation is complex. All of it is administered or put into effect by civil servants, local government servants and other agencies acting on behalf of Minsters or Government departments. All the social services described in the following pages are the creatures of Parliament, i.e. the services as we know them are brought into being by Statutes. Reference is made in the chapters to the relevant law.

Although Parliament may hope to produce a better life for everyone by the provision of necessary services, we find in practice that things go wrong. A doctor may not attend a patient when called; a social worker may place a child in the care of a person quite unfit to have charge of the child; a perfectly normal and sane person may be committed to a mental institution; persons eligible for benefits may be denied them by a careless civil servant. The list is endless.

Machinery has been set up to ensure that where maladministration has occurred the matter is investigated by persons specially appointed to investigate cases. Thus the **Parliamentary Commissioner for Administration** is charged with investigations into matters affecting the central government and the various ministries. The Parliamentary Commissioner also holds the post of **Health Service Commissioner** and in that capacity makes investigations into maladministration in the National Health Service (see page 432). **Local Commissioners** have been appointed for England, Wales and Scotland (see page 432) to investigate maladministration by local authorities.

Complaints against the police may also be dealt with by a chief constable together with two lay commissioners. It is hoped that any fears that the public may have as to misuse of powers by police will be allayed.

We deal with the subject of complaints in more detail in Chapter 16. This is more suitably dealt with towards the end of the book. The first requirement is to know and understand the services themselves and the particular groups for whom special arrangements are made – the old, the sick, children and young persons, the disabled and other persons.

(More details on the matters raised in this Chapter can be found in *British Constitution Made Simple*, Heinemann and in *Local Government in Britain*, Penguin).

Questions

1 What is meant by (a) the legislature, (b) the executive and (c) the judiciary?
2 What do you understand of the doctrine of the Separation of Powers?
3 The rule of law is fundamental to our Constitution. What do you understand by the phrase 'the Rule of Law'?

4   Describe the process of law-making from the presentation of a Bill to the final Act.
5   What are the money functions of the Commons?
6   What are the main functions of the Department of Health, the Department of Social Security, the Department of Employment, the Home Office and the Department of the Environment?
7   Describe the structure of the local authorities (a) in England and Wales, and (b) in London.
8   What are the functions of (a) county councils and (b) district councils?
9   Some powers of a local authority are described as (a) mandatory and (b) permissive. What is meant by this statement.
10   How does the central Government maintain control over local authorities, and what is the justification for this control?

3
Social security

Definitions of poverty

The existence of widespread poverty presents an obvious problem in any society – obvious in the sense that:

1 It is *overt*: the ragged beggar is instantly seen as poor; it is not so easy to see if people are ill-educated, sick or troubled.
2 It is *basic*: the lack of means is a fundamental deficiency for it denies access to sustenance and shelter, and other necessities of life, and may thus cause premature death or a more chronic stunted existence.

This extreme kind of poverty, where a person lacks the necessities of life, is called **absolute poverty**, and it is rarely found in Britain today. Instead we tend to think in terms of **relative poverty**, where people are able to survive adequately, but where they are either (a) less well off than they used to be – for example, when they retire from paid employment – or (b) at a serious disadvantage in their ability to experience or enjoy the standard of life of most other people – for example, not being able to afford an annual holiday. By analogy we could say that Pakistan is poor compared to Portugal, but the latter is poor compared to Britain.

We are, it is said, as old (or young) as we feel. The same can be said about poverty: you are as poor as you feel. This is called **'felt poverty'**, and is obviously very subjective and not very susceptible to measurement. It is not unimportant, however, when we are concerned with people's peace of mind, sense of justice or wage claims.

In the early twentieth century, Seebohm Rowntree used the concept of **secondary poverty**, by which he meant the condition of those people who, though having enough resources to avoid absolute (or primary) poverty, nevertheless fell into that condition because they misspent their income on inessentials, such as cosmetics instead of clothing. This still occurs on a substantial scale where, for example, excessive gambling or drinking leaves the family deprived of food.

All these definitions are important because, by affecting the way we perceive the problem, they affect the way we try to deal with it.

And deal with it we should for poverty may:

1 Undermine the development of the **individual** physically (through malnutrition, squalid housing); mentally (through anxiety, humiliation); and socially (through despair and marital discord).
2 Damage the **community** by creating slums, ill-health, delinquency and discontent, and by depriving society of fully developed citizens.

To deal effectively with poverty, however it is defined, requires a whole battery of social and economic approaches, control of inflation; maintenance of employment; manipulation of foreign exchange rates; decent housing; educational opportunity, etc. The principal and most immediate mechanism, however, is that of **social security**, which can be described as the income-maintenance arrangements which society, through the State, has made available for the alleviation and avoidance of poverty. These arrangements are examined in the remainder of this chapter.

Arrangements for dealing with poverty

Viewed historically there has been a wide range of provision for the poor including:

(a) family, friends, relatives, local community;
(b) the Church, trade guilds, individual and group charities;
(c) employers and businessmen;
(d) mutual self-help (trade unions, friendly societies);
(e) the State (central, local and intermediate government).

We are primarily concerned with (e), the State, but the continued importance of many of the others should not be overlooked.

The social security arrangements for most of this century have comprised *three* financial elements:

(i)   Assistance on proof of need, e.g. Income Support.
(ii)   National insurance, e.g. retirement pension.
(iii) Universal allowances, e.g. Child Benefit.

In the nineteenth century, state aid was almost entirely confined to assistance on proof of need, and this took the form of the Poor Law.

The Poor Law

As we have seen (page 8) the ancient laws regulating the movement and care of the poor were revised in the *Poor Law Amendment*

Act, 1834. This attempted to apply throughout Britain the principles of the 'workhouse test' (i.e. no help outside the workhouse for able-bodied poor) and 'lesser eligibility' (i.e. lowly conditions in the workhouse). The application of the Act met with much hostility in some areas, especially in the North, and consequently the 'new' Poor Law began to crumble soon after its inauguration. But it lasted a long time and its legacy in terms of attitudes has been substantial, even up to today.

The **break-up of the Poor Law** occurred in three directions:

   (i)   changes in administration;
  (ii)   the undermining of the Poor Law principles;
 (iii)   the loss of 'clients'.

(i) Changes in administration

At central level, responsibility for supervising poor relief lay originally with the Poor Law Commissioners (1834–47) and the Poor Law Board (1847–71). This function was transferred to the Local Government Board in 1871, and in 1919 it became the responsibility of the new Ministry of Health, which supervised local government generally. But the more important changes happened at the 'delivery end', i.e. locally. Since 1834 the authorities responsible for the poor were the Boards of Guardians, single purpose *ad hoc* bodies. In 1929 these were abolished and their functions handed over to local authorities. Then in 1934 and finally in 1948 the relief of poverty function was entirely taken over by the central government. This transfer is important for a number of reasons, but in particular because it:

(a)   Removed the dependence upon local generosity or parsimony which led to substantial variations over the country. Uniform scales of relief could now be applied nationally.
(b)   It removed some of the humiliation and reluctance to seek relief by those who had to reveal their circumstances to their neighbours (the local magistrate committees and relieving officers) when making a claim.

(ii) Undermining the Poor Law principles

This occurred in a number of ways, many of which also illustrate and reflect the factors which have influenced the development of the Welfare State generally.

(a)   A number of **social inquiries and surveys** demonstrated that poverty was not a blameworthy condition. For example, in their separate studies of poverty at the end of the nineteenth century,

Charles Booth* and Seebohm Rowntree† showed that the main causes of poverty were unemployment, low wages and old age. How could you save for your retirement years when you were paid so little during your working life? Similarly, the Rev. A. Mearns‡ showed that a slum upbringing virtually guaranteed an existence of poverty for many thousands of people.

(b) **Royal Commissions** such as that of 1885 investigating the trade depression, helped to give some official support to the inquiries of individuals. Of more direct importance were the Royal Commissions of 1895 and 1905. The former was concerned with 'the Aged Poor' and concluded that there ought to be more humane conditions for the 'deserving', by which they meant those who had worked and led an upright life before becoming impoverished. The *Royal Commission on the Poor Laws, 1905–09* was of fundamental importance. It published two Reports which recommended:

1   Abolition of Boards of Guardians, passing their function to local government.
2   Poverty to be no longer regarded as reprehensible.
3   Poor relief should be renamed 'public assistance'.
4   Labour exchanges be established to help the unemployed.
5   The general mixed workhouse should go.

The Second or Minority Report was more outspoken and radical: its authors were against so much emphasis on charity and voluntary aid. They wanted more State involvement and better standards. In short, they wanted to break up the Poor Law by creating separate services.

(c) **The economic depressions** of the 1880s and the 1930s provided plenty of evidence that unemployment was not the result of being work-shy and idle. The principle of welfare began to seem more appropriate than the principle of deterrence.

(d) **Modern wars** have had a marked effect on our social policy in requiring new skills, in creating casualties and perhaps above all in revealing the social problems and conditions under which 'the other half lives'. Both the Boer War (1899–1901) and the First World War (1914–18) shocked the nation when they revealed the appallingly low standard of the health of the recruits. This was largely attributed to their impoverished background and upbringing. But so many were turned away as unfit that even if

---

*C. Booth, *The Life and Labour of the People in London* (1889).
†S. Rowntree, *Poverty: A Study in Town Life* (1901).
‡Rev. A. Mearns, *The Bitter Cry of Outcast London* (1883).

it was their own fault (which people were increasingly to doubt), in the interests of the nation's future security it behoved the State to take a more positive approach to the needy.

(e) **The limited role of the State** was being seriously questioned at a more philosophical level. In the late nineteenth century organisations like the Fabian Society and the Labour Party were advocating Socialism and were gaining support and influence. At the universities political theorists like T. H. Green and B. Bosanquet began to write and expound the notion that State activity could increase people's liberty by removing the hindrances, such as poverty and slums, to personal development.

(f) **The spread of the franchise** (the right to vote), both locally and nationally, resulted in:

1 Existing MPs, Ministers and councillors having to start 'courting' and canvassing the working man and taking some account of his opinions and ideas.
2 Working men themselves beginning to get elected to positions of influence, as a result of which provision began to change. Perhaps the best illustration of this was the 'Revolt of Poplar', when the newly elected members of the Poplar Board of Guardians under the leadership of George Lansbury began to pay outdoor relief to the able-bodied ('decent treatment outside the workhouse, and hang the rates!'). Some other Boards followed suit until 1921, when the Poplar Guardians were jailed.

(g) **Foreign examples** of alternative means of dealing with poverty began to influence both the practices and the principles of Britain's Poor Law. New Zealand had introduced an Old Age Pension Scheme in 1898. Germany had developed in the 1880s a system of social insurance which gave cash benefits in times of sickness, unemployment and retirement. At the beginning of the twentieth century Europe generally was moving towards a system of national insurance, and when it happened in Britain it was the beginning of the end of the Poor Law.

(iii) The loss of clients

The Poor Law began to break down because it was becoming redundant, not just as an idea but also as a mechanism; it began to lose 'customers'. At the end of the nineteenth century more people were being helped by private charity than by the poor law, and many people were helping themselves (through savings banks and building societies) and one another (through trade unions and friendly societies). Above all, after the beginning of the twentieth century the Guardians themselves started to become 'unemployed' as the State began to provide alternatives to the Poor Law.* Thus the following Acts should be noted:

1905   *Unemployed Workmen Act* – provided public works employment.
1906   *Education Act* – arranged for the provision of subsidised school meals for elementary school children.
1908   *Old Age Pensions Act* – introduced a non-contributory provision of 5*s*. (25p) per week (maximum) for those over 70.
1909   *Labour Exchanges Act* – established a system of employment exchanges.
1909   *Trade Boards Act* – set up machinery to fix minimum wages to prevent low pay.

All these helped to diminish people's reliance on the Poor Law; but the most important development was the *National Insurance Act, 1911*.

The National Insurance Act, 1911

This was perhaps the most important of the 'Liberal reforms'. It was to transform our system of social security through the provision of cash benefits when earning was interrupted through sickness or unemployment.

On the **health** side it:

1   Required weekly contributions from employees (4*d*.), employers (3*d*.) and the Government (2*d*.). The scheme was commonly called 'ninepence for fourpence'.
2   Covered all manual workers and non-manual workers earning under £160 p.a.
3   Included benefits in the form of a cash payment of 10*s*. (50p) per week, and a free 'panel' doctor service.
4   Provided that the scheme be administered by 'Approved Societies', i.e. friendly societies and insurance companies approved by the Government.

On the **employment** side it:

1   Required weekly contributions of 2½*d*.

*It could be argued that any state provision which improved people's overall welfare reduced their call on the Poor Law, so that housing, health and education legislation could all be considered relevant here. We shall confine our attention to the purely social security aspects.

2 Provided unemployment benefit of 7s. (35p) per week for a maximum of 15 weeks.
3 Was limited to certain trades at first, covering about 2½ million people.

In many ways the National Insurance Scheme was simply an extension on a national scale of insurance arrangements which had been developed in the nineteenth century by trade unions and friendly societies. This enabled the system to gain public acceptance, but it found special favour from those who argued that it gave people greater self-respect to receive benefits on the basis of having made contributions. Apart from this it was a system which appealed to the Treasury since it provided an acceptable method of raising money. Consequently, in 1921 the Unemployment Scheme was expanded to cover 11 million employees and introduced dependents' allowances; and in 1925 a **contributory pension scheme** was introduced for the elderly (aged 65–70) and for widows and orphans.

The result of all these measures was substantially to reduce the numbers seeking relief from the Poor Law authorities. But the economic recession of the 1920s and 1930s put this development in jeopardy and threatened to lead to wholesale reversion to the services of the Guardians.

The inter-war period (1919–39) was characterised by heavy unemployment, averaging over 14 per cent. Many were out of work for long periods and exhausted their entitlement to insurance benefit. However, the Government decided to allow them to continue claiming; hence it was variously called 'extended', 'transitional' or 'uncovenanted' benefit. There was, however, a limit to what the Government could afford, and it was in fact seeking to reduce public expenditure. In 1931 it reduced benefits by 10 per cent and those receiving 'uncovenanted' benefits (i.e. the dole) were to be 'means' tested. Consequently many of the unemployed and their families had to resort to the local Poor Law either to supplement or replace their expired unemployment benefit.

Yet the strain of unemployment was too great for many Boards of Guardians as well. Some had to borrow money, some even went bankrupt. Others struggled on, but the result was considerable variation in standards over the country. Thus, quite apart from the 'snooping' and the indignity of treatment, it was apparent that the Poor Law system was failing to cope. Consequently, in 1929 the Boards of Guardians were abolished and their functions transferred to **Public Assistance Committees** of the local authorities. Then in 1934 the **Unemployment Assistance Board** was created to pay out public assistance instead of the pretence of 'insurance' (mentioned above) to those who exhausted their benefit entitlement. It would not be very long before this Board, renamed the **Assistance Board** in 1940, took over the work of the local authority Public Assistance Committees in order to apply uniform scales of relief.

The Beveridge Report, 1942

In 1941, on the suggestion of the trade unions, the Government set up a committee to review existing national insurance arrangements. Sir William Beveridge (later Lord Beveridge), who had a lifetime's interest and experience in employment and welfare matters, was appointed its chairman. He virtually assumed sole responsibility for the subsequent Report called 'Social Insurance and Allied Services' (HMSO, Cmnd. 6404).

The Government was seeking a tidying up of the social security system, but Beveridge believed it was 'time for a revolution, not patching'. In particular he was critical of the existing arrangements in respect of:

1   Coverage – far too many people were excluded from the insurance schemes.
2   Scope – certain risks or life events, such as marriage or death, were not covered.
3   Benefits – often inadequate, inconsistent or short-lived.
4   Administration – this was untidy and wasteful.
5   Underpinning – the system lacked strength without the support of certain other services such as employment and health services.

As a result of these deficiencies there were far too many people still dependent upon the Poor Law. In 1942, of those receiving outdoor relief, some 40 per cent (90,000) were receiving it in supplementation of some form of State benefit.

Outline of Beveridge proposals

The Report speaks of 'five giants' in the road of post-war reconstruction – namely Disease, Ignorance, Squalor, Idleness and Want. The **aim** of the proposals was to eliminate the latter: Want, i.e. poverty.

The **method** was to consist of a thoroughly revised scheme of (a) national insurance, topped up where necessary by (b) national assistance, and the whole system to be underpinned with (c) full employment, (d) a National Health Service, and (e) a system of family allowances (see Figure 3).

(a)   **National Insurance.** This was to be the most important element and was to be based upon certain *principles*:

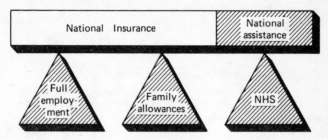

Figure 3 *The Beveridge social security scheme*

(i) **Universal** coverage, bringing into the scheme all people whether workers, self-employed, non-employed or dependants.

(ii) **Comprehensive** scope in the coverage of risks.

(iii) Adequate, or **subsistence**, levels of benefit (a 'national minimum').

(iv) **Flat-rate** contributions and benefits, i.e. paid at the same rate regardless of income.

(v) Benefits to be paid as **of right**, provided that contributions are complete.

(vi) **Unification of administration** through payment of a single contribution (the NI stamp) to a single Government department.

(b) **National Assistance.** This was to be completely centralised and the Poor Law abolished. National Assistance was a 'safety net' to catch those who failed, through insufficient contributions, to qualify for insurance benefits. This would normally be a small number of people, though at the beginning many pensioners would have to rely on allowances until the passage of time and regular contributions entitled them to full retirement benefit.

(c) **Full employment.** This was seen as a prerequisite to the success of the scheme. As the 1930s had shown, no national insurance scheme could survive the strain of mass unemployment.

(d) **A comprehensive health service.** This would reduce sickness, and therefore claims on the insurance fund for sickness benefit. After that, it was hoped, health services themselves could contract as people became healthier.

(e) **Family allowances.** These were to be introduced partly to alleviate poverty in large low-wage families, and partly to boost the sagging birth rate. The main reason for this proposal, however, was to avoid the 'Why work?' attitude by maintaining an income differential between the wage-earning family and the family on benefit.

Importance of the Beveridge Report

Most of the recommendations were adopted by post-war Governments, to a large extent because they caught the public imagination and became overwhelmingly popular.

In many ways the reforms did not amount to 'a revolution'. In the first place, they built substantially on existing arrangements, and second, levels of benefit were not altered very substantially since they were to provide no more than subsistence.

The Report has been criticised as 'born of the 1930s' and too influenced by the past; that it should have allowed for the possibility of inflation; and it should have sought adequacy (in the relative sense) rather than subsistence (in the absolute sense). Yet a more radical report might not have received official acceptance, as indeed was almost the fate of the Beveridge Report itself. In many ways the Report was important because it:

(i)   Provided a universal system which made the scheme truly national.
(ii) Produced a complete system instead of a collection of different schemes.
(iii) Abolished the Poor Law and instituted a national minimum of support.
(iv) Supplied the basis of our social security system even up to the present day.

The Beveridge legislation

The following is a summary of the legislation which resulted from the Beveridge Report.

National Insurance

1944   *National Insurance Act* – set up the Ministry of National Insurance to administer the new scheme.
1946   *National Insurance Act* and *National Insurance (Industrial Injuries) Act.* Together these two Acts:
    (a)   Embodied the National Insurance Scheme, operative in 1948.
    (b)   Replaced existing provisions for pensions, unemployment National Insurance and Workmen's Compensation Acts.
    (c)   Provided that everyone of working age be insured, except some of the non-employed, including married women.

(d)   Set up classifications for every contributor as:

employee (Class I)
self-employed (Class II)
non-employed (Class III)

(e)   Laid down entitlements (for a single person) of:

Sickness benefit	£1 6s. (£1.30) p.w.	
Unemployment benefit	£1 6s. (£1.30) p.w.	
Retirement pension	£1 6s. (£1.30) p.w.	
Industrial injuries	£2 5s. (£2.25) p.w.	
Death grant	£20.00	
Maternity grant	£4.00	
Maternity allowance	£1 16s. (£1.80) p.w.	
Widow's benefit	£1 6s. (£1.30) p.w.	
Guardian's allowance	12s. (60p) p.w.	

(f)   Said that benefit rates were to be reviewed every five
years.

(*Note:* Benefit depended on contribution record and the insurance class. Only Class I persons were entitled to the full range of benefits.)

Family allowances

1945   *Family Allowances Act* – Payments of 5s. (25p) per week
payable for each child, after the first, up to leaving school.

National Assistance

1948   *National Assistance Act* – This established the National Assistance Board which replaced the Assistance Board and took over the remaining functions of the Public Assistance Committees of local authorities. The function of the National Assistance Board was to give assistance to those not, or inadequately, covered by National Insurance. It was a non-contributory allowance, and it was financed by the Treasury. The allowance paid by the NAB was based on an assessment of the needs and means of the claimant. Typical examples of allowances were: single person £1 4s. (£1.20) p.w.; married couple, £2 p.w., plus rent allowance.
(*Note:* Part III of this Act left welfare services, including ex-workhouses, in the hands of local authorities.)

Comments

While this legislation substantially followed Beveridge's recommendations it differed in detail. Thus:

(a) Benefits were not paid at subsistence levels, e.g. family allowances were paid at 5s. (25p) p.w., which was well below the recommended subsistence of 8s. (40p).

(b) Retirement pensioners, instead of waiting 20 years for their contributions to build up and 'mature', were actually paid from the start, although at the lower rate as in (a) above.

(c) Unemployment benefit was not payable for the duration of unemployment if it exceeded 30 weeks.

Changes in the Beveridge system

Since the founding legislation of the 1940s there have been a number of developments in the field of social security. Some of these have substantially removed the Beveridge elements. The changes have occurred in four directions:

1 In the rates of benefit/contribution.
2 In the administrative machinery.
3 In the form of benefits and contributions.
4 In the underlying principles.

1 The rates of benefit/contribution

These are bound to alter over time, either in response to the changing cost of living or to changing views about what is a reasonable level of payment. The Beveridge Plan allowed for a regular (five-yearly) review. In practice the pace of inflation has been such that much more frequent reviews have been necessary, and while legally obliged to review pensions annually, the Government usually revises most benefit rates each November (and contribution rates each April).

The figures are given for the purposes of illustration. They show dramatic increases since 1948, and Ministers are often proud to announce 'biggest ever' rises in the rates of benefit. But the increases are only massive in *money terms*. In *real terms* (what the money or benefits can buy) the overall levels of benefit have only kept pace with average earnings (benefits for a married couple usually amounting to about 30 per cent of the average wage – see M. Young, *Poverty Report 1974*, page 7). So there have been real improvements for the less well off; but no more than for society as a whole, and in recent years there has perhaps even been a relative fall (see A. Walker, *The Growing Divide* and CPAG *Poverty The Facts*).

Weekly rate of Payment	1948	1969	1976	1989
Insurance benefit (pension, sickness, unemployment) for single person, basic rate	£1.30	£5.00	£15.30 (pension) £12.90 (unemployment) £12.90 (sickness)	£43.60 £34.70 £36.25 (after 28 weeks or £52.10 of SSP)
National Assistance/ Supplementary Benefit/**Income Support** (without rent) for single person	£1.20	£2.80	£12.70	£34.90
Family Allowance/ **Child Benefit**	25p	40p	£1.50	£7.25
National Insurance **Contributions**	23p	88p	5.75% of wages (= £3 approx, average)	9% (= £20 approx)

2   Changes in administration

The legislation which followed the Beveridge Report established the Ministry of National Insurance and the National Assistance Board (NAB). They were to be separate because it was felt desirable to distinguish between insurance benefits and assistance allowances. In 1953 the old Ministry of Pensions, which paid war pensions, was merged with the Ministry of National Insurance. But of more significance were the changes of 1966.

In 1966 the **Ministry of Social Security** was created to assume overall responsibility in that field and thus replace the Ministry of Pensions and National Insurance. At the same time the NAB was replaced by the **Supplementary Benefits Commission (SBC)**, which was to be a semi-autonomous body, acting as a subdepartment of the Ministry of Social Security. (This was unlike the NAB, which was more of a separate department.)

The status of the SBC was based on a compromise to keep questions of assistance out of politics, yet to allow greater coordination of benefits and allowances, rates and claims. By linking Supplementary Benefits more closely to National Insurance it was also hoped that the inferior status of the former might be diminished. Besides, Supplementary Benefits had long been *supplementing* insurance benefits. The change of name was significant too, because it got rid of the stigmatic term 'assistance' which was so closely associated, since the 1930s, with the dreaded Poor Law.

In 1968 the **Department of Health and Social Security (DHSS)**, was created from the amalgamation of the Ministry of Social Security and the Ministry of Health. Internally it contained separate sections or divisions of government to deal with social security, health and personal social services, and each had an Advisory Committee with members drawn from public authorities, trade unions and the professions. The purpose of creating such a 'super-Ministry' was essentially to attempt to coordinate benefits in cash with benefits in kind since 'the services needed to deal with social insecurity are not cash benefits only, but health and welfare services as well'. (V. George, *Social Security*, page 77.) Thus a lonely widower may need a home help, sheltered accommodation or meals-on-wheels, as well as income in the form of a pension. Whether such accommodation is actually *achieved* is another matter; clearly it was not regarded as particularly important for in 1988 it was separated into two once more (partly because it was felt that it had become too big a responsibility for one person to carry).

3   Changes in principles

Many of the principles explicitly stated in the Beveridge Report have been amended over the past 30 years. Some were deliberately changed; others were just allowed to lapse. They include:

(i)   **The subsistence principle.** Beveridge thought it crucial that benefits be paid at the subsistence level, by which he meant the 'poverty line' measure used by Rowntree and others in their social surveys of the 1930s. Yet when they were introduced, National Insurance benefits and family allowances were below this level. Although the rates of benefit did improve, the overall result was that many people found them inadequate and had to resort to National Assistance, later Supplementary Benefit and now Income Support.

(ii) **National Assistance.** Beveridge had seen the means-tested National Assistance as a residual and diminishing element of the new social security system; in effect 'a safety net' for those who missed out on National Insurance and could not claim full benefit. As we have seen above, the reverse occurred: assistance on proof of need, now called Income Support has expanded enormously, providing claims worth over £5,000 million a year, for some 5 million claimants (compared to 1.6 million in the mid 1950s). There is also an estimated £500 to £1,000 million of benefits not claimed by about one million of those eligible.

(iii) **The flat rate principle.** This simplified the social security scheme, and reflected the spirit of equality which was engendered by the war. Everyone was to receive the same subsistence benefit. But in 1961 and 1966 the insurance scheme was modified to allow contributions and benefits to vary with individual earnings (see page 50). The immediate reason for this change was to raise money. In the late 1950s the National Insurance

Fund was being drained by the rising numbers of pensioners, yet it was difficult to raise the flat-rate contributions because it would hit the lower-paid. So the new system, in so far as it related contributions to earnings, was more equitable. The revised system was seen as more equitable in another sense: it took account of the notion of 'relative poverty'. It did this in two ways: (a) it meant that when people stopped earning they fell back on benefits which were related to their former income rather than a uniform flat-rate level; (b) since benefits were now related to incomes (which were rising in real terms) the benefit levels were becoming linked to the general standard of living. It was an attempt to allow claimants to share the affluence of the 1950s and 1960s. 'Thus the Beveridge revolution spent itself with the rise in national prosperity.' (V. George, *Social Security*). Thus it was hoped that in time, these improved levels of insurance benefit would diminish claimants' need for recourse to Supplementary Benefits. However, partly to reduce State spending, and partly to reduce the temptation of those in benefit to delay their return to work, the Government abolished earnings-related benefits in 1981 (except for pensions).

(iv) **Universality.** In 1942 the Beveridge Report said: 'In a matter so fundamental [as social insurance] it is right for all citizens to stand in together, without exclusions based on differences of status, function or wealth.' In 1961, in incorporating the earnings-related system, the Government allowed 'contracting out', i.e. employers with their own benefit schemes could, on behalf of their staff, opt out of the State earnings-related part of National Insurance. This breached the principle of universality, as not everyone would have access to an occupational scheme, and these will vary in quality from one to another. This has been reinforced by the pensions legislation of 1975 and 1986 (see below).

(v) **Funding.** The Beveridge Plan was to be 'funded'. This means that contributions were to be built up over a sufficient period of time so that claims could be adequately met as they fell due. The principle applies particularly to retirement pensions, and this is why the Report planned to phase in pension entitlement over a 20-year period. In practice the scheme was jeopardised from the outset when the Government decided to pay after 10 years (i.e. from 1958) full pensions to those joining the scheme in 1948, while those already retired under the 1925 Act got full pensions straight away. Subsequent pensions plans have given rise to discussion about the wisdom of funding, but the new provisions for pensions, operative from 1978, are firmly wedded to the idea of a 'pay-as-you-go' system, which is the opposite of funding.

These changes in principle have both reflected, and have been reflected in, the changing **form** of social security.

4   Changing forms of benefit

Some of these changes are variants of existing payments; others are completely new payments which may imply a fundamental change or simply the filling of a gap. We may summarise the changes as follows:

Date	Name of Payment	Date	Name of Payment
1957	Child's Special Allowance	1975	Earnings Related Pensions
1961	Graduated Pension	1976	Child Benefit
1965	Redundancy Payments		Invalid Care Allowance
1966	Earnings Related Benefit		Mobility Allowance
1970	Pensions for over-80s	1982	Unified Housing Benefit
1971	Attendance Allowance;	1984	Severe Disablement Allowance
	Invalidity Allowance	1986	Personal Pensions
	Widows Age-Related Pension		Income Support
	Family Income Supplement		Family Credit
1972	Rent Allowance/Rebate		Social Fund

Some of these developments are of such fundamental importance that we must examine them in detail. We shall be in a position to give an overall assessment.

Changes up to 1979

The National Insurance Act, 1959 introduced **graduated pensions**, operative from 1961, i.e. in return for additional contributions you became entitled to an extra pension, on top of your flat-rate State retirement pension.

(a)   In addition to flat-rate contributions, contributors paid 4.25 per cent of their earnings, within £9–£15 p.w. band (later extended).

(b)   The extra revenue was used partly to raise flat-rate pensions and partly to pay the extra (i.e. graduated) pensions, according to people's contributions.

(c)   Employees could **'contract out'** where an occupational scheme existed (see page 49) but would then be required to pay a higher flat-rate contribution, because they gained from the increased flat-rate pension, as in (b) above.

The National Insurance Act, 1966 introduced **earnings-related be-**

nefits, i.e. other than pensions:

(a)   In addition to the flat-rate contributions, contributors paid 0.5 per cent of their income (on £9–£30 p.w.).
(b)   'Contracting out' was not permitted.
(c)   Extra revenue was used to pay extra (i.e. earnings-related) benefits, on top of flat-rate benefits for unemployment, sickness and widowhood.
(d)   The additional benefit would normally amount to one third of average earnings, but flat-rate *plus* earnings-related supplement could not exceed 85 per cent of average earnings.*
(e)   The addition ran for six months. (*Note:* This earnings-related scheme ceased in 1981 (see below).)
(f)   The earnings-related part of contributions were to be paid through the tax system (PAYE), but under the *Social Security Act, 1973*, all **contributions** were to be earnings-related, so in 1975 the traditional insurance 'stamp' was dropped and contributions are now mainly collected as a fixed percentage of earnings through the PAYE system (broadly 9 per cent of earnings between £41 and £305 p.w. in 1989).

The Family Income Supplements Act, 1970. This Act introduced the Family Income Supplement (FIS) for working parent(s) on low incomes:

(a)   Where family income (gross) falls below an officially prescribed level, a supplement is paid equal to half of this deficiency, up to a maximum sum (e.g. of £22 p.w. in a one-child family, £24 for two children).
(b)   The prescribed level varies with the number of children (e.g. in 1984 for a one-child family it was £85 p.w., £94.50 for two children, £104 for three).

This Act breaches the principle that employed persons cannot receive Supplementary Benefit, and it resembles the old Speenhamland system (see page 6). Apart from single parents and single-child families it was intended to benefit those on low incomes who may be subject to the 'wage stop', as FIS would now be regarded as part of their normal income.*

*This limitaiton of 85 per cent is known as the 'wage stop'. It is similar to that which until 1975 operated in the Supplementary Benefits Scheme, in which no claimant must receive from State benefits more than s/he would normally have earned from being employed. The aim was to avoid work disincentive by a modern form of 'lesser eligibility'. Under the 'work shy' rules of 1968, however, Supplementary Benefit could be withdrawn from anyone regarded as making insufficient effort to find work, but this has been rarely used. However, entitlement can be lost if claimants are found to be 'moonlighting' i.e. drawing benefit *and* working.

The Child Benefit Act, 1975. This Act ordained that Family Allowance and Income Tax Allowance for dependent children were to be phased out and replaced with a new Child Benefit. This non-contributory benefit is payable for all children, including the first. It represents part of the Government's response to the 1974 Finer Committee's Report, *One Parent Families*. It started in 1976 with the benefit going to the first child of single-parent families; in 1977 all first children became eligible.

The Social Security Pensions Act, 1975. This act is based on the Labour Government's White Paper of 1974, *Better Pensions*, though its proposals really go back to the 1969 White Paper *Superannuation and Social Insurance*. The proposed legislation was interrupted by a change of Government, at which point the Conservative Government published its own proposals in the White Paper '*Strategy for Pensions*'. The legislation for this (the *Social Security Act 1973*) did not have a chance to become operative owing to another change of Government in 1974. Thus we have pensions, like housing, becoming something of a political football, and the main issue has really been the extent to which the State or private enterprise should be made responsible for the earnings-related portion which is added to the basic pension.

Under the 1975 Act (operating from April 1978):

(a)   The pension has two parts: the basic flat rate *plus* a certain percentage (about 25 per cent) of earnings.

(b)   Contributions are earnings-related, and tripartite (i.e. employee, employer and Government).

(c)   The basic pension is paid by the State: the additional pension known as SERPS would be based on a person's best 20 years' earnings and paid by the State, *or* by employers where they operate an acceptable occupational scheme and 'contract out' (which reduces the rate of contribution to be paid into the State scheme).

(d)   The scheme will mature over 20 years: anyone retiring within 20 years will get a proportion of his full entitlement.

(e)   Women will belong to the scheme in equal terms with men in respect of both contributions and benefits.

(f)   Benefits include not only retirement pensions, but also invalidity pensions, widows' pensions and widowed mothers' allowance.

(g)   Pensions are to be revalued to keep pace with prices (the intended link with earnings was dropped in 1979).

(h)   Pension rights are safeguarded during absences or changes of employment. Rights under the old Graduated Pension Scheme, which ceased in April 1975, will be preserved until retirement.

Briefly, the aim of the Government in this pension arrangement was, in partnership with occupational schemes, to give an adequate pension so that resort to Supplementary Benefits becomes unnecessary. 'It will take the worry out of old age; the sting out of retirement' (Barbara Castle).

The changes outlined before show how far we have departed from the Beveridge Plan. Further important changes have occurred since 1979.

Changes in the 1980s

Beveridge, Bevan, Titmuss and others saw the Welfare State as the outward form of the responsible and caring society. Mrs Thatcher on the other hand sees what she calls the 'Patronage State' as divisive rather than cohesive: that it divides honest workers and savers from the prolific spenders who live from day to day. In 1987, the Secretary of State for Social Services, John Moore, criticised what he called 'the dependency culture'. Not surprisingly, therefore, the Conservative Government has taken a more radical and less supportive approach to the social services. Besides, the Government was elected in 1979 on a programme of restoring economic incentives to business and individuals through cuts in both taxation and State spending, though in practice spending on social security has grown – mainly to support the higher unemployment. This overall growth masks a number of important changes in detail since 1979. Limitations of space allow only a brief summary of these:

(a)   Earnings-related supplements to short-term benefits ceased in 1981.
(b)   Short-term benefits are now taxable (as was already the case with long-term benefits, e.g. pensions).
(c)   The link between benefits and prices and/or earnings (known as 'indexation') is now confined to prices; and usually after a time-lag.
(d)   For workers on strike, benefit (payable only to family dependents) is reduced by an assumed amount of union strike pay (£17.70 p.w.).
(e)   Employers now pay sickness benefit (SSP) for the first 28 weeks (at a flat rate, with no additions for dependents). Self-certification operates for the first week: doctors' notes are then required.
(f)   The Supplementary Benefit system was re-cast by merging various rates of payment (e.g. for different aged children) and

by standardising many payments (for exceptional circumstances and needs – ECPs and ENPs) which were formerly discretionary (and overseen by the SB Commission).

(g)   The Supplementary Benefits Commission was abolished in 1980 (partly due to (f) above).

(h)   Entitlement to Income Support for most 16–18-year-olds was withdrawn by the *Social Security Act, 1986*. Post-school students may claim Income Support during term time only if their college hours do not exceed 21.

(i)   Insurance tribunals and Supplementary Benefit Appeal Tribunals were merged into Social Security Appeal Tribunals.

There are various **reasons for these changes**. Firstly, to reduce public expenditure (including the administrative savings from the new system of *monthly* Child Benefit payments); total savings were officially estimated at £1,500 million. Secondly, to reduce the 'poverty trap' and increase the incentive to find work by making life on the dole less relatively financially attractive. Thirdly, to simplify and make administratively tidier (as with the alignment of some Supplementary Benefit and insurance benefits, and injury and sickness benefits).

These motives also help to account for the Government's fundamental review of Social Security in 1984 (the '**Fowler reviews**'). In addition, the Government was concerned about the mess the system seemed to be getting into as a result of all the changes; the social security system had become like a house with lots of odd extensions, conversions and additions.

The results of the review were published in 1985 as a Green Paper *Reform of Social Security*, followed in the same year by a White Paper *Reform of Social Security: Programme for Reform*. This resulted in the *Social Security Act, 1986*, declaimed by the Minister as 'the Beveridge of the 1980s' and intended to take the social security system well into the twenty-first century. Indeed, echoing the words of the original Beveridge Report (see page 42) the White Paper declared that 'the need is not for trimming but proper reform'. Before looking at this important reform, we shall outline the faults which were detected during the review.

The review criticised the social security system on the following grounds:

(a)   Having developed piecemeal, it now consisted of too many different benefits – over 30 of them – each with separate rules and regulations.

(b)   Its great complexity for the public in general and for claimants and the (40,000) social security staff in particular, and the consequential probability of errors (e.g. a report by the Parliamentary Public Accounts Committee in February 1988 revealed overpayments of £87 million).

(c)   That help does not always go to where it is most needed, especially low-income families.

(d)   It was leaving too many in the poverty and unemployment traps (see page 66).

(e)   It was failing to take account of the likely costs of the system to future generations (when, in 2035, there will be 4 million more pensioners).

Thus the key features of the new scheme, which was detailed in the *Social Security Act, 1986*, involved:

(i)   A sharing or off-loading of the state through an extension of occupational pensions and a new right to personal pension, since, in the words of the White Paper:

> In building for the future we should follow the basic principle that social security is not the function of the state alone. It is a partnership between the individual and the state – a system built on twin pillars.

(ii)   More direction or 'targeting' of help to those in need (especially the low-income families and disabled).

(iii)   The reduction or removal of the dependency 'traps'.

(iv)   Simpler and more sensible rules.

(v)   A financial base which the country can better afford

i.e. partnership, target, un-trap, simplify and reduce cost.

The Social Security Act, 1986

This Act, supplemented by numerous Government regulations, and implemented mainly in 1988, fundamentally reformed two areas of social security – pensions and means tested benefits (or assistance on proof of need; see page 61).

(a)   The additional State earnings-related part of the pension (SERPS) is scaled down to 20 per cent (from 25 per cent) of lifetime earnings (rather than the best 20 years; see page 52), though this will not affect anyone retiring before 2001. In addition, employees have the option of transferring from SERPS entirely into either an occupational scheme or a personal pension arrangement. Apart from widening choice, the aim is to reduce costs. It was estimated that pension costs could rise over three-fold between 1985 and 2035 owing to the growth in pensioners, and that workers/contributors per pensioner will fall from 2.3 to 1.6.

(b) **Income Support** replaces Supplementary Benefit and simplifies the old rules and categories. As before, payments depend on claimants' means (income and savings) and their requirements or needs. Income is now calculated *after* tax, and savings only partially affect entitlement between £3000 and £6000. Claimants receive payments called 'personal allowances' (which vary with age and family status) for themselves and their children, plus 'premiums' for particular client groups (pensioners, the disabled etc.). The latter in effect replaced the Supplementary Benefit additional allowances (for special diet, heating etc. costs). Anyone receiving Income Support is automatically entitled to Housing Benefit and to exemption from NHS charges (though they are liable to pay at least 20 per cent of rates/community charge). And Income Supplement cannot be claimed by those in full-time employment or education.

(c) **Family Credit** replaces Family Income Supplement (FIS; see page 51). It is an income-related benefit paid to low-income working families with children (where at least one partner works 24 or more hours a week). Payment depends on (i) level of income (now after tax) (ii) number and age of children (iii) savings (over £3000), and takes the form of 'credits' for adults and children. These are paid in full (tax-free) when income is at, or below, the Income Support level/rate; above that level (broadly from £55 to £100 p.w.) payment of Family Credit is reduced (or 'tapered'). Families on Family Credit will continue to receive exemption from NHS charges. But automatic entitlement to free school meals and welfare foods ceases (though the level of Family Credit child credits has been raised to compensate). Once application for Family Credit has been accepted, it runs for six-monthly renewal periods.

(d) **The Social Fund** is established to provide special additions for people with exceptional expenses (formerly met by Supplementary Benefit through Exceptional Circumstances Allowances and Exceptional Needs Payments). Payments are determined by the specially-trained staff and most take the form of loans; most of the grants are payable for community care purposes (to enable ex-patients and others to move back to, or remain in, the community).

(e) **Housing Benefit** was modified in various ways. In particular, there was the alignment of qualifying income levels with those of Income Support, and assessment is now based on *net* income (to help avoid the unemployment and poverty traps where it may hardly pay to seek employment or a better paid job).

These radical reforms have been praised for: (i) introducing greater simplicity; (ii) aligning the conditions or rates of the various benefits; (iii) focusing more help on families with children; (iv) reducing the poverty traps; and (v) enhancing claimants' self-respect by replacing free services with cash allowances. But critics have pointed to (i) the many who have lost benefit or suffered reduced payments; (ii) the greater complexity or difficulty in getting benefits; (iii) the nonsense of repayable loans; (iv) the excessive discretionary power of officials; and (v) claim the whole exercise as a way of reducing social security expenditure.

At this stage it is too soon to make a judgement, though there is some early evidence to suggest that many people are living in poverty in spite of, or because of, the present system (see below). Meanwhile, it appears that the Government is considering further, perhaps longer-term, changes. Child benefit has been frozen for two years (losing some 7 per cent of its real value), suggesting that it may be phased out entirely. The Government has also hinted that benefits (such as flat-rate state pensions) may be targeted or means-tested. However, at this point it is appropriate to summarise Britain's social security system.

An outline of current cash benefits

Basically there are three kinds of benefits: (a) Contributory (or National Insurance); (b) Non-contributory; and (c) income-related (or means-tested).

The figures for these, given on pages 57–64, were operative from April 1989, and are illustrative in that only *one* figure is given, mostly a *weekly* sum, and one relating (usually) to the *single adult male*. Many benefits carry additions for dependents or special circumstances.

Contributory benefits (i.e. NI contributions are required)

1	Unemployment Benefit £34.70	(a)	Flate-rate *benefit* payable after 3 days and continuing for up to a year (then replaced by Income Support).
2	Sickness Benefit/SSP £33.20	(a)	After 4 days of illness, for most people this is paid (for up to 28 weeks) by the employer, as *Statutory Sick Pay*, at different rates according to earnings e.g. £52 or £36 p.w. for those earning over or under £84.

Contributory benefits (i.e. NI contributions are required)

Those not eligible for SSP (self-employed, unemployed etc.) may claim flat-rate Sickness Benefit for up to 28 weeks, after which time invalidity pension (see below) is applicable.

3   Invalidity Benefit
£43.60

(a)   Flat-rate invalidity *pension* replacing sickness benefit after 28 weeks and payable for as long as incapacity for work continues.

£9.20 or £5.90 or £2.90
(up to age 40 or 50
or 60)

Invalidity *allowance*, paid in addition to (a); varies with age at which incapacity began, providing this was more than five years before retirement age; payable as long as incapacity continues.

4   Maternity Benefits
90 per cent of earnings
for 6 weeks then £36.25
p.w.

(a)   For those in employment and paying National Insurance the employer pays *Statutory Maternity Pay* for up to 18 weeks.

£33.20

(b)   Those without an employer but with National Insurance can get *Maternity Allowance* for up to 18 weeks.

5   Retirement Pension
£43.60

(a)   Flat-rate *pension* paid on retirement at or after age 60 for women, 65 for men. (Pension was reduced where earnings exceeded £75 per week. This 'earnings rule' ceased in October 1989.)

(b)   Earnings-related addition (see page 000).

(c)   Increments earned by deferring retirement.

(d)   Addition for pensioners over 80.

6   Child's Special Allowance
£8.95

Payable to divorced mother if ex-husband dies while he was contributing to the child's upkeep.

7	Widow's Benefits £1000	(a)	Lump sum *widow's payment* of £1000 for those under 60 (and those over 60 if husband died before retirement).
	£43.60	(b)	Widowed *mother's allowance* payable when widow's allowance ceases, for as long as the widow has a son or daughter under 19 living with her or dependent on her.
	£13.08–£40.55	(c)	Widow's *age-related pension* payable to women widowed at 45 or over who have no dependent children *or* who are 45 or over when widowed mother's allowance ends. Pension rate varies with age. May be earnings-related additions for (b) and (c).
8	Industrial Injury	(a)	Industrial *injury benefit* ceased to exist as such when it merged with Sickness Benefit in 1983. Anyone suffering from an industrial accident or disease is thus entitled to SSP for 28 weeks, and if necessary (after 6 months) invalidity benefit – see above. If disablement or death results from injury, other benefits may be payable – see 16, page 60.

Non-contributory benefits (i.e. NI contributions are not required)

9	Guardian's Allowance £8.95	Payable to a person providing a home for a child whose parents are both dead, or where one parent is dead and the other cannot be traced or is serving a long prison sentence.

Non-contributory benefits (*contd*)

10	Old Person's Pension £26.20		Flat-rate *pension* for those over 80 not entitled to sufficient Contributory pension.
11	Attendance Allowance £34.90 or £23.30		Flat rate *allowance* for severely disabled (physical or mental) people needing attention or supervision from another person day and/or night.
12	Child Benefit £7.25	(a)	Flat-rate for each child up to leaving school/college. Replaced Family Allowances 1975.
	£5.20	(b)	*One parent* benefit: this supplements (a).
13	Invalid Care Allowance £26.20		Flat-rate payment to people (except wives) of working age who cannot work because they have to stay at home to care for a severely disabled person (not necessarily a relative).
14	Mobility Allowance £24.40		Flat-rate *allowance* for severely disabled people aged 5 to 75 (but no new claims after 65).
15	War Pensions £71.20 (for private, 100 per cent disabled)	(a)	*Disablement pension* is payable for lifetime for those disabled in the forces. Amount depends on rank and degree of disablement.
	(Mobility supplements may be payable too)	(b)	*Widow's and dependants pension* – of those killed in armed service: sum varies with rank, and with age of claimant; additions for children and rent.
16	Industrial Injury £71.20–£14.24	(a)	Industrial *disablement benefit* is payable if disablement results from industrial injury (whether or not the person works). The amount varies with the

extent of disablement and
certain conditions (constant
attendance, unemployment,
etc.).

£60.65

(b) Industrial *death benefit* is
payable for death resulting
from industrial accident or
disease. Paid to dependant
(usually widow) at flat rate.

£43.60 or £13.08

After six months one of two
lower rates is paid.

17 Severe Disablement
Allowance
£26.20

A flat rate payment to those
of working age unable to
work for at least 28 weeks
because of severe mental or
physical disablement but
cannot claim Sickness
Benefit or Invalidity
Benefit.

Means-tested benefits i.e. you do not need to pay NI contributions;
but any income received may reduce entitlement. Certain amounts
(between £5–£15 income and £3000 savings) are disregarded. The
general aim is to augment a person's income when his resources fall
below his requirements as set by Parliament, but this is usually not
payable to those in full-time employment or to full-time students.

18 Income Support
Personal allowance
- adult £34.90
- couple £54.80
- child (0–11) £11.75
- child (11–15) £17.35
Premium
- disability £13.70
- lone parent £3.90

Is a weekly payment (by
giro or order book) for
those whose financial
resources do not meet State
assessed needs, known as
'the applicable amount'.
Those able to work must
normally sign on as
available for employment or
training (and will lose IS
entitlement if they refuse
reasonable offers of these);
this includes part-time
students who can claim IS if
their college course does not
exceed 21 hours p.w.
Claimants are paid IS for
basic living expenses in the

Means-tested benefits (*contd*)

19   Social Fund

20   Family Credit

form of personal allowances, child allowances and (for those groups with extra expenses e.g. disabled) premiums. The total of these is the applicable amount and where a person's financial resources are smaller, IS is payable.

This provides for occasional lump sum payments to help with exceptional expenses. They may (largely at the discretion of the Social Fund Officers) take the form of *grants* or more likely *loans*. There are six types of payment (grant or loan); funeral payments, maternity payments, crisis loans, budgeting loans, community care grants, cold weather payments. Some of these are only available to those on IS (mainly through which loans will be repaid).

Is payable (normally to the woman) to working families with low income (net of tax and Housing or Child Benefit). Savings must not exceed £6000, and at least one parent must work at least 24 hours p.w. Adults and (according to age) children are allocated 'credits' (adults £33; child under 11, £7; child 11–15, £13; 16–17, £16). These are paid in full where income is no more than the Income Support threshold allowances/applicable amount (e.g. couple £54.80

plus young child £11.75: see above). Where income is above that level, FC payment is reduced or 'tapered' (e.g. couple with child aged 16; income £80; Family Credit = £27).

(*Note:* Hospital in-patients lose some of their cash benefits: single people on Income Support can only receive £8.70 p.w. (known as the Hospital Pocket Money or HPM rate) and those on National Insurance have their benefit reduced by £17.40 (i.e. 2 × HPM).

Other payments – miscellaneous

21   Redundancy Payments

For staff made redundant after at least two years' service. Receive lump sum from employer which varies with length of service and age, viz. one week's pay per year of service at age 22–40. Employer reclaims part from Redundancy Payments Fund to which he contributes per head of employees.

22   Housing Benefit

This scheme provides (i) payments, called rent allowances, for private tenants, (ii) rent rebates for council tenants and (iii) rates rebates for those on low (net) incomes (and savings under £8000). The amount of HB varies with income, rent/rates, family size and needs. Needs (as in IS) are called the 'applicable amount' and are calculated by adding together personal allowances and premiums as above (e.g. couple £54.80 plus young child £11.75). If income is no greater than the applicable amount, HB

Other payments – miscellaneous (*contd*)

covers all rent and 80 per cent of rates. Where income is greater, HB is tapered (i.e. 65 per cent) of excess income is deducted from HB for rent and 20 per cent is taken from the HB for rates e.g. adult with net income £44; applicable amount is £33.40; excess income is thus £10.60, of which 65 per cent = £6.89 and 20 per cent = £2.12. If rent is £20, deduct £6.89 and rent allowance/rebate is £13.11. If rates are £5.68 then 80 per cent of that = £4.54; less £2.12 (20 per cent of excess income) and rate rebate is £2.42. In all HB is £13.11 plus £2.42 = £15.53.

Note: Rates are replaced by community charge/poll tax 1988 (Scotland) and 1990 (England and Wales).

Some comments on the social security system

Our present social security system is certainly very comprehensive: a glance at pages 50–64 will show that. Yet a number of criticisms have been levelled at it. These include:

1 The rates are not high enough. This applies particularly to National Insurance benefits, for 75 per cent of those who resort to Income Support/Supplementary Benefit are already receiving (inadequate) National Insurance benefits e.g. 2 million pensioners currently top up their NI pensions. This situation is exactly the reverse of what Beveridge intended. Yet the same criticism can be made of Income Support/Supplementary Benefits: in 1977 even the Chairman of the SBC declared the rates were too low, with one million existing claimants (about one third) having to be given extra discretionary payments because of hardship on the standard payments (e.g. on the ordinary scale a claimant receives an extra £11.75 p.w. for a child under eleven which is only £1.70 per day). In 1981 the Chairman of the Social Security Advisory Committee (which superceded the SBC made similar critical comments. Under the new system, Family Credit families are no longer entitled to free school meals; instead the FC payments have been raised to compensate. But this amount is less than school meal charges. Overall, on a relative plane, benefits are only about 30–50 per cent of national average earnings.

2 Benefits are difficult to obtain. This may be because of (a) Ignorance through inadequate publicity. (b) Non-availability of forms in Post Offices, etc. (c) Complexity of rules and regulations – enough to fill a fat book, and to baffle officials themselves (see the Ombudsman reports). There are 150 different social security leaflets. (d) Obscure language of leaflets requiring a high reading age to understand them (e.g. the Family Credit application form is 15 pages long and at one point says send the form 'as soon as you can . . . We cannot deal with your claim if you send it in too soon. And if you send it in late you could lose money'!! (e) Stigma involved in making claims (partly through fear of being labelled a 'scrounger' or accused of making fraudulent claims). (f) Brusqueness of the 117,000 officials in 500 offices (who are often over-worked, under-prepared or lacking in job-satisfaction, e.g. Birmingham strike 1982).

We do not know exactly how many do not claim their rightful benefits. There is a widespread belief that if you don't claim *all* your entitlements there is a better chance of obtaining *something*. The current estimate (1988) of take-up of Family Credit is 40 per cent (and the Government's target figure is a pessimistic 60 per cent). Until they were recently reformed or discontinued, the take-up rates were 76 per cent for Supplementary Benefit, 77 per cent for Housing Benefit, and a mere 7 per cent for those (non-FIS or non-SB) entitled to Welfare Foods. And an estimated 810,000 (33 per cent) retirement pensioners failed to claim Supplementary Pension. Altogether some £760 million of Supplementary Benefit was left unclaimed annually. In 1986, the Association of County Councils estimated that there were £2,000 million of unclaimed benefits, and it urged more local authorities to set up schemes to promote welfare rights take-up (e.g. as Strathclyde did in 1981 and increased claims by over £1 million). Such a figure compares with the estimated £500 million saved through social security fraud investigation, and over £5,000 million lost tax revenue from undeclared 'black economy' earnings.

In addition, some groups have their benefits deliberately reduced for various reasons. These include those on strike, those who make insufficient effort to find work and those who pay excessive rents. Individuals can appeal to a tribunal (see page 54) yet many fail to do this, again out of ignorance or feelings of intimidation or through lack of legal or other representation.

3 'Poverty trap' and problem of overlap. This refers to the fact that many people receiving cash benefits may have them drastically reduced if they have a small increase in income. Many benefits are subject to tax and many are 'means tested'. Thus, for example, up to 1988 a pay rise of £1 a week would amount to only 50p for those on FIS. In fact, a rise in income can jeopardise people's entitlement to a host of benefits such as free school meals, Income Support, Housing Benefit or retirement pension, and can even bring some into the taxation net. All these, together with Insurance contributions, mean that low-income groups can be subject to severe financial penalties if they improve their gross income: hence they can become 'trapped' in their poverty. One consequence of this is that some people may be better off not working, especially those on very low wage rates who are not entitled to Income Support/Supplementary Benefit because they work: they thus fall into the 'unemployment trap'. The SBC in 1978 estimated that perhaps one in ten of the unemployed may be better off or as well off on benefits, and the DHSS estimated that 50,000 of the low paid became worse off for every extra £1 earned. Hence the recent taxing of benefits; and hence too the regular call for up-rating the universal Child Benefit (i.e. since it is paid to the employed and the non-employed it helps to maintain an income differential between workers and non-workers).

Recent reforms have reduced the incidence of these 'traps' by changing the definition of income from gross to net (of tax and NI contributions). But universal Child Benefit has not been regularly uprated (losing 10 per cent of value since 1979), thus reducing the differential incomes between those parents in work and those not working. For example, a lone mother with two children would have disposable income of £85 if she earns £60 p.w., and only £100 if she earns £140; a married man with two children would have an income of £86 if he earned £80, but only £95 if he earned £140.

4 Inconsistencies or deficiencies. Certain benefit groups claim that they do not receive equal or fair treatment e.g. the war (and until 1983 the occupationally) disabled get higher benefit rates than other disabled people. Similarly, some groups (such as pensioners) have managed to keep their incomes closer to average earnings than others (such as the unemployed, who are also denied a long-term supplement). Do one-parent families get a fair deal? Should Child Benefit be restored to its real value, having been allowed to lose value since 1979? Should men and women continue to qualify for retirement pension at different ages? Does Family Credit (ex-FIS) merely encourage employers to pay lower wages? How can those on Income Support realistically repay loans to the Social Fund? Why are there great disparities between DSS offices in awarding grants and loans? Why is the standard of service so low? (A 1988 report on the DSS by the National Audit Office was severely critical about the 'oppressive' benefit offices, their lack of facilities or privacy, the lack of information offered to claimants, the undue hours of waiting to be seen, the delay in processing claims, their inaccuracy and their disparity.)

In other words, perhaps the whole social security system and its order of priorities on spending is open to question. Indeed, the problem may be that there is no one system, but a muddled compromise of three conflicting sub-systems – National Insurance, universal benefits and means-tested benefits.

Perhaps the best way to assess our present social security system is to see if it does its job properly, i.e. does it adequately maintain incomes and so relieve or prevent poverty?

Poverty in modern Britain

We no longer judge which people are poor by reference to an absolute (physical survival) standard. Nor do we judge them by the standards of the past. It is little comfort to the farm-worker today to be told that his income exceeds that of most people of 100 years ago; he must be compared to his contemporaries. We must judge who is poor by the standards of our own time.

Consequently, as we have said earlier (see page 35) the modern concept of poverty is cast in *relative terms* i.e. that those people are poor who cannot afford the life-style of the average person or family in society – see page 468. Such a definition implies that poverty exists because *inequality* exists. If we accept this to be valid it still leaves open the question of the magnitude: how *much* inequality must there be for us to declare a state of poverty?

There is bound to be a lot of inequality in a social system which rewards things like skill, qualifications, responsibility, effort, risk-taking, status or sheer bargaining power. But incomes in Britain are made more equal through (a) the system of **direct taxation**, which, being progressive, takes proportionately more from the better off, and (b) the **social wage** (worth an estimated £2,000 p.a. in 1980), which is the collection of benefits which an individual receives from social services and other State expenditure. Just *how* equal incomes have become is impossible to say: the evidence is obscure, conflicting or out of date (see Chapter 18).

At first sight it would seem that direct taxation takes substantially from the rich and that social security gives mainly to the poor. On top of this it would seem self-evident that the less well-off make most use of the other social services such as health, housing or personal social services. *Economic Trends* (No. 278, HMSO) provides confirmation and concludes that the overall effect is to redistribute income *from* people with higher incomes and few children, *to* those with more children and lower incomes. (See also *Social Trends*, HMSO.)

However, there are some deficiencies in the figures, and they need to be treated with caution. For example, better-off people may derive more benefit from some of the social services than the less well-off (e.g. in higher education and health – see page 111 and Chapter 18). Furthermore, what is striking about the redistributive effects is that the degree of reduction in inequality appears to have changed very little since 1937 despite the Welfare State (see D. Wedderburn, *Poverty, Inequality and Class Structure*, Chapter 3). This is a difficult issue which was studied by a Royal Commission until it was abolished in 1979. Fortunately, to assess the extent of poverty in modern Britain we can move away from the discussion of inequality because we have a ready-made measure of poverty in the Income Support/ Supplementary Benefits allowance scales which are the State's 'safety net', and being in the range of 30 per cent–70 per cent of national average income (according to circumstances, additions and disregards) represents a relative poverty level. (For example the weekly IS allowance, excluding HB for a family of 2 parents and 2 children is £79, while average household expenditure for such a family is about £200.)

The poverty line

In the early 1950s it was felt that poverty had been eliminated from Great Britain, with only a few isolated pockets remaining. Yet by the end of that decade there was mounting evidence that poverty existed on a large scale. Poverty had been rediscovered.

Poverty had also been redefined, for instead of the 'absolute' measure used earlier in the century, investigators now based the poverty line on the scale of allowances laid down by the National Assistance Board (later Supplementary Benefits Commission). These scales bear some limited relationship to average earnings, but they have no necessary connection with absolute needs. They can be regarded as the standard set down by society below which no one should fall. It is the poverty line agreed by society through Parliament.

In the 1950s and 1960s surveys showed there to be variously between 4 and 12 per cent of the population living below the Supplementary Benefits' scales. In 1969 Professor A. Atkinson (*Poverty in Britain and the Reform of Social Security*) said: 'It seems fair to conclude that the proportion of the population with incomes below the National Assistance/Supplementary Benefits' scale lies towards the upper end of the 4–9 per cent.' In other words, some 2–5 million of the population were living below the official national minimum. In addition, some 2.6 million were in receipt of Supplementary Benefits and, therefore, living on the poverty line. At the very least this would mean 10 per cent of the population were in poverty.

However, some would go further and argue that the Supplementary Benefit scales themselves are an inadequate yardstick because (a) they provide allowances which amount to only 50 per cent or less of average manual earnings, and (b) because the DHSS does allow, through 'disregards', for up to £15 (or more for single parents or disabled) per week additional income before Benefit is reduced. Thus in 1965 Professors Abel-Smith and Townsend in *The Poor and the Poorest* thought it reasonable to measure poverty on the basis of the SB scales, *plus* 40 per cent. With this poverty line they found some 14 per cent (i.e. 7.5 million) of the population in poverty, i.e. with incomes below 140 per cent of the SB scales. The main groups were:

Retirement pensioners	2½ million
Full-time workers on low incomes	3 million
Single-parent families	¾ million
Sick and disabled	¾ million
Unemployed	½ million
Total	7½ million

Poverty today

Recent evidence suggests that in the past 20 years poverty has not diminished. In fact certain trends appear to have exacerbated the problem; since 1965 there have been increases in:

(a) The number of retirement age (from 8.5 million to 10 million).
(b) The scale of unemployment (from ⅓ million to over 2 million).
(c) The scale of short-time working and early retirement.
(d) The number of one-parent families (from 570,000 to 940,000).
(e) The cost of living due to inflation (at over 20 per cent in the 1970s).
(f) The number of students (following the 1960s' high birth rate).

Today 7 million people are dependent on Income Support/ Supplementary Benefit. Yet even this 'is still too low to keep many people who depend on it out of poverty' (SBC Annual Report for 1978). Their living standards are 'appreciably lower than those of most wage earners, even amongst the lowest paid'. For the average family 'the rates are below generally accepted measures of low earnings' (*Social Assistance*, DHSS 1978). And a DHSS-sponsored survey in 1982 found 56 per cent of families on SB ran out of money most weeks.

When we add the 2 million who cannot, or do not, claim* (including a million pensioners), we have an estimated 9.38 million people living at, or below, the IS/SB poverty line in Britain. If the definition were extended to SB plus 40 per cent (as above) then there are 15.4 million (or 29 per cent of the population) living in, or on, the margins of poverty. Of these:

36 per cent are pensioners†	(51 per cent in 1979)
24 per cent are unemployed	(10 per cent in 1979)
19 per cent are employees on low pay	(21 per cent in 1979)
4 per cent are sick or disabled	(5 per cent in 1979)
17 per cent are others (such as carers, students, lone parents)	(14 per cent in 1979)

Thus, the pattern of poverty is changing. Indeed, while there has been an increase in numbers *on* the SB/IS poverty line, there has been a fall both in those *below* it and in those up to *40 per cent above* it.

Much of this has been analysed and massively documented by Professor Townsend in *Poverty in the UK* (1979) in which he suggested a figure of 15 million for those in, or on, the margins of poverty (increased to 18 million in 1984). He also argues that income measures alone are really inadequate, and that there is a need to take account of housing standards, employment, peoples' environment, etc. to get a proper measure of relative deprivation.

A recent survey has attempted to provide what might be called a *social definition of poverty* by asking people what they think all families must have to be able to live at an acceptable standard. It revealed that 7.5 million people failed to reach that standard; these are the poor. See page 468 for further details.

Reducing poverty

The reduction of poverty in Britain cannot be achieved either simply or quickly. Here we shall outline some possible strategies. They fall into two groups: (a) Those dealing with the social security system. (b) Longer-term measures which are preventive rather than remedial.

---

*'Social Security Statistics 1981' (HMSO) showed there to be 2 million people living *below* Supplementary Benefits level. An estimated 2.6 million fail to claim their apparent entitlement to Supplementary Benefit (*Pressure Points*, NCC, 1983).

†A report in 1988 showed that poverty among Britain's elderly helped cause a shorter life expectancy for them compared to many (21) other nations. *Promoting Health Among Elderly People*, King's Fund and Age Concern.

Strategies for (a) can be suggested as follows:

1 Improve access to benefits, whether through greater publicity, simplifying procedures or greater uniformity. (The 1986–8 reforms achieved some of these e.g. alignment of the different needs scales. There is also a Freephone Social Security number (0800 666555) which deals with inquiries.

2 Reform present benefits, by paying really adequate National Insurance and Child Benefits, perhaps coupled with an indexing of benefits to keep up with inflation; consider new benefits such as for single parents, carers or deserted wives; alter the retirement ages; give the long-term unemployed same (higher) rates as the sick.

3 Indexing of tax allowances and benefit disregards (i.e. income allowed before benefit is calculated), to diminish the poverty trap. Alternatively, implement 'negative income tax' (see 4).

4 Abandon National Insurance, by paying all benefits out of taxation so that anyone who is ill, unemployed or retired collects an automatic allowance without means test. Alternative to this is **negative income tax**, which at its simplest means: everyone submits a tax form declaring his income and claiming allowances; those over the tax threshold pay tax, but those below instead of paying tax receive cash benefits, i.e. a 'negative' tax. In 1972 the Government outlined plans for a **tax credit system** which, while similar to NIT, would have retained National Insurance.

5 Clarify the objectives of the social security system for these appear to be both numerous and sometimes inconsistent. The over-riding objective is to provide a reasonable basic minimum, yet because higher rates might destroy incentives benefits are often paid at rates which are officially admitted to be inadequate. For similar reasons people even in poorly paid employment cannot claim Income Support, and claimants may have been subject to rules such as the 'four-week rule', 'the rent-stop' and the 'cohabitation rule' which keep them below the minimum. The social security system has acknowledged one aspect of the concept of relative poverty by developing the earnings-related system so that a person does not fall so sharply from his accustomed lifestyle when he ceases to earn. Yet in the long run, this system maintains relative poverty in that inequalities which arise through the wage structure are carried over into the non-working situation, i.e. retirement.

Strategies for (b), longer-term measures, may be summarised as follows:

1 Encourage economic growth and reduce unemployment.

2 Introduce a national minimum wage or maintain an incomes policy which benefits the low paid (including equal pay for women).
3 Break into the 'cycle of deprivation' which manifests itself in (a) problem families, i.e. bad parents → bad children → bad parents. Intercept by intensive counselling, extra cash and family planning (see also Chapter 18) and (b) derelict environment, squalid housing and poor public services e.g. as in many inner urban areas (see Chapter 12).

Conclusion

In so far as poverty is rooted in inequality, then ultimately its elimination can only really be achieved through a redistribution of incomes and wealth, and the foundation of the egalitarian state. Just how equal people will need to be depends on the point at which 'having less than others' becomes 'poverty'. The dividing line is bound to be hazy; and differences may well be allowed to exist since most contemporary commentators declare relative poverty to exist only where individuals fall 'significantly' or 'seriously' behind the rest of society (see P. Townsend, *The Concept of Poverty*).

On the other hand, some people see the poor as serving some useful functions: apart from cheap labour, they provide a warning to others, and they provide a basis for 'social distancing', so that those who are better off are more aware of their superior status. A recent survey of views on poverty in the EEC revealed that in Great Britain over 40 per cent of those interviewed thought people were poor because of 'laziness and lack of will-power'. And the 1981 Gallup poll revealed that only 31 per cent wanted greater redistribution in favour of the less well off. (See also page 469.) If these views are an accurate reflection of British attitudes then the prospects for the poor are bleak indeed.

However, opinions do appear to be changing: only 19 per cent now see laziness or lack of willpower as the main cause of poverty, believing instead that circumstances (37 per cent) and sheer injustice (25 per cent) are more to blame. Consequently, 72 per cent of those surveyed thought it the government's responsibility to reduce income differences between rich and poor. (*British Social Attitudes, 1987.*)

Questions

1 Distinguish between absolute poverty and relative poverty.
2 Name the main constituents of social security.
3 Give three reasons why the principles of the Poor Law were undermined.

4 Name three landmarks in the history of the social security system 1900–48.

5 In what ways was the Beveridge Report revolutionary?

6 Give three ways in which we have moved away from the Beveridge Scheme.

7 How much poverty is there in Great Britain today?

8 Which groups in Great Britain's society are likely to be poor?

9 Name two reforms which would improve our social security system.

10 Suggest three methods of reducing poverty in Great Britain.

11 'Welfare has become discredited both among those who depend on it and those who pay for it. The social security system is inherent, a jungle of 'poverty traps' and disincentives, lacking form and principle.' Discuss.

12 Explain and discuss the following: (a) 'Poverty is exclusion.', (b) 'Poverty is inequality.', (c) 'Poverty is being unable to buy your own identity.' Give examples.

4
The health service

We all want to live to a ripe old age. Yet we tend to take our health for granted – at least until we are ill. Then we worry about it, and accord high esteem to those who can cure: from the witchdoctor in primitive communities to the medical practitioner in our own society.

However, there is more to health than doctors. They can help us to overcome illness, but they do not create health. 'Health is a state of complete physical, mental and social well-being and not merely the absence of disease or infirmity'. (World Health Organisation 1946.) Thus it is difficult to say exactly what creates health. But there are some well-established prerequisites for healthy bodies: minimum food intake, avoidance of poisons, personal hygiene, exercise and keeping clear of diseases. The body can, of course, resist disease, but there is a limit to this power of resistance, as has been made clear in periods such as the fourteenth, seventeenth and nineteenth centuries when a number of killer diseases spread through Great Britain at the cost of thousands of lives and much suffering. Those days are now safely behind us.

The development of the health service: 1840–1940

In Britain over the last hundred years the battle against ill-health has been fought on four main fronts and in three overlapping phases:

1 During the second half of the nineteenth century attention was focused on improving the **environment** (housing, planning, sanitation). This concentration on preventive measures was known as 'the Public Health Movement'.
2 From the late nineteenth century attention was turned to the protection and improvement of the health of **children** (clinics, meals, etc.). This involved a more personal approach to health provision.
3 From the early twentieth century there was greater concern with the **treatment of the sick**. This was partly due to improvements in medical science (drugs, X-rays, antibiotics, etc.).

4   From 1911 there was increasing **access** to health services, culmi-
nating in the creation of the National Health Service.

The Public Health Movement

The background to this Movement lay in the problems created by a
combination of population growth and industrialisation.

Between 1801 and 1851 the population doubled from 9 million to
18 million. Much of this growth was concentrated in the industrial
urban areas:

	Birmingham	*Liverpool*	*Sheffield*	*Leeds*
1801	73,000	82,000	46,000	53,000
1851	233,000	376,000	135,000	172,000

As a result housing accommodation was scarce and overcrowding
occurred; not just in the houses themselves, but also in terms of
housing density per acre of land. Workmen had to live near their
work; and there were then no buses. There were no planning or
building regulations, so dwellings were built back-to-back or in large
tenement blocks. There was, in addition, a general lack of adequate
or suitable drainage, sewerage and water supply, and there were deficiencies in paving, ventilation and refuse disposal. Lavatories, when
they existed, were shared in some cases among hundreds of people,
and they often emptied into open cesspools; other people used the
open fields. Piped water was rare, stand-pipes for whole districts
operated only at certain times of the day. The rest was provided by
water sellers or the local river. No wonder gin and beer were drunk in
such quantities.

The consequence of all this was often appalling living conditions,
frequent epidemics of disease and a generally high death rate. The
average life-span of the working man was about 40 years in the early
nineteenth century. Only about one person in ten died of old age.
These problems became so widespread and stark that they could not
be ignored, and there emerged in the early nineteenth century what is
known as 'the sanitary idea' or the Public Health Movement.

A number of individuals, especially doctors, wrote reports or
commentaries on the conditions they witnessed. Many advocated
reforms. But these lone voices achieved little, partly because of the
general ignorance about diseases. Many thought it was God's displea-
sure for their wickedness. Others believed that bad air was the cause.
In addition, the administrative machinery of the central government
and local government was not really able to take effective action
because of lack of expertise or conviction or because of corruption.
Some of the very worst situations were, however, dealt with in some
areas by the Improvement Commissioners.

In the early nineteenth century diseases such as typhoid, smallpox, tuberculosis and diphtheria took about 20,000 lives per annum. Countless others suffered severe discomfort through illness. These attacks of disease were a regular occurrence, and people got used to it. But this complacency was shattered when in 1832 the cholera epidemic spread to Great Britain and killed about 100,000 people.

In that year the Royal Commission on the Poor Laws was set up. It reported in 1834 and drew attention, among other things, to the close relationship between poverty and sickness. It pointed out that sick workmen and bereaved families became a charge on the Poor Rate, thus suggesting an improvement in health would help in the battle against pauperism.

A number of inquiries followed: in 1840 the Health of Towns Committee reported; 1842 saw Chadwick's report of the Poor Law Commission on the Sanitary Condition of the Labouring Population; and there were the Royal Commission Reports of 1844 and 1845. The 1840s thus became 'the most exciting period in the history of public health, which forced questions of public health into politics' (Asa Briggs).

The result of this and of subsequent agitation – for example, by the Health of Towns Association, a pressure group – was a mixture of (a) local initiative, (b) Private Bills and (c) national legislation:

1   The *Nuisances Removal Act, 1846*, permitted local authorities to clean up their districts. The Boards of Guardians were largely responsible, but were slow to act.
2   In 1847 the first Medical Officer of Health was established in Liverpool, under powers of a Private Act.
3   The *Public Health Act, 1848*, was passed in the same year as a further epidemic of cholera struck. The Act established a Central Board of Health; allowed local areas to set up local Boards of Health (this was compulsory where the death rate exceeded 23 per thousand); the Boards of Health were enabled to appoint Medical Officers of Health and were to secure adequate sewerage, draining, water supply and street cleansing.

Although some 200 local Boards of Health were established, covering 3 million people, the overall result was limited. There was opposition to the idea of the central government interfering in local matters, and Chadwick, one of the three members of the Central Board of Health, was widely disliked. *The Times* declared that: 'We prefer to take our chance of cholera and the rest than be bullied into health.' Meanwhile in 1849 about 400,000 people were affected by cholera.

Subsequent Acts dealt with sewage disposal, scavenging, water supply, control of burials and sale of foods. In 1866 the appointment of sanitary inspectors was made compulsory, and some public money was made available for building houses. Useful as all this legislation was, the result was something of a tangle of regulations and authorities.

A further epidemic in 1866 (the last cholera outbreak) led to renewed public agitation and further inquiry. The Royal Sanitary Commission reports of 1868–71 showed the need for a more unified system of public health provision. The result was the *Public Health Act, 1872*, which required the appointment of Medical Officers of Health, and the *Public Health Act, 1875*, which extended and consolidated all the previous legislation. Public Health authorities were required to be established over the whole country, and the Local Government Board (a Government department) was to supervise all Public Health and Poor Law administration.

By 1875, therefore, local authorities were forced to install adequate draining and sewerage systems and water supplies. They were also allowed to provide amenities such as parks and hospitals and to undertake slum clearance. Great Britain had now become a place fit for human habitation, and the death rate had fallen significantly from 2.3 per cent in 1850 to 1.7 per cent fifty years later. Not that everything was perfect: in the early twentieth century it was quite common for dozens of families to queue at stand-pipes for water and communal lavatories. Indeed, some households do so even today.

The health of children

So far the nineteenth century approached health as a 'collateral aid', i.e. as a means of providing an environment in which people could take care of themselves. But it was becoming evident that such an attitude could not be taken towards children – a highly vulnerable section of the population for whom mortality rates had altered little. The infant mortality rate in 1850 was 15.6 per cent of live births, and in 1900 it was still 15.1 per cent. In some areas it was staggeringly high; for example, in Liverpool in 1840 the infant mortality rate was 23 per cent, and the death rate for children up to age 5 in Manchester was 57 per cent.

Some attempts had been made to protect the health of children through the various factory reforms of the nineteenth century. Acts of Parliament regulated the form, conditions and duration of employment of child employees. But employment was only part of the problem.

The major diseases of the nineteenth century – typhoid, scarlet fever, diphtheria – particularly affected children. Vaccination against smallpox had been developed by Jenner (1749–1823) at the end of the eighteenth century; but even sixty years later deaths from smallpox could still amount to a quarter of the deaths in certain areas.

Consequently, in 1858 vaccination was made compulsory for all. Compulsory vaccination was abolished only in 1948.

At the height of the nineteenth century the reports of Booth and Rowntree highlighted the poor conditions in which children lived. These were substantiated by the many recruits (40 per cent) who were rejected on medical grounds when they applied for enlistment for the Boer War. This led to an official inquiry, the significant title of which was 'The Inter-Departmental Committee on the Physical Deterioration of the Young'. It reported in 1904 and provided the stimulus for the Education Acts of 1906 and 1907 which provided, respectively, for the provision of school meals and milk by the local education authorities and for school medical inspections. Some local education authorities had already taken action along these lines on their own initiative. With the introduction of compulsory education in the late nineteenth century, teachers had long been aware of the material and emotional handicaps of pupils.

The greatest danger to children, however, occurred at birth and in the immediate post-natal stage of life. As we have seen, in 1901 the infant mortality rate was 151 per 1,000 live births. By 1939 this had fallen to 46 per 1,000. This was due to:

(a) **Better nursing.** The Midwives' Institute was founded in 1881, and the *Midwives' Act, 1902*, confined the practice of midwifery to properly trained nurses.

(b) **Welfare facilities** were increasingly provided by progressive local authorities, often taking the lead given by voluntary organisations in, for example, health visiting, or by copying France who pioneered child welfare clinics in 1892. The *Maternity and Child Welfare Act, 1918*, encouraged all local authorities to provide services to safeguard the health of mothers and children, including ante-natal clinics. This was the result of the nation's shock at the poor state of recruits to the forces in the First World War, when something like two thirds were rejected on medical grounds.

(c) **Medical improvements.** The work of the 'microbe hunters', like Koch and Pasteur, increased the scope, efficiency and popularity of vaccination. Antiseptics were developed, and the pasteurisation of milk in the 1880s helped to eliminate epidemics of scarlet fever and diphtheria. Antibiotics were soon to follow.

As a result, infant deaths from specific diseases of measles, smallpox, scarlet fever, diphtheria, croup and whooping cough fell from 10 per 1,000 births in 1900 to 2.7 per 1,000 by 1940.

Treatment of the sick

In the mid-nineteenth century the availability of personal health services was very limited, partly because people were normally charged for medical treatment and partly because the medical service was itself of a very low standard, based often on ignorance, guesswork, and, in some cases, superstition. It was a great misfortune to be ill in the nineteenth century.

The training of doctors was limited owing to the state of medical knowledge, and many unqualified people (known as 'quacks') practised until the *Medical Registration Act, 1858*, which established registration for medical practitioners.

Treatment was often worse than the original illness. Doctors were often accused of making money by playing on people's fears of disease, and offering cures which were cheap but useless: bleeding (with leeches or scalpel incisions) and purging with laxatives or induced vomiting were the most common techniques. But surgical operations were feared most, and **hospitals** were often dirty and ill-ventilated and lacked adequate sanitation. They often promoted rather than prevented the spread of diseases such as typhoid, since wards were usually mixed rather than isolated, and infection spread. The nurses were normally untrained and often illiterate and immoral.

Some hospitals did not charge, and doctors often gave their services free. But admission was not always easy; one often required a letter of recommendation from a person of consequence. Nevertheless, there was considerable reluctance to enter hospitals because of the bad name which hospitals had gained through their high mortality rates – due at least in part to the fact that they got the worst cases.

Apart from hospitals and private practice, doctors might also treat patients who were members of friendly societies, whose regular subscriptions would entitle patients to free treatment by the doctor who contracted to work for the societies.* Alternatively, doctors might become salaried employees of the parish Board of Guardians at about £20 per annum. Here he would treat the inmates of the workhouses and also the local poor who applied for medical help either at home or at the workhouse infirmary or dispensary. The Poor Law did therefore provide a rudimentary system of health services throughout Great Britain, but usually with an eye on the rates with the result that minimum standards only were observed.

The image of medicine began to change in the later nineteenth century. Research had produced the **germ theory** of disease, and in the 1850s and 1860s anaesthetics and antiseptics had been discovered.

---

*There were also private insurance arrangements and doctors' clubs which entitled the subscriber to medical attention which was free or at a reduced charge.

The pioneering work of Florence Nightingale (1820–1910) helped to make hospitals cleaner and safer, and nurses became competent, dedicated and respectable. **Medical science** by the beginning of the twentieth century had made substantial progress, and public acclaim was growing. The problem now was one of **access** to the health services.

The health service: 1900–1939

Access to health services depended on (a) availability of the services and (b) ability to meet the fees charged. In the late nineteenth and early twentieth centuries access increased on both fronts.

The health services provided by the Poor Law Boards of Guardians continued to be provided with some expansion of hospitals (see Table 1). In the early twentieth century local authorities built hospitals especially for isolation (from infectious diseases), maternity and convalescence (especially for tuberculosis). Both local authority and voluntary ('cottage') hospitals charged fees, though these could be remitted in cases of low incomes.

Local authorities expanded their personal health and welfare services in the form of home nursing, health visiting, family planning, vaccination and children's clinics. The *Maternity and Child Welfare Act, 1918*, provided for the growth of the latter, especially as a result of the First World War (1914–18) where only one in three of the recruits were found to be fit and healthy. The *Local Government Act, 1929*, abolished the Board of Guardians and allowed local authorities to take over their functions. The 1929 Act was part of the move to rationalise the health services and their administration. This began in 1919 with the creation of the Ministry of Health. The Ministry took over many of the health responsibilities of a host of government departments, including the Home Office, the Board of Trade, the Board of Education and the Local Government Board.

Meanwhile **medical science** continued to make progress; new vaccines were discovered, together with new antibiotics (sulphonamide, prontosil). Insulin for diabetes and penicillin were produced in the 1920s. There were also developments in the production of synthetic drugs ('magic bullets'), aspirin, DDT and radium. Techniques of surgery were improved, blood transfusion was practised and the electrocardiograph was invented for heart cases.

Many of these were still in their development stage and were often an expensive form of treatment. But even the more straightforward forms of treatment were not easily available to much of the population. This was because of the **fees**. Charles Booth (1840–1916) and B. Seebohm Rowntree (1871–1954) showed that at the turn of the century some 30 per cent of the population were at or below the poverty line, and, apart from the free medical services of the parish

Table 1 Number of Beds for the Physically Ill and Percentage Distribution in Voluntary, Poor Law and Municipal Hospitals 1891–1938, England and Wales

Hospital type	1891		1911		1921		1938	
	number	per cent	number	per cent	number	per cent	number	per cent
Voluntary	29,520	26.2	43,221	21.9	56,550	24.7	87,235	33.2
Poor Law								
infirmaries (a)	12,133	10.6	40,901	20.7	36,547	16.1	7,909	3.0
sick wards (b)	60,778	53.9	80,260	40.6	83,731	36.6	44,556	16.9
Municipal	10,319	9.2	33,112	16.8	51,728	22.6	123,403	46.9
Total	112,750	100.0	197,494	100.0	228.556	100.0	263,103	100.0

Notes: (a) separate institutions (b) in workhouses.
Source: Robert Pinker, *English Hospital Statistics 1861–1938*, Heinemann, 1966. Ministry of Health 'Annual Reports'.

doctor and dispensary, could not afford even the often nominal charges made by many doctors and hospitals. The death-rate was still unacceptably high at 17.7 per 1,000 in 1900; and there were some 1,000 deaths per week from tuberculosis alone. Consequently, the Government was urged to adopt the insurance principle being operated by friendly societies to provide sickness benefits. The German Government had set an example when it developed a national insurance scheme in the 1880s, followed later by other countries such as Hungary and Norway.

Lloyd George (1863–1945), a leading Minister, whose father died from tuberculosis, took up the idea in 1908 and, amid great opposition from doctors, employers, friendly societies and insurance companies, implemented the *National Insurance Act, 1911*. It involved:

(a) Contributions from employees (4*d*. per week), employers (3*d*. per week) and the Government (2*d*. per week – 'ninepence for fourpence'.

(b) Benefits of 10*s*. (50p) per week during sickness and free ('panel') doctor service. In addition, the contributor might get free dental, home nursing and other medical services (known as 'additional benefits').

(c) Initially the service was confined to the working poor, i.e. those in employment and earning up to £3 per week, and was administered on behalf of the Government by 'approved societies', i.e. friendly societies and insurance companies which were 'approved' by the Government's Insurance Commissioners. The scheme was later extended to those earning up to £5, and by

1940 £8 per week, thus covering a substantial part of the population.

The health service in 1939

By the outbreak of the Second World War much had been achieved. Some diseases, like cholera and typhus, had been virtually eliminated. Deaths from other killer diseases were greatly reduced – for example, the death rate from tuberculosis had fallen from 1.4 per 1,000 in 1910 to 0.6. Infant and maternal mortality rates were also well down. Children generally were taller and heavier compared to previous generations. And the National Health Insurance system relieved many of both illness and the anxiety and stress which had previously accompanied it. The overall death rate was down to 12 per 1,000 and the average life span was 60 years or more compared with 45 years in 1900.

However, all was not well; for there were serious **deficiencies and anomalies** in the health service provision:

1   More than half of the population were **not covered** by the National Health Insurance, including employees earning over £8 per week (the equivalent of £200 per week today), the self-employed and, above all, the families of contributors were not covered.

2   There were considerable variations and uncertainties in the provision of **additional benefits**. Entitlement depended on where you lived and your health history; for example, it is estimated that in 1939 only 4,834 approved societies provided free dental services out of a total of 7,000 societies.

3   The **distribution** of specialists and general practitioners was very uneven; for example, in Hastings there was one general practitioner to every 1,178 people, and in South Shields the figure was one to 4,105.

4   There was considerable variation in the adequacy and efficiency of **local authority** health services. These disparities were due to differences in the resources and the enterprise of the local councils.

5   **Hospital** services too were unevenly distributed, since they depended on the existence of fee-payers and on local authorities and voluntary effort (street collections and charity), which were not only unreliable in themselves, but in failing to cooperate also precluded a coordinated system. A number of critical reports drew attention to these deficiencies and provided force to those who had been long arguing the case for a National Health Service.

The National Health Service: development of an idea

The suggestion of a state medical service was put forward by individual thinkers in the nineteenth century, and received its first semi-official backing in the minority report of the *Royal Commission on the Poor Laws* (1905–09). This document, largely attributed to Beatrice and Sidney Webb, argued the desirability of a unified and comprehensive health service, though not necessarily a free one. The 1911 National Health Insurance arrangements provided an important step in this direction by providing the 'panel' (free) doctor service for insured workers.

In 1919 the Ministry of Health was created, and its accompanying Consultative Council, under the Chairmanship of **Lord Dawson**, produced a report in 1920 dealing with the organisation of medical care in the re-construction period after the First World War. This report criticised existing arrangements as being too fragmented and badly distributed. It sought a more unified approach based on a series of health authorities and health centres, and pursuing a distribution according to the needs of the community and available to all citizens. Support for comprehensive health provision also came from the *Royal Commission on National Health Insurance, 1924–26*. This suggested not only extending National Insurance coverage but also ultimately separating health entirely from insurance and financing the service from general taxation. Opposition from insurance bodies coupled with depressed economic conditions prevented any action along these lines.

In the meanwhile the idea of a fully-fledged state health service was being promoted by a growing number of individuals and groups: the Fabian Society, the Labour Party and a group of doctors who formed themselves into the **Socialist Medical Association** in 1930. The SMA published many articles, held conferences and, through its MP members, raised the issue in Parliament. They wanted:

(a) Medical services to be free of charge;
(b) Doctors to be full-time state employees;
(c) Health centres and large district hospitals;
(d) Administration by local authorities (reorganised into larger units).

Support for these principles, with some variations, came from other sources, such as the National Association of Local Government Officers, the Society of Medical Officers of Health and the Walton Plan. The British Medical Association was more cautious: the general practitioners were worried about the prospect of a salaried service and the specialists were afraid that a state medical service might threaten their private practice, upon which they depended to allow them to give free services in many of the public wards of hospitals. Generally the BMA showed a preference for extending National Insurance cover both in terms of persons and benefits. The BMA, however, along with the Sankey Report (1937) and the PEP Report of 1937 did advocate coordination of hospitals on a regional basis.

The **Second World War** (1939–45) intervened in the national debate and forced events along in two ways:

1   The creation in 1939 of the Emergency Hospital Service for war casualties, through which the State took over and expanded all hospitals to secure a more widespread provision and rationalisation. One consequence was the movement of specialists to different areas of Great Britain and away from the towns where they tended to be concentrated. They often found their new environments poor in medical terms, with the result that they became more sympathetic to the idea of a national system with more uniform standards.
2   The **Beveridge Committee Report**, 1942, though dealing primarily with social security, emphasised the necessity for a national system of health services. No details were given, though Beveridge did emphasise accessibility. The Report caught the public's imagination, and its very popularity alone was probably enough to commit the coalition Government to action. So the **principle** of a NHS was accepted: the problem now was its **form**.

In 1942 the Minister of Health published a draft plan for a unified health service. There was some strong reaction by doctors who said that a salaried service would destroy the opportunities for choice for doctors and patients. In 1944 a revised plan, in the form of a White Paper, proposed that:

1   Free health services would be available to all.
2   The administrative areas would be based on joint local authorities.
3   These area health authorities would incorporate (though not absorb) voluntary hospitals with the local authority hospitals and would also run health services in health centres.
4   General practitioner services were to remain independent, but GPs would work under contract for the health service, receiving payments on a capitation basis, i.e. according to the size of the doctor's 'list'.

Discussions on the White Paper were extensive, but were not completed owing to the General Election of 1945. The new Minister of Health, **Mr Aneurin Bevan**, did not continue to negotiate with the doctors, and published his National Health Service Bill in March,

1946. The various proposals aroused strong antagonisms, and in the end the NHS, which came into existence in 1948, embodied many compromises. Its overriding aim was to eliminate the 'well of misery'.

The *National Health Service Act, 1946*

The main provisions of this important Act were:

1 The **hospitals** (with some exceptions, including the teaching hospitals) were taken over and administered by the Government through agencies called Regional Hospital Boards and Hospital Management Committees. Consultants and hospital doctors were to be salaried, but they could undertake some private work. Patients were to be referred to the hospitals through general practitioners.
2 **Family practitioner** services (which included general medical services by GPs, and dentistry, etc.) were provided, under contract, by individual practitioners with the option for some of working together in local authority Health Centres.
3 **Local authorities** became responsible for Health Centres and ambulances, as well as retaining responsibilities for public health, immunisation, school health and maternity services.
4 All health services were **free of charge**: it thus became based on *service* rather than on insurance as abroad.
5 **Freedom of choice** was retained in two ways: (i) doctors could choose to refuse patients, and patients could change doctors; and (ii) private practice was permitted so that not all patients or doctors had to use or join the National Health Service.

The NHS was thus created with a **tripartite structure**. This was to be expected to some extent since there had been virtually three sets of health services operating beforehand. But this structure was also due to the pressure exerted by (a) doctors who insisted on remaining self-employed; (b) the voluntary hospitals who found the *ad hoc* administrative arrangements were less objectionable than outright takeover; and (c) the local authorities who had lost their hospitals and had to be left with some health functions.

The NHS: aims and achievements

The principles and aims underlying the *National Health Service Act, 1946*, were:

1 **Optimum** standards of service. In contrast to the social security legislation of the time, which provided for a basic minimum, the new health services aimed '*to secure improvement in the physical*

and mental health of the people and the prevention, diagnosis and treatment of illness'. The service was designed 'to meet health needs wherever and whenever they arise'.

2   The services were to be **comprehensive** in scope and **universal** in population coverage.

3   To facilitate this last point, services were to be **free of charge**.

4   **Expenditure** was to be financed mainly from **general taxation**.

5   Services (especially hospitals) were to be **integrated** and more effectively planned and distributed.

6   Underlying all this was the notion of **freedom**: no one was compelled to join, and while patients could change their doctor or dentist, the medical practitioners could also undertake private work.

The service became and remained exceedingly popular; the vast majority of both patients and medical practitioners have joined. The private sector is small and takes up a fraction of the time of most of the practitioners who supply it. In spite of people's grumbles, surveys show that the NHS is given a high rating in the opinion of the public.

The NHS has been described by an American observer* as 'one of the great achievements of the twentieth century'. The creation of the NHS has eliminated the financial barrier between doctors and patients, and the public are freed from money worries when ill. The achievement is also notable in that (a) there is a better distribution of doctors and hospitals, and (b) there are improvements in certain of the indicators of the health of the nation:

Deaths from tuberculosis	1939 –	25,623
	1986 –	376
Deaths from diphtheria, polio,	1948 –	1,394
measles and whooping cough	1986 –	16
Infant mortality rate	1947 –	43 per 1,000 live births
	1986 –	9.5
Maternal mortality rate	1934 –	4 per 1,000 live births
	1986 –	0.07
Percentage of people under	1947 –	11%
30 with no natural teeth	1978 –	3%

The overall death rate has continued to fall and life-expectancy to rise, so that today it stands at 71 years for men and 77 years for women (in 1931 it was 58 and 62 respectively). Infant mortality rates have fallen significantly and are among the lowest in the world. Furthermore, the height and weight and the general health of chil-

*A. L. Lindsey, *Socialised Medicine in England and Wales*.

dren are, on average, better than those obtaining before the introduction of the NHS.

Criticisms of the NHS

Critics of the NHS, both before and since its creation, have made the following points:

1 Its achievements have been **modest**, rather than outstanding, and the rate of improvement has perhaps been no greater than it was in the 1930s.
2 Health, as indicated by mortality or morbidity statistics, has improved as a result of **other factors** (higher standard of living, housing, changes in work patterns, reduced smoke pollution, scientific advances, etc.) rather than the existence of the NHS as such.
3 There are too many significant **deficiencies** in the NHS after 40 years, including the number and distribution of doctors, hospitals and health centres.
4 The nation **cannot afford** the NHS. Its founders claimed that the health bill would diminish as the pool of ill-health was mopped up. Instead, however, health costs have escalated (see page 112).
5 The NHS is a virtual **monopoly**. Consequently there is too little choice and a lack of competition which engender a 'take it or leave it' attitude. The system has become too big, impersonal and inflexible. A further consequence may be that, compared to a private or more mixed system, the state-run NHS has inhibited the provision of resources to, and growth of, health services.
6 A free health service **disables** and **demoralises** people by causing them to rely on medicine instead of healthy ways of living, and by encouraging abuse of a free service.
7 The tripartite system (see Figure 4) has meant a **fragmented** and uncoordinated system which was little different from that prevailing before the NHS was created.

The reorganisation of the NHS: 1974

As we have seen, the NHS has been criticised on the grounds of inadequate coordination among the virtually self-contained parts of the tripartite structure. This fragmentation was a barrier to a proper balance of services. More specifically, reform of the structure was desirable for four reasons.

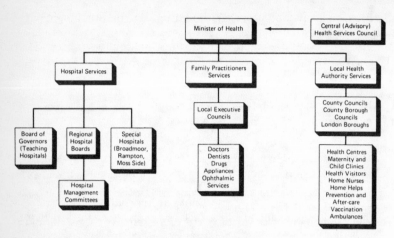

Figure 4   *Structure of the NHS, 1948–74 ('tripartite')*

1   Economic

There was a wasteful duplication of services and especially of administrative structures. More importantly, there was a danger of a waste of resources because of independent decision-making by each of the three 'arms', each one seeking to maintain its own 'empire' and safeguard its own budget. As a result there was a distortion of priorities and a neglect of consideration for overall cost-effectiveness of health spending.

2   Professional

As a result of the separate administrative and medical arms of the service, the medical practitioners tended to be isolated, breeding a certain amount of mutual distrust and suspicion – for example, by hospital doctors of Medical Officers of Health. In particular there had developed a decline in the morale of GPs, who felt cut off from the work, the facilities and, to some extent, the glamour of hospitals. And for each group of doctors there was the irritation of having to decide the appropriate treatment, and then having to arrange its provision by another 'arm' of the NHS.

3   Technological developments in medical science

Conditions that were once near hopeless are now amenable to treatment and conditions that were once life-threatening are treated as routine. These are the consequences of improvements in antibiotics, chemotherapy, anaesthetics and surgery. The overall consequence of this is a changing pattern of disease and treatment, with the patient more frequently moving from hospital to GP and domiciliary care (i.e. in his own home), then perhaps readmittance to hospital for another short stay, and then back to the community services. The NHS had developed a 'revolving door' process, especially for the mentally and elderly sick.

4 Patient care

The objective of the NHS is to provide adequately for the general public. In a variety of ways, including those mentioned above, the structure was inhibiting the provision. The structure was creating gaps in communications, not merely because of the tripartitism but also because many of the various health authorities did not coincide geographically and their boundaries overlapped. Patient care was also undermined by the wasteful use of resources. Many patients were remaining in hospital unnecessarily because community services were not available. It was increasingly apparent that there should be a closer integration of the three parts of the NHS, and positive moves in this direction began in 1968.

An integrated service

The notion of an integrated service is not new. The Dawson Report of 1920 favoured single health authorities; so did a number of the NHS proposals in the 1930s. A number of other proposals for integration were made in post-war years: the Gillie Report (1963) suggested that health services should be coordinated through **family doctors**; the Guillebaud Report (1956) and the Royal Commission on Local Government (1969) suggested that **local government** might take over responsibility for the NHS; other schemes suggested the absorption of the Executive Councils by **hospital authorities**, and that the NHS should be 'hived off' to a **public corporation**. What was finally decided was to reorganise the NHS very much along the lines suggested in 1962 by the Porrit Report, 'Social Assay'; that is, by creating *ac hoc* **health authorities**.

The preliminary steps in the process were by public discussion and negotiation. In 1968 a **Green Paper** on the administrative structure of the NHS proposed a virtually single-tier system of 40–50 area health boards. This idea was dropped because of strong criticism that it might make the service too remote from the public, and also because of the strong opposition of doctors who feared for their independence. A **1970 Green Paper*** expanded the proposed number of health

---

*A Green Paper is a tentative document of ideas produced by the Government for discussion only. The Government does not state this is the final policy. A White Paper is a Government's *declared* policy prior to actual legislation.

boards to 90, but added the idea of advisory regional health councils to provide some coordination, and it suggested the creation of some 200 district committees whose function would be to keep a 'grass roots' eye on the services provided by area health boards. A 1971 **Consultative Document** of the Conservative Government was quickly followed by a White Paper (1972) and the *National Health Service Act, 1973*. This Act provided the basis of the present structure which came into operation in 1974.

The NHS structure since 1974

This new structure unified the three parts of the service (Hospital Services, Family Practitioner Services and Local Health Authority Services), but had three operating levels: (1) **Region**; (2) **Area**; (3) **District** – see Figure 5. In 1982, these were reduced to two when the Areas were abolished (see below).

In effect, the different authorities run the health service as agents of the DHSS, but each has its own **statutory** functions:

The Department of Health (until 1988 DHSS) is responsible for:

1   Overall policy objectives of the NHS. 2   Central strategic planning. 3   Monitoring of performance. 4   Allocation of resources to Regional Health Authorities (since 1976 on the basis of RAWP – see page 111). 5   Giving guidance, support and direction to the Regional Health Authorities regarding priorities and scale of service provision in the regions and districts. 6   Obtaining and developing resources: finance, buildings, staff forecasting and training. 7   Research, statistics, superannuation. 8   It also runs special hospitals (e.g. Broadmoor, Rampton).

The Regional Health Authorities. There are 14 of these (plus the Welsh Office and the Scottish Office), and each must contain within its boundaries at least one university medical school. The RHAs itself consist of a chairman and members (about 20) appointed by the Secretary of State for Social Services after consulting the health professions, the local authorities, universities and health employees' organisations. Members are unpaid, but are entitled to allowances. The chairman is paid a part-time salary. The *functions* of the Regional Health Authorities are:

1   Determination of regional priorities (e.g. how much kidney transplant surgery).
2   Regional planning (e.g. location of specialities such as neurosurgery).

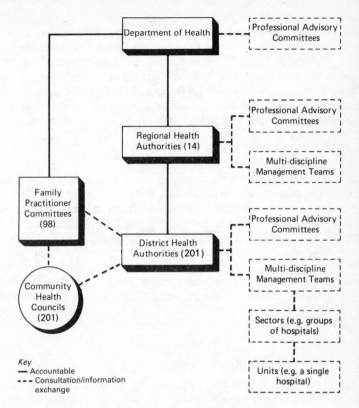

Figure 5 *Structure of the NHS from 1982 ('unified')*
Note: 1974–82 there were 98 Area Health Authorities in place of Districts – see below.

3 Allocation of resources to District Health Authorities.
4 Monitoring District Health Authorities' activities and relative costs.
5 Provision of major building projects.
6 Securing coordination among District Health Authorities.
7 Employment of medical and dental consultants and senior registrars except in health teaching areas where there is a university medical school).

The District Health Authorities. Prior to 1982 there were 98 Area Health Authorities (AHAs) in England and Wales. They comprised about 20 members of whom one third were appointed by local authorities and one third were professional and university appointments. AHAs broadly covered areas of counties and metropolitan districts (except in London). They were responsible for planning and administering health services for the area. They were abolished in 1982 and replaced by 201 District Health Authorities (DHAs), following criticism by the *Royal Commission 1979* (see later) and the *Health Services Act, 1980*. There had been some criticism since 1974 that the AHAs were too small for proper planning and too large for delivery of services. Others accused them of duplication and waste, of creating excessive bureaucracy and of slowing-up decision making. The Government claimed that their replacement should save some 10 per cent (£30 million) in management costs – though in practice it has only been £10 million.

The 201 new *District Health Authorities* (192 in England, 9 in Wales) are responsible for assessing local health needs, for the employment of medical and other staff and for planning and administering the appropriate health services (under guidance from the Regional Health Authority, based on RAWP principles – see page 111). Each DHA has a chairman appointed by the Secretary of State for Health, and normally 16 other members (four of whom are appointed by local authorities and the others by the RHA who must include at least one nurse or health visitor, a GP, a consultant and a nominee from a university medical school). There is generally a four-year term of office. In practice, in many places the substitution of the District for Area Authorities has involved little obvious change.

The Family Practitioner Committees

These bodies administer the contracts of the family practitioners (GPs, dentists, opthalmic practitioners, opticians and pharmacists), i.e. paying fees and allowances and plan the development of the service. They have links with the DHAs but are largely independent of them, being directly financed by the Department of Health. Each FPC has 30 members: 15 appointed by the professions, 11 by the DHA and four by local authorities. They do not exist in Scotland where FP services form part of the 15 Health Boards.

At each level of this management structure, there are strong professional **advisory committees** whose function is to ensure that decisions are taken in the full knowledge of expert opinion. These committees have a statutory right to be consulted about plans and proposals for the operation of the health service.

Health care delivery

So much for the formal **administrative** structure. Running parallel to this is a similar two-tier structure for the **operational** or delivery side of the NHS. This consists of a multi-disciplinary **Management Team**, which thus operates at (1) Regional, (2) District levels. Here medical, nursing, financial and administrative staff function as a *team* in actually providing health care. This is an example of the 'consensus' or *'corporate approach'* to management; but following criticisms by the *Griffiths Report*, 1983, this has changed (see page 95). The basic operational unit is the District, and the day-to-day running of the NHS is discharged through these Health Districts. Each district normally contains a District General Hospital and has a population of 150,000–300,000. The District Management Team (DMT) consists of six members of whom the most important or interesting is the 'community physician' – the medical planner for the health needs of the district.

Community Health Council

We have seen above that the NHS structure comprises two parallel hierarchies – an administrative and a professional. To provide for an explicit representation of the consumer each District is 'shadowed' by a **Community Health Council** (CHC) which watches over the public interest and can take up issues with the DHA. In Scotland local Health Councils relate to the 15 Health Boards. CHCs are created on the basis of one for each Health District. With up to 30 members, at least half are appointed by the relevant local authorities, at least one third by the local voluntary organisations concerned with health, and the rest by the Regional Health Authority after consultation with other organisations. Each CHC appoints its own chairman from among its members. The council meets at least four times per annum, and expenses are paid.

Though financed by the District Health Authority, the Community Health Councils are independent. Their *function* is **to monitor the health services** and to represent the health interests of the public. Unlike the DHAs they have no management responsiblities. Community Health Councils have the right to visit health institutions, make representations to the District Health Authority and draw attention to consumer problems. They each publish a report annually (to which the District Health Authority must publish its reply) and they have the right to obtain information and access to the DHA and its officers. The DHA must consult the CHC on any plans for the health service (e.g. closing a hospital) and there is at least one formal meeting each year when the DHA meets CHC representatives.

CHCs were created to compensate for the somewhat remote position of the Area Health Authorities. Some would now therefore question the need for CHCs since the replacement District Health Authorities are generally smaller. However, the Royal Commission (1979) recommended that CHCs be given additional resources and powers (e.g. access to FPCs), and that they be encouraged to play a more positive and active role by acting as patients' advocates or 'friends' in cases of complaint (see page 119).

Criticisms of the structure

The new structure aimed to overcome the divisions of the tripartite structure, i.e. to present a unified and closely coordinated system. Has it succeeded? Critics see the following defects in the reorganised system:

Lack of unity. This has several aspects:

(i) The NHS does not include occupational and environmental health services, nor those of the armed forces.

(ii) Family practitioner services are not fully integrated with hospital and community health (and FPCs are further detached under the *Health and Social Security Act*, 1984 – see page 118). The Royal Commission recommended that the FPCs be abolished and integrated as in Scotland and Ulster.

(iii) District (and former Area) Health Authority boundaries are based on local government boundaries, which are not necessarily appropriate for medical needs.

(iv) The health services are separated from housing, education and personal social services.* There are joint-funded schemes, overlapping DHA membership and joint consultative committees linking DHAs with Social Services Departments, and medical social workers have been transferred from the health service to local authority employment. But many feel that liaison and coordination are still inadequate.

Response to the public. The reorganisation aimed deliberately to secure effective management, by choosing members with ability, judgement and drive. The representative function was separated off to another body, the Community Health Council, in order to avoid confusion of function. But some would question the acceptability of such an arrangement in a predominantly social (rather than economic) service. Have the Community Health Councils enough weight, and are they adequately representative? Is the service too manage-

---

*The need for these social services to work closely together is most apparent in such areas as child guidance, accommodation for ex-mental patients and for most aspects of the work of the Personal Social Service departments. The distinction between health and welfare is very blurred, and services such as home helps, residential accommodation, aids and occupational centres are in many ways extensions of and supportive of health services. In Northern Ireland these welfare services are actually administered by the Health Authorities.

rial? Should it be more democratic, perhaps even elected like local government?

Administration and management. The criticisms here have several aspects:

(i)   The system is too bureaucratic, which slows decisions and absorbs resources. Doctors are also fearful of interference from excessive monitoring. The criticism that the NHS has too many tiers has now been met (with the abolition of AHAs). The Royal Commission has recommended greater delegation of powers from the DHSS to the RHAs; it appeared unconvinced about the allegation of 'too many administrators' in the NHS.

(ii) The form of management (variously described as consensus, team or corporate) has been criticised as inefficient and slow because all members of the management team have an equal say and have to agree decisions. Following the recommendations of the *Griffiths Report*, 1983, the Government has introduced general managers (or chief executives) at regional, district and unit levels, to provide leadership. (At national level there is now a thirteen-member **Supervisory Board**, chaired by the Minister, to determine policy objectives and strategy, and a **Management Board** (with a Chief Executive) to allocate resources and review performance.)

(iii) The management structure is described and decried as 'syndicalist' or as a 'medical technocracy', i.e. excessive participation and power in the hands of the medical profession. Is there a danger of the medical view dominating decisions which are often *social* rather than medical in nature?

However, there are other more fundamental criticisms of the reorganisation. These include those who say: 1   The NHS should have been passed into the hands of **local government**. 2   The NHS should be established in the form of a semi-independent board or **public corporation**, like the nationalised industries (e.g. BBC, British Rail, British Coal). The Boards in (ii) above are a move towards this. 3   The NHS should be dismantled and health services be left to **private enterprise** and insurance. 4   Reorganisation was **unnecessary** as the liaison of the former three 'arms' was steadily improving, and a large cause of the trouble in the 'old' NHS was lack of resources or faulty attitudes and poor cooperation rather than the structure as such being wrong. In some respects the reorganisation occurred at a bad time, and has suffered the effects of the squeeze on public resources, the trend to unionisation and the growth in demand for health services. Perhaps the structure is being made into a distraction or scapegoat for other problems in the NHS.

Although the structure of the NHS was changed in 1974 and 1982, the actual services provided are the same; and it is still convenient to examine these under three headings: (a) hospital-based services; (b) family practitioner services; and (c) other community health services.

Hospital-based services

Since the NHS began in 1948, the hospital sector has predominated, both in terms of its command of the NHS resources (absorbing over 60 per cent) and in terms of public esteem. Indeed, the NHS has often been dubbed the 'National *Hospital* Service'. In many ways the hospital sector acts as the powerhouse of the NHS, for it brings together a variety of technical and scientific resources and skills for the purposes of diagnosis and treatment, care and rehabilitation as well as research and teaching. This combination of skills is most completely found in general hospitals and teaching hospitals. Many hospitals, on the other hand, tend to specialise. Out of the total of approximately 2,500 hospitals in England and Wales are some 200 hospitals for maternity, 300 hospitals for mentally disordered and 300 for long-stay patients.

Beds and waiting lists

There are about 400,000 beds in Britain, which is little different to the number in 1948 when the NHS began, and contrasts to the 100 per cent increase in the number of hospital medical, nursing and other staff during the same period. However, as a result of better distribution and utilisation of resources, the 'productivity' of hospitals has increased. More cases (nearly double) are being treated with the same number of beds, so that there are now nearly 7 million in-patient (and over 40 million out-patient) attendances per annum, together with 15 million accident and emergency attendances. Thus the actual number of beds is not in itself a useful measure of NHS progress. What is important is bed utilisation (e.g. average hospital stay for medical cases has fallen from 18.6 days in 1966 to 10.2 in 1981 and 8 in 1984, especially by using quicker through-put and day surgery).

In spite of this, it is still true that waiting lists are about the same as they were about 30 years ago (i.e. 700,000 or some 10 per cent of admissions p.a.). Understandably the waiting list is criticised. But it does discriminate between urgent and less urgent cases; it is the latter who have to wait, perhaps years, for hernias, varicose veins, hip-joint, etc. problems to be treated. For various reasons, about 1 in 7 drop out of the 'queue' – some of them paying for quicker attention by going private.

Staff shortages

Both the quantity and quality of health services have been limited by shortages of staff, especially medical and nursing staff. For hospital doctors, the problem has been not just overwork and inadequate pay, but also complaints about inadequate opportunities for promotion, for post-graduate study facilities and, for senior hospital doctors (the consultants) the threat of losing their opportunities for private practice. There was also a mistaken policy decision in the 1950s when medical training was reduced in the light of the then falling population trends. One consequence of the doctors' complaints has been the emigration of doctors: one aspect of the 'brain drain'. In recent years some 800 doctors left UK annually, though about 500 return per annum, making a net annual loss of about 300. However, the number of immigrant doctors virtually balances this figure. About one third of hospital doctors and 20 per cent of general practitioners were born overseas.

Between 1976 and 1987 the number of hospital doctors increased from 36,600 to over 44,000. The increasing numbers of consultant posts (currently 14,500) provide more opportunities for junior hospital doctors and improves their morale (though many still work excessive hours – an average of 86 hours per week, with 16 per cent

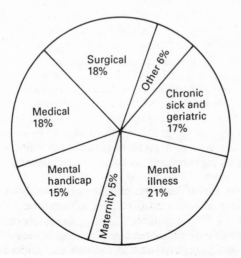

Figure 6   *Hospital beds, England and Wales, 1987 (350,000)*

working over 100 hours). On the other hand with the trend to lower birth rates, we may be heading for an *excess* of doctors whilst still leaving the problem of shortages in particular specialities, e.g. geriatrics and psychiatry (which contain high proportions of overseas doctors). In 1987 the Government proposed a limit on medical training, having already (in 1985) placed restrictions on more doctors from overseas and (1988) imposed a retirement age of 70 on doctors (and dentists). However, problems in maintaining recruitment levels of the 400,000 nurses is anticipated with the dramatic fall in the number of school-leavers during the rest of this century. In addition there are growing shortages of staff in the paramedical professions (including occupational-, speech- and physiotherapy, and clinical psychology).

Buildings

In 1948 the NHS inherited a very mixed bag of hospitals: big asylums, prestigious teaching hospitals, Poor Law infirmaries, small cottage and isolation hospitals. These were haphazardly located and often very old. There has been spasmodic progress in replacing them, so that today about 50 per cent of beds are located in hospitals built before the First World War (a third pre-1900 and only 45 per cent are post-Second World War (1945)).

Table 2   Hospital (capital) allocations (£million at 1978 prices)

1948–58	52
1958–68	190
1968–78	425
1978–88	380

(*Source: Hospital and Health Services Yearbook, 1988*)

With the 1962 Hospital Plan, hospital building received much attention and resources. But with periodic financial and economic problems, projects were delayed and piecemeal upgrading and renovation substituted. However, since then resources have been significantly increased and new (and expensive) hospitals have appeared under the 300 new hospital schemes, each costing over £1 million, undertaken 1981–7. Nevertheless, many hospitals remain unsafe, unhygienic and ill-maintained, and require (according to Parliament's Accounts Committee, 1988) an estimated £1,800 million to bring them up to acceptable standards.

What sort of hospitals?

The problem is not only one of resources. There is the question of how to deploy those buildings resources. The 1962 Plan envisaged the nationwide provision of **district general hospitals**, with some 600–800 beds each and covering the whole range of treatments: acute, geriatric, psychiatric, maternity, ear, nose and throat, etc. This would have the advantage of concentrating resources and allowing a team approach to treatment and care. In 1969 the Bonham-Carter Committee Report reasserted this principle. But the Committee also allowed for the possibility of some local or community hospitals, especially for convalescent cases, and manned by general practitioners and local nursing staff. Many people have expressed fears that the concentration on district general hospitals would not be in the best interest of patients, that they might be too big, impersonal and isolated from the community, and many local hospitals have survived only as a result of local protests. However, with the emergence of economic problems and public expenditure cuts, the Government announced in 1975 (and re-confirmed in 1981) that further wholesale building of large district general hospitals was to be abandoned; instead local hospitals were to be retained and 'nucleus' hospitals (with about 250 beds and based on a standardised design system) were to be developed (the first of which opened in 1982). In general, there is now at least one general hospital in each health district.

Family practitioner services

These front line or 'primary care' services have the most frequent contact with patients, often over a considerable period of time; they have important preventive as well as diagnostic and curative roles to play in medical care. The services are:

General medical practice	(there are about 32,000 general practitioners or 'family doctors')
General dental service	(there are about 17,000 dentists)
General ophthalmic service	(there are about 9,000 ophthalmic opticians)
Pharmaceutical service	(there are about 12,000 retail pharmacies under contract for prescriptions with the NHS)

General practitioner services

For most people, the family doctor or 'GP' is the first line of defence in case of illness, and he acts as a link with the other parts of the

NHS. On average 70 per cent of the population see their general practitioner at least once a year and the average patient consults about four times per annum.

All members of the public are entitled to register with a GP of their choice. Some 97 per cent of the population are so registered, but they may change doctors if they wish. GPs are also free to choose their patients. Thereafter the GP has complete clinical freedom to treat the patients on his 'list' according to his professional discretion. There are no regulations as to which drugs or treatments he should prescribe, though excessive prescribing can be investigated by the Family Practitioners' Committee. In some areas the doctor will dispense as well as prescribe medicines.

Numbers and distribution. Owing to the cutback in medical training in the 1950s, the number of doctors was slow to improve since the NHS was introduced. However, following the Todd Report on Medical Education, 1968, medical training has expanded, and in 1971 the number of doctors began to keep pace with, and exceed, the growth of patients. Moreover, distribution has been improved by a quota system operated by the Medical Practices Committee, which surveys the need for doctors throughout the country and can refuse doctors permission to practise in certain areas called 'restricted areas'. While the average list today is 2,000 patients (c.f. 2,300 in 1977 and 2,200 in 1980) some have less than 2,000, and some even have over 3,000. (Some of the latter, as 'designated' areas, receive funds from the Department of Health to pay doctors extra to work there.)

Demoralisation and regeneration. For a long time after the NHS started, general practitioners felt they had suffered a decline in status both in society generally and in medicine in particular. There were many reasons for this:

(a)   The enhanced importance of the hospital service, with its superior resources and equipment, its well-publicised achievements and its drama.

(b)   Hospital doctors were now salaried, and no longer therefore relied on referrals by general practitioners. Many general practitioners feel they have become no more than 'filters and signers of certificates'.

(c)   The development of antibiotics and drugs has eliminated some of the more dramatic medical episodes and made the work of the general practitioner more routine and lacking mystique.

(d)   Many general practitioners resented their exclusion from hospitals and began to feel somewhat isolated from the medical developments within the hospital sector.

(e)   Some doctors complained of the insatiable demand for health services, the trivial complaints and the overwork.

(f)   Inevitably there were complaints over pay. This was aggravated by the 'captitation system' of payments (i.e. fixed sum per person on the doctor's list) which gave no encouragement or recognition to the good doctor who might seek to improve his premises or qualifications, but tempt him to develop a long list.

In 1966 there was an important agreement, the 'Doctor's Charter', which introduced allowances for rent and ancillary staff. It increased the pay scales substantially (the average salary of a GP is £25,000), and changed the structure of payments to reflect both qualifications of doctors and the form of their practices, i.e. group practice. The result has been: 1   A boost in the modernisation of practices (buildings, equipment, appointments systems). 2   Growth of group practices and health centres. 3   A boost in morale. 4   Increased use of ancillary staff (80 per cent of district nurses, midwives and health visitors are now attached to group practices).

Since then we have seen the establishment of the Royal College of General Practitioners (1967) and the publication of the Todd Report on Medical Education (1968), which sought an improvement in the specific training of general practitioners. Furthermore, general practitioners have been increasingly associated with hospitals, often as clinical assistants on a part-time attachment basis. Access to hospital equipment has been increased, and many more family doctors are meeting their hospital colleagues in the growing post-graduate training centres (over 200 work as 'hospital practitioners'). In addition, developments in technology and drug treatment allow more opportunities to run local, community hospitals, undertake surgery diagnosis and treat cases at home which formerly went to hospital (e.g. duodenal ulcers).

Organisation. The face of general practice has changed significantly since the early days of the NHS when the majority of doctors worked single-handed, usually in their own homes, and lacked nursing or secretarial assistance and equipment. Today over 80 per cent of doctors work in partnerships or **group practice** (and 25 per cent work in health centres). More than 60 per cent have appointments systems. Today general practitioners not only have better premises but also have the diagnostic and treatment equipment to go in them (perhaps assisted by Government loans from the General Practice Finance Corporation). Some GPs have formed Practice Committees with patients to discuss health matters and the running of the practice.

Nevertheless, it is perhaps paradoxical that while the general practitioner deals with 90 per cent of medical cases (known as 'episodes'), their share of the NHS budget is only 8 per cent. In 1950 it was 12 per cent.) Finance no doubt still accounts for the emigration of many general practitioners. But for some the reason is dissatisfaction with their role in or uncertainty with the NHS. The Royal Commission 1979 recommended offering the option of salaried employment to GPs who wanted greater security perhaps in combination with a smaller list to attract them to less popular areas, e.g. inner cities. This is being actively considered by the Government – see *Primary Health Care: an Agenda for Discussion*, HMSO, 1986.

The role of the general practitioner. Many general practitioners used to come into this branch of medicine as a second best option, having been denied the opportunity of specialisation. However, it has now become a much more attractive profession, especially since 1981 when a three-year vocational training requirement was introduced. And those with a comprehensive range of high-quality provision will in future receive extra 'good practice' allowances. But what is the *proper role* of the general practitioner. Should his work remain general? If so should the general practitioner: (a) be concerned with relatively routine general physical complaints, filtering off the more difficult? (b) develop a more social and psychological approach, bearing in mind that many, perhaps 30 per cent, of patients' symptoms are psycho-social rather than physical in origin? (The attachment of counsellors to practices can significantly reduce patients' demands on GP time and drug prescribing.) (c) specialise within the group practice or health centre in, say, health problems of particular age groups or particular branches of medicine (e.g. psychiatry) so that colleagues can make referrals on the spot (this development might also strengthen their case for retaining local cottage hospitals)?

It is also argued that with the development of appointments systems, group practices and 'practice nursing', relationships with patients are becoming less personal and continuous, and so the traditional role of being a 'family doctor' (GP) is no longer viable. Indeed, in 1963 the Gillie Report advocated that he become the coordinator and director of the community care team. On the other hand, a more radical move would be to adopt the US practice of replacing the general practitioner system as such and have all medical services based at hospitals.

Health centres

These were advocated in the Dawson Report (1920) and a few did become established before the Second World War. The *National Health Service Act, 1946*, envisaged a widespread development of them by making their provision by local authorities mandatory. However, up to 1960 only 12 were created. Part of the problem was the reluctance of doctors to get involved with local authorities (who provided them) and partly the building costs involved. Since the mid-1960s their numbers have grown substantially, so that there are now 1,000 in operation (provided by District Health Authorities).

In their developed forms, they comprise multidisciplinary teams of doctors, dentists, nurses, midwives, health visitors, pharmacists and social workers, plus visiting hospital specialists. Their **advantage** is that they can provide an all-round primary service at one centre, costly equipment can be shared and ancillary staff can be more easily attached, above all the staff can work as a team. But some patients find them inconvenient (e.g. old people who have to travel to the centre rather than pop round the corner to the GP) and some GPs fear for their independence.

General dental services

Unless receiving private treatment the patient receives family doctor services free of charge (except for prescriptions at £2.60 per item – 13 times the 1978 figure – though in hospital even medication is free). Dentists, however, charge for treatment except for those on low income. NHS patients currently (1989) pay 75 per cent of the cost (up to a maximum of £150; it was £30 in 1982). And in 1988 a charge of £3 became payable for dental check-ups. Costly treatment requires the prior approval of the Dental Estimates Board. Dentures are also charged for, though there are remissions for young people, expectant mothers, nursing mothers and the elderly. As with the family doctor service, there is complete freedom of choice by patients of dentists, and by dentists of patients. Unlike GPs, however, dentists do not require patients to register with them. The normal practice is to visit a dentist's surgery by appointment.

There is one dentist to every 3,500 people. Altogether, more than 32 million courses of dental treatment are given per annum, compared with 8 million in 1949, plus those provided at dental hospitals as part of the hospital service.

General ophthalmic services

These provide for the testing of sight and supply of spectacles by qualified practitioners, registered by the Family Practitioners' Committee. There are three groups of these: ophthalmic medical practitioners, i.e. doctors who test sight and prescribe glasses; ophthalmic opticians, who test, prescribe and supply glasses; and dispensing opticians, who simply supply glasses to prescription. Again there is complete freedom of choice for the patient using the service, but the person using the service for the first time must obtain a note from his doctor. Since 1988 eye tests (10 million p.a.) have become subject to charges for adults (£10 minimum), and supplies (7 million) have been charged for since 1951, though remissions using vouchers are obtainable for low income groups. Since the *Health and Social Security Act, 1984* anyone can supply glasses (the Government hoped that free competition would reduce prices). Consequently, NHS supplies are now confined to children and those on low incomes.

Pharmaceutical services

The dispensing of medicines and appliances is undertaken mainly, via prescriptions, by pharmacies as part of the NHS. These chemists' shops are required to keep open at reasonable hours, and there is usually a rota system for evenings and holidays. In 1986 (England) 323 million prescriptions were dispensed at a cost of about £1,500 million, of which 10 per cent is recovered in charges; three-quarters are free due to exemption (for children, elderly, expectant and nursing mothers, low income groups and certain chronic sick). Chemists are paid, via the Family Practitioners' Committee, the cost of the items dispensed, plus a professional fee. Smaller chemists depend on NHS dispensing for over 60 per cent of their trade.

A current problem is that with the development of health centres and group practice, neighbourhood chemists are losing trade, and are closing down, so that in some areas many people, especially the elderly, cannot find chemists, or even doctors, within easy reach.

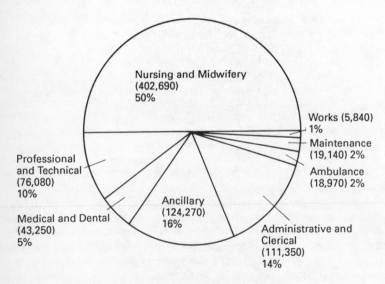

Figure 7   *NHS directly-employed staff, England, 1986*
Total = 801,590 (whole time equivalents)

Other community health services

Costing over £1,500 million p.a., these cover a wide range of medical supportive and preventive services. These include ambulances, school health, family planning, health visiting, home nursing, midwifery, epidemiology (checking epidemics), maternity and child health care, aftercare and preventive medicine, including vaccination and health education. It is evident that these are geared primarily to the needs of the very young and the elderly.

Maternity and child welfare services

These include the provision of welfare foods, ante- and post-natal clinics, child welfare clinics and the advisory services of health visitors. Some 70 per cent of babies are taken to clinics. It is felt, however, that attendances should be increased, if only to help screen and prevent non-accidental injury to children. One suggestion has been made to make payment of family benefits conditional on regular attendances.

These centres may also provide **family planning** services which were pioneered and developed by the Family Planning Association. It is now an integral part of the NHS and available to all irrespective of age or marital status. The service is provided mainly at family planning clinics, hospitals and by general practitioners, though the voluntary clinics also continue to make provision (see page 175). However, in recent years, the non-GP provision has experienced significant reductions in funding.

Abortion

This was legalised under the *Abortion Act, 1967*, provided that *two* doctors are of the opinion that: (i) continuance of the pregnancy would involve risk of the woman's life, or of injury, mental or physical, to the mother or her other children; or (ii) there was a substantial risk that the child would be born seriously handicapped. In 1986 there were 157,000 (legal) abortions in Britain (compared with 95,000 in 1971) with about half each in NHS or private hospitals or clinics. A complementary service is that of **family planning** provided by clinics and GPs. And a **fertility** service has also been developed, mainly through drugs; but in 1982 the first 'test tube' or artificial insemination (AID) baby was born within the NHS. With an estimated 15 per cent of couples being infertile in 1984 the Warnock Report *Human Fertilisation and Embryology* recommended that surrogate motherhood be permitted (within limits) genetic manipulation be banned and an independent statutory Licensing Authority be set up to regulate certain infertility treatments.

In this section we have been primarily concerned with the NHS. However, we should not overlook the fact that health services are provided in other forms and by other authorities. Apart from the small private sector and a fairly substantial sector of self-medication, there also exists the important areas of public health and occupational health. Within the latter we can include the public health services provided by the Armed Forces.

Public health

This developed in the nineteenth century and continues to play a vital role in an overall health care. But in dealing essentially with the environment it tends to get overlooked in discussions of health. Public health functions are directed at maintaining living conditions conducive to health and to checking the spread of disease. The more important of the services include:

1 **Water** supply and **sewerage**, the responsibility of the ten Regional Water Authorities (due to be privatised in 1990).
2 **Clean air** regulations and **noise** abatement.
3 Controls to secure minimum **housing** standards.
4 Control of **infectious diseases** and prevention of **food poisoning**.
5 **Health control** at seaports and airports to check the introduction of diseases from overseas.
6 Control of **medicinal products** and of addictive drugs.
7 **Environmental health** in the form of street cleaning, refuse, disinfestation and provision of burial grounds and baths.

Many of these functions lie with the local authorities, but obviously there is need for close consultation with the health authorities. Consequently **District Community Physicians** have now been appointed, with dual responsibilities to both the health authorities and the local authorities. They thus replace the former Medical Officers of Health.

Occupational health

These services are essentially preventive and protective. In effect they are an extension of the public health services into places of work and are thus complementary to the personal health services (see page 319). Relevant powers and duties derive from public health legislation, Factory Acts and, more recently, the *Health and Safety at Work Act, 1974*. Similarly, the law relating to employment of children and young persons is relevant.

Many employers voluntarily maintain medical services for their staff in addition to those required by law, including regular medical examinations and various preventive measures (many initiated by EMAS – see page 322). Some factories operate 'on the spot' medical care, provided by industrial medical officers i.e. doctors, and industrial nurses (mostly part-time appointments). Medical care provided by industry amounts to over £100 million per annum. There is particular concern these days because of the evidence of the effects of stress (such as that resulting from relocation) which is growing with the increasing pace of change in work and society. For example, it is estimated that stress-related illness costs over £4,000 million a year in absenteeism and inefficiency. In addition, a St John's Ambulance survey in 1988 revealed 'horrifying' public ignorance about first aid procedures.

The private sector

The private sector consists of (i) health services provided by the commercial 'off the shelf' sales of medicines, drugs and appliances in chemists' shops and supermarkets (this informal or self-care is an estimated £450 million p.a.) and (ii) private treatment provided by the various family practitioners and the specialists who are mainly hospital based. The latter group of services are frequently financed by private insurance. Some 70 per cent of private hospital admissions are covered by insurance, especially that provided by BUPA (British United Provident Association) and the PPP (Private Patients Plan) schemes. Altogether there are over 2 million subscribers covering nearly 6 million people and worth some £1,500 million (compared with 0.7 million subscribers covering 1.5 million in 1966), mainly employees in large organisations. It is estimated that the private sector amounts to the equivalent of about 5 per cent of NHS expenditure. There are altogether about 150 private hospitals plus nursing homes providing some 300,000 treatments a year in 7,200 beds.

The existence of a private sector in health is controversial partly because of the tax relief involved. The main **advantages of a private sector** are:

1 It reduces the NHS waiting lists by taking patients away;
2 It provides competition with the NHS, and a standard by which to measure the NHS;
3 It provides a choice for the public;
4 It provides greater freedom for doctors who are not, as a result, bound to join the state system;
5 If there were no private sector, doctors might emigrate to practise;
6 It produces a 'financial discipline' on people who, in having to

pay, realise the true cost of health services and so do not abuse the system or take up time and resources with trivial complaints.

One result of its existence is that many doctors work both privately and also for the NHS. For example, some 50 per cent of hospital consultants do not work full-time for the NHS, but undertake some part-time private work. They do this partly for the extra income (it may raise their income to over £100,000 p.a.) but partly too because it enables them to practise medicine with more freedom.

Disadvantages of a private sector:

1   It withdraws resources, e.g. doctors, from the NHS;
2   It creates a maldistribution of resources – for example, geographi-
    cally private practice goes to those areas where the money is;
3   It introduces two standards of health care, and there may even be
    some malpractice by doctors to exaggerate the failings of the NHS
    to boost their own practices;
4   It provides the possibility of 'jumping' the queue or waiting list;
5   It may tend to more wasteful, unnecessary or extravagant expend-
    iture.

However, it could be argued that private patients pay twice (having already paid taxes), and if they choose to, say, sacrifice a £500 holiday in order to have an early operation that is reasonable freedom of choice. The obviously theoretical solution to the dilemma is to raise the NHS standards and cut the waiting lists so that there is no gain in going private.

Another dispute concerns the private treatment which occurs *within* the NHS, i.e. the 'paybeds' reserved by doctors for their private fee-paying patients. There are today 3,250 pay beds (i.e. under 1 per cent of the total). In 1966 there were 5,400 and in 1948, 6,500. The *National Health Service Act, 1976*, began to phase them out (except for overseas patients); it set up the Health Services Board and introduced a licensing system for private nursing homes and hospitals; it also established a common waiting list for serious cases. However, the *Health Services Act, 1980*, abolished the Board and restored the Minister's discretionary powers to allow pay beds (hence their expansion from 2,400 in 1980).

The arguments against phasing out paybeds are: 1   Many feel that this is the beginning of the end of all private practice and a move towards state monopoly. 2   Patients should have the right to choose; to pay for privacy or to choose their consultant and date of entry to hospital. They are paying twice, taxes *and* fees (a bed can cost nearly £200 per day in London). 3   It brings in an income to the NHS, variously estimated at between £12 million per annum (1978) and £40 million per annum. 4   It will break the link between the State and private sectors so that standards might more seriously diverge. 5   For some doctors, paybeds provide the only opportunity for private practice. This helps to spread the distribution of doctors as well as keep some of them from emigrating abroad. 6   It will create wasteful duplication and the under-utilisation of expensive resources; for example, the existence of private beds within NHS hospitals saves the waste of time through travel of valuable specialists. (Paradoxically the NHS buys some 3,000 bed/places in private hospitals.)

The arguments for phasing out paybeds are: 1   Introduces queue jumping. 2   Contravenes the NHS principle of treatment according to medical need. 3   Blocks NHS beds and increases the waiting lists. 4   Consultants abuse their part-time system by poor attendance to NHS duties and off-load their work on to junior doctors. 5   Rather than keep up NHS standards, the existence of paybeds may actually lower them as doctors, consciously or not, may lower their standards of courtesy or attention in order to give private patients the appearance of something special for their fees. 6   Increases the NHS costs, i.e. the income does not cover the actual costs of using NHS facilities (premises, equipment, staff). In 1979 the Royal Commission recommended that pay bed charges be raised to meet their proper cost.

One other aspect of the dispute over private practice was the Government plan of 1974 to make more attractive the pay and conditions of those doctors who opt to work full-time for the NHS. It was intended that extra rewards should go to those working in the 'twilight' areas of medicine – geriatrics and mental disorders – where opportunities for private practice are very limited. However, the doctors objected to this and it appears to have been dropped.

Inequalities in the NHS

Fundamental to the NHS is the concept of equality and ease of access to doctors, hospitals, health centres. A continuing criticism has been that of disparities and variations in the provision of health services. These variations have three aspects.

1   Medical. This has to do with priorities, the general point being that certain areas of medicine seem to be neglected relative to others. E.g., do the community health services get sufficient resources when hospitals absorb 65 per cent of the NHS expenditure? In particular, do the elderly and handicapped get a fair share of resources? e.g. the mentally disordered occupy 43 per cent of beds, but get only 25 per cent of the hospital budget.* Overall, about 60 per cent of NHS expenditure goes to services for children, elderly, disabled and mentally disordered.

Another indication is the 'merit award' system whereby special payments are made to consultants, amounting in some cases to an extra £22,000 p.a. on top of the average consultant's salary of £26,000 (1984). Most of these are engaged in general medicine and surgery; less than 20 per cent go into geriatric or mental health. By and large geriatrics and mental patients tend to be in older hospital buildings, have more crowded conditions and far fewer beds in teaching hospitals. Should more resources be diverted to the health services for the chronic sick and to community and preventive services? Is the balance of NHS expenditure† the right one?

2   Geographical. Despite closer integration and better planning since 1948, regional disparities in the distribution of health services still amount to what has been described as 'territorial injustice', i.e. the standard of care depends very much on where you happen to live, e.g. in 1972 the South-West Metropolitan Region was spending over £48 per patient in health care, while in Sheffield Region the figure was only £30; in East Midlands 25 per cent of GPs had lists over 3,000, compared with only 8 per cent of those in the South-West; in 1977 spending in Westminster was £192 per head, in Leicestershire and the Trent region only £62. And teaching hospital areas tend to be particularly favoured with resources.

Inequalities like this might be justified if the money was being concentrated in areas where people needed health care most. But this does not happen. In fact the relationship is often inverted (and known as 'inverse care law'): the NHS often provides least services to those parts of the country where the death rates are highest and there are higher morbidity rates. Broadly speaking, the North has more illness but relatively fewer NHS resources per head than the South. However it is measured, whether by beds, or nurses per head, dental services, or waiting lists, there are great variations which are not usually rational. In recent years the Government has introduced a plan to eradicate the worst of these through a process of identifying 'health deprivation areas' and by channelling resources to them (similar to the Education Priority Area policy – see page 245) through

---

*In its 1975 Annual Report the then Hospital Advisory Service was very critical of the accommodation provided for the elderly (HMSO).

†In 1988 the balance of NHS expenditure was:

Hospitals	65.0%	Dental	3.0%
Pharmaceutical	11.0%	Ophthalmic	1.0%
Community	11.0%	Other	3.0%
GP	7.0%		

allocation of funds to allow differential growth. This is based on a formula devised in 1976 by the Resource Allocation Working Party or **RAWP** which takes account of population size and age, regional rates of morbidity (illness), etc. But the RAWP system is difficult to operate at a time of minimal or nil growth; nor does it affect differences among the different parts of the UK (Wales, Scotland, etc.); and although it is also applied to Districts within Regions, it does not include general practitioner services. It was replaced in 1989.

3 Social class. Similar criticisms apply here. Generally speaking, health statistics, e.g. mortality and morbidity, show that the working-class people are among those most in *need* of medical care, and yet paradoxically they appear to derive relatively and proportionately *fewer* NHS resources. There seem to be three reasons for this:

1 **Geography.** The semi-skilled and unskilled workers tend to be more highly concentrated in the North and East, yet these areas get a less than average allocation from the NHS budget (see **2** above).
2 **Poorer quality** of services. For example, although they may use the services more often, e.g. in visits to the GP, those GPs have more patients, inferior premises, etc., so treatment may be inferior. In inner city areas, GPs tend to be older (10 per cent over 70 compared with 3 per cent nationally), have longer lists and work single-handed rather than in groups.
3 **Under-utilisation.** Some evidence exists to suggest that the working class does not use the NHS as much as they are entitled to. This may be due to inadequate knowledge about illnesses or about the NHS and its workings, and perhaps a reluctance to use or sustain a regular contact with certain (middle-class, officious?) health services. On the other hand, it is suggested that middle-class people consult earlier, consult over minor ailments and use more expensive sectors of the NHS. For example, a far higher percentage of working-class women than middle-class have confinements at home rather than at hospital. Middle-class families proportionately have more tonsillectomies for their children. Working-class people tend still to feel a stigma attached to mental disorder compared to middle-class; and middle-class people make more calls on elective and cosmetic surgery.

The Royal Commission (1979), the Black Report *Inequalities in Health* (1980) and *The Health Divide* (a report by the Health Education Authority, 1987) confirm, document and condemn the disparities in health and health services (e.g. pointing out that the death rate for unskilled workers is double that for professional people). Thus in terms of both social justice and efficient use of resources it seems desirable to reallocate resources and make the service more accessible. In the long run, as Lord Taylor has said, 'In the quest of health for our patients we have to embrace social and economic pathology,' i.e. inequalities in health arise from inequalities in social and economic circumstances: equalising the latter will equalise the former (see Chapter 19).

Financing the NHS

When it was introduced, the NHS aimed at providing an optimum, rather than a minimum, standard of service. But in practice there are gaps and delays in provision, and standards are often criticised. Clearly such deficiencies have much to do with resources:

1   Are we devoting insufficient resources to the NHS?
2   Are the resources wastefully used in the NHS?
3   Is it the case that while standards of health provisions are improving, the aspirations and demands for health care are growing even more quickly?

The cost of the NHS

In 1951 the NHS was costing £500 million per annum, which represented some 4.0 per cent of the National Income. Since then the actual expenditure has increased steadily every year so that in 1974 the figure was over £7,000 million and today some £15,000 million (net), i.e. over 5 per cent. However, other countries seem to be devoting more resources to health and getting better results, e.g. in terms of lower death rates and higher life expectancies (see *Demography Yearbook*, United Nations). (1974 figures in brackets.)

> United States 10.8% (6.4)   Italy 7.4% (1.2)
> France   9.4% (2.7)   Japan 6.6% (1.8)
> W. Germany   8.1% (1.8)

On the other hand, it may be that Britain spends relatively more on housing and welfare services, which underpin health; or that its smaller percentage is spent more effectively. Nevertheless, the question remains: should we spend more? Indeed, will we *have* to spend more to meet future demands: the number and percentage of old people; the increased survival of handicapped persons; developments in medical technology – plus the problems associated with unemployment (sickness, suicide, demoralisation) as revealed in the DHSS Report *Unemployment and Health in Families* (1981) and *Forsaken*

Families by Fagin and Little (Penguin, 1984) (which help explain the 20 per cent higher death rate of the North of England).

In 1988 an *Age Concern* report drew attention to the similar plight of the elderly (see page 139).

Can we afford it?

In 1987 the NHS was costing some £15,000 million p.a. (net of charges and property sales) or 5.9 per cent of the National Income (of which 0.6 per cent is the private sector provision). This amounts to over £25 per family per week. Much of the increased expenditure goes to pay increased medical, nursing and ancillary staffs (since three-quarters of expenditure goes on pay). This was financed mainly by general taxation:

	1987	%	**1961**
Taxes	85		78
National Insurance Contributions	11		16
Charges	4		6

If we wanted to raise the percentage spent on NHS the contribution of one or all of these items would have to be increased. Before we examine this possibility, consider the overall impact of raising the percentage of National Income devoted to the NHS. What is to be *sacrificed*? (i) Other Government expenditure. But which: Education? Housing? Defence? Highways? (ii) Private consumption, i.e. increased taxation, where the Government then diverts proceeds to the NHS (a 1p on tax raises £1 billion). (iii) Private investment, i.e. more taxes on business, corporation tax etc.

The obvious problem with this is tax 'saturation'. Is there a danger of **overtaxation** with the demoralising and disincentive consequences? And does not the economy require more, not less, private investment? If the taxes raised are indirect (e.g. VAT) this could be both unfair as between rich and poor, and inflationary. (In a period of economic *growth*, of course, we would not need to devote a greater proportion of the Gross National Product to increase the NHS resources.) It may be easier to raise the level of National Insurance **contributions** (a small portion of which go to the NHS), since contributors can feel they are getting a direct benefit in return; or perhaps even introduce a separate 'earmarked' health contribution. Increases have been made more acceptable too by the replacement of the flat-rate system by the earnings related scheme. Nevertheless, in the end, contributions are just another tax, and are perhaps high enough for most contributors (employees and employers alike). The Royal Commission (1979) felt that an insurance-based NHS, like compulsory car insurance, would be costly to administer and would penalise those least able to pay (thus creating two levels of service). Existing **charges** could be increased, i.e. charges for amenity beds, for dental treatment and spectacles, for appliances and for prescriptions. These charges are well below cost. In addition, charges could be introduced for general practitioner consultations or for hospital 'hotel' facilities, i.e. bed, food, laundry, etc. Charges have the **advantages** of: (i) Raising essential funds. (ii) Reducing unnecessary demands, e.g. for trivial complaints. But there are a number of **disadvantages**. Charges would (i) be objectionable on principle; it would be a tax on sickness. What of the chronic sick? (ii) Distort the doctor's pattern of prescribing (i.e. choosing the cheapest for poorer patients); (iii) reduce demand and might increase the incidence of ill health in the nation; (iv) yield only a small amount (unless the charges were very high); since allowance must be made for exemptions (currently about half the population). On 1978 prices, a charge of £2 per GP consultation would bring in £300 million p.a.; and a £20 per week hospital charge, £500 million. Costs of collection would have to be off-set too. The Royal Commission (1979) was against charges and recommended their complete extinction. However, the Government has (1989) increased the **prescription charge** (or 'tax') to £2.80 per item (from 20 pence in 1979, though the average cost to the NHS is £5 per item) and has introduced eye (£3) and dental (£10) examination charges. It has also introduced medical charges for patients from overseas (estimated to raise £6 million a year).

Alternatives

1   Better use of **existing resources** and eliminating waste. Before 1974 it was often believed that NHS reorganisation itself would help in this respect by bringing managers and clinicians closer together, and by increasing the professional management of the NHS. However, critics allege that the new structure has made matters worse; that too many man hours are being wasted, especially where doctors and nurses are having to attend numerous (consensus) management committees (e.g. in multi-disciplinary management teams); and that there are too many young and not particularly expert administrators (following a 30 per cent increase in numbers since 1973). The Royal Commission did not accept this last point (which has now been superseded by the introduction of general management, following the Griffiths Report; see page 95) but was aware of an excessive proliferation of medical advisory bodies. The Commission was also critical of the NHS financial control system. Do doctors have too much freedom to determine medical treatments regardless of costs? Should they be made responsible for managing cash-limited

budgets? Are they sufficiently aware of the costs of treatments; and aware of the efficacy (or rather in-efficacy) of many standard treatments (e.g. tonsillectomies, intensive coronary care units, etc.)? Is there an excessive range of drugs available on prescription, and are there too many unmonitored repeat prescriptions? In 1981, the Government envisaged that increased efficiency in the NHS would 'create' some £17 million worth of resources for spending. As a result of competitive tendering and contracting out laundry and cleaning services to private firms, the Government's anticipated efficiency savings are now £150 million a year. Managers are also being given more scope to buy and sell medical services with other Health Authorities and the private sector (together with opportunities for income generation through leasing hospital forecourts, providing testing for private laboratories etc.). But there are those who fear that the drive for efficiency will lower standards of health care e.g. as with patients who relapse because they are discharged too soon. On the other hand there is evidence of waste in the management of NHS property. A report by the National Audit Office, in 1988, estimated savings of £500 million here e.g. 20 per cent of Health Authorities have been found to own land of which half is surplus to requirements. A more recent development in the attempt to get the best from the resources devoted to health services is the use of QALYs (or quality-adjusted life-years) which seek to compare health outputs with the costs of treatment. See page 476 for an illustration. But it is a controversial subject. Equally controversial is the Government's policy of contracting out hospital services to private firms (catering, cleaning, laundry) and selling off surplus assets (land and buildings). And in the future hospitals could be allowed to opt out of local health authority control and become self-governing bodies within the NHS (employing staff and buying in services from health authorities and doctors, see page 123).

2 Should there be a review of **priorities**. Would it be more economic, for example, to devote more resources to the relatively low cost 'front line' services of the home nursing, health visitor and home help (personal social services)? Good examples of this in recent years have been: (i) Quicker turnover in hospital bed utilisation as with quick through-put surgery and day admissions. (ii) Rehabilitation work, especially with mentally subnormal hospital patients, enabling them to become self-supporting in the community. Some studies suggest that one third of hospital patients could be treated at home or as out-patients (though this does pass costs on to the family and community services) e.g. Holland has more home confinements than Britain and experiences lower infant and maternal mortality rates. Are our present priorities too largely the result of historical accident? (However,

can priorities ever be fully *rational*, e.g. as between medical attention for the middle-aged worker and services for the aged or mentally handicapped; between providing geriatric day-trips or kidney machines?)

3 Should more attention be given to health **education** – better self-care (diet, smoking, jogging) and wider use of preventive services (family planning, well-women clinics, less lead in petrol, etc.)? By devoting more resources here it may actually become a National *Health* Service. Note here the role of the Health Education Authority and the College of Health. In 1988, in his report *On the State of the Public Health for the Year 1987* the Government's Chief Medical Officer referred to the 'tragic waste of human resources' from the preventable deaths, illness and disability of people from drinking and smoking (e.g. some 40,000 a year die from lung cancer and many children die at birth owing to the mother's smoking). This was reiterated and reinforced by another group of health specialists in *The Nation's Health* (1988) who urged increased taxes on drink and tobacco, compulsory immun-isation, the use of rear seat belts in cars, and regular screening for cancer and blood pressure. Meanwhile, the Government has initiated publicity campaigns on drug-taking and AIDS (which has killed 1,352 and currently affects 1,500 people in Britain). And in 1988 it launched a new vaccination campaign (in view of the fact that only 67 per cent of children are currently immunised against whooping cough and 70 per cent against measles). More attention is now being given to environmental medicine and health with the growing realisation of the pervasive impact of environmental factors on health. There is evidence to suggest that some illnesses (e.g. arthritis, migraine, asthma, eczema, irritable bowel, be-haviour disorder) may be caused by chemical pollution (fertilis-ers, pesticides), visual display units, chlorine in water, foam-filled furniture, chemicals in paint, clothing and insecticides, and aller-gies associated with plastics, dust, pollen, bacteria and a wide range of foods. Food poisoning too has increased from 500 cases in the 1960s to 17,000 per year today.

4 Make greater use of the **voluntary sector**. There is a long and varied tradition of service here. The supreme example today is the *hospice movement* for the care of the dying. It began in 1967 and has depended throughout on voluntary effort and resources. With its 140 hospices (1988) it is currently supported by Health Author-ities to the extent of some 40 per cent of its expenditure. A more recent development here is the creation (in 1988) of a NHS lottery. This is expected to raise some £40 million per annum.

5 Expand the **private sector**, i.e. the fee-charging sector outside the NHS which includes chemists' sales, private consultations and treatment by medical practitioners, all amounting to about 10 per

cent of NHS expenditure. In addition to private hospitals there are the controversial 'pay beds' within NHS hospitals. Other ideas for expanding the private sector include giving tax relief for those taking out private health insurance and a scheme for giving health vouchers to everyone (which can be cashed in for NHS or private medical care). Any substantial expansion of private health services implies that the state health service will become less universal and more selective – which raises many issues, some of which were dealt with by the Royal Commission.

The Royal Commission on the NHS (1975–79)

This was appointed to 'consider in the interests both of the patients and those who work in the NHS the best use and management of the financial and manpower resources of the NHS'. The Report (Merrison, 1979) covers (a) the aims, achievements, defects and opinions on the NHS; (b) a review of individual health services; (c) NHS manpower; (d) relations with other organisations; (e) NHS structure, management and finance. Apart from references in the text, limitations of space here allow only the briefest indication of some of its **findings and recommendations**:

1 Whilst it is not the envy of the world, the NHS is fundamentally sound and gives good value for money: '. . . we found much about which we can all be proud . . . If in considering some aspects in detail we have made specific criticisms, we have done this in the hope that in the future the NHS can provide a better service, not because we think it is in danger of collapse.'
2 Whilst cautious about advocating more NHS expenditure, it did want extra resources for replacement hospitals, for primary care services in declining inner cities and better services for the handicapped and elderly; it also called for an occupational health service to be established.
3 It saw a continuing place for mental hospitals; and cast some doubt on the appropriateness of the District General Hospital units for the elderly and mentally disordered.
4 More preventive measures were recommended – fluoridation, compulsory seat belts, screening, chiropody, more health education and restrictions on adverts which induce bad dietary habits.
5 There should be more training for those caring for the elderly and others needing long-term care; and perhaps the development of Continental-type nursing homes (which combine hospital with residential care).
6 Health and social services links and inter-professional collabora-

tion could be improved in the education and training of health and
social work professionals.

7 Urgent attention should be given to training in industrial relations
(the NHS is the nation's biggest employer, with some 1.2 million
workers).

8 Health departments should enforce their priorities in the medical
staff shortage specialities (e.g. geriatrics).

9 In regard to GP services, it recommended that the controls
exercised by Medical Practices Committees be strengthened; that
auditing of GP services be strengthened; that health departments
should introduce a limited list of drugs and encourage more
generic (i.e. not branded) prescribing; that there should be research into the feasibility of common budgets for family practitioner, hospital and community services.

We have seen that the Commission did recommend the shedding of
a tier in the 1974 structure. What it did not suggest was the transfer of
the NHS to local government; nor the transfer of local authority
welfare functions to the NHS. But it did not condemn such ideas, and
it did commend the continuation of the arrangements in Northern
Ireland where health and social services are administered together
through *ac hoc* boards.

The Government's response to the Commission's ideas has been
swift in some respects (e.g. the abolition of Area Health Authorities). It has been zero, weak or dilatory in others (e.g. enhanced
health education, or a strengthening of the CHCs). For others it has
adopted contrary policies (e.g. increasing charges; seriously considering Continental-type insurance schemes; further detaching FPCs
which became health (and employing) authorities in their own right
in 1985 with their chairmen and members (15 lay and 15 from the four
professions) appointed by the Secretary of State for Health (see page
92). But Commissions frequently fail to effect changes; indeed they
are often allegedly set up to stall action or allay discontents. Meanwhile like most Royal Commission Reports, it provides a fund of
useful, interesting and readable information.

Controls and complaints

The NHS is held in high public esteem, e.g. a Gallup survey in July
1988 revealed that 84 per cent of people are satisfied with the NHS.
However, it is not free from criticism.

One of the general criticisms of the NHS is that it is not sufficiently
subject to democratic control; that while the administration and
medical professions are well represented, the patient (and taxpayer)
is not. The Royal Commission dismissed the idea of **elected** health

authorities (as in New Zealand) because it feared the loss of the present mixture of professionals and lay members; it also feared the intrusion of party politics and envisaged very low voting figures.

Community Health Councils are a useful, if limited, device for giving voice to the consumer. One of their problems, however, is finding out what the consumers want to say with this voice. Another problem is deciding their role. Do they criticise the management over poor services, or do they side with management in the demand for more NHS resources? To what extent also should they involve themselves in long-term planning matters, such as allocation of resources, as opposed to matters of detail, such as a pram shed at a clinic, design of hospital lockers, etc. Some are still uncertain about their powers, e.g. the right to visit schools to inspect toilet facilities. One useful change has been to allow the Community Health Council to attend and speak (but not vote) at District Health Authority meetings.

The Davies Committee report (1973) on Hospital Complaints recommended a code of principles for recording and investigating complaints of patients in hospitals. It suggested (i) patients should be automatically informed of their right to complain; (ii) there should be a definite procedure (to include lay members) for investigating a complaint; (iii) regular analyses of health complaints by Health Authorities. This was partly implemented in 1976 when a code was introduced. Then, in 1981, a 'second opinion' procedure was devised whereby two independent consultants can be called in to investigate hospital complaints.

The Health Advisory Service (formerly the Hospital Advisory Service) began in 1969, to consider the problems of long-stay psychiatric and mentally subnormal hospitals, following a number of scandals (e.g. Ely, 1969). It visits institutions and (perhaps in conjunction with the Social Services Inspectorate) community homes, etc. It may offer advice and produces reports and recommendations; the latter may be followed up by a further visit. It is difficult to judge its success, but it does provide something of a safeguard for a very vulnerable sector within the health services. Its work is complemented by Mental Health Review Tribunals and by the newly-formed, 90-member **Mental Health Commission** (see page 164).

The Health Service Commissioner In addition to consumer safeguards provided by the CHCs, the *National Health Service Act, 1973*, also created the Health Service Commissioner. His function is to investigate complaints from members of the public who consider they have suffered injustice and hardship as a result of (a) failure by a Health Authority to provide a service it should provide; (b) failure in the service provided; (c) maladministration which adversely affects action taken by a health authority.

Members of the public can complain directly to the Health Service Commissioner, though normally only after it has been brought to the attention of the responsible Health Authority and it has been given an opportunity to respond. However, there are certain circumstances in which he cannot investigate a complaint. He **cannot** investigate a complaint if it (i) is made after 12 months following the incident complained of; (ii) can be dealt with through the courts or a tribunal; (iii) relates to purely **clinical** matters; (iv) relates to services provided by family practitioners (who have a separate complaints machinery in the FPC); (v) involves staffing matters (pay, promotion, etc.); (vi) involves a commercial transaction; (vii) comes from a public body (local authority, board, etc.).

Each year the Commissioner receives about 700 complaints, but rejects 80 per cent of them because they are outside his jurisdiction (the Royal Commission recommended that he be allowed to investigate cases involving clinical matters). Of those he investigated in 1987–88 he found 60 per cent were justified in whole or in part. Complaints concerned delay or failure to treat; ill-treatment; inadequate or insensitive communication; mishandling or poor recording of patients' monies. Subsequent remedies included apologies, change of procedures or occasionally financial compensation.

Professional bodies

By definition, professional people are concerned about the standards of practice in their own field. Consequently, in the medical field we find some surveillance and control exercised by:

(a)   The **General Medical Council**, established in 1858, is a registering body for all registered medical practitioners. Registration with the GMC carries with it certain privileges for the registered practitioner, and constitutes a guarantee of competence in medicine. The training for the medical profession occupies six to seven years in a medical school and hospital. On successful completion the trainee can become fully registered. After registration the medical practitioner may engage in general practice in the NHS. The GMC is also the **disciplinary body** for the medical profession and those found guilty of offences against the discipline code i.e. of 'serious professional misconduct' (such as gross negligence, sexual advances to patients or non-fulfilment of contractual duties) may be struck off the register. However, a report in 1988 shows that very few cases get beyond the preliminary proceedings. In 1987 of 1,019 complaints received by the GMC, only 52 went through (and 11 doctors were admonished, 11 suspended and 7 struck off).

(b) The **British Medical Association** was established in 1832 and is a voluntary organisation which acts as the doctors' trade union, making representations on pay and conditions of service affecting doctors. Thus, in respect of those doctors employed within the NHS the representations would be made first to the system of councils established on Whitley Council lines, and finally to the Secretary of State in the event of disagreement. Apart from these 'trade union' functions the BMA is also concerned with the standards of medical practice and the furtherance of medical progress. To this end, it organises numerous conferences, exhibitions and study groups, and it publishes a variety of journals of which the best known is the *British Medical Journal*.

Know your rights: practical points

The following is a summary of the rights which you may pursue.

Introductory

All patients have the right to expect **reasonable standards** of care and skilled medical practice from doctors, dentists, nurses and other professional people within the health service. Reasonable care and skill is based on the sort of treatment that the **average**, not ideal, doctor would give.

There is no right to demand a particular form of treatment. Patients must give their consent for any treatment or operation. Operations without consent would be legally defined as assault. Normally patients are requested to sign a consent form. Patients who are mentally unfit cannot give legal consent and these constitute an exception.

Let us suppose you have suffered from a lack of care or skill by a professional person – to take a simple case, the nurse has tied the tag on a wrong thumb so that the healthy thumb, not the diseased thumb, is amputated. Mistakes do occur in all human organisations. You may sue the person or persons responsible, and, if that person is employed directly by the hospital, you may also sue the particular Health Authority.

Proving negligence is sometimes difficult (though not in the above illustration which speaks for itself) for the reason that you will need to call members of the same profession as witnesses to testify in court as to their colleague's lack of skill. There is the problem of the heavy protection provided by medical defence unions; and there is the problem of professional solidarity, the heavy protection provided by medical defence unions and the problem of distinguishing *negligence* from *professional misjudgement*. But it can be done. All persons, including the most highly skilled surgeons and consultants, are subject to the Rule of Law. The function of the court is to get at the truth and administer justice. Damages may then be awarded to you for the loss of the thumb, or limb, or loss of life. A deceased person may sue through his personal representatives. These issues may be settled out of court.

Complaints about your family doctor, dentist, optician or chemist. The complaint should be sent (within eight weeks of the incident) to the local Family Practitioners' Committee (see page 92) or Health Board (Scotland). Libraries and Post Offices have the addresses. In response you may be offered an *informal* procedure, where a lay member of the FPC will make inquiries on your behalf and give advice. If this is not appropriate or sufficient, the *formal* procedure takes place whereby the Service Committee of the FPC will investigate and perhaps hold a hearing, before it makes a decision.

Complaints about hospital treatment. For example, a patient is left alone for a very long period, particularly when the patient is frightened and nervous; has no food; or receives rough handling by a nurse or doctor. These do not usually give rise to a cause of action at law. Write to the General Manager of the District Health Authority. The address can be obtained from local libraries. Usually a letter addressed 'c/o the Hospital concerned' will reach the official who must take action. Send a copy of your letter to the local Community Health Council, whose function is to represent 'consumer' interests. CHCs cannot investigate complaints, but they make sure they are dealt with fairly.

Complaints to the Health Service Commissioner. If you have made your complaint but have got no satisfaction the next step to consider is to write to the Health Service Commissioner, Church House, Great Smith Street, London SW1 (see page 432). (First appointed 1973.)

How to complain. Here are some tips: 1　Type your letter, and always keep a **carbon copy** or **photocopy**. 2　Be clear and concise in what you allege, and be **accurate** about times, dates and places. 3　If you have the names and addresses of witnesses record them and keep them safely for future reference. 4　If you consider you have a **legal claim** for damages go to the Citizen's Advice Bureau or a solicitor and take advantage of free or assisted legal aid and advice if you have modest means (see page 445). 5　Formal letters: use recorded delivery or registered post. Keep the counterfoil as proof of posting. 6　Make sure your complaint is **reasonable**, and not trivial.

7 Finally, you may write to the Patients' Association, 335 Gray's Inn Road, London WC1. This body, which is independent, will give you more details of what your rights are and how to make your complaint effective. Alternatively you may contact an organisation called Action for the Victims of Medical Accidents, 135 Stockwell Road, London SW9. (See also *Patients' Rights* National Consumer Council, 1982.)

There is, however, a growing dilemma here. As more patients go to law over alleged medical negligence (and increasingly win very substantial payments) so have the premiums of medical defence insurance societies been raised (from £25 to over £1,000), with a consequential tendency for medical practitioners to reduce their willingness to provide high-risk services (e.g. anaesthetics or surgery). In 1989 there were proposals to give Crown immunity to hospital doctors (i.e. the NHS would pay out claims for damages).

NHS reform plans 1989

In a White Paper *Working for Patients* (February 1989) the Government outlined its proposals for reforming the NHS. It seeks to raise medical services 'to the level of the best' by eliminating the wide variations which exist between parts of the NHS, such as the different waiting times for the same operations, GP referral rates and prescribing habits, and costs of hospital treatment (which can vary by up to 50 per cent). This is to be achieved by giving health authorities and hospitals more control over their own affairs (and even allowing some hospitals, from 1991, to become self-governing i.e. opting out like schools, see page 254). All hospitals will be able to offer services to different health authorities and the private sector and thus generate additional funds. It also aims to make it easier for patients to change GPs and the latter will be encouraged to provide better services, with some doctors being allocated their own NHS budget with which they can 'buy' services direct from hospitals. The various health authorities are to be slimmed down (by removing local councillor representatives) and their expenditures are to be scrutinised by the Audit Commission to secure value for money. Overall, the declared aim is to secure efficiency, better standards and more patient choice by the creation of an 'internal market'.

The proposals have been heavily criticised (by the medical profession and others) on the grounds that: they will create fragmented and variable standards and a two-tier system may emerge; that while some hospitals will thrive and expand, this will be at the expense of others; the consumer voice is weakened with the removal of elected local councillors from the health authorities; doctors will become obsessed with financial management rather than treatment; there is no provision for more preventive medicine; and overall, some see the reform as heralding the destruction of the NHS.

Questions

1 Explain the constitution and functions of (a) Community Health Councils, (b) Family Practitioner Committees and (c) the Health Service Commissioner.
2 What are the arguments for and against insurance schemes for private medical or surgical treatment?
3 Explain the reasons for the reorganisation of the NHS in 1974.
4 What are the functions and powers of the British Medical Association and the General Medical Council?
5 What is the present law on legalised abortion?
6 Describe the services offered by (a) health centres and (b) family planning clinics.
7 Describe the function of the Health Advisory Service.

5
The aged

The care and welfare of the old or elderly in years gone by were matters outside the scope of Government. The old were the responsibility of their children or relatives, good neighbours or the Church. Many people died young so that the problem of care and welfare simply did not arise. For those who did survive the prospect of advanced years was generally grim. The simple fact was that if you did not or could not work there was a risk of starvation which in turn caused ill health and sometimes death.

Towards the latter part of the nineteenth century public attention was drawn in the Press and in Parliament to the needs of the elderly, and a demand was made that something be done about it. There were the Poor Law institutions (see page 5) in which the old could be kept. There were almshouses and old folks' homes provided by the Church, by the Merchant Guilds of London or by private benefactors. Altogether the aged poor were a neglected group of people who depended largely for survival on the charity of richer groups who were concerned about the plight of their fellow human beings and on the care given by children or relatives.

The first general financial provision for the elderly on a national basis was the *Old Age Pensions Act, 1908*, which introduced pensions (at 25 pence per week) for those over 70 years of age whose income did not exceed £25 a year. Though small in amount, it may have helped to keep some of the elderly away from the ministrations of the Poor Law. It was taken further in the *Widows, Orphans and Old Age Contributory Pensions Act, 1925*, which was financed by National Insurance contributions rather than from general taxation.

But generally, apart from the residential institutions of the Poor Law and these pension arrangements, provision for the elderly was little developed by the State before 1939. Reliance was placed essentially on family, neighbours and voluntary organisations.

Numbers

The improvements in sanitation, diet, medical care and new medical treatments have all combined to lengthen life. Thus today the average man lives to 71 and women to 77, in 1911, it was 49 and 52 respectively. Consequently we have proportionately more older folk in Britain today. The same tendency is seen in other advanced countries (in contrast to Africa, South American and Asia where the population is predominantly young).

Greater life expectancy, which has occurred mainly through a fall in infant mortality, raises considerable problems. The average cost of health and welfare services for an old person is about eight times that of a person of working age; and about one third of all State social policy expenditure is attributable to the elderly (compared with 3 per cent for the under 5s). How much of the country's wealth *should* be devoted to the elderly compared to, say the handicapped or children? All are deserving cases. Such difficult choices have to be resolved by the Government and MPs.

Ageing occurs over a period of years, and parts of the body age at different rates. Thus to name a particular age or year for the definition of 'old age' is bound to be arbitrary and often misleading (all averages are). In this chapter the elderly are defined as those aged 65 and over (though at age 60 women qualify for retirement pension, compared to 65 for men).

In the last 20 years, the population over 65 has increased by a third. In 1980, there was in Britain a record high figure of 8.7 million people aged 65 and over, equal to 1 in 7 (or 15 per cent) of the population. There were 5.25 million women and 3.4 million men. This compares with the 1901 figure of 1.8 million (or 4.7 per cent of the then population). Within the present figures nearly 3.7 million (1 in 15) are aged over 75, and contain twice as many women as men. And the Queen has to send nine times as many telegrams to centenarians as she did when she ascended to the throne (from 200 to 1,700 p.a.). The number of old people will not increase much by the year 2001, but those over 75 will increase by about 20 per cent – see Table 3 (where 'elderly' includes women over 60). It is in the years 2001–2031 that a sharp increase in the elderly is expected such that in 2025, as a percentage of the working population, the elderly (men of 65+ and women of 60+) will form 38.5 per cent compared to 30 per cent today, as indicated in Table 3.

The majority of the elderly live healthy and active lives. But they differ widely in needs, lifestyles and expectations. It is often forgotten that they have emotional and human needs like younger people in society. It behoves us all to understand the process of ageing and its problems, and to treat the older generation with consideration.

Table 3 Elderly population in UK (in thousands) actual (or estimated)

	1911	1971	1986	(1991)	(2001)
Men aged 65 and over	965	2,804	3,428	3,581	3,576
Men aged 75 and over	249	828	1,227	1,335	1,461
Men aged 85 and over	28	124	166	222	294
Women aged 60 and over	1,914	6,211	6,853	6,805	6,701
Women aged 65 and over	1,282	4,502	5,255	5,307	5,270
Women aged 75 and over	374	1,765	2,451	2,588	2,706
Women aged 85 and over	50	349	543	636	773
Total men 65+/women 60+	2.9m.	9.0m.	10.3m.	10.4m.	10.3m.
Elderly as a percentage of total population	6.8	16.6	18.0	18.2	17.3
Elderly as a percentage of working-age population	11.0	27.9	29.0	29.9	29.9

Source: *Annual Abstract of Statistics 1988* (HMSO) and *Social Trends 1988* (HMSO)

A significant proportion of the elderly (between 15 and 50 per cent according to definition) have some chronic illness or disability, e.g. heart disease, hypertension, bronchitis. There are over 8 million visits a year to doctors for arthritis and rheumatism. About 1 in 7 of those over 75 have some degree of mental disorder. About 1 million of the elderly (including those in hospitals and homes) are severely or appreciably disabled, i.e. they are handicapped; about a quarter of these live alone.

In recent years retired people are tending to move to holiday resort towns to spend their retirement. The consequence of this is that some 20 to 50 per cent of the total populations of such towns as Bexhill, Worthing, Hastings, Seaton, Eastbourne and Grange-over-Sands is made up of elderly residents. On the other hand, in the New Towns recently settled with people of working age and their families, the proportion of the elderly may be 5 per cent or less. There is, therefore, no even spread of the elderly over the country as a whole. And there is the growing problem of adequate provision of medical services in those areas where there are heavy concentrations of elderly (such as those named above).

Health

The *National Health Service Act, 1946*, and the corresponding Act of 1947 applicable to Scotland provided for a comprehensive system of almost entirely free medical treatment and health services.

Recent developments in medical organisation (see Chapter 4) and practice show a more positive approach to the health care for the elderly. The modern practice seeks to anticipate and check the drift into inactivity and invalidity, to deal with specific ailments in the elderly and to promote a return to active life. Where that is impossible the duty imposed on the medical services is to try to 'alleviate the irremediable' and to try to improve the patient's condition as much as possible.

The primary health care team. This includes the **general medical practioner**, (or GP), the health visitor and the home nurse. The GP may prescribe treatment, medicines and appliances, as he considers necessary. Prescribed medicines are free to those of pensionable age or with chronic illness requiring medication over a long period. Elderly patients are encouraged to visit the doctor in his surgery if they can. If they cannot because they are immobile the doctor will visit them in their homes. The elderly account for 20 per cent of GP consultations (about two thirds take place at the patient's home for those over 75). The general practitioner receives a higher capitation fee for patients aged 65 and over. But the elderly increasingly face the problem of access due to the concentration of GP surgeries in health centres and the recent closures of local pharmacies.

Health visitors spend about 15 per cent of their time with the elderly, treating about 600,000 old persons a year. They endeavour to promote health, prevent and detect disease and conditions that cause handicaps. They also teach the elderly how to look after themselves, by giving personal advice on nutrition, how to keep warm and by distributing pamphlets.

Home nurses spend an increasing amount of time (currently about 50 per cent) in the care of the elderly who may need skilled attention in their homes or elsewhere. They saw 1.6 million cases in 1986 (England). They work under the general direction of the general practitioner and visit patients to give the nursing attention required, changing surgical dressings or bathing. In addition, home nurses may arrange for the provision of commodes, bed-rests and disposable bedding supplies – all of which are provided free.

The teamwork of the above three agencies enhances the effectiveness of the services since effort is coordinated, information and records can be pooled and regular discussion between members ensures that the best treatment is available to the patient.

Spectacles. Most elderly people need spectacles. Sight testing and general ophthalmic services are carried out by (a) ophthalmic medical practitioners, (b) ophthalmic opticians (both groups can test eyesight, prescribe and supply glasses); and dispensing opticians who supply glasses to prescription. All the above services are available under state schemes (and are free to low income groups).

Hearing aids. For those aged persons who are hard of hearing, hearing aids are available free under the NHS. The first approach is to a GP who may refer the patient to a suitable hospital where he is seen by a consultant.

Dental treatment. Again this form of treatment is available under the state scheme. If the patient is poor he may receive dental treatment free, under arrangements with the local office of the DSS. Otherwise charges are made to each patient (see page 103).

Chiropody. Many old people suffer from painful or deformed feet. Chiropody services at home or at clinics are increasing (and now cover about one million people) thus contributing much to the comfort and mobility of the elderly. About 1.2 million were treated in 1986 (England) – 20 per cent at home.

Hospital services. Older people may receive the same care and treatment at hospitals as others. If it is an emergency they may go straight to the casualty department in the same way as other younger people.

Age, it is said, does not come alone, and some older folk have multiple medical (and social) problems. Thus, on average, the cost of an elderly person to the NHS is eight times that of a person of working age. Such persons are best catered for in units specially staffed and equipped to deal with clinical, preventive, remedial and social aspects of health in the elderly. These are called **geriatric units**. The object is to make them part of all district hospitals so that the elderly may have ready access to a range of diagnostic and treatment facilities. People with physical and mental disorders may thus be treated in the unit. The aim is to try to rehabilitate the patient if this is at all possible, so that he or she may return home.

The provision of geriatric units is one of special priority under current hospital plans mainly because of the large numbers of elderly people in the UK. This treatment and impetus to get the patient out again and discharged from the hospital or unit represents a new approach. While the average person goes to hospital once every 10 years, those over 75 go twice as frequently. And while only 2.0 per cent of the elderly are in hospital, they occupy nearly half of the beds (the over-75s take one-third of the beds).

Day hospitals (including mobile ones) are also coming into being. Patients, including some hospital in-patients nearing discharge, attend the day hospital for the whole day for physiotherapy and occupational therapy as well as medical treatment, and for instruction in using aids for the handicapped. Some day hospitals give instruction in cooking simple and nourishing dishes. By this means elderly people are helped to continue to live at home and to enjoy active lives in spite of their disabilities.

Outpatient clinics are available at most hospitals for diagnosis or for treatment. Patients can use the facilities in such clinics and so ensure a minimum interference with ordinary life.

Mentally ill and infirm. Advancing years are often accompanied by mental deterioration, which can present serious problems. Affected persons fall into three main groups: 1. Patients who entered hospital for the mentally ill before modern methods of treatment were available and have grown old there. 2. Elderly patients with functional mental illness, i.e. the sort of mental disturbances from which people of any age may suffer. 3. Elderly patients with dementia (feebleness of mind – which currently affects 3 per cent of 65–74 age group, 13 per cent of 75+ and 22 per cent of those 80+).

Overall, the elderly occupy about half of the psychiatric beds (and a quarter are occupied by the over-75s). Much depends on the degree of disability. Wherever possible the illness (mental or physical) is treated and the patient is returned home or arrangements may be made for him or her to be admitted to geriatric hospitals as long-stay patients or in residential homes where they may be under medical supervision. Some who are allowed to go home are encouraged to attend hospital as out-patients or day patients e.g. those suffering depression but who can live normal lives at home while taking appropriate medication. There are plans to develop nursing-home type provision within the NHS to provide for the more dependent elderly who do not really require hospital care.

Personal social services

Statutory provision of personal social services for the elderly is made under the *National Assistance Act, 1948*, the *Health Services and Public Health Act, 1968*, and the *Chronically Sick and Disabled Persons Act, 1970*. Services which local authorities are required or empowered to provide, either directly or through the agency of voluntary bodies include:

Domestic help	Meals services	Visiting
Laundry service	Sitters-in	Holidays
Centres and clubs	Incontinence supplies	Transport
Recreation workshops		

Home helps (or home carers) of which there are 130,000 are particularly valuable to the older and less able elderly. They can help with house-cleaning, shopping, cooking, etc. There may be a charge for the service (it varies among local authorities). While there are about a million calls a year, the expanded service (50 per cent up on 1970) has barely kept up with the growth in the elderly and is thinly spread, covering under 10 per cent of the over-65s, and thus leaving many needs unmet. Some councils give priority to this home care service in order to maintain as many people as possible in their own home. (There is also a large private market in domiciliary care.)

Meals ('on wheels') are provided by local authorities either direct (50 per cent) or via voluntary bodies such as WRVS or Red Cross. About 20 million a year are provided at day centres and clubs for the elderly, and some 30 million are delivered to the homes of those elderly who are housebound or do not attend clubs. The figures sound impressive, but only 3 per cent of the elderly receive meals, many only once or twice a week.

Social workers and social work assistants are spending a greater proportion of their time in helping old people and their families with their problems, including the problem of terminal illness. In this respect the voluntary 'hospice' movement is an important development (see page 116). (The question of euthanasia has also been made prominent in recent years by the movement 'Exit'.)

Home adaptations and aids for the elderly to help them to maintain their independence may be provided by local authorities. Adaptations include heat insulation, provision of handrails on stairs or grips near the bath and lavatory, ramps on steps, alterations to kitchens, widening of doorways for a wheelchair, or adding downstairs showers or lavatory.

Day centres and clubs. These may be run by local authorities to prevent loneliness and to relieve relatives who may themselves be under stress from the care of the elderly. They also provide a focus for various services, e.g. chiropody, laundry facilities and the provision of meals. There are some 500–600 such centres in existence, providing over 30,000 places (for 4 per cent of those 65+), many of them organised by voluntary groups. They are an important means of combatting isolation as 30 per cent live alone.

Alternatively, 'good neighbour' and 'adopt a granny' schemes exist in some areas to provide voluntary help by **visiting** and finding out whether the elderly person wants some service, e.g. books, shopping, collecting pensions, writing letters or even a meal. This is an important service since 34 per cent of the elderly live alone (compared to 52 per cent who live with their spouse); for the over-75s, the figure is nearly 50 per cent. Overall, 20 per cent receive a weekly visit from a statutory or voluntary social worker. Local authorities also provide some 36,000 of the elderly with **holidays**.

Transport is another means of preventing isolation in the elderly. With increasing costs and diminishing public services (especially in rural areas) the Government is encouraging concessionary fares both locally and nationally (e.g. British Rail) and novel forms of community transport (such as post-buses, community buses, social car services and car-sharing).

Powers to move elderly persons. Occasions arise where a person suffers from grave chronic disease or, being aged, infirm or physically incapacitated, is living in insanitary conditions and is unable to devote to himself, or is not receiving from other people, due care and attention. Under the *National Assistance Act, 1948*, power is vested in an approved medical practitioner, specially appointed by each local authority, to certify in writing that in the interests of the person concerned, or in order to prevent injury to the health of, or serious nuisance to, other persons, it is necessary to remove such a person from her or his present accommodation. The local authority may then apply to a magistrates' court (sheriff's court in Scotland) for an order for the removal of the person to a suitable hospital or other place and to be detained there.

Housing

Over a quarter of elderly households lack at least one basic amenity, i.e. a bath, hot water or inside lavatory. Many of their dwellings are also too large and in poor condition. Attempts to meet the special housing needs of the elderly are made by local authorities and voluntary housing associations. Government grants encourage them to provide:

1 Small bungalows or flats for those able to look after themselves.
2 Grouped flatlet schemes where the elderly retain independence while having support from a resident warden, called 'sheltered' dwellings.
3 Old people's homes for those whose infirmity prevents them continuing to live independently.

Over half of the houses now being built by local authorities are small and convenient for the elderly and handicapped. Sometimes two-storey blocks of flats have proved to be convenient and to use less land; and in some cases flats for the elderly are provided in multi-storey blocks.

Interior design and fitments. Research has been carried out to ensure that accommodation is suitable e.g. room temperature is important, and windows, stairs, baths, lavatories, cookers and shelves need to be specially designed for the elderly. Bathrooms are a particular source of danger. Cookers should be fitted with safety devices, and so on.

Sheltered housing. This is groups of flats with a warden in charge. Usually each flat has an emergency call system so that the warden can be called in case of accident or other need. The presence of a warden on the site provides some reassurance to the group of folk for whom the warden is responsible. It has been described as 'independence with a safety net'. Some councils provide 'specialised' sheltered housing with communal facilities and care assistants.

Housing associations. These associations exist independently of the State or local authorities. They are *voluntary bodies* which are financed chiefly by loans from local authorities and the Housing Corporation (a national State corporation) and by donations and grants from charitable organisations. There are now about 2,250 housing associations affiliated to the National Federation of Housing Societies. The object of housing associations is to provide, *inter alia*, rented accommodation. Most housing associations provide some housing specifically for the elderly and about 670 of the 2,250 associations are predominantly concerned with housing for this class of person. Some housing associations operate nationally (e.g. Abbeyfield) and some provide accommodation locally. Some provide accommodation for the retired members of a particular trade, e.g. the Linen and Woollen Drapers' Cottage Homes and the Licensed Victuallers' National Homes for retired publicans.

Almshouses. These are charity houses, some of which have existed since the sixteenth century. They were built and endowed for the elderly who live in them free or for a nominal sum. There are some 26,250 separate almshouse dwellings in Britain administered by about 1,950 almshouse trusts which provide independent accommodation for single elderly people and for couples. Local authorities make grants for improvement of these dwellings, as do also charities and private benefactors. Generally a qualification such as residence, membership of a trade, profession or religious group is required for admission to an almshouse.

Old people's homes. This name is given to those residential institutions which may be owned and run by local authorities, by voluntary organisations or by private persons (the *Registered Homes Act, 1984* regulates the latter – see below). The primary aim of the old people's home is to create an atmosphere in which residents can live as normally as possible and in which their individuality, independence and personal dignity are respected. The function is to provide considerate and skilful care in comfortable surroundings for elderly people, who, even with help, are unable to live independently at home but are not in need of continuous nursing care. Only 2.5 per cent (200,000) actually live in such homes, about half in local authority homes and half in voluntary and private homes.

Local authorities have a duty, under Part III of the *National Assistance Act, 1948*, to provide accommodation for all who need care and attention, regardless of financial circumstances: hence it is known as 'Part Three accommodation'. Since the 1950s, the size of these homes has been diminished and it is usual for new ones to hold about 40 residents.

Most residents now enter homes at an advanced and more dependent age (average 82) in expectation of living there for the rest of their lives. Sometimes, the homes may be used to give respite or temporary relief to families to may need rest and recuperation from the work entailed in looking after a demanding elderly relative. It is argued also that too often homes are seen as a permanent 'last refuge' whereas they should be more versatile, e.g. be open for local day-care facilities, and used for the rehabilitation of the elderly with a view to their returning to a more independent life back in the community.

Old people's homes usually have a staff of a matron, who may be a qualified nurse, and/or a warden superintendent, with deputies, attendants and domestic staff. A standard charge is made to cover costs of running the local authorities' homes, and where the elderly person cannot afford the charge discounts are available so that the resident is left with a weekly pocket money amounting to not less than one fifth of the basic state pension (thus equal to £9.55 in 1989). The fees and charges in private homes vary.

Private old people's homes must be registered with the local authority, and are inspected periodically to ensure satisfactory standards are maintained and that the elderly are not maltreated. However, private homes have increased by over 100 per cent since 1979 (having been much encouraged by the State Social Security board and lodging allowances, though this was restrained in 1985 owing to the cost). Consequently, not all councils manage the mandatory annual inspection, under the *Registered Homes Act, 1984* (partly because the fees charged by local authorities do not cover their monitoring costs).

Boarding-out schemes. A new scheme is being developed in some areas: that of boarding out elderly people in private households ('granny fostering'). Again local authorities may organise these, or they may be sponsored by hospitals or by a voluntary old people's welfare committee. Some schemes provide for people to stay permanently, others for short stay only.

Much care has to be used to ensure that the elderly person suits the host family, and vice versa, so that welfare and happiness of the parties are ensured as far as possible. Boarding-out schemes require a trained organiser who must work in collaboration with various services, including the DSS, the Hospital Service and voluntary organisations.

Employment

With unemployment in 1989 over 2 million the question of the employment of the elderly seems somewhat inapt. Any jobs available should go to those who are younger and who shoulder the responsibilities of family life. So runs the argument.

Some people welcome retirement and may seek early retirement (or job-release; see page 332) looking forward to spending time on hobbies, adopting new interests and pleasing themselves as to what to do or not to do. In fact early retirement has been increasing in recent years such that in the five years before the basic state retirement age, only 60 per cent of men and 50 per cent of women are working. However, others become anxious and may become ill physically or mentally following retirement: they may feel they are not wanted or that their work was everything to them and their sole interest. They may feel they are no longer important. People vary in their reactions to the same situation.

Some on reaching retirement age find alternative work themselves, through advertisement or by personal contacts. Others may seek the help of local State employment offices (Jobcentres) or the voluntary **employment bureaux** which have been set up in certain towns (e.g. Cambridge, Stoke, Luton, Brighton) to assist older folk to find employment. They keep records of employers willing to employ older workers, and the bureaux maintain contact with the local Jobcentres whose work they complement. An example is REACH (the Retired Executives Action Clearing House).

Continuing employment. About 7 per cent continue working beyond retirement age. Some industrial and commercial firms make special arrangements for employees who wish to continue working for the company after reaching retirement age. The continuance of work depends much on the policy of the individual firm. The older person may be given less exacting work, may be offered part-time work or work at peak periods, depending on requirements. Much depends on the economic factors facing the company, which may want to maintain full production with all the skilled and reliable workers of all ages. Many companies provide a variety of services for their retired staff – e.g. club and sporting facilities, parties and outings – and an increasing number of companies run special courses on preparing for retirement.

Workrooms. In certain parts of Britain workrooms may be set up to provide part-time work for the elderly. The work is usually light and provides a purposeful occupation for, say, two hours each day. The work helps to prevent loneliness and the feeling of not being wanted, as well as promoting mental and physical health. Local authorities under the *Health Services and Public Health Act, 1968*, are empowered to maintain workshops for the elderly either directly or through the agency of a voluntary body. The majority are in fact run by voluntary groups, who receive financial grants from local authorities or charitable trusts or local fund-raising committees. And indeed an alternative to gainful employment is **voluntary work** itself. At present only about 20 per cent of the elderly belong to a voluntary organisation.

Pre-retirement courses. Like most things, the secret of successful retirement is adequate preparation. Hence the need for these courses which are run by further education colleges, the WEA and private firms. They usually include information on pensions, other income and savings; leisure and employment; exercise, health and social services, and voluntary work. However, only about 6 per cent of the ½ million who retire each year receive any formal preparation.

Some key features of the elderly (mainly 1986 figures)

---

30 per cent live alone
40 per cent of these are aged 75+
44 per cent of elderly women are not married
64 per cent of women over 75 are widows
38 per cent of over-75s (England 1977) have never had children or have outlived them
55 per cent of over-65s (England 1980) have long-term illness

Among households containing people over the age of 60:

68 per cent have no car
55 per cent have no central heating
34 per cent have no telephone
40 per cent have no washing machine

55,000 have to share a lavatory with another household
750,000 have to share a bath with another household
173,000 have no inside bath or lavatory
Nearly half of pensioner households depend on State pensions or benefits for at least 75 per cent of their income; 2.8 million pensioners live at, or below, Supplementary Benefit (IS) level

---

Problems, defects and criticisms

Concern has been expressed about the services for the elderly on the following grounds:

Numbers. We do not know the number of the old who could be helped, for no register is kept. So many of the elderly do not receive the services or benefits available to them. Referrals may be made to the social services department by a neighbour, by a GP or in emergencies by the police; but otherwise, help may be missed. The *Chronically Sick and Disabled Persons Act, 1970*, required local authorities to discover the number of those disabled in their communities, and this did include many of the elderly. The *Disabled Persons Act, 1986* gives them a right to claim services (see page 144). Should a permanent register be kept? It is important to realise that most people, old or young, resent intrusion into their private lives.

Variation in provision of services among the different localities is inevitable and justified where it matches differences in need (e.g. variations in the population age structures). But many such differentials in service standards are not related to need, but vary with resources, local tradition, local politics, differing priorities and the level of local voluntary support. Thus in 1982 old people in the North of England had a 50 per cent better chance of getting home help services than in Scotland or the South West; four times as many pensioners receive meals on wheels in Doncaster as in Sheffield or Croydon. Some areas have fewer than seven home helps per 1,000 over-75s. There can be a 100 per cent difference between local authorities in the number of places per 1,000 elderly in old people's homes. While some councils do little, others devote considerable resources to keeping the elderly warm in winter e.g. by providing thermometers to check room heat, draught proofing, insulation and moving beds and furniture into one well-heated room. (Yet Britain's death rate rises in winter – by some 40,000 – while in Canada and Scandinavia it remains constant.)

Coordination. There should be closer cooperation and coordination of services, in housing, health and social service care. Doctors regard their relationships and files as confidential and hence are reluctant to disclose details of patients. Community services are not always informed or alerted when patients are discharged from hospital though some local authorities provide 'family aides' to support and resettle people at home after hospital. This was recently reiterated in the Griffiths report *Community Care: Agenda for Action* (1988) (see page 416).

Medical knowledge. Geriatric medicine and psychiatry are not popular with doctors and consultants. There is a need in view of the increasing number of the old to make this branch of medicine more attractive.

Employment. There is no doubt that a lot of skill and knowledge is wasted when people have to retire. It can also be personally disheartening, tearing the meaning out of life of some. Should retirement be made more flexible? Or is employment opportunity really more important to the young? Perhaps with the severe decline in the numbers of school-leavers over the next 40 years – when 15–24 year-olds will decline by over 2 million – employment opportunities will increase for the elderly.

Incomes are a problem for many old people. They find their pension inadequate, and nearly 2 million have to claim Income Support. (It has been estimated that pensioners have lost around £10 p.w. because pensions, since 1980, are no longer linked to national average earnings.) Many still find difficulty paying for food and rent. Heating bills are a particular problem because elderly people are at home more. And many are disabled (with those over 70 constituting two-thirds of the severely disabled. An *Age Concern* survey drew attention to the link between low incomes and life span; see page 70).

Leisure. Sporting facilities for the young in schools must be provided (*Education Act, 1944*), but do local authorities bear in mind the needs of the elderly? Some do not give much thought to physical exercise and sport (e.g. golf) for those citizens in their areas. And many LEAs are raising charges or closing courses in Adult Education.

Institutional care. There are grave shortages of places in homes for the elderly (and long waiting lists) and many are forced to 'go private' or remain inappropriately in either hospital or at home (and at risk). The Government itself has said, 'During the last 25 years there has been a growing recognition that community care would be far better . . . than prolonged periods in hospital . . . Encouraging progress has been made [in the development of community services] but there is still a long way to go'. (*Heath Care and its Costs*, DHSS, 1983).

In 1985, the Audit Commission said that local authorities were wasting money and providing bad service by mismatching provision with those who needed residential or community care (*Managing Social Services for the Elderly More Effectively*). It also suggested that coordination could be improved both between local authorities and hospitals and between housing authorities (the *district* and borough councils who provide sheltered housing) and social services departments (over half of which are in *county* councils). Private homes are inadequately monitored and many cases of poor provision and perhaps harsh conditions, even violence, occur. This may be partly due to the low levels of trained staff. But in local authorities the level of training among residential staff is only 15 per cent (see Chapter 15). And it has been suggested, in the Wagner Report *Residential Care: A Positive Choice* (HMSO, 1988) that council homes should be subject to inspection too (in 1989 the Government agreed to this: see page 416). The Wagner Committee was reviewing provision homes (not just for the elderly) at the time of the scandal over great cruelty in a local authority home for the elderly (Nye Bevan Lodge in Southwark, London). Camden Borough had also been recently criticised for its low level provision. But cruelty does not have to be violent: many homes are accused of inducing passivity among their residents by undue sedation and doing too much for them, failing to stimulate or provide opportunities for self-determination. Some say the homes are too isolated from the local community and ought to open their doors more. Consequently both the Wagner and the Griffiths (1988) reports recommended paying special allowances so that people could choose (by 'buying' services, perhaps with the advice of a social worker who would help assess needs) whether to have residential or community care (see page 416).

Support for families and neighbours – the informal carers – is clearly inadequate. More needs to be done to help sustain them as there is a limit to what family and friends can given in terms of time, money and effort (e.g lifting and bathing). Cash benefits (attendance allowance, invalid care allowance, mobility allowances) and experimental paid 'good neighbour' schemes are helpful, but more needs to be done by way of respite breaks and help through care assistants help with bathing, lifting, laundry and social work guidance and reassurance: this is relatively cheap compared to institutional care, and yet many old people continue to come into care simply because their family can no longer cope. There are currently about 1½ million people caring for a dependent adult relative or friend in the community. Three-quarters of these carers are women. As the birth rate has fallen, so has the number of potential carers. Many of these are drawn into the labour market: over 50 per cent of married women now work compared to 30 per cent in 1951. And for the very old, even their offspring are old or pre-deceased. Carers cannot always be expected to cope. The responsibility is tiring and often stressful. Many carers feel overloaded and isolated. They may feel trapped or resentful, and may be driven through their stress to behaving violently towards or neglecting their elderly relative (a speaker at the British Geriatric Society conference in September 1988 suggested that as many as one elderly person in 20 may be subject to such abuse). Clearly more needs to be done to 'care for the carers' including practical help and relief care (such as that provided by local authorities) as well as advice and support (such as that provided by the King's Fund Informal Caring programme). And for the same reason, hospitals should avoid pushing patients out too soon if there are inadequate community support services (see pages 152 and 161).

Meeting the cost. The increased numbers of the elderly, the emergence of 4- or even 5-generation families and the possibility of a 'third age' with some 20 years of life in retirement is an achievement we should be proud of. But the elderly, like youngsters, are dependent and have to be provided for by the working generation(s). This should be done willingly: not only have our parents and older relatives made (and perhaps continue to make) their contribution to society, but the measure of a civilised society is the support it gives to its disabled, disadvantaged and elderly members. However, it is evident that while the numbers of the elderly will increase substantially by the year 2045 (thus increasing the demand for care), equally the relative size of the working population (the 'supply' side) is forecast to fall, so that whereas today there are 2.3 contributors per pensioner, there will only be 1.6 contributors or taxpayers for each pensioner by 2035. This situation will require policy decisions such as increased taxes, more private pensions, perhaps postponing the retirement age or equally controverial, reducing benefit levels or targeting (means-testing) them on those in greatest need. We have already seen some policy adjustments, as with the 'Fowler Reforms' (see page 54). Which policies lie ahead will depend on political party fortunes and pressure group influences. In recent years we have witnessed greater political activity and lobbying by groups of the elderly and retired ('grey power'). We can expect to see more such activity (e.g. as with the recent formation of the over 50s Association of Retired Persons), as numbers grow and the general standard of fitness of the over 65s improves, as they are increasingly drawn from less deprived backgrounds and childhoods.

Questions

1 Give an account of the services available for the elderly.
2 What problems does increased life expectancy create for Britain? What measures to solve the problems have been undertaken by recent governments?
3 Advise someone about to retire how best to cope with life after work.
4 'Women retire at 60, yet live to 80 plus, while men retire at 65 and live till 70. Therefore men must work harder than women and the rule should be: men retire at 60 and women at 65.' Discuss.
5 Find out what you can about the aims and methods of voluntary groups working for the elderly, such as Age Concern and Help the Aged.
6 What is meant by 'the mismatch between institutional and community care'?

6
The handicapped

In this chapter we are concerned with the problems of and the services provided for the **physically** and **mentally** disabled. Together the mentally and physically disabled currently constitute between three and six million, according to definition of the population. The mentally and physically handicapped groups are similar in so far as (a) their everyday functioning is impaired, and (b) the degree of incapacity can range from minor to very severe.

Consequently, many of the same services are provided for both groups. However, since many of the underlying and presenting problems, and the services provided for each group are often distinct and specific, it is wise to consider each of the groups – i.e. the physically and the mentally disabled – separately.

The physically handicapped and disabled

Definition

It has been said there are no such people as 'the handicapped' though there are handicapped individuals. The implication is that people cannot be grouped in this way, for each person has his or her own physical disability to meet, and each has his or her own psychological, physical or social problem to overcome if at all possible. Further, not everyone who is disabled is necessarily handicapped: much depends on the activities which are restricted as a consequence of the disability and to what extent he/she is unable to lead a full life, to work and play an active role in the family. The World Health Organisation gives the following definitions: '**Impairment:** a permanent or transitory psychological, physiological or anatomical loss or abnormality of structure or function. **Disability:** any restriction or prevention of the performance of an activity resulting from an impairment, in the manner or within the range considered normal for a human being. **Handicap:** a disability that constitutes a disadvantage for a given individual in that it limits or prevents the fulfilment of a role that is normal depending on age, sex, social and cultural factors, for the individual.' However, both generally and officially the terms 'disabled' and 'handicapped' are used interchangeably; and in this chapter we shall treat them as synonymous.

There are, of course, different types of disablement and handicap. The most notable are the blind, the deaf and the physically disabled by injury or disease. Among the more common diseases are diabetes, epilepsy, haemophilia, multiple sclerosis, Parkinson's disease, cerebral palsy and many other simpler diseases which are found the world over. Some disabilities may be caused by the use or misuse of drugs during pregnancy, e.g. Thalidomide, so that the disability is congenital; some disease may attack suddenly; and some may be of slow growth resulting in final and complete disability.

History

The general care of the disabled and handicapped fell on family and neighbours in the Middle Ages. The Church had always shown concern for the blind, the lame, the poor, the sick and the needy. The essential Christian message was one of compassion and Christian love and care. Its resources were poor but it started the hospitals, encouraged learning, the study of medicine and the care of the needy.

The first Act was the *Poor Law Act, 1601*, which imposed a duty on the local authorities to provide for the sick, the needy and the homeless with the means of subsistence.

The eighteenth and nineteenth centuries witnessed an advance in medical science (see page 79). The number of doctors increased and hospitals were built with private endowments. Free infirmaries were provided for the poor. These generally were grim forbidding institutions, some of which lasted until the twentieth century and have been converted and altered to suit modern requirements.

In 1893 local school boards (see page 218) were empowered to ensure that blind and deaf children received an elementary education. In 1914 the education authorities were obliged by law to provide special education for epileptic and mentally handicapped children.

The *Workmen's Compensation Act, 1897*, and the *National Insurance Act, 1911*, began to make material provision, i.e. pay and pensions, for the sick and people injured in industrial accidents. Disablement at the end of the nineteenth century was regarded as confined to the blind, the deaf and the crippled. Provisions by the Government and local authorities were quite inadequate and unevenly distributed. Doctors were primarily concerned with treating the particular disease, and voluntary workers, motivated by charity and compassion, operated in watertight compartments. Rehabilitation was not yet appreciated or attempted.

We must, therefore, look to the twentieth century for the improvements in rehabilitation we have today. The first step was taken by

Pendrill Varrier-Jones, who, in 1917, founded a village settlement in Bourne Colony, later transferred to Papworth, Cambridgeshire, which provided a special environment for tuberculosis patients who could work and live normally under medical supervision.

The First World War saw the introduction of massage and remedial exercises in the treatment of orthopaedic cases. Military hospitals for members of the Armed Forces disabled by war were organised under Robert Jones. These provided a rehabilitation regime, and included physiotherapy, hydrotherapy, remedial exercises and occupational therapy. The British Red Cross Society helped in this rehabilitation work. St Dunstan's Hospital for blinded soldiers and sailors showed how experts with a medical approach could train the disabled to acquire self-reliance and compensatory skills. Between the wars little was done except to introduce occupational therapy into mental hospitals.

Two official reports,* one by the BMA and one by the Government, emphasised the need for rehabilitation services in hospitals to aid functional recovery. These recommended centres to provide post-hospital reconditioning in certain cases. Employers were encouraged to employ disabled persons, and the Government set up Government Instructional Factories for ex-servicemen. In the seven years after the First World War some 100,000 were trained, most resuming employment in occupations for which they were trained.

The Second World War added impetus to the rehabilitation and treatment of the disabled. The *National Health Service Act, 1946*, provided free medical treatment. The *National Insurance Act, 1946*, made available weekly benefits, and the *National Insurance (Industrial Injuries) Act, 1946*, provided for benefits and pensions for those injured at work. The *Education Act, 1944*, made special provision for the education of handicapped children. The *Chronically Sick and Disabled Persons Act, 1970*, obliges local authorities to ascertain the number of disabled people living in their areas and to provide them with social services. The Act also concerned itself with ensuring that public premises were adapted so that the disabled could get in and out of the premises, e.g. in wheelchairs and the like. This was reinforced by the *Disabled Persons Act, 1981* (and by the *Local Government (Miscellaneous Provisions) Scotland Act, 1981*) which seeks to enhance access to public buildings and to better protect parking spaces designated for the disabled. The *Disabled Persons (Services, Consultation and Representation) Act, 1986* requires local authorities to inform the public of the services available and to involve representatives of disabled persons groups in their decision-making procedures.

*The Fracture Committee of the BMA (1935) and the Interdepartmental Committee of the Ministry of Health and Home Office on the Rehabilitation of Persons Injured by Accidents (1939).

The above measures in broad outline have done much to provide the legal framework within which the benefits and facilities are made available for the disabled within our communities. But law and regulation do not provide the personal care, sympathy and understanding to make life tolerable for those suffering disadvantages not known to the normal individual.

Numbers of disabled

For 1971 and 1981 the estimated numbers of disabled people over the age of 16 in private households are shown in Table 4. Of the 1.3 million handicapped, some two thirds were over 65 (one third over 75), and two-thirds were women. We should add to these survey figures an estimated 100,000 or more handicapped children and perhaps 200,000 handicapped in homes and hospitals, thus giving a total estimate for the handicapped in excess of 1½ million.

New figures were published in *The Prevalence of Disability in Adults* (OPCS, 1988). This gives a total figure (for adults) of 6.2 million (with about ½ million in communal establishments and the remainder in private households). The figure is larger because since 1971 (i) there are more elderly people (see Chapter 5), (ii) there are more disabled able to survive and (iii) the measure or definition of disability is more generous. As the Report says: 'Disability is a restriction or lack of ability to perform normal activities, which has resulted from the impairment of a structure or function of the body or

Table 4   Numbers of disabled in Britain over age 16

	1981	1971
Very severely handicapped needing special care	193,000	170,000
Severely handicapped needing considerable support	416,000	380,000
Appreciably handicapped needing some support	717,000	660,000
	1,326,000	1,210,000
Impaired but needing little or no support for normal living activities		1,942,000
		3,152,000

Source: J. Wilson, *How many disabled people are there?*, Disability Alliance, 1980. A. Harris, *Handicapped and Impaired in Great Britain*, OPCS, HMSO, 1971.

Table 5   Estimates of numbers of disabled adults in Great Britain (1988) by type of disability and age (thousands)

Type of disability	Total population			
	16–59	*60–74*	*75 and over*	*TOTAL*
Locomotion	1,009	1,565	1,758	4,332
Reaching and stretching	275	426	529	1,230
Dexterity	418	613	705	1,737
Seeing	293	445	930	1,668
Hearing	557	871	1,161	2,588
Personal care	593	781	1,109	2,483
Continence	293	330	521	1,142
Communication	376	332	494	1,202
Behaviour	650	311	385	1,347
Intellectual functioning	604	333	537	1,475
Consciousness	158	41	31	229
Eating, drinking, digesting	78	94	104	276
Disfigurement*	163	141	87	391

*Excluding those in establishments.
Note: There are no totals as many have multiple disabilities

mind . . . Disability is a continuum in terms of severity, from the very slight to the very severe.' The Report provides ten categories, from 1 (the lowest severity category e.g. deaf in one ear) containing a million people, to 10 (the highest e.g. stroke, cannot walk, cannot feed or self-care) containing 200,000 (half of whom are in communal establishments). An example of category 6 is someone with arthritis who cannot bend, cannot walk 200 yards without discomfort and has difficulty opening the lid of a jar.

About 70 per cent of the adult disabled are over 60. And 64 per cent of the severely disabled are over 75. Disabilities and their incidence are shown in Table 5.

Nature and causes of handicap

We do not know the numbers of *handicapped* in Britain; we have to rely upon estimates and local surveys. One guide is the **register** of disabled persons which local authorities are obliged to keep. Registration itself is voluntary and therefore the figures are always an underestimate. In 1984/6 in England and Wales there were:

registered blind or partially sighted   191,500
registered deaf or hard of hearing   97,500
registered with other handicaps   1,102,500

The latter include such conditions as arthritis, rheumatism, stroke, heart disease, spasticity, multiple sclerosis and paraplegia.

Some disabilities are inheritable (e.g. muscular dystrophy) and others may occur before birth (e.g. through drugs such as thalidomide or certain vaccines). Apart from these *congenital* factors, handicap may result from illness and disease, from accidents (e.g. car crashes) and injury at work or in war.

Services for the handicapped

Apart from the support given by the informal network of family, friends and neighbours, services are provided by a number of statutory (i.e. central and local government) and voluntary bodies. These fall into five main categories:

1   Income. In addition to any earnings or unearned income, State benefits may be payable for disability and industrial injury, and may include additionally attendance allowances and mobility allowances (see Chapter 3).

2   Education. Where possible, the disabled are placed in ordinary schools and educational settings. Where this is not possible or advisable, special schools (some residential) exist or special arrangements are made such as hospital teaching, home visiting teachers, supply of Braille or Moon books (see Chapter 10).

3   Medical treatment and rehabilitation is available under normal NHS provision, together with certain special services including rehabilitation. All new general hospitals now include rehabilitation departments, and in some of the older hospitals adaptations have been made to enable rehabilitation departments to be set up. Apart from these there are now special centres named Rehabilitation Demonstration Centres, where what can be done, new techniques and services and recent advances are shown. The work is carried out under the supervision of a medical consultant who supervises physiotherapists, remedial gymnasts, occupational therapists, together with social workers acting as a team.

Occupational therapy aims to stimulate interest, occupy time constructively and restore confidence. Some hospitals have rooms filled with domestic equipment, where disabled people, especially housewives, can be trained to overcome their disability and re-learn common domestic tasks. Many household appliances or 'aids' are adapted for the training needs of specific groups, such as the one-armed or the chair-bound.

Medical rehabilitation includes the provision, free of charge, of hearing aids, surgical supports, invalid wheelchairs, certain types of invalid vehicle and artificial eyes and limbs. The **Artificial Limb Service** was developed during the First World War for war pensioners. The service is now administered by the Department of Health and the Scottish and Welsh Offices through hospitals and local offices (or ALACs – Artificial Limb and Appliance Centres, now run by the Disablement Services Authority, since 1987). They currently provide some 20,000 legs and 2,000 arms. (There are about 63,000 amputees in Britain.)

On the question of **mobility** a full range of artificial limbs and appliances (including power-driven wheelchairs) is provided for patients who have undergone amputation or who suffer limb deformity. Wheelchairs from the Department of Health or Red Cross are on free loan, but some people prefer to purchase their own. In 1986, 463,000 wheelchairs were supplied (compared to 209,000 in 1976). A car or three-wheeled carriage may have been provided (up to 1976) for those with difficulty walking (in 1980 about 22,000 of these two vehicles were in use). The Government's mobility allowance (£23.00 per week, 1989) is replacing the supply of vehicles. 'Motability' (started in 1978) is a private scheme which helps disabled people to put their weekly allowance towards the leasing or hire purchase of a car – for which concessions are often available. 100,000 vehicles have been so acquired. (A useful publication for the disabled is *Door to Door*, published by the Department of Transport.) The Orange Badge Scheme (OBS) enables disabled drivers to find on-street parking easier. This now applies to 5 per cent of cars (and in 1987 there were 840,000 badges compared to 730,000 in 1986).

After a patient is released from medical care and rehabilitation the **social worker** assists in solving problems (of patient and his family) of making adjustment to the condition of handicap. A case conference (involving social worker, employment resettlement officer, medical and nursing staff, etc.) may consider the patient's employment potential.

4   Employment and training. Apart from ordinary employment in 'open employment', there are a number of special services to help resettle handicapped persons into suitable work. These are dealt with in more detail in Chapter 13, but it is appropriate to indicate its main features here.

The *Disabled Persons (Employment) Act, 1944*, requires (i) the Secretary of State to maintain a Disabled Persons Register, (ii) employers to engage a certain proportion of disabled employees, (iii) empowers the Secretary of State to reserve certain kinds for work for the disabled, (iv) authorises the provision of 'sheltered' employment for *severely* disabled people, (v) provides for courses of employment rehabilitation and vocational training to be given where needed.

To **register** with the local office (Jobcentre) of the Department of Employment an applicant must be disabled within the terms of the Act. 471,000 were so registered in 1980 though it is believed that many of those eligible fail to register. Following registration, it is the responsibility of the Disablement Resettlement Officers (DROs) in the Jobcentre to advise and if possible to place the handicapped person in employment. They may refer the client to a rehabilitation centre and may propose a course of special training. DROs work closely with social workers, members of the medical professions and perhaps local Careers Officers.

Most disabled people are able to hold their own in competition with able-bodied persons in **open employment** once they have been found suitable work (often through the DRO), though car-park attendance and lift attendance have been **designated** by the Minister as occupations reserved for the disabled. Elsewhere where an employer engages more than 20 workers he is required to employ a quota of registered disabled people. This **quota** is 3 per cent of total staff. Thus failure to employ is not in itself an offence, but an employer who is below the quota may not engage a non-registered worker without a permit from the Minister. However, 'The Times' (December 10, 1977) pointed put that, 'Only two of the 30 government departments met the quota . . . Only one of the 32 London boroughs was meeting the quota; only one of the 53 county councils; none of the nationalised industries . . . and none of the 14 regional health authorities. Two thirds of companies in the private sector also failed to meet the quota . . . The main criticism was that government, which was free with advice and directives, failed to act up to its own advice and legislation'.

Severely disabled people may need special **sheltered employment** conditions to work in, e.g., where they are unable to take the strain or keep up to the pace of ordinary employment. Under the 1944 Act the Minister has power to make provision for sheltered employment, e.g. by making grants to local authorities or voluntary undertakings. (In 1984 this amounted to some £60 million and provided jobs for about 14,750 disabled people.) Or by setting up non-profit-making public companies for this purpose, such as **Sheltered Industrial Groups** or **Remploy Ltd** (established 1945).

The **rehabilitation** of disabled people is the responsibility of the Department of Employment. Employment Rehabilitation Centres have been established in some 27 places (the first being in Egham, Surrey in 1943) for some 16,000 people. Recommendation is made by

DROs who consult with the medical authorities to assess whether a course is likely to render the disabled person fit for work.

Government sponsored **training** in Skillcentres is open to the disabled on the same basis as other workers. Training is free and maintenance allowances are paid to the trainees. About 80 per cent of the 4,000 disabled trainees train alongside the able-bodied.

5   Personal social services. These are the main focus of this chapter. They are mainly the responsibility of local government through their housing departments, their education departments (or LEAs) and particularly their Social Services or Social Work Departments (variously known as SSDs, SWDs, LASS or PSS). However, a host of *voluntary* agencies play an important part here: they complement the official provision and may on occasion be employed by local authorities as agents providing services to specific groups of handicapped people. Most of these voluntary bodies specialise in their concern for or care of groups of the handicapped, e.g. the Royal National Institute for the Blind (RNIB), the British Deaf Association, the British Epilepsy Association, the Multiple Sclerosis Society, the Spastics Society, etc. The Disability Alliance is concerned with the income resources of the disabled. Many such bodies are affiliated to RADAR, the Royal Association for Disability and Rehabilitation. There are also some 60 voluntary Disablement Information and Advice Centres.

The personal welfare services provided by local authorities and voluntary organisations for the physically disabled can be divided into (a) those which provide residential care, and (b) those which are designed to help the disabled to continue to live with some degree of independence in the community. Local authorities are required to keep a **register** (not to be confused with the Department of Employment's register, page 336 above) of the disabled, and this forms the basis for the provision of many of the services; but registration is voluntary and services are not confined to the registered disabled.

(a) **Residential services.** Under the *National Assistance Act, 1948*, local authorities have to provide suitable accommodation for all who through age, infirmity or for any other reason are in need of care and attention not otherwise available. Social services (PSS) departments may provide the accommodation or (apart from hospital) may supervise accommodation in voluntary or private (commercial) homes (which must be registered with PSS).

Local authorities must lay down charges for their homes, though these may be adjusted to the resident's means, and the DSS can help out in cases of hardship. Residential homes are being transformed from the big, old buildings to modern, small (20–40 beds) homes. Hostels may also be provided for young, single workers and the disabled undergoing training courses.

(b) **Community-based services.** Under the *Chronically Sick and Disabled Persons Act, 1970,* local authorities must find out the numbers of disabled in their areas and must publicise their services available to them. More specifically, where they are satisfied that they are needed by the disabled, local authorities *must* provide or make arrangements for the provision of the following: (a) practical assistance in the home; (b) provision of, or assistance in obtaining, radio, television, library or similar facilities; (c) provision of lectures, games, outings, or other recreational facilities outside the home, or assistance in taking advantage of educational facilities; (d) facilities for or assistance in travelling to participate in any services provided by the local authority, or similar services (e.g. sheltered employment); (e) assistance in arranging for the carrying out of any works of adaptation in the home or the provision of any additional facilities designed to secure greater safety, comfort or convenience; (f) facilities for taking holidays, whether at holiday homes or otherwise and whether provided under arrangements made by the authority or otherwise; (g) provision of meals at home or elsewhere; (h) provision of, or assistance in obtaining, a telephone and any special equipment necessary to enable use of the telephone.

There are variations in the amount of provision by local authorities according to their assessment of 'need' (among other things). There are also variations in their charges. Many of the services – whether residential (i.e. homes), community (i.e. day centres) or domiciliary (i.e. provided at home) – are the same as those provided for the elderly (see Chapter 5). Thus a regular contact, as well as material support, is provided by the midday **meals** on wheels service and by **home helps** (the latter dealing with 55,000 cases of handicapped people under 65 in 1980).

Social workers visit the handicapped to give advice and information about local services and to assess the need for a particular service. They may arrange for adaptations and aids in the house, for transport to day centres and clubs, for residential ('Part Three') accommodation, for training or occupational therapy, or for sheltered employment, etc. They also provide valuable guidance and reassurance to the handicapped person and his family, and increase links with the 'outside world' by helping to arrange for a telephone or appropriate equipment for isolated housebound people. (In England in 1986 some 542,000 aids were provided for disabled people, including 120,000 telephones, telephone equipment or rentals, and 22,000 televisions or licences.)

Occupational therapists (or 'rehabilitation advisers') visit the disabled (on the advice of social workers) to assess the need for **aids and adaptations** to the home, to make daily life easier for them; apart from walking frames, hoists, easy switches, water taps and kitchen gadgets, adaptations can include fixing rails, fitting ramps and widening doorways. There were 65,000 adaptations to property for the disabled in England in 1986.

Many PSS departments or voluntary organisations have **day centres** or social clubs where the disabled and housebound can meet socially, have a meal and perhaps make use of other facilities which may be provided, such as occupational therapy (or OT), physiotherapy, chiropody, hairdressing. Some centres are multi-purpose and combine to provide light employment as well as social and welfare facilities. Outings, holidays and sports days may also be provided – 100,000 disabled people enjoyed such holidays in 1986.

Social services departments usually provide transport to day centres and workshops for the less mobile disabled. For those who can travel independently there are usually fare concessions and the orange car badge system to ease problems of parking. **Access** to car parks and to public lavatories was made easier for the handicapped by the *Chronically Sick and Disabled Persons Act, 1970*. Community Service Volunteers arrange to live with or near individual severely disabled people living alone in order to sustain their living in the community.

Problems and criticisms

1   Numbers. As with the elderly, the number of handicapped is increasing as more people survive into old age and as modern medicine saves the lives of many more of the injured or congenitally deformed. This raises questions about the ethics or morality of more or less deliberately allowing badly handicapped babies to die (see the case of Dr Arthur in March, 1982).

2   Level of services. Growing numbers strain existing services. There are considerable variations in the level of local services for the handicapped (arising partly from differences in definition and registration). Recent years have witnessed the decline of some service provision, e.g. in 1976 holiday provision covered over 103,000 disabled people in England and Wales, while the figures for 1979 and 1980 were 94,400 and 87,200; similarly home adaptations in the United Kingdom fell from 83,900 to 65,700 between 1979 and 1980 (though both have increased since then). It has been suggested that the handicapped should be able to demand legal rights to services (though this might cause local authorities to readjust downwards their definition of handicap and to their fulfilling the statutory *minimum* of service rather than trying to meet properly assessed needs). All this is compounded by the fact that 75 per cent of the disabled rely on State benefits as their main source of income, and two-thirds of them are estimated to live on and around the poverty line (*The Financial Circumstances of Disabled Adults*, OPCS, 1988). And added to this is the problem of the confusion created by having so many different agencies involved in the provision of services for the disabled (see *Last on the List*, King's Fund, 1988)

3 Support for the carers. Apart from services for the handicapped in general there is criticism that those particular services which help sustain the informal carers – friends, neighbours and family, especially daughters – are lacking. These include such services as home helps, meals, visiting, sitters-in, day and/or night care attendant schemes, incontinence services, aids, help with lifting and bathing, day hospitals, day centres, and home nursing. Without an adequate supply of these, many family carers, especially women, undergo considerable physical and emotional strain as well as loss of income (employment, promotion and earning power*) and loss of social contacts and social life. This can create resentment and tensions which can lead to sullen resignation or to abuse and violence – and ultimately to a collapse of informal care. At such a point, the statutory services have to take over and assume the full caring and financial burden – see page 162.

As the Griffiths Report (see page 416) stated in 1988:

> The first task of the publicly provided services is to support and where possible strengthen these networks of carers. Public services can help by identifying such actual and potential carers, consulting them about their needs and those of the people they are caring for, and tailoring the provision of extra services accordingly.

4 Unemployment among the handicapped who are able and willing to work is higher than the average – about double. Handicapped workers are among the first to be made redundant, though the question of who should get priority in employment – young, old, able-bodied or handicapped is difficult to resolve when jobs are scarce. Less excusable are the low rates of pay given to the handicapped working in some industrial centres and sheltered workshops. The report on *The Financial Circumstances of Disabled Adults* (OPCS,

---

*It was estimated that it costs £3,000 p.a. to look after a disabled person at home and overall, the value of such 'free' informal care is £5–7 billion a year. Indeed if only 10 per cent of those living at home were transferred to residential care, it would cost an additional £1 billion p.a.

1988) showed that disabled adults are only half as likely to be working as able-bodied people, and those who do work usually earn less e.g. the average earnings for disabled men are 80 per cent of the national male wage.

5   NHS-PSS liaison. The administrative structure of the NHS is such that the boundaries of the District Health Authorities largely coincide (are co-terminous) with those of local authorities, and they have also (by law) established joint planning committees, joint Community Assessment and Treatment Teams and joint funding schemes (e.g. for after-care hostels). Joint funding amounted to £96 million in 1984 (c.f. £8 m. in 1976 when it began). But there is still evidence of insufficient liaison and cooperation arising from the two organisations' differing perspectives, priorities, income bases and both internal and external pressures e.g. in this field, local government serves two masters who may not have the same plans for local services – the DHSS may encourage spending while the Department of the Environment may penalise it through cuts in grant-aid. All this applies particularly to the services for the mentally disabled.

6   Independence. Paradoxically, some provision may be excessive, in that too much may be done for (or to) the disabled, such that it deepens their dependency and lowers their dignity and self-esteem (e.g. reading to visually-impaired people instead of providing sight-enhancing equipment so they can read themselves). A recent development here is the Independent Living Scheme (a CSV initiative) where volunteers live with, and help support, the severely handicapped in such a way that the users control their own lives more and the helpers work with the users as advocates in dealing with others.

The mentally disordered

The dividing line between health and sickness is blurred. No one is *completely* healthy: people are only more or less healthy. This is particularly true of the field of mental disorder, which often shows itself in odd, unusual or deviant behaviour. The term covers two broad categories: (a) **mental handicap** (or subnormality) which is the result of retarded development of mental powers. For those with such **learning disability** it can range from mild simple-mindedness to severe sub-normality and virtual helplessness. Whilst it cannot be cured, improvement is possible through care and training. It is usually measured in terms of intelligence – or IQ – with an IQ of under 50 representing 'severe' handicap and an IQ of 50–70 representing mild or 'moderate' handicap. However, it may be argued that a preferable definition or measure would take account of behavioural aspects and ability at *social functioning*. There are currently about 160,000 severely handicapped in Britain (of which 60,000 are children), plus perhaps three times that number who are less disabled and who can live quite independent lives without great dependence on special support services (detailed below). The 1988 OPCS report on disabled adults (see page 145) gives an overall estimate of 1½ million for those whose handicap is 'intellectual functioning'. (b) **mental illness** (or abnormality) is a condition which can affect ordinary people, i.e. whose intelligence has developed normally. It can range from mild depression or anxiety to violent psychopathy. It is largely curable or self-correcting. Over half a million people suffer from a diagnosed mental illness; 1 in 6 females and 1 in 9 males will experience some mental illness. Thus it could be any one of us, though society has created stereotypes and extreme images of the 'mad' and 'insane' which distorts the true picture.

We are still a long way from a complete understanding of these disabling states of mind. Yet it is important that as a society we make the effort to do so – both in the interest of the individuals and families affected, and in the interest of society generally (e.g. over 25 million working days p.a. are lost through mental disturbance).

Causes

A number of different factors can cause mental disorder: (a) genetic inheritance, (b) the process of birth (e.g. premature birth, anoxia), (c) maternal health in pregnancy (e.g. German measles), (d) body chemistry, diet, poisoning (e.g. lead in petrol fumes), (e) environment and experience (e.g. stress, bereavement). We cannot say with any certainty which of these, if any, is predominant; there are over 300 possible causes. But our general approach is now both more confident and more humane than it was in the past – though some old attitudes and practices do linger on.

History

It was not until the nineteenth century that special provison was made for the mentally disordered: nor was any real distinction made between mental handicap and mental illness until that time. But even then provision for both disabilities was primarily custodial and containing, rather than curative or preventive. Very broadly, society's view of mental disorder has moved through four phases:

1 The *ethical* phase (from the Middle Ages to the eighteenth century) when superstition and punishment predominated. Madness was 'badness', and affected people (e.g. 'witches') were whipped, and burned as 'evil' beings.

2   The *legal* phase (nineteenth century) where madness was 'nuisance', and affected people were controlled and locked away in asylums and private madhouses. But since this could lead to abuse (i.e. wrongful custody) safeguards were established in the form of 'certification' (signed by doctors and, after the *Lunacy Act, 1890*, by JPs) and the setting up of Lunacy Commissioners to inspect premises. Separate institutions for the handicapped began to be provided under the *Idiots Act, 1886*, and special education under an Act of 1899.

3   The *medical* phase (twentieth century) where madness is 'illness' and important strides have occurred in treatment, especially through drugs, more enlightened approaches and earlier treatment. The latter was encouraged by the *Mental Treatment Act, 1930*, which permitted voluntary and informal admission to mental hospital (the new name for asylum): this avoided the trauma of certification and facilitated freer movement to and from hospital. Meanwhile, since the *Mental Deficiency Act, 1913*, local authorities were permitted to make community provision where appropriate for the subnormal, classified under the Act as 'idiots, imbeciles, feeble-minded and moral defectives – many of whom remained 'inside' as certified (partly through fear of their breeding and degenerating the nation's stock).

4   The *social* phase, where madness is 'sadness' rather than illness. This is the current phase, reflected in considerable argument about how far mental disorder should be based on the 'medical model', i.e. viewed in medical terms. This social 'model' view sees the application of medicine to the disordered as of limited relevance: that disorder has more to do with personality than with organic, measurable sickness; that it is more often socially induced and thus needs to be treated in and by society itself. Radicals here (including the 'anti-psychiatry' school of thought) condemn much of the drug treatment (the 'liquid cosh'), ECT and psycho-surgery (see below). Indeed some, such as Thomas Szasz, even question whether mental illness exists at all – it is perhaps a myth, involving a misinterpretation of normal people reacting quite reasonably to *abnormal* circumstances (undue pressure of work, excess tension, lack of affection in the family, etc.).

The *National Health Service Act, 1946*, was important because it stated that ordinary health services were to secure improvement in physical *and* mental health and was to seek prevention as well as treatment of both. This parity of concern was made explicit by the Royal Commission on Mental Illness and Mental Deficiency, 1957, when it asserted that, 'Disorders of the mind are illnesses which need medical treatment . . . and most people are coming to regard mental illness in much the same way as physical illness and disability'.

Many of the Commission's recommendations were enacted in the *Mental Health Act, 1959*. This Act defined mental disorder in terms of three kinds of mental condition: (1) mental illness, (2) arrested or incomplete development of mind, which it sub-divided into (i) sub-normality and (ii) severe subnormality, and (3) psychopathic disorder.

The Act also emphasised the concept of **community care** and spelt out in detail what was needed for preventive and after-care services. It did not actually extend the range of community services but it did emphasis their importance and sought (without great success) to encourage their development and use (making some mandatory on local authorities).

Present services

We have indicated that there are at any one time an estimated 1 million Britons who suffer mental disorder, either illness (½ million) or handicap (½ million). Services for the disordered take two main forms – medical and social (or community).

(a) Medical services – hospitals

Hospitals are the traditional source of treatment, deriving originally from asylums (i.e. the 'haven' established by William Tuke in 1792.) The legislation of 1930, 1946 and 1959, the modern drug treatment 'revolution' and the modern attitude towards mental disorder have done much to reduce the stigma formerly attached to those who were admitted to mental hospitals. The result is that more people are encouraged, through 'informal' admission, to attend for voluntary treatment. Those detained by force of law (i.e. placed under a 'section') constitute about 10 per cent (20,000) of mentally ill admissions and under 5 per cent (600) of handicapped admissions. Altogether, of the 1988 psychiatric hospital population (England) of 103,000 (65,000 ill, 37,000 handicapped), detained patients comprise 5 per cent. Among the handicapped, those most in need of hospital care are usually the more severely disabled; and among the mentally ill, it is the psychotic rather than the neurotic (the latter having some insight or understanding that they are ill or have a problem). There are also about a quarter of a million day- and out-patients.

Hospital treatment. Much depends on the nature of the disorder. For most patients, psychiatric treatment involves: (1) **chemo-therapy** – taking certain medicines and drugs (tranquillisers, sedatives, anti-depressants) which can relieve symptoms and control the condition or modify mood. Some may even positively help to cure it, but greater reliance for this is placed on psychological treatments or therapy. (2)

psycho-therapies – fall into two broad groups: (a) individual therapy, which includes such processes as *psychoanalysis* (giving the patient a chance to talk, reflect and gain some insight into his problem); *behaviour therapy* (such as aversion treatment for alcohol or gambling addiction, or to overcome irrational fears of spiders, open space, etc.). And (b) *group therapy*, which may involve patients and staff talking about their problems; or more developed is the 'therapeutic community' approach which involves patients (and perhaps their relatives) in making decisions about the running of their hospital ward, the routines, responsibilities.

Clearly such 'talking' therapies have limited or nil relevance for the seriously handicapped, but others can be useful, including *occupational therapy* (*OT*) which seeks rehabilitation through engaging in activities which may enhance physical abilities (e.g. manual dexterity) but more importantly provide constructive and purposeful activity, especially with others, which helps to build self-confidence (e.g. art and crafts). *Industrial therapy* is a somewhat more structured and demanding development of OT, based on semi-industrial production lines in 'sheltered' workshops, or in Adult Training Centres (the latter also providing some formal education in basic subjects and life skills – including sign language where necessary: for children there are special hospital schools). Some patients are actually found daytime employment outside the hospital. (3) **physical therapy** – is more dramatic and controversial. It may include electro-convulsive treatment (ECT) which involves passing a small electric current through the brain to help ease or cure depression (and perhaps schizophrenia). It may occasionally take the form of psycho-surgery (e.g. leucotomy) to destroy or remove offending brain cells to relieve severe anxiety or obsessional-compulsive states of mind; this is rarely used and is usually a last resort.

Hospitals have changed a lot in the last 30 years, and they continue to change. Many old, large, isolated mental hospitals have been run down (to under a fifth of the total) as patients have been transferred to the community services or to psychiatric units in ordinary district general hospitals. Most patients are voluntary, wards are unlocked and often divided into smaller units; patients generally stay for shorter periods (e.g. for mentally ill new admissions 50 per cent stay for under a month and 90 per cent under three months). There is generally a great sense of achievement and optimism.

Hospitals also attempt to relate more to the community – through patients' visits to town for shopping or attending the local 'tech' or cinema; by having visitors and volunteer helpers and friends; open days; adult education classes, etc. Hospitals are used more for treatment rather than custody – hence the 'open door' policy, though for some this becomes a 'revolving door' as they return to the hospital after discharge (especially where community facilities have not been available). The aim is to prevent 'institutionalisation', i.e. becoming so dependent on the hospital way of life that self-will is lost. For some it is already too late and they have to live out their time in the hospital back wards, together with those who have to remain as long-term patients owing to the complication of other illnesses (especially among the elderly). This applies too to many of the handicapped for whom suitable provision outside the hosptial does not exist. The Government's consultative document *Care in the Community* (DHSS 1981) estimated that 15,000 handicapped (including 2,000 children) and 5,000 mentally ill need not be in psychiatric hospital if suitable facilities were available out in the community. Another aspect of the 'open door' policy is the expansion of both **out-patient** treatment (attendances for the mentally ill and handicapped increased respectively from 1.6 million and 9,000 to 1.9 million and 23,000 in 1966–80) and of **day hospitals** (with attendances of the disordered together rising from 3.4 million to 3.5 million in 1976–80).

Medical services – primary care. General Practitioners usually assume responsibility for ex-patients when they leave hospital or after a period of out-patient treatment. In practice they are also often the first to deal with psychiatric cases and actually deal with more cases than the hospitals. It is estimated that one tenth of their time is taken up with patients' psychiatric problems, and that they see some 5 million patients a year with such problems. They will refer some to hospital for specialist treatment; others they will deal with themselves (especially through drug treatment). Unfortunately doctors are not always well trained for this side of their work and may not always recognise psychiatric problems presented to them. But the advent of group practice and health centres does increase opportunities for consulting colleagues. GPs may also be assisted in this work by psychiatric community nurses who treat patients at home.

In the 1970s, the Government published White Papers and plans for half the population in psychiatric hospitals by providing for their transfer to community-based services (both NHS and LASS). The document *Better Services for the Mentally Handicapped* (1971) envisaged a 20-year time scale. In 1975 *Better Services for the Mentally Ill* thought it might be 30 years. Progress has undoubtedly been made, as Table 6 shows.

However, until the 1980s progress has been slow and sporadic, largely because of hostile public attitudes to, and financial restraints on, community provision. The problem now may be too rapid an implementation (see pages 162–3).

(b) **Social services**

What services are required here will depend on the person's disorder (i.e. handicap or illness) and his circumstances (i.e. whether he is a

Table 6   Expenditure on health and social services (England and Wales)

	1977 (%)	1986 (%)
Mentally ill		
Health	97	95.5
PSS	3	4.5
Residential	90.7	86.2
Community care	9.3	13.8
Mentally handicapped		
Health	73.8	64.5
PSS	26.2	35.5
Residential	82.3	79
Community care	17.7	21

Source: New Society, 8 September 1987

member of a family or is alone, with or without employment, accommodation, etc.). A key role after discharge from hospital is played by the **social workers** – normally the psychiatric social workers attached to the hospital, who give guidance and advice to the patient and his family. They will if necessary help find suitable **accommodation** for those who are unable or are advised not to return home; this will include local authority residential accommodation in homes or perhaps shorter stay hostels. (In England, 1986, 16,000 handicapped ex-patients were so placed, plus 9,500 in registered private or voluntary homes; corresponding numbers for ex-mentally ill patients were 4,500 and 3,800.) An alternative is suitable lodgings or in some cases fostering.

An important development in recent years has been the creation of **minimum support units** for the mentally handicapped, i.e. ordinary houses containing small groups of ex-patients over whom the social worker keeps a distant (non-residential) but watchful eye. In **medium support units** more staff support is provided. Such patients are usually given training and a trial run in independent residential units and flats within the hospital.

Social workers may help in the search for **employment**, e.g. through registration with the Department of Employment, taking advantage of the services of the DRO or perhaps finding a job through the quota scheme (see pages 149 and 335). The alternative is sheltered employment in special industrial units. Where this is inappropriate (especially for the handicapped) there is ordinary school or special school **education** or, for adults, special education in Adult Training Centres (also known as Special or Social Education Centres). The latter provide some 45,000 places for the purpose of basic education and training (e.g. in such things as home-making, shopping, personal care, and the use of money and transport). ATCs also provide occupational therapy.

Local authorities also provide a range of **community facilities** for the disordered or their families (especially parents of handicapped children) which include day nurseries, fostering or short-term respite and residential care, holidays and holiday play schemes together with a number of day and/or evening social centres and clubs. The trouble is that such service provision is often inadequate and patchy, e.g. the 55 or so day centres for the mentally ill are no where near enough. (Note the important voluntary provision e.g. by MENCAP).

Problems and criticisms

Limitations of space allow only the briefest indication of these:

1 Stigma, old attitudes and unnecessary fears continue to abound. The result is that (a) disordered people often avoid treatment or come to it too late, (b) medical practitioners find psychiatric medicine a less attractive specialism, and (c) employers and society generally often confuse handicap with illness, and may discriminate against the disordered and so frustrate moves towards community care.*

2 Inadequate knowledge and uncertainties about appropriate treatment. Within the psychiatric field there are rival theories of causation and treatment, e.g. whether ECT is ever valid; or whether to treat symptoms for quick results or search longer and deeper for the roots of patients' problems, which may cause frustration or anxiety to the patient and his family.

3 Inadequate services exist in the fields of hospital and community services. (i) Regarding *hospitals*, some big, old buildings are still in use; some chronic sick and handicapped in-patients are given up and left to languish or follow dull routines; medical and other staff (e.g. speech therapists) have little time to spend with patients, particularly in a one-to-one and constructive basis; there are often very low nurse-

*In June 1988 the Health Service Commissioner himself was accused (by the National Association of Health Authorities) of 'legitimising' prejudice against mentally handicapped people and setting back their rights by his ruling that local residents should be consulted before mentally handicapped people were moved into minimum support or community group homes.

to-patient ratios, any many nurses are poorly qualified; there have been numerous scandals and inquiries about ill-treatment (e.g. Ely hospital 1969, Rampton 1978 and St Lawrence's 1981 where a small boy was chained to a pillar in the ward for several hours a day) often caused by overwork of staff (and leading to the creation of the **Hospital Advisory Service** in 1969 whose role is to visit hospitals and nursing homes and generally keep their procedures under review: see page 119); it is often alleged that patients are over-sedated with drugs to keep them quiet, and that there is generally an insufficient check on treatments (including those administered under compulsion – see below); it is sometimes suggested too that the 'talking' therapies favour articulate middle class patients. (ii) Regarding *community services*, some local health authorities and PSS departments are providing very few or no day centres, hostels, ATCs or residential accommodation (especially for the young handicapped and elderly mentally confused). Provision of some of these nationally is only 50 per cent of the required level. As the Government admits, although there has been 'steady progress . . . in the shift in the balance of care between hospital and social services, provision has been slower than was originally hoped' (i.e. in 1971. See *Health Care and its Costs*. HMSO, 1983). Consequently many discharged patients return to hospital or become homeless, perhaps offending and ending up in jail. Many too are isolated and lonely, and may be subject to exploitation (e.g. sexual) by the community. For some, the only community support is a regular injection from a community psychiatric nurse and perhaps an occasional visit from a social worker. There are considerable variations in the levels of services across the country e.g. some councils spend £12 per head of population on the mentally handicapped and £7.50 on the mentally ill, while others spend only £2 and 50p respectively. There are also variations in the relationships and degree of cooperation among health, housing and social services authorities (see page 163). This point has been made in a host of recent reports, including the Audit Commission in *Making a Reality of Community Care* (1986) and *Community Care: Developing Services for People with a Mental Handicap* (1987), the Griffiths Report *Community Care: Agenda for Action* (1988), the Public Accounts Committee of Parliament (1988), the Social Services Committee of Parliament (1985) and the National Audit Office 1988. Indeed, with responsibility for community care in so many hands (the Departments of Health, Social Security and Environment, and at local level hospitals, local authority housing and social services departments (SSDs)), the Griffiths comment seems most apt that community care seems to be 'a poor relation; everybody's distant relative but nobody's baby'. Thus, at local level, there is often a lack of coordination between health authorities and SSDs such that patients remain unnecessarily (and expensively) in mental hospital because community services are not available; or, increasingly patients are discharged into a community care-*less* society. Central imposition of rate-capping has not helped progress. Consequently many feel that hospital closures and discharges are now happening too rapidly, and groups such as Schizophrenia Fellowship and Rescare (a society for the mentally handicapped in residential care) are urging a slow down until community services are improved. (Indeed in August 1988, the Department of Health has indicated such a policy.) Finally it may be asked whether community care passes too much of a burden on to the family; far too often for example, the choice for parents of the severely handicapped child is between coping with keeping him at home with little support or guidance (except where there are voluntary groups such as local Down's syndrome groups) or sending him (far) away to a long-stay hospital.

There are plans to strengthen community care: under the *Health and Social Services and Social Security Adjudications Act, 1983* the powers of health authorities to make payments to local authorities and voluntary bodies are extended to help in the provision of education and housing, such as 'core and cluster units', i.e. houses in the community to enable broadly independent living for groups of ex-patients. In 1984 the Government announced a scheme of 'Helping the Community to Care'. Over three years £10½ million will be provided to help families, volunteers and others to care better for their elderly or handicapped dependents. (Since 1975, National Development Teams have been visiting health and PSS establishments to advise on how services can be improved for the mentally handicapped.) Meanwhile, pioneering integrated NHS-PSS schemes for services for the mentally handicapped have been developed in a number of local authorities (e.g. Hillingdon and in Wales). And the **Griffiths Report** has recommended that a Minister be appointed with specific responsibility for community care policy; that local authorities should be responsible locally for assessing the care needs of their area and developing community care plans (perhaps 'buying in' from private and voluntary sectors); and local authorities should receive a special grant (of up to 50 per cent) to develop community care (see page 416). However, it is important that the community services be truly part of the community; there has been a tendency for some councils, in effect, to re-institutionalise (or trans-institutionalise) some ex-patients from hospital settings to residential home settings (partly encouraged, as the Audit Commission pointed out in 1986, by the central payment of board and lodgings allowances).

4 Abnormal offenders need psychiatric treatment rather than imprisonment. Yet none is available, apart from the overcrowded special DHSS hospitals (Broadmoor, Moss Side, Park Lane and Rampton and in Scotland, Carstairs) which provide for the 2,000 violent or more disturbed offenders. But large numbers of lesser offenders with psychiatric problems require different 'secure' places and treatment. The Butler Committee (1975) recommended separate institutions or separate units within NHS hospitals: these have yet to materialise. The Government has now announced plans to provide a network of regional secure units, between maximum security special hospitals (above) and open NHS hospitals, for patients likely to respond to programmes of active treatment and rehabilitation but who need some security. In the meantime, existing NHS psychiatric hospitals frequently refuse to accept offenders (even where the problem is minor in nature) and as a result, many end up in prison: in 1979 there were 192 in the special hospitals and 581 in prisons who should really have been receiving medical treatment in psychiatric hospitals.

5   Compulsory powers may be exercised when a person becomes so disordered as to be incapable of managing his or her own affairs, and refuses to see a doctor or enter hospital. A social worker or the person's relative can override his or her wishes by applying for compulsory admission to hospital for: (i) observation up to 28 days (section 25 of the 1959 Act), (ii) emergency observation for 3 days (section 29), or (iii) treatment for up to 12 months (section 26). All these require the signature of two doctors before admission (except emergencies when one signature can be given after admission) and must be explicitly in the interests of the patient's health or safety or to protect others. Whilst being detained a patient can ask for a second opinion and he (or his relative) can appeal for release to a **Mental Health Review Tribunal**.

These provisions represent a serious threat to people's liberty and interference with their bodies and minds. Consequently, following persistent pressure from MIND and others, the *Mental Health (Amendment) Act, 1982* and the subsequent *Mental Health Act, 1983* changed the law relating to the mentally ill. The 1983 Act: (a) reduces section 26 to 6 months, (b) provides automatic review by Tribunal and makes legal representation available there, (c) creates a Commission to inspect and review patient care (Scotland already had a Mental Welfare Commission), (d) provides for a Code of Practice for treatments, (e) provides for a second opinion, plus patient consent, where treatment is hazardous or irreversible (e.g. surgery) or where a patient refuses consent to other forms of treatment (e.g. ECT, drugs), (f) confines social worker involvement in compulsory admission to those specially trained (the Approved Social Worker), (g) increases opportunities for 'guardianship', i.e. compulsory care in the community, (h) detained patients and those most concerned with them (e.g. relatives) must be informed of their rights, (i) health and local authorities have a duty to provide after-care services, (j) voluntary patients now have the right to register and vote in elections.

All this is very commendable as it seeks to safeguard the rights of patients when they are in a very vulnerable position. Yet it undoubtably throws additional problems and strains on others, such as nurses and social workers. Moreover there are still criticisms concerning the inadequacy of safeguards against incompetence, peremptory examination and wrongful admission; and overall standards of care may still be inadequate.

Questions

1 What is (a) disablement and (b) medical rehabilitation?
2 What is meant by sheltered employment, designated employment, Remploy Ltd?
3 Outline the provisions of the Chronically Sick and Disabled Persons Act, 1970.
4 What local authority services are provided for the physically handicapped?
5 What is meant by 'mental disorder' under the Mental Health Act, 1959?
6 Discuss the variety of care and services for the mentally handicapped.
7 Explain the procedure involved in compulsory hospital admission.
8 Discuss the nature and extent of 'community care' for the mentally disordered.
9 The 'open door' has become the 'revolving door' following the medical treatment of the mentally disordered. Explain this statement and consider the extent to which this is true and why it may occur.
10 Find out what you can about the aims and methods of the voluntary organisation MIND.
11 In 1979 the Jay Committee on Mental Handicap Nursing and Care suggested that residential care staff should be 'socially' trained (with say the CSS – see page 000) rather than medically trained as many are today (especially in nursing). Comment on this suggestion.
12 The Government White Paper *Better Services for the Mentally Ill* (1975) envisaged that a satisfactory network of services would take 25 years to build up. What progress has been made?
13 About 5,000 children a year are born with serious handicaps such as spina bifida, heart disease, kidney disease, Down's Syndrome, muscular dystrophy, cystic fibrosis or severe haemophilia. It is claimed that 2,000 of these could be avoided through prenatal diagnosis and genetic screening. Suggest reasons why such action is not taken.
14 Between 1976 and 1986 some 15,000 people moved from long-stay hospitals into community care. Assess and comment on the significance of this.

7
Mothers and young children

In this chapter we consider the welfare services for mothers and young children.

'By the present Declaration of the Rights of the child, commonly known as the Declaration of Geneva, men and women of all nations, recognising that mankind owes to the child the best that it has to give, declare and accept it as their duty that beyond and above all considerations of race, nationality or creed:

1 The child must be given the means requisite for its normal development, both materially and spiritually;
2 The child that is hungry must be fed; the child that is sick must be nursed; the child that is backward must be helped; the delinquent child must be reclaimed; and the orphan and waif must be sheltered and succoured;
3 The child must be the first to receive relief in times of distress;
4 The child must be put in a position to earn a livelihood and must be protected against every form of exploitation;
5 The child must be brought up in the consciousness that its talents must be devoted to the service of its fellow men.'

('Declaration of the Rights of the Child', adopted by the Assembly of the League of Nations in 1924.)

So runs the concerted wisdom of the leaders of the nations of the world as expressed in their Declaration. Alas we are all too well aware that the Rights expounded are by no means universally honoured even among the developed or civilised nations.

History

We have already referred briefly to the history of the social and welfare services and the problems faced from the *Poor Law Act, 1601*, to the nineteenth century when the effects of the industrial revolution in this country were plain for all to see. Side by side with apparent national material prosperity and expansion there existed bad social conditions harmful to many of the young.

Child welfare services, like other social services, grew up piecemeal. Originally the Church did its best to discharge its obligations and to practise its philosophies, and the local authorities tried to discharge their duties under the *Poor Law Act, 1601*. These were woefully weak, and inadequate. The *Public Health Act, 1848*, and the *Public Health Act, 1875*, were important developments in public health generally but they were unable to relieve the conditions faced by those who were the weakest in the social scale. Something more needed to be done and it was left to pioneering indivduals such as Dr Barnardo, Lord Shaftesbury, Margaret Beaven of Liverpool and Mary Carpenter and other inspired and industrious leaders who founded voluntary organisations. Josephine Butler, for example, challenged the leaders with the injustices meted out to the unmarried mother in Victorian times.

What was needed was central organisation by the central Government and more efficient administration of elementary services. There was much opposition to simple ideas. Some argued that feeding and general caring for the family was a matter for the parents, and that these responsibilities should remain with them. The independence of the family would thus be ensured. Some argued that the State could do too much, that it could 'feather-bed' too many of the so called 'needy' who should work harder and fight to keep the family together and sustain them. Adversity can in many instances bring out qualities of independence, self-reliance, courage and confidence. Sharing of burdens and distress is the very stuff of family life. Adversity can, however, be overwhelming and crushing.

Gradually in the **twentieth century** there grew an awareness that more should be done to promote the health of mother and young child. There were several reasons for this. Firstly there was general concern over the high infant and child mortality particularly among the poor. Secondly the Government realised that the recruits for the Boer War (1899–1902 in South Africa) were in poor physical condition, though reputedly the fit and fighting youth. Thirdly compulsory education from 1880 revealed to local and central authorities that many of the school children were in poor health and received a poor diet.

One of the first steps to be taken was to ensure that **midwives** be properly trained in their duties of assisting at the deliveries of young babies. The *Midwives Act, 1902*, laid down that midwives be properly trained. In 1936 local authorities were required to ensure that there was an adequate number of midwives in their areas.

The *Maternity and Child Welfare Act, 1918*, permitted local authorities to provide services for expectant mothers and children up to the age of five. The central Government gave financial grants to authorities providing these services and gave them power to appoint **health visitors** to visit the young infants in their homes after the fourteenth day of life. In 1981 there were 2½ million cases attended.

After the Second World War there was a strong desire for improvement in welfare services generally. The *National Health Service Act, 1946*, was passed to ensure the provision of **welfare foods**, such as orange juice, vitamin tablets, cod liver oil, which had been supplied at clinics during the war to ensure the fitness of mothers and young children during the critical years when most people were on rations. During the war the clinics were staffed by nurses and doctors who maintained a general watch over mothers and infants.

Services today for mothers and young children

All expectant mothers and nursing mothers may use any of the maternity and child welfare services of the NHS. Medical services and nursing services are in general free, but charges can be made for welfare foods and for some local authority services such as 'home helps'.

Maternity and child health services. All District Health Authorities must provide maternity and child health services.

Health Authorities are now operating a more relaxed regime so that parents can more easily visit and stay, day and/or night, in hospital with their ill children. An important part of these is organised around the local health clinics for mothers and young children. Some 6,000 of these centres exist in England and Wales, and more are planned. The clinics do not give treatment for illness; patients are referred back to their own doctor or, sometimes, direct to a specialist or hospital.

These child health centres, although primarily concerned with giving **advice** for expectant mothers and babies and general medical **supervision**, now also provide for the distribution of welfare foods, vaccination and **immunisation**, and examining and weighing babies. Some provide social clubs and discussion **groups** for mothers (especially useful for isolated and depressed or anxious young mothers); crèches and play groups; special clubs for premature babies, toddlers and children under school age; and health visiting and midwifery services. The majority of expectant and nursing mothers attend these health centres of clinics, which have proved popular and most useful for this priority class in the community. But it is the more educated among the mothers who attend and make most use of the services, while mothers with a poor standard of care with large families, or with illegitimate infants – those who most need advice and help – are less likely to attend. Thus only half of the under-5s attend in the course of a year (though the Court Report, 1976, was critical of standards in the maternity services generally). Much help in running the centres is given by voluntary workers at the centre in keeping records, organising the distribution of welfare foods, etc.

Vaccinations. Health authorities arrange for vaccination against diphtheria, poliomyelitis, tuberculosis, whooping cough, tetanus, rubella and measles. Vaccination against smallpox is no longer recommended as a routine procedure in early childhood. Cases of brain damage to children following some vaccinations have caused some reluctance by parents to have their children vaccinated.

Welfare foods service. Under the Welfare Foods Service free milk is available to: an expectant mother and all children under school age in families in receipt of Income Support; school-age children who are severely disabled and not at school; children up to 5 attending approved day nurseries, play groups or child-minders. Free vitamins are available to low income expectant mothers and their children under 5. Welfare foods provided by health authorities at special prices comprise: dried milk for expectant mothers and children; vitamin A, D and C drops for children; and vitamin A, D and C tablets for expectant and nursing mothers. Some authorities also provide, through clinics, other proprietary foods at reduced prices.

Home or hospital confinements. Whether an expectant mother has her baby at home or in hospital depends on a number of factors: the mother's own wishes; her home situation (e.g. whether she has other infants at home); her own medical condition; and the availability of medical resources.

If admission to hospital is preferred or necessary on medical and obstetric grounds the family doctor makes the arrangements directly with the hospital consultant. Much thought is given to good human relationships and to the creation of a home-like atmosphere in the maternity ward. The post-natal stay in hospital is now about six days; some 17 to 18 per cent of women are discharged home within 48 hours of delivery to the care of the family doctor and domiciliary midwife or nurse. About 90 per cent of all expectant mothers are confined in NHS hospitals. About six weeks after the birth of the baby the mother is given a post-natal examination to confirm that she has returned to normal health and activity. **Health visitors** make some 2 million visits p.a. to the 4 million under-5s.

Abortion. The circumstances in which a doctor is justified in terminating a pregnancy are defined in the *Abortion Act, 1967*, the purpose of which was to amend and clarify the law relating to abortions so that the operation could legally be performed where certain criteria were met. The Act states that a doctor may terminate a pregnancy if two registered medical practitioners are of the opinion, formed in good faith: (a) that the continuance of the pregnancy would involve risk to the life of the pregnant woman, or of injury to the physical or mental health of the pregnant woman or any existing children of her family, greater than if the pregnancy were terminated; or (b) that there is a substantial risk that if the child were born it would suffer from such physical or mental abnormalities as to be seriously handicapped.

In determining whether the continuance of a pregnancy would involve such risk of injury to health as is mentioned in (a), account may be taken of the pregnant woman's actual or reasonably foreseeable environment.

The Act further allows termination of pregnancy by a registered medical practitioner where he is of the opinion that the termination is immediately necessary to save the life of the woman or to prevent grave permanent injury to her health, without requiring the recommendation of a second doctor. The Act also requires that, such cases of immediate necessity excepted, a termination should be carried out in a State hospital or in a private nursing home approved for that purpose by the Secretary of State. The woman's age, marital status, duration of pregnancy, previous obstetric history, any complications consequent on the operation, and whether a sterilisation was performed have to be notified to the Chief Medical Officer at the Department of Health within seven days of the operation.

In 1986 there were 168,000 legal abortions (of which 30,000 were to non-residents, and over 4000 were under 16s). Overall, 65 per cent were unmarried. In 1970 there had been 50,000 legal abortions. Groups opposed to abortion (such as 'Life' and the Society for the Protection of the Unborn Child) have sought to have the law changed or abolished.

The unmarried mother and child

In Victorian times the unmarried mother was usually regarded as 'fallen' and outcast. Even those who tried to help her were looked upon with some misgiving and criticism as condoning immorality. Many outstanding women, however, defied public opinion and went to the help and rescue of their 'fallen' sisters (for example Agnes Jones and Josephine Butler in the nineteenth century). In that general atmosphere official local authority services were slow in developing their assistance. Religious organisations and voluntary bodies were, however, the prime movers in providing that care and help which the unmarried mother and her child needed.

The National Council for the Unmarried Mother and her Child (NCUMC) was set up in 1918 and was an important coordinating and propaganda body, working to improve the social services available to the unmarried mother and her child and to encourage more sympathy and understanding for them. However, it is no longer just concerned with the unmarried mother and it has now become the **National Council for One-Parent Families** in view of the massive growth of the one-parent family to one million today, of which 11 per cent are men; and of the women, 19 per cent are widows, 38 per cent divorced, 25 per cent separated and 18 per cent never married (though three-quarters of the latter are cohabiting). The National Council acts as a pressure group for better provision for the one-parent family. It also seeks to provide a variety of services e.g. finding jobs, legal advice, small grants for clothes, debts and fares, finding 'foster mothers' who will provide for the young unmarried mother and her child, and advising on maintenance. Several thousands of problems are dealt with each year. Some women are helped directly by the NCUMC's own social workers, but most are referred to local organisations and social workers near the home of the unmarried mother.

Help for unmarried mothers. Attitudes have changed and illegitimacy is more accepted today. Nevertheless there are many problems to be faced. First the expectant mother may want a place to stay before and after the birth of her child. There are about 150 mother-and-baby **homes** in the country; some have been converted into flatlet accommodation. Some homes and hostels are provided by local authority social services departments, but most are run by voluntary organisations with religious affiliations, often subsidised by local authorities. Girls and women who go into traditional mother-and-baby homes can stay for about six weeks before and after the birth.

After the birth the unmarried mother usually has to go out to work and earn a living. The majority have to fend for themselves. Frequently they will have to live with friends or relatives or find a bed-sitter, a child-minder or a day-nursery. Some will seek support of the DSS and some will consider making application for an **affiliation order** against the putative father in the Magistrates' Court (see page 365). A decision will have to be made whether or not to keep the child or arrange for **adoption**.

Medical care through the NHS is available for all expectant and nursing mothers whether married or not. For obvious reasons unmarried mothers tend to use **ante-natal** and **post-natal** services less frequently than married mothers. But the services are there, nevertheless, for their use. Unmarried mothers who have paid the necessary contributions are also entitled to maternity benefits (see pages 56 and 58), equally with other mothers. If she is not eligible, or needs additional financial help, she can apply to the DSS so long as she is over 16.

The under-16s who have no other provision, e.g. from parents or relatives, can be helped financially by the PSS, though these do not give regular support of this kind. Voluntary organisations, such as Dr Barnardo's, now sometimes assist with maintenance grants. Unmarried mothers who want to return to work are given priority for **day-nursery** vacancies.

All kinds of social workers, including moral welfare workers, probation officers and health visitors, do their best to help unmarried mothers who come to them. However, they often refer them to voluntary organisations who employ social workers with special training for work with unmarried parents. Today these spend more time than formerly on the special problems of 'schoolgirl' mothers (some 8,500 p.a.). These social workers work closely with social workers in the official services. Addresses of the voluntary organisations can be found from local authority social services departments (SSD), health visitors, Citizens' Advice Bureaux or libraries.

Divorce. Many unmarried mothers are literally un-married, i.e. divorced. We now experience 160,000 divorces a year, at which rate it will affect one marriage in three (and one child in five). There was an increase from 150,000 following the *Matrimonial and Family Proceedings Act, 1984* which allows divorce after only one year of marriage. The Act also reduces the liability of husbands for maintenance payments to their former wives – to overcome the so-called 'meal-ticket for life' or 'alimony drone' syndrome which exploits ex-husbands. However, in practice 25 per cent of maintenance orders are never paid; 55 per cent are in serious arrears and 57 per cent are for sums of between £1,000 and £11,000. Wives are often reluctant to seek enforcement for fear of reprisal from former husbands.

In 1971 there were 500,000 single parents. Today there are over a million, with 1.5 million children. The typical lone parent is a woman (see above) since the mother usually gets custody of any children in cases of divorce. Significantly, over 400,000 single parent families depend on Income Support. And since most divorcees re-marry, it is also significant what happens to the two sets of children when families merge, and perhaps a third set of siblings emerge from the new union; indeed such are some of the problems that a counselling service has been developed specially (called 'Stepfamily', 162 Tenison Road, Cambridge).

Day care for pre-school children

Day care services for those children with special needs – for health or social reasons, or whose mothers have no option but to go to work – are provided by various bodies, local authorities and private. The unmarried mother especially has a good claim for these services since she will often have to work to provide for herself and her child.

There are State (LEA) **nursery schools** (no longer mandatory since 1980) providing some 300,000 places, and voluntary playgroups and private kindergarten provide over 570,000 places, but both of these are only available for limited hours in the day and close down for holiday periods.

Apart from a few voluntary establishments (e.g. NSPCC) there are about 450 State (PSS) **day nurseries** with some 30,000 places. Some are called 'Family Centres' since they increasingly involve the parents in the care of the children at the nursery. Whilst they charge fees, in practice many are remitted since places are largely confined to single-parent or problem-family children (usually on the recommendation of a health visitor or social worker). There are vast differences in the scale of provision locally and nationally there is a waiting list of some 12,000. The Children Bill 1988 will compel provision.

Private nurseries and firms' creches help provide another 25,000 places. This is a growing area of provision, especially in view of the decline in school-leaver employees (see page 63) but it does raise the problems of adequate regulation. Apart from providing creches, some firms (such as Penguin Books, Thames TV and Oxfam) are paying allowances to some staff to offset the cost of childminding while they are at work. **Childminders** add (officially) another 80,000 or so places. Under the *Nurseries and Childminders Regulation Act, 1948* all these private or voluntary providers should register with local authorities to ensure that the premises and their managers are satisfactory. It is estimated that up to 300,000 child-minders do not register, and even those who do so are sometimes given official approval even when they fail to reach required standards (so that they can at least be monitored and encouraged to improve, rather than go completely 'underground' – see page 195).

Working mothers

Before the Second World War it was general practice for a woman to give up employment and devote herself to the raising and care of her children. However, during the war there was a need for as many women as possible to enter war work. Local authorities and factories employing female labour thereupon arranged for the care of their children by providing their own nurseries (or 'creches'). Since that time (especially recently) the demand for women workers has continued and the climate of opinion has changed. Thus, today, the 'typical family' of a working father, two children and the mother at home applies to only 5 per cent of households. About 60 per cent of all mothers go out to work, including 30 per cent (up from 25 per cent in 1973) of those mothers with children (about 1 million or a quarter of the age group) under 5. A recent survey (by the EOC) found that 63 per cent of mothers would like to go to work but for lack of day-care facilities for young children. Only two out of five lone mothers have paid jobs, which leaves the rest (650,000) dependent on State benefits and largely poor (see page 69). In 1988, under the Government's Employment Training programme (see page 353) parents on the scheme may receive up to £50 a week per child minded. An estimated ¾ million under-5s have mothers at work but without access to local authority day nursery or child-minding services.

There is a division of opinion about this practice: some women regard the care and nurture of the family as a full-time occupation until the child or children reach adolescence; others take the view that employment outside the home provides interest and social contact and enables them to provide greater economic advantages for themselves, their children and their home. Much, therefore, depends on individual choice and personal circumstance. There are advantages and disadvantages. One special risk is that where children ('latch-key kids') attending school return home and find it empty (the parent being at work) there is greater opportunity for mischief which may land the child before the Court, where it is shown that the child is then in need of care or control (see page 187). One recent survey has found that 300,000 of 5–10 year-olds and 375,000 of 11–15 year-olds are left unsupervised during school holidays.

There have been considerable changes in public opinion and in the law on this subject: e.g. the *Equal Pay Act, 1973* (as a result of which women get something like 70 per cent of men's hourly pay c.f. 60 per cent in 1970); the *Sex Discrimination Act, 1975*; and the *Employment Protection Act, 1975*. The latter gives three important new rights to a woman who is expecting a baby, including the right not to lose her job (pregnancy itself will not be a valid reason for dismissal); the right to return to her job after the baby is born; and the right to maternity pay.

Women also seek the right to protection from their **violent husbands**. 60,000 acts of domestic violence in London alone were reported in 1989; one estimate suggests there may be ¾ million such assaults a year there. The PSS and probation service help here, often in conjunction with voluntary groups (e.g. there are over 200 **refuges** established under the aegis of the National Women's Aid Federation; they received 3,000 requests 1983–84). But whereas a recent Parliamentary Committee has recommended one such place for every 10,000 of the population, in practice the figure for 1981 was only one in 60,000. The *Domestic Violence and Matrimonial Proceedings Act, 1976*, provides some protection since it enables courts to make non-molestation and exclusion orders, barring violent spouses and cohabitees from the matrimonial home.

The family planning service

A family planning service is now available on the NHS to all irrespective of age or marital status. NHS clinics may be run and staffed by doctors and nurses directly or they may be run on an agency basis by organisations such as the Family Planning Association. Clinics and hospitals may also provide free advice and treatment, and the supplies which they prescribe and dispense are also free. This includes normal methods of contraception. Family planning and advice is increasingly available from GPs. Yet in spite of this, a recent survey indicates that as many as 2 million sexually active women are at risk of unintended pregnancy through not using reliable birth control methods. More recent developments in this area include the administration of fertility drugs and artificial insemination ('test-tube' babies) as a means to parenthood. The health services (in conjunction with the Marriage Guidance Councils – now called 'Relate') also provide sexual therapy clinics. Sex obviously plays an important part in the life of couples. Where there are problems, this can undermine and threaten the relationship or marriage.

Comment

The services described in this chapter have been seriously criticised for their low level of provision. For example, only 1 per cent of under-fives in Britain attend day nurseries and 40 per cent (mainly 4 year-olds) receive nursery education. This compares with pre-school care of the 3–5 year-olds of 99 per cent in Belgium, 93 per cent in France, 95 per cent in the Netherlands and 70 per cent in West Germany.

Equally there are great variations in provision among local authorities, especially as there is no legal obligation on them to make such provision. Thus some councils make no provision for day nurseries, nursery education or grants to playgroups, childminders or community nurseries.

Questions

1 Describe the services available for mothers and young children.
2 *A* is an unmarried mother who needs help. Advise her of the social services she may take advantage of. Name some of the voluntary organisations specially concerned with the unmarried mother.
3 Justify an increase in expenditure on day-care provision for young children.

4   How do you account for baby battering? Should those convicted of baby battering be helped or punished?
5   Briefly indicate the main regulations regarding child-minding.
6   'If a society values its children, it must cherish their parents' (J. Bowlby). In what ways and to what extent do we 'cherish' parents in modern Britain?
7   Britain has the highest rate (14 per cent) of lone parent families in Europe. Why do you think this is so?

8
Children and young persons

History

Today's children are tomorrow's parents. We owe it to them and to society in general to see that they have a stable home life and happy upbringing, since the quality of the physical and emotional care they receive will greatly affect what kind of adults they become. Before the nineteenth century children and young persons were looked upon as forms of cheap labour, unless they were the sons and daughters of wealthy parents. When the Industrial Revolution was under way the factories in the industrial towns exploited the reservoir of pauper or free children who, from age seven, were hired from the workhouse (ostensibly as 'apprentices') to work long hours in factory, mine or mill.

The first legislation to protect children was the *Health and Morals of Apprentices Act, 1802*. Then the *Factory Act, 1833*, provided for an inspectorate employed by the central Government to enforce the provisions of the Act which controlled the hours worked by women and children and to ensure safety precautions were complied with. The *Elementary Education Act, 1870*, provided for the establishment of schools managed by popularly elected school boards. Public funds were made available to educate the children in basic skills – the three Rs. Medical officers were later appointed to inspect the schoolchildren. Other legislation followed, viz. the *Education (Provision of Meals) Act, 1906*, giving permissive powers to local authorities to provide food for children who were undernourished. Gradually improvements were made until the passing of the *Education Act, 1944*, which laid down the present structure (see page 225).

Treatment of young offenders. Adults and children were dealt with in the same way in the courts until the beginning of the nineteenth century. Generally the treatment at the hands of the law was harsh. In 1838, however, Parkhurst Prison was opened for the detention of children *separately* from adults. The *Reformatory Schools Act, 1854*, provided for the building of Reform Schools to offer an alternative form of treatment from imprisonment with adults.

In 1847 the magistrates were empowered to deal with children summarily in the Magistrates' Courts for certain offences instead of committing them to the Assizes and Quarter Sessions Courts for jury trial. Gradually the Justices held separate sittings of their local courts to try all children's cases. The *Children Act, 1908*, enacted that all magistrates dealing with offences by children should hold separate sittings, i.e. separate from adult courts. The *Juvenile Courts (Metropolis) Act, 1920*, laid down that only magistrates who were specially selected and suitable should be able to deal with offences at these special children's courts. The *Children Act, 1908*, abolished imprisonment as a form of punishment for anyone under 14.

The poor and orphaned. The child without a family or one with a family who ill-treated him faced a grim situation. Many were housed with the **Poor Law Guardians** (see page 8). These controlled large institutions where the children lived with adults, some of whom were ill or mentally unfit. The children were harshly treated. But certain public-spirited people tried to help, e.g. Dr Barnardo (1845–1905) who worked for four years among the destitute children in the East End of London. He opened his first boys' home in 1870. That was a success and he established more, and began to experiment with 'boarding out', training ships and emigration (mainly to Australia and Canada) so that the young people would have work and opportunity overseas.

In 1884 the **National Society for the Prevention of Cruelty to Children (NSPCC)** was founded (sixty years after the founding of the RSPCA!). This tried to deal with neglect and ill-treatment of children. Parents formerly had complete rights over their children, until the *Poor Law Amendment Act, 1868*, made it an offence for a parent wilfully to neglect to provide adequate food, clothing, medical aid and lodging for his children. The *Act for the Prevention of Cruelty to and Better Protection of Children, 1889*, established penalties for ill-treatment and neglect.

Parents would sometimes allow their children to be adopted. Later, when the child had grown old enough, the natural parents would reassert their right to the child, particularly when they saw the prospect of gain as the child became old enough to earn money from employment. The *Adoption Act, 1926*, ensured safeguards where parents of this character intervened to the child's detriment and harm (see page 183). Of particular significance were the *Children and Young Persons Act, 1933*, and the *Children Act, 1948*.

At the same time as these developments were taking place there were pioneers in youth work in the nineteenth century – e.g. Boys' Brigade, Church Brigade, Scouts, Girl Guides, YMCA, YWCA and similar groups. In 1918 the Government urged local authorities to form committees to mobilise local resources in the service of youth.

Present services

Officially, a child is aged up to 14; a **young person** is aged between 14 and 17; and a **juvenile** is aged up to 17. Children and young people today enjoy a range of services which seek to promote their general welfare. Some of these services are of direct benefit, others are indirect; some seek to prevent distress among children, others resolve stressful situations. Traditionally, the social care services for children are divided into those for *deprived* children, those for young *offenders* and those for *ill-treated* children. Thus we shall examine these services under five categories: (i) family and legal status, (ii) care and protection of those at risk, (iii) care of deprived children, (iv) young offenders, (v) general protection. In addition there is (vi) a whole range of services which support children and their families, including health, social security and education. These are mentioned further below.

Who administers the services?

There is no single service or government department responsible for these services as such. There is a hotch potch of government departments, local authorities, public corporations and voluntary bodies:

1 Central government administers family benefits and other social security benefits throughout Great Britain. The Department of Social Security is the responsible government department.
2 Local government administers (a) education, careers and youth services, (b) care of deprived children and (c) school health services.
3 Health services are administered by various bodies, groups and boards (see page 90). These are independent corporations but under the general control of the Department of Health.
4 The Home Office is responsible for police, prisons, borstals and similar institutions, and the probation and after-care service.
5 The Department of Employment is responsible for a range of employment, education and training services and for enforcing employment and health and safety regulations (see Chapter 12).

The arrangement of services distributed among various government departments and local authorities is further complicated by the voluntary bodies. These include the NSPCC, the Church of England Children's Society, Mencap, Share and many other bodies too numerous to mention. All this is untidy; but it is not so important if each of the services work together in the interests of children and society generally.

Legal and family status

Parents' rights and duties

(a) **Equal rights.** Before 1973 the father was recognised in law as the natural guardian of his legitimate child until that child reached 18. Now, as a result of the *Guardianship Act, 1973*, the father and mother both have equal rights of guardianship over their legitimate children up to the age of 18. These equal rights relate to taking decisions about (a) the upbringing of children and (b) the education or (c) the religion in which the child is to be brought up. Moreover, consent has to be given by *both* parents to the adoption of their child or to the marriage of a young person aged under 18.

(b) **Access to courts in disputes.** In most families the parents come to a sensible agreement over such matters. However, where there is a fundamental disagreement between the mother and the father over the upbringing of the child, either may bring the matter before a Magistrates' Court or a County Court.

(c) **Custody.** A parent may either apply for a decision on the matter in dispute or to be awarded sole custody or care and control of the child. When faced with this sometimes difficult decision the court must have the *welfare of the child* as its prime consideration. The court makes such orders as it thinks fit regarding such matters as (a) custody and (b) the right of access to the child by either parent. Thus, for example, Mrs *W* may be awarded custody of the child, and Mr *W* may be allowed access one or two week-ends in four to see the child and take him out. When hearing an application for custody, the court may also ask for a **social inquiry report** from a local authority or probation officer; or commit the child to the care of a local authority if it appears to the court that there are exceptional circumstances making it impracticable or undesirable for the child to be entrusted to either parent or to any other individual. Parents are nowadays divorcing more frequently than ever before. Sometimes an application is made for judicial separation. In either case the *Matrimonial Proceedings and Property Act, 1970**, applies to parents residing permanently in England and Wales. This act makes provision for the welfare of children of parents about to divorce or be judicially separated. Similar provisions apply to Scotland. Here again a Divorce Court is required to place the welfare of the child as the paramount consideration, and there is no presumption in favour of either spouse. In other words, the court does not assume that a mother, as such, is the better person to be granted custody of her child. The court, moreover, is not bound to commit custody to either party and may in exceptional cases commit a child to the care of a local authority, or order that he should be placed under the supervision of a probation officer or social worker.

(d) **Contribution by parents.** If custody is given to the mother, or a third person, or if the child is committed to local authority care, the court may require the father to contribute to the child's maintenance. Furthermore, in cases where custody is not given to the mother, she too may be required to contribute to the child's maintenance. Parents enjoy equal rights of application to the court on matters relating to their children. Under the *Matrimonial Proceedings and Property Act, 1970**, courts have wide powers to order financial provision for children. Thus if the husband is at work and his wife is not the court may well order the husband to contribute to the child. However, it may well be that the wife is working and the husband is not, in which case the wife may be compelled to contribute to the upkeep and maintenance of the child. Such payments generally continue until the child's first birthday after reaching school-leaving age of 16. If the child remains in education or training the payments can be extended by the court.

(e) **Marriage.** A marriage between persons either of whom is under 16 at the date of the marriage is void. In England and Wales young persons between the ages of 16 and 18 must usually obtain the consent of the parents or guardian to the marriage. If the consent is refused, a court may give consent to the marriage. No parental consent is required in Scotland for children 16 and over.

(f) **Chastisement** is an emotive and sensitive subject. A parent or guardian has the right to chastise a child. That right may be delegated to a nurse or teacher or other person by the parent or guardian. (In 1982, the European Court declared that schools could not use physical punishment on children where parents object.) The punishment must be moderate and reasonable. Where it is unreasonable and cruel an offence is committed. The offender may be fined or imprisoned by a Magistrates' Court or Crown Court (*Children and Young Persons Act, 1933*). The difficulty of detecting this type of offence is obvious, particularly when committed against a very young child. Where an offence is reported the NSPCC may make inquiries and may bring a case to court if the police do not themselves prosecute the offender. The court may then make any suitable order, e.g. placing the child in the care of the local authority or other person.

---

*As modified by the *Matrimonial and Family Proceedings Act, 1984*.

(g)   **Education.** The *Education Act, 1944*, makes it a duty of every person who is a parent or guardian or has the actual custody of a child of compulsory school age to cause him to receive efficient full-time education suitable to his age, ability and aptitude, either by regular attendance at school or otherwise.

Illegitimacy

A child born during wedlock is *prima facie* legitimate. Similarly, a child born within the normal time after the termination of a marriage by the death of the husband or by divorce is presumed legitimate. That presumption of legitimacy can be rebutted by evidence showing beyond reasonable doubt that the husband could not have been the child's father – for example, where the husband was in Mongolia from January 1 to December 31 and his wife gave birth to a child on, say, December 30.

A child will only be illegitimate when the mother does not marry the father. If the mother does, however, marry the father following the birth of the child, the child may be legitimated, the legal effect of which is that the child is treated in most respects as the legitimate or lawful child. If the mother marries some person other than the natural father, her husband is not liable to maintain the illegitimate child. However, the mother and the husband may in such a case jointly adopt the mother's illegitimate child (see page 183). Roughly 20 per cent of the adoptions of illegitimate children are of this kind.

Custody. The mother has the right of custody of the illegitimate child, and the right to determine his religion. She has a duty (so long as she is single or a widow or separated from her husband) to maintain the child until he is 16.

Affiliation. The mother may apply to a Magistrates' Court for an 'affiliation order' against the man alleged to be the father. If the court grants the order, the father may be ordered to contribute a limited sum (no limit applies in Scotland) to the child's maintenance up to the age of 13, or 16 if the court so directs, or, where the child is engaged in a course of education or training, until the child reaches 21. In Northern Ireland an order may be made until the child, if a boy, reaches 15, or, if a girl, 16.

An illegitimate child and his parents have the same right to share in each other's estates on an intestacy as if the child were legitimate. (The word 'intestacy' means 'leaving no will'.) But even where a will has been made by a parent an illegitimate child may apply to the court (Family Division of the High Court) for some provision to be made to him out of the estate of his parent. Similar provisions apply in Scotland. The law of wills and succession to property is special, and a person who wishes to pursue his claim is wise to see a solicitor, and, if need be, obtain legal aid and advice (see page 445).

The attitude of the public generally has changed for the better over recent years, and this is reflected in legislation regarding birth certificates. The *Births and Deaths Registration Act, 1953*, and the corresponding legislation in Scotland and Northern Ireland, make provision for a short form of birth certificate which contains no particulars of parentage, and thus does not disclose an illegitimate birth.

Adoption and custodianship orders

The law has always accorded important rights to the members of a family – for example, rights of succession to property of a parent whether the parent left a will or not. The relationship of parent and child is not always one of blood: it can be created by adoption, first introduced into England in 1926 by the *Adoption of Children Act, 1926*. The present law is contained in the *Adoption Act, 1958*, the *Adoption Act, 1976* and the *Children Act, 1975*.

What is the effect of adoption? Adoption puts the adopted child (i.e. a person under 18) for all practical purposes in the same position as a child born in lawful wedlock to the adopter, except that the adopted child cannot inherit a title (e.g. a peerage) of its adoptive parents. Thus the adopter assumes all rights of custody, education and maintenance of the normal natural parent (unlike fostering where these rights remain with the natural parent or care authority). After the date of the adoption order, the adopted child is treated in law as the child of the adopter, and not the child of its natural parents.

Who may adopt? An infant (i.e. a person under 18) may be adopted by one person, male or female, or by a married couple. In either case the applicant must be (i) 25 years of age or over; or (ii) 21 years of age or over *and* a relative (grandparent, brother, sister, uncle or aunt) of the infant; or (iii) the mother or father of the infant, irrespective of age (see page 182).

A married couple may jointly adopt an infant, but unless one of them is the mother or father of the infant, conditions (i) and (ii) above must be satisfied in respect of one of the applicants, *and* the other spouse must have attained the age of 21. Orders of adoption will not usually be made for a man to be *sole* adopter of a girl.

The courts and their jurisdiction. The High Court (Family Division), County Courts and Magistrates' Courts have jurisdiction in adoption. All courts must be satisfied that certain requirements are fulfilled. On hearing an application, the court has to give first consideration to safeguarding and promoting the welfare of the child. It has also to ascertain, as far as practicable, the wishes and feelings of the child and to give consideration to them, having regard to the child's age and understanding.

The court must appoint a guardian *ad litem* (curator *ad litem* in Scotland) to safeguard the interests of the child before the court. The guardian is required to investigate the relevant circumstances and to report to the court.

When making an adoption order, the court may impose certain conditions; it may also make an interim order giving the custody of the child to the applicant for a probationary period not exceeding two years.

Consents. The consent is normally required of the parents or guardian of the child and of the other spouse where the adopter is married. The court may, however, dispense with parental consent in certain specified circumstances:

(i)   if the parent cannot be found;
(ii) if the parent has abandoned the child;
(iii) if the parent has persistently ill-treated the child.

Under the *Children Act, 1975*, the court may dispense with parental consent if the parent or guardian has seriously ill-treated the child and it is unlikely that the child will be able to live with such a parent. The court has to satisfy itself that the child's welfare cannot be secured if he is returned to his own family. A mother's consent to adoption is not valid if it is given before the child is six weeks old.

Religious preferences. Adoption agencies are required, under the *Children Act, 1975*, to consider, as far as practicable, the natural parents' religious preferences in placing a child for adoption. It is no longer possible, however, for such parents to make their consent to adoption subject to a condition about the child's future religious upbringing.

Payments. From 1982 (under the *Children Act, 1975*) adopters can be paid 'bed and board' allowances such as those paid to foster parents (see page 194).

Private adoption

If a person who is not the parent or guardian of the child participates in arrangements for placing a child below school-leaving age in the care and possession of another person who is not his parent or guardian or relative, he must notify the local authority not less than two weeks before the child is placed. After that, the person in whose care the child is placed must notify the local authority of changes of address or of the death of the child. Officers of the local authority must visit and give advice on the care of the child.

In 1986 there were 8,000 adoptions (mostly within families, by step parents). This contrasts with 24,000 in 1968 and 9,200 in 1982. The decline is due to the wider use of contraception (the birth rate has fallen from 17.9 per 1,000 in 1961 to 13.3 in 1987) and of abortion; thus there are fewer unwanted children. In addition, as a result of greater social acceptance, there is a growing tendency for unmarried mothers to retain and bring up their children. Consequently, only 20 per cent of adoptions involve babies (under one year). There are, according to the National Association of the Childless, an estimated 2 million people – one couple in six – who have problems conceiving. Couples wishing to adopt are becoming more willing to adopt the 'hard-to-place' children, and for some of these, (especially those over 12) the usual criterion of being a young married couple may not be required.

Adoption agencies

There are nearly 50 adoption societies in England, Scotland and Wales. Some are national and others are local societies. Some restrict services to certain groups, such as those of a particular religious denomination. Some adoption societies offer a range of child-care and family services; others deal with the selection of adoptive homes and the placement of children.

All adoption societies must be registered with the local authority in whose area their administrative centre is situated. The local authority must be satisfied that the society is a charitable organisation, properly administered, and its employees are competent. An Adopted Children Register is required to be kept by the Registrars-General for England and Wales, Scotland and Ulster. Local authorities now have a duty to provide an adoption service as part of their general social services for families and children.

The *Children Act, 1975* (being implemented over a number of years), provides that courts and adoption agencies should give *first* consideration to the need to promote the welfare of the child in any decision relating to adoption.

Local authorities are obliged to ensure that a comprehensive adoption service is available throughout their area. Such a service is operated in cooperation with any *approved* voluntary adoption society in the area. Adoption societies have to be approved in England by the Secretary of State for Social Services, in Scotland by the Secretary of State for Scotland and in Wales by the Secretary of State for Wales.

The Act introduces a new procedure for 'freeing a child for adoption'. This enables questions of parental agreement to be resolved before a child is placed for adoption. It will also ensure that arrangements can proceed in the knowledge that there are no last-minute changes of mind by parents. Applications to free a child for adoption may be made in the following circumstances:

(a)   A parent wishing to give early agreement to adoption may consent to an adoption agency applying to a court for parental rights to be transferred to the agency.

(b)   The agency may apply to a court for an order transferring parental rights in the case of a child in the care of a local authority or approved voluntary adoption society. This can only be done if the parents have refused to make up their minds about the child's future or have virtually abandoned the child and there is no realistic prospect of their being able to resume care of the child. The agency may then apply to the court for an order transferring parental rights and for parental agreement to adoption to be dispensed with on one of the statutory grounds. Parents will be able to contest the application and be eligible for legal aid.

Before making such an order the court has to satisfy itself that each parent or guardian had been given an opportunity to declare that he preferred not to be involved in future questions concerning the adoption of the child. If the parent or guardian did *not* make the declaration, he would have the right, 12 months after the making of the order, to be informed if an adoption order had been made or if the child had been placed for adoption. The Act provides that such a parent or guardian may apply for the revocation of the order freeing the child for adoption at any time 12 months from the date of the order, if no adoption had been made in respect of the child and if the child did not have his home with a person with whom he had been placed for adoption.

The Act, as under previous legislation, restricts the removal of a child from applicants for an adoption order where the parent has agreed to the making of the order. It also provides that people who have looked after a child for five years or more will be able to apply to adopt the child without the fear that the parent may remove the child before the hearing without leave of the court and so frustrate the application. In addition, the Act restricts the removal of a child once an adoption agency has made application for an order freeing a child for adoption without the consent of the child's parents.

Another provision of the 1975 Act enables adopted persons over the age of 18 in England and Wales to be given access to their birth records.

Custodianship. The *Children Act, 1975*, contains provisions under which, as an alternative to adoption, relatives and other people looking after children on a *long-term basis* would be able to obtain the legal custody of the children. This will be achieved in England and Wales by the creation of a new legal relationship conferred by a custodianship order. As the order will be revocable by a court, the link between the child and his natural parents will not be completely severed as with adoption.

The Act says that a child should have had his home with the applicant for at least three months before the application in the case of relatives and step-parents and 12 months for other applicants. The consent to the application by the person having legal custody of the child would be required unless the child had had his home with the applicant for at least three years. There would be restrictions, pending a court decision, on a child's removal from an applicant who had looked after the child for three years or more.

Protection and control of children

There are occasions when a court may make an order for the securing of the 'care and control' of a child or young person. Take the example where a father has been charged with wounding a member of his family – let us say, his daughter. If, on being charged, the case is remanded and the alleged offender is released on bail is it safe for him to go back to his home where he could harm another member of his family? There are many occasions where a child may be ordered to be taken into a 'place of safety' – such as a local authority foster home or a community home – in the best interests of the child. The order may be temporary or may be until the young person reaches 18.

The statutes. Laws providing for the care, protection and control of children include the Children and Young Persons Acts of 1933, 1963 and 1969 and the Children Acts of 1948 and 1975. These have been consolidated and largely superseded by the *Child Care Act, 1980* though there is to be further consolidation and some important changes in the *Children Bill, 1988* (see page 190). The 1933 Act stipulated that a Juvenile Court dealing with a child should have regard for his welfare, and, if necessary, take steps to remove him from undesirable surroundings and secure proper provision for his education and training. The 1948 Act required local authorities to set up Children's Departments with responsibility for the care of children deprived of a normal home life or committed to care by order of the court. The 1963 Act conferred on local authorities a *duty* to undertake preventive work with children and their families. If there was financial need, help could be provided, the principle being that it would be less costly to the State in the long run if aid were given early before a crisis in a family came about. The 1969 Act modifies the 'care' provisions of previous legislation and provides new options or alternative forms of treatment of children in trouble (see page 195).

The *Local Authority Social Services Act, 1970*, abolished the children's departments and set up a social services department (SSD) in each county council and metropolitan district council with staff to carry out the social work where need is shown.

A child in need of **care *or* control** is defined as one who is:

(a)   beyond the control of his parent or guardian; or
(b)   exposed to moral danger; or
(c)   is of compulsory school age and is not receiving efficient and suitable education e.g. through truancy; or
(d)   is guilty of an offence (excluding homicide); or
(e)   whose proper development is being avoidably prevented or neglected or his health is being avoidably impaired or neglected or he is being ill-treated.

Who starts proceedings? Any local authority, police constable or officer of the National (in Scotland, Royal) Society for the Prevention of Cruelty to Children (NSPCC) may bring before a Juvenile Court a child or young person whom they have reason to believe (perhaps as a result of inquiries following a neighbour's phone call) is in need of care, protection or control. It is the *duty* of the local authority to bring 'care proceedings' where there appear grounds for doing so, unless it is satisfied that action is undesirable in the child's interest or the public interest, or that some other person is taking action. Under the *Children and Young Persons (Amendment) Act, 1986* grandparents now have the right to become party to the proceedings.

If the court is satisfied that a child or young person is in need of care or control it may:

(a)   Issue a **care order** under which the child is committed to the care of the local authority.
(b)   Order his parent or guardian to enter into a **recognisance** (see page 198) to exercise proper guardianship.
(c)   Make a **supervision order**.
(d)   Issue a **hospital** or **guardianship** order under the *Mental Health Act, 1959*. (For this order to be made medical evidence is required by the Justices before they make their pronouncement.)

Note: The court can make an order only if: One or more of the conditions set out above has been complied with (e.g. is 'beyond control' or 'exposed to moral danger', etc.), and the court is of the opinion that the child is in need of care or control which he is unlikely to receive unless the order is made.

What is the effect of a care order? In effect, the child or young person is held in care by legal compulsion; parents have no choice. The local authority has *legal* custody of the child and the power to restrict his liberty where necessary. The order is reviewed every six months by the local authority and may be discharged at any time by the court following an application by (a) the local authority, (b) the child, or (c) his parent or guardian.

Care orders normally expire on the child's eighteenth birthday when he is in law an adult. But the order may be extended to the nineteenth birthday if a court is satisfied that it is in (a) the child's interest or (b) the public interest for him to continue to be accommodated in a 'community home'.

The 1969 Act provides that 'approved schools', 'remand homes' ('List D'schools in Scotland) and local authority and voluntary children's homes now become part of a comprehensive system of **community homes** available for all children in care. There are some 34,000 places in all, of which about 5,000 are in observation and assessment centres (see page 194) and 5,000 in community homes with education (known as CHEs). The aim of the latter is to provide care, treatment and education to build up the self-image of the children, increase their self-discipline and enable them to adjust better to the outside world. (It is estimated that each place in a CHE costs £15,000 a year.)

Where a court makes a **supervision order** the supervisor is (a) the local authority or (b) the probation officer (see page 199) depending on age. Either way, the supervisor is supposed to assist and befriend the child.

The above arrangements apply to England and Wales only. **Scotland** has its own legal system and judicial officers, and broadly similar measures have been enacted in Scotland for children and young persons there. The main Act is the *Social Work (Scotland) Act, 1968*, which created new local authority social work departments (SWDs) that include within their scope the probation services (kept separate in England and Wales) and the children's services.

In Scotland there are what are known as **Children's Hearings**, which have to a large extent replaced Juvenile Courts. The object of the hearings is to discuss in an informal way (e.g. with the child and parents present) the difficulties of children and to provide the most appropriate measures of care and treatment for those who need them. In Northern Ireland, the provisions are similar to those in England and Wales.

In recent years there has been alarm at the extent of non-accidental injury (NAI) to children (including baby battering). An estimated 1.5 million children are now suffering cruelty in Britain, and the NSPCC estimate that there are 44,000 children on child abuse registers (a 20 per cent increase since 1985, though this may be due to better detection or reporting, especially since the setting up, in 1986, of

'ChildLine', a free national helpline for children in trouble or danger; the number is 0800 1111). To try to deal with the problem, local authorities have drawn up 'risk-registers' based on reports of social workers, doctors, health visitors and teachers.

Since the death of Maria Colwell, there have been 35 child abuse inquiries. Recent cases concerned Doreen Mason (1989), Lucy Gates (1982), Reuben Carthy (1985), Jasmine Beckford (in a report *A Child in Trust*, 1985), Heidi Koseda (1986), Tyra Henry (in a report called *Whose Child*, 1987), and Kimberley Carlile (in a report *A Child in Mind*, 1987). These reports have variously put the blame for the tragedies on such factors as inexperience, inadequate training, bad timing or laxity by social workers, health visitors, doctors, magistrates or police; lack of management supervision and of child protection information systems; poor teamwork or communications, muddle and confusion arising from multi-agency involvement; insufficient powers to enter and inspect and if necessary remove children from their homes, coupled with an ignorance of the legal powers or opportunities available in this respect. A 1988 study by the London Boroughs' Training Committee suggests that it would cost over £1 million in London alone to train social worker staff in new child care legislation. Yet another factor is lack of resources and reduced staffing levels.

Child *sexual* abuse has become an area of particular concern. In 1988 the NSPCC estimated that over 7,000 children are subject to sexual abuse (though the official notified figure is 2,266 – a four-fold increase in five years). This was publicly highlighted as a result of the discovery of massive alleged child sexual abuse in Cleveland, in 1987, when 121 cases of abuse were diagnosed in five months and the children removed from their homes (through 'place of safety orders'). Most of them were subsequently returned home and there was a judicial inquiry, led by Lord Justice Butler-Sloss, into the evident excessive zeal and over-confidence of some of those involved. Like other child abuse reports, the inquiry (July 1988) attributed blame to lack of communication, ignorance, management failure as well as particular individuals. The report also made a number of recommendations concerning training, monitoring, inter-agency cooperation, the composition of child abuse committees, the rights of parents regarding access and information, and the application of various court orders (including place of safety, emergency protection, interim care and custody care orders).

A number of these recommendations have been incorporated in the **Children Bill, 1988** which aims to 'strike the balance between the need to protect children from harm and to enable parents to challenge any action which is taken', and it has been heralded as 'the most important change in child law in decades'. It proposes to: (a) Create a more unified legal code by bringing together the often fragmented and overlapping law on children scattered through some seven Acts (covering both the private sphere i.e. disputes between private individuals over custody and guardianship, and the public sphere i.e. regarding public authority intervention through care proceedings, supervisory orders etc.); (b) Replace the 28-day place of safety order with an 8-day emergency protection order; (c) Allow parents to challenge such an order after 72 hours, and to be represented at proceedings, and have new rights of access to children in care; (d) Strengthen the rights of children to be represented at care proceedings; (e) Limit the power of local authorities to pass a parental (or 'section 3') resolution whereby they can take over the rights of parents in relation to those children who have been *voluntarily* placed in the care of the council; there will be similar restriction on the use of wardship (i.e. where children are made wards of court); (f) Care orders for criminal offences are to go and be replaced by supervision orders for school truancy; (g) Care orders will be confined to situations where the child suffers 'significant harm' by parents or is beyond their control; (h) In the private aspect, replace custody and access orders with residence, contact, specified issues and prohibited steps orders; (i) Reform the law on private fostering and children's homes.

The Government has also published new guidance for social workers setting out a systematic approach to assessment and long-term planning in child protection cases, and emphasising the importance of involving the child and family throughout.

Abuse and cruel behaviour by parents cannot be excused. But many of them are themselves the products of bad parenting; many are young and immature (8,500 schoolgirls are pregnant by the age of 16); 1 in 10 mothers are separated or have no spouse; unemployment, poor housing and low income create strain and pressure (families with children in bed and breakfast accommodation increased from 11,000 in 1983 to 22,000 in 1986); some mothers just do not 'bond' with their child and others may 'blame' the child for their being unable to have a social life or career. Some of these problems are increased in the case of reconstituted or step families.

The reasons or excuses are many and varied, and the statutory organisations do not and should not always take a penal attitude. Instead, they may seek to provide positive and preventive help, such as day nursery provision or advice and assistance (e.g. in the form of substitute mums – known variously as 'homemakers', family aides or family helps – who visit or live with the family to guide and support the mother).

Similar help is provided by voluntary bodies, among which the best known are the NSPCC, the Family Welfare Association, Family Service Units, Family Groups and Mothers in Action. Others include Parents Anonymous, New Parent Infant Network ('Newpin') and the Crying Baby Relief Scheme. They may provide material aid. Equally they may provide counselling or advice and contacts about finance or housing or school problems. Clearly while some of the problem lies in individual and personal deficiencies, much is also rooted in the patterns and pressures of society at large.

Care of children deprived of normal home life

The *Child Care Act, 1980* (section 2), (which replaces the *Children Act, 1948* but note the *Children Bill, 1988*) states:

Where it appears to a local authority with respect to a child in its area appearing to be under the age of 17:

(a)   that he has neither parent nor guardian or has been and remains abandoned by his parents or guardian or is lost; or

(b)   that his parents or guardian are, for the time being or permanently, prevented by reason of mental or bodily disease or infirmity or other incapacity or any other circumstances from providing for his proper accommodation, maintenance and upbringing; **and**

(c)   in either case, that the intervention of the local authority under this section is necessary in the interests of the welfare of the child,

it shall be the **duty** of the local authority to receive the child into their care under this section.

A high proportion of children come into care under this provision (rather than by compulsion of a court order – see page 188). In other words many children are voluntarily brought into care by their parents (especially because of the latter's physical or mental illness or child-birth) and they can take them home again at will. Of course, local authorities do not accept all requests (parents must be genuinely unable to provide) and they may suggest day nursery as an alternative in order to keep families together. Also, there are financial charges involved.

They have a duty to return a child home as soon as possible consistent with the child's welfare and thus normally accede to a parent's request to have their child back (cf. care orders under which children are removed by court order and parents or the local authority must go back to court to free the child). Some children who are in care on a voluntary basis may nevertheless remain in care until they are 18 (e.g. orphaned or abandoned children). But many voluntary admissions (an estimated several thousand each year) may be converted to a compulsory status (under a 'parental rights resolution' or section 3 of the *Child Care Act, 1980*) if it appears to the local authority that 'a parent is of such habits and modes of life as to be unfit to have the care of the children'. Such a decision need not necessarily go before a court, and it is alleged that local authorities abuse their power in this respect, leaving the parent(s) at a loss and in despair. The Family Rights Group has been formed to protect such parents, and has recently succeeded in enhancing parental right of

Table 7   Admissions to the care of local authorities, England and Wales, 1985

	Sub-total	Total
In voluntary care (under the *Child Care Act, 1980*)		
• illness, incapacity of parent	4,800	
• death, desertion, imprisonment of parent, abandoned	11,900	33,650
• homeless, unsatisfactory home	8,400	
• other reasons	8,550	
In care by order (under the *Children and Young Persons Act, 1969*)		
• neglect or ill-treatment	17,000	
• exposed to danger	3,000	
• not receiving education	2,900	34,000
• beyond control	2,800	
• guilty of offence	9,300	
Other reasons (divorce, on remand etc.)		11,100
		78,750

Source: DHSS Statistics 1987

access to children in care (clarified in the *Health, Social Services, Social Security Act, 1983*); see too *Children Bill, 1988* (page 190).

Numbers received. We live in troubled times. Divorce (at 160,000 p.a.) is at record levels. One family in 8 (with 1½ million children) is headed by a lone parent, and 20 per cent of children can expect to experience a divorce of their parents (40 per cent if we include separation). Once a marriage is broken down, Marriage Guidance (now called 'Relate') and the Courts Family Conciliation Service try to ease disputed matters (such as custody of children, access, property and finance). Unemployment too is high at over 2 million plus many (especially women) workers who have become redundant but have not registered. And there is the perennial problem of ill-health which may prevent parents from adequately looking after their children.

Consequently the numbers in care increased in the 1970s: from 62,200 in 1961, to 87,400 in 1971 and to 105,000 in 1981. This represents an increase from 0.5 to 0.8 per cent of the age group (under 18). However, part of this increase is explained by a change of definition (to include those in remand homes and approved schools – List D schools in Scotland – after the *Children and Young Persons Act, 1969*) and the numbers in care have fallen since to 6.5 per cent today. This is due partly to more children being retained by their unmarried mother (see page 171), to the increased belief that separating children from their parents can cause more damage than leaving the family together and to the increased preventive work of local authorities and others.

Where children are placed. The general aim should be to find a substitute home as much like a good, normal home as possible. The work of Dr Bowlby has shown how important a close, secure and loving atmosphere is for a child's development. In practice there is a range of possibilities, and they are currently used to the following extents:

- fostering   48%
- community homes (council)   22%
- guardian, relative, parent, friend   17%
- lodgings, flat   10%
- voluntary homes   3%

Of these community homes are the most expensive, costing over £15,000 per child – six times the cost of fostering. In addition, some children are adopted. We consider some of these options below:

(i) **Residential homes.** Most of these are now provided by local authorities themselves who staff them with a house mother and other helpers depending on the size of the home. Compared to the past, children's (or 'community') homes today are generally smaller – typically holding about 10 children. However, some children do seem better suited to the less emotionally demanding larger homes and teenagers may prefer hostel-type accommodation. Other children (admitted by court order) are often placed in the **community homes** which replaced approved schools and remand homes in the 1970s. There is thus a range of community home provision to cater for the different types and condition of the children. In addition, there is the accommodation provided by voluntary bodies (e.g. the National Children's Home) who have about 12,000 places. Allocation of the children occurs at **observation and assessment centres** or reception homes. Altogether, about one third of children in care are placed in community homes. (ii) **Foster homes.** Since the 1948 Act (and the preceding 'Curtis Report', 1946) these (technically known as 'boarding out') have been the preferred form of care, since they involve children living in with ordinary (though carefully chosen) families. The foster parents are paid a weekly allowance to cover their additional costs. About half of children in care are boarded out with 27,000 foster parents. However, there is a shortage of willing couples and some 8,000 children are on a two-year waiting list of placements. Part of the problem is inadequate payments to cover the costs of caring. But according to the National Foster Care Association, there is also a lack of training and emotional support, especially for those who have the more difficult job of fostering teenagers, handicapped children and those who have been sexually abused. Foster care does not suit all children and there are breakdowns in the arrangement, with much upset to child or host family. There is also the risk of inadequate supervision of such placements by the local authority social services departments (PSS). Local authority and voluntary homes are subject to central government inspection. (iii) **Adoption**. This has been dealt with on pages 183–6. It may be mentioned, however, that the aim of the new arrangement to pay adopters is to make it less difficult for foster parents (who are paid) to adopt (and not lose their allowances).

Private provision. In addition to voluntary and local authority community homes and boarding out, there is private provision. A number of such profit-making homes exist in the South East of England. Private fostering (which excludes the short-term good neighbour arrangements) is more widespread, and may or may not involve payments. Either way it is regulated by the *Foster Children Act, 1980* (which replaces the *Children Act, 1958*, in England and Wales): thus the foster home must register with the local authority, must be open to inspection and may have to comply with certain regulations.

Similarly, premises used for **child minding** have to be registered if children are looked after on a daily basis for two hours or more each day. Conditions may be imposed regarding staffing and standard of accommodation (though while some 80,000 are so registered, it is estimated that perhaps 100,000–300,000 are not; see page 173).

Treatment of offenders

This century has witnessed a revolution in our attitude to juvenile offenders; firstly in the setting up of separate Juvenile Courts (1908). Secondly the *Children and Young Persons Act, 1933*, declared that the welfare of the child offender should be considered alongside the offence itself. Then in the 1960s, it was argued that the welfare of the young offender should take precedence over the offence itself. Consequently, where the 1933 Act recognised the impact of environment on a child's behaviour and it sought to remove the child from that (harmful) environment, the *Children and Young Persons Act, 1969*, seeks to keep the young offender in his community but work with him in that context – especially the family context. The importance of the family in the creation and prevention of maladjustment and delinquent behaviour is now recognised and it is widely accepted that the young offender and his family are in need of help like that given to the deprived child and his family. In other words, there is a case for treating disturbed, delinquent and deprived children in the same way since the child is the product of his home and not a separate responsible individual. The problem is one of discovering the causes of child offending, and of deciding at what age a child can be held to be rational or truly guilty of his offence.

Law relating to children and young persons

A child **under 10** (in Scotland 8) is not criminally liable for any offence. Thus if, say, Tom aged 9, has broken into premises and stolen money, nothing will be done by way of charging him with the offence and bring him before a law court.

Between the ages of **10 and 14** a child is liable for any crime he commits if the court finds that such child **knew** his conduct to be wrongful. Generally it is held that a juvenile of this age is not capable of knowing his actions are wrong: it is presumed that he cannot form 'a guilty intent'. Consequently, he is dealt with under the ambit of *civil* (i.e. care) proceedings. But this presumption is 'rebuttable', i.e. it may be established that he did know what he was doing was wrong. In this case the young offender is prosecuted under *criminal* proceedings. The net result either way is little different since the Juvenile Court procedure (see below) is similar in each case, and the subsequent decisions (orders or penalities) are substantially the same (see below).

Juveniles **over 14 and under 17** are fully liable for their criminal acts, in the same way as an adult. The main difference is that the offender is charged before a Juvenile Court and he will be treated in a different way once a finding of guilt is established. Furthermore if a young offender (10–17) is believed to be in need of care, protection or control he will be dealt with under (civil) care proceedings.

The situation is somewhat fluid and complex because the *Children and Young Persons Act, 1969*, introduced fundamental changes, but these are yet to be fully implemented and some are being superseded by subsequent legislation. However, one intention of the 1969 Act is to raise the age of criminal responsibility to 14; thus anyone under 14 would only be liable to care proceedings. Alternatively, the current practice would continue, so that in some cases the police consult with the social services department and may decide that a caution will be sufficient, so that the child is formally warned by the police and there are no further proceedings. At the moment about 50 per cent of juvenile offenders are dealt with in this way (plus an unknown number who are informally cautioned or 'ticked off' by police officers and are thus not recorded).

The general procedure where a juvenile has committed a very serious offence is that he will be committed for trial by a Magistrates' Court and the proceedings will be finally determined by a Crown Court.

Procedure in juvenile courts

Special rules apply. The main rule is that the magistrates in a Juvenile Court must explain the substance of the charge ('You are brought before us because the police found you at 1 a.m. on December 1 in

Woolworth's Stores in the High Street and when you were searched you had £500 in notes on you', etc.). The object is to let the juvenile know precisely and clearly why he is at the court. Where an application is made for the child or young person to be taken into care, again the procedure and reason for it is explained to the child or young person if he is capable of understanding.

The parents or guardians may be required to attend at court during all stages of the proceedings – for example, when the child is remanded or the case adjourned, or (if the child is committed for trial) at a Crown Court.

The courts show great care in the use of language. The words 'conviction' or 'sentence' (each has an unpleasant overtone) are not used in relation to children or young persons. The phrases 'finding of guilt' and 'order of the court' are substituted for them.

Once the court has determined the guilt of the offender on the evidence before it, the court must, before deciding on his treatment, consider any information concerning school record, health, character, home conditions. The information may be provided by a social worker or probation officer who will gather information from his own knowledge of the offender's home, etc., and from the school by an approach to the headmaster. The social worker or probation officer gives his evidence to the court so that the magistrates may make up their minds as to the most suitable treatment or 'order' which they may prescribe.

Remand. This is the process by which a court in England and Wales adjourns the case in the course of hearing a charge and remands the accused. Thus, let us assume that the magistrates sitting in a Juvenile Court cannot conclude the inquiry that day. The court may remand the accused either (i) on bail or (ii) in a remand centre, or to the care of a local authority. If the court is satisfied that the accused is of so unruly a character that he cannot safely be committed to local authority care, the accused will be remanded to a remand home. Very exceptionally he may be sent to a prison, e.g. where it is impossible to control him in a remand or community home.

Orders which the court may make

In *care* proceedings the court may:

(a) Issue a 'care' order.
(b) Order the parent or guardian to enter into a recognisance to exercise proper guardianship.
(c) Make a supervision order.
(d) Issue a hospital or guardianship order under the *Mental Health Act, 1959.*

In *criminal* proceedings, the court may additionally:

(e)   Impose a fine up to £50.
(f)   Order payment of compensation to the person injured.
(g)   Grant a conditional discharge.
(h)   Grant an absolute discharge.
(i)   Order attendance at an attendance centre.
(j)   Order detention in a detention centre.
(k)   Commit the offender to the Crown Court with a view to borstal.

These orders are described in more detail below.

1   **Care order.** Where a child or young person commits a criminal offence the magistrates may, after considering all the factors of the case, order that the child be committed to the care of the local authority. The care order places the local authority in *loco parentis* to the child or young person. The local authority assumes the entire discretion of what to do with the person committed to their care and may: (i) board the child out with foster parents; (ii) maintain him in a community home or a voluntary home; (iii) place him in the charge of a parent, guardian, relative or friend (about one third of all children in care are placed here).

Magistrates have no power to send a child direct to a home or order that he be kept in a secure home. The magistrates may suggest what might be done, but the actual decision is made by the local authority social services' department. However, under the *Criminal Justice Act, 1982*, JPs now have the power to issue 'residential care' orders and also extend community service orders to 16 year olds (see page 391).

Many difficulties arise in regard to seriously disturbed or difficult children. These may require residential places in community homes. Wardens of community homes have been known to refuse to admit particularly difficult children or young persons. The admission of one particular person might upset the home itself and the progress of the other children and young persons already in care. Consequently special secure units are being established (e.g. in Surrey, Lambeth and Leicestershire). See page 201.

2   **Binding over parent by recognisance.** Where a court finds that the parent(s) have not exercised proper control over a child or young person it may order that they enter into a recognisance (i.e. a bond) to exercise proper control in the future. The effect of this order is that if the child falls into trouble – for example, by committing a criminal offence – and it is found that the effective cause of this is lack of proper parental control and guardianship, the court may order the parent to forfeit the sum of money named in the recognisance.

3   **Supervision order.** A supervision order for a specified period of

up to three years may be imposed. Supervision of a child under 13 years of age is carried out by a local authority social worker (a probation officer may be appointed if he or she is already working with the child's family). For children aged 13 to 16 supervision is carried out either by a social worker or a probation officer. The supervisor is intended to assist and befriend.

Certain conditions may be attached to a supervision order such as: a requirement to undergo treatment for a mental condition, to reside with a named person (e.g. relatives), to participate in specified activities or a requirement to undergo 'intermediate treatment' (or IT).

Intermediate treatment is a form of provision which falls between complete removal from home (to a custodial institution) and leaving the child at home. It consists of participation in a variety of constructive and remedial activities either through short residential courses or through attendance at day or evening centres. The object is to bring the child into contact with a new environment, giving him an opportunity to develop new interests and give a sense of involvement and achievement. Often treatment involves the child in activities with children who have not been before the courts.

The weakness of the supervision order is that where a child or young person refuses to follow the direction of the supervisor there is no way the court can enforce obedience. Social workers do not, as a general rule, regard themselves as a punishing body, and the magistrates who imposed the order cannot follow it up or ensure that supervision is in fact being exercised. Where a person is placed on probation and commits a breach of the order, the matter is reported to the court who may punish the offender for the breach committed, or he may be sentenced for the original offence commmited. While there have been some enthusiastic developments here, intermediate treatment is generally underdeveloped, largely through lack of resources.

4 **Order under Mental Health Act, 1959.** This order may be made by a court to ensure that where a child or young person is found to be in need of treatment for his mental state he may be ordered to be detained in a mental hospital or to attend on a day basis.

5 **Fine.** A court may fine a child or young person any sum up to a maximum of £50. This power is in practice difficult to enforce. There is also a power to order a parent or guardian to pay a fine, but here too the power is hedged by qualifications and unavailable in a great many cases when it would otherwise be useful.

6 **Compensation order.** The maximum compensation which a defendant may be ordered to pay to a person who has been attacked or

whose property has been damaged is £1,000. The intention behind this provision is that the culprit should make good the damage or injury he has caused. However, the order is of no great use where the culprit is without the means to pay compensation, as when he is a child or young person or an adult who is unemployed or receiving a low wage.

7   **Conditional discharge.** Here the offencer, being found guilty, is discharged subject to the condition that he does not commit another offence. If he does, he will be liable to be sentenced for the original offence. The condition cannot remain in force for more than three years.

8   **Absolute discharge.** This order may be made by a court where it finds the accused guilty, but, having regard to all the circumstances, thinks it inexpedient to inflict any punishment or to impose a probation order.

9   **Attendence centres.** There are some 60 centres for boys under 17 in England and Wales. These will continue in existence for the time being until some alternative form of treatment is devised for such boys for whom probation and fine are inappropriate. So, where a boy is convicted of an offence for which, were he an adult, he would have been sentenced to imprisonment, the Juvenile Court may order that he attended at one of the centres.

The boy must attend during his spare time on a Saturday. The period he spends there may be up to three hours on any one occasion and for a total of not more than 24 hours. So the boy could be ordered to attend for eight Saturdays consecutively on each occasion for three hours. The activities include physical training and instruction in handicrafts or other practical subjects. Efforts are made by the staff at the centres to induce boys to join a youth club or other similar organisation.

10   **Detention centres.** These centres provide a form of treating young offenders for whom a long period of residential training in an approved school (now a community home) or borstal does not seem necessary, but who cannot be taught respect for the law by fines or probation. There are four **junior centres** in England and Wales for boys between 14 and 17 years of age, and 13 **senior centres** for boys between 17 and 21. In Scotland there is one senior centre.

The period of detention in England and Wales may not be for less than three months and not more than six months (amended to 3 weeks–4 months under 1982 legislation – see page 391). If an offender is sentenced to consecutive terms of detention (as when a boy is sentenced to two periods of detention for two separate offences, such detention to 'follow on' as it were) the *total* term may not exceed nine months at any one time. If the offender is of good conduct during the period of detention he may earn remission of sentence of up to one third.

In Scotland the fixed period for *all* detention centre sentences is three months, and the age of the detainee ranges from 16 to 21.

The intention behind the detention centres is to provide a 'short, sharp shock'. The life at the centre is strict and vigorous, and there is emphasis on high standards of discipline and behaviour. The keynote is positive training in a routine. The normal working week is 44 hours, including one hour daily devoted to physical training. Boys of compulsory school age receive full-time education, and for others over 16 there are classes of further education which are provided in the evenings. In 1980, several such centres were nominated to provide especially rigorous routines for detainees. On discharge from the detention centres the boys are placed under statutory supervision for up to 12 months by probation officers.

11 **Borstal or youth custody centres.** There are 23 such institutions in England and Wales for the treatment of young persons between 15 and 21, male and female. Different types of young offender are classified according to age, intelligence and criminal sophistication. There are a few borstals for special purposes; for example, for allocation or recall. The period of detention in a borstal varies from six months to two years. After release the young offender is subject to supervision for two years from the date of release. The supervision is undertaken by the probation service. Scotland has a somewhat different procedure: the maximum period of detention is two years (there is no minimum period) and supervision on release is for one year only. In Northern Ireland the period of detention ranges from six months or two years, which is followed by supervision for one year from date of release.

Many borstals are 'open' establishments, and there is much freedom of movement in these. Emphasis is placed on vocational training in skilled trades and education. For these purposes the staff at the borstals are carefully chosen. When an offender is sentenced to borstal, the first step is one of classification so that the particular offender is sent to the institution most suited to his personality, character and ability.

12 **Young prisoners' centres.** As a general rule, no person may be sent to prison who is under 17 years of age. A few who are unruly and cannot safely be detained in any other institution may, however, be sent to prison even if they are younger. Young prisoners' centres are those centres for persons over 17 and under 21 who are sentenced to imprisonment. The centres provide special training suited to the age and character of the offenders. On release the offenders are subject

to supervision under licence for a period equal to the amount of remission (usually one third of the full sentence). The minimum period of supervision is six months. The probation service undertakes the supervision of the young offender. The distinction between borstals and young persons prisons is to disappear under the *Criminal Justice Act, 1982*, with the creation of 'youth custody' sentences.

Success or failure?

There are two different judgements on the achievement of the 1969 Act and its underlying philosophy. The first sees it as having failed: not only is Britain one of two countries which imprison the most young offenders (with over 3,000 so held in 1980, awaiting trial or sentence: another estimated 2,000 are locked up in secure units in children's homes and youth treatment centres), but our juvenile crime rate is alarmingly high and many JPs feel that their powers (especially the imposition of care orders) have become too restricted and provided a 'soft option' for delinquents. As a result they have allegedly over-reacted by seeking to impose heavier and custodial sentences, especially the use of detention centres and (via the Crown Court) borstals. (In fact the number of young offenders sent here has increased fivefold during 1965–79. And yet the reconviction rates, after discharge, are between 75 and 83 per cent.)

The other view is that the 1969 Act's community approach has not failed because it has not really been tried, i.e. many elements have not been implemented, e.g. only 25 per cent of juvenile offenders were given supervision or care orders during 1978. In particular is intermediate treatment underdeveloped and social workers as a result are themselves placing more delinquents in residential care (where re-offending rates are high) rather than at home supported by community-based schemes.

Experimental schemes. The increase in crime among children and young persons (including those under 21) is alarming. The question of how to treat this class of offender is one which bothers the responsible governments in all civilised countries. Experiments are therefore continually being made to find the best form of treatment.

One of these is Northorpe Hall, Yorkshire, which enables boys between 12 and 16 *voluntarily* to spend short periods away from home at weekends, etc. The boys' families are much involved, developing something of a partnership, and are given help or advice if needed. The scheme is supported by the probation service, local authority social services and voluntary organisations.

The Rainer Foundation also runs experimental schemes for boys on probation at day and evening centres. They aim to encourage self-discipline, self-confidence and group discipline. Thus physical education and outdoor pursuits (climbing, camping, canoeing, etc.) are provided together with basic education and life skills for those with social and educational disabilities. Young Concern in Hastings provides full-time residential care for disturbed or delinquent young people.

A further development is that of special **fostering**, i.e. having selected families to take in difficult youngsters. Apart from thus keeping them in the community, this 'professional' fostering is also cheaper (at £70 a week) than residential (at over £200 p.w. in Community Homes or CHEs, which have superseded approved schools – see page 189).

In the meantime, the aim must be to take preventive action where possible, by working with and through families.

General protection of children

Offences against children

In most civilised societies there is a considerable amount of law to protect children and young persons from harm, though, it is one thing to make the law, but it is quite another to enforce all its provisions.

The *Children and Young Persons Act, 1933*, is the main statute for England and Wales. Scotland and Northern Ireland have similar statutes. It is an offence punishable by fine or imprisonment for *any* person over 16 who has the custody, charge or care of any child or young person under 16 wilfully to: (a) assault, (b) ill-treat, (c) neglect, (d) abandon him, or (e) expose him, or (f) cause or procure him to be assaulted, ill-treated, neglected, abandoned or exposed in a manner likely to cause him unnecessary suffering or injury to health. These offences may be committed by parents, guardians, foster parents – or, *any* person, as the statute states. Other offences are: (a) Causing or allowing persons under 16 to be used for begging. (b) Giving intoxicants to children under five. (c) Causing or allowing children under 14 to be in bars of licensed premises. (d) Selling tobacco to persons under 16. (e) Preventing children from receiving education. (f) Exposing a child under 12 (7 in Northern Ireland and Scotland) to the risk of burning. (g) Failing to provide for safety of children at entertainments.

Sexual offences are prosecuted under the *Sexual Offences Act, 1956*. For example, it is an offence to cause or encourage the seduction or prostitution of girls under 16. The *Consumer Protection Act, 1961*, requires that nightdresses designed for children shall be made of a material which meets a prescribed standard of low inflammability.

The main statute which prohibits offences commited against children and young persons is the *Offences against the Person Act, 1861*. This is a general statute but there are other particular statutes and, indeed, the common law which, taken together, provide the legislation dealing with all sorts of offences including murder, manslaughter, infanticide, wounding, sexual offences of rape, incest, indecent assault and other assaults.

Where there is reasonable suspicion that an offence has occurred the police should be informed and if an offence is disclosed suitable action will be taken to prosecute the offender. The child or young person will be cared for as shown on page 187. Cruelty cases are sometimes notified to the NSPCC who may take appropriate action if an offence is disclosed.

Employment of children and young persons

The *Employment of Women, Young Persons and Children Act, 1920*, prohibits the employment of children below the limit of compulsory school age (now 16) from employment in mines, factories, building and engineering construction works, railways and transport undertakings. Similarly, the employment of children in ships at sea is also prohibited. There are exceptions in respect of members of the same family employed upon the vessel, or where it is approved work on a school or training ship.

The law on employment of children is contained in the *Children and Young Persons Act, 1933* and *1969* (as amended), and the *Children Act, 1972*. Broadly, the legislation imposes considerable restrictions on the employment of children under school-leaving age, but gives local education authorities (LEAs) power to make bylaws which modify or supplement the statutory provisions in certain respects.

Employment of a child **under 13** is prohibited (unless authority is given in local bylaws for him to be employed by parent or guardian in light agricultural or horticultural work). **Over 13**, while at school, he may not be employed before the close of school hours on any day on which he is required to attend school (unless local bylaws authorise his employment for not more than one hour before school hours); before 7 a.m. or after 7 p.m. in the evening on any day; for more than two hours on any day on which he is required to attend school; or on any Sunday. A child may not be required to lift, carry or move anything so heavy as might injure him.

Young persons under 18 employed in industrial premises (factories, docks, warehouses, etc.) are protected by the *Factories Act, 1961* (which is enforced by the Factory Inspectors of the Department of Employment). Those between **16 and 18** may normally work up to 48 hours in a week (nine in any one day). Extra hours are allowed (e.g.

up to 6 hours per week) but not more than 100 in a year. Those **under 16** are limited to 44 hours a week. The Act also prescribes intervals for meals.

Bylaws

Local authority bylaws may prohibit absolutely the employment of children in any specified occupation or may prescribe conditions, such as the age below which children are not to be employed. Thus a local authority may prescribe a later minimum age, say 14, than that provided by the general legislation applying to all parts of England and Wales; or again a local authority may prescribe the maximum number of hours which may be worked, the meal and rest intervals and the holidays to be allowed. Occupations deemed unsuitable for children and prohibited by most local authorities are employment in: barbers' shops; kitchens or catering shops; billiard saloons (as an attendant); slaughter-houses and similar establishments.

Delivery of newspapers and milk are subject to special rules. Bylaws permit these employments by children before school hours, but a condition is imposed that the employment shall not begin before 7 a.m.

Bylaws commonly adopted require the employer to see that a child employed out of doors is suitably clad for protection against bad weather. Some bylaws require the child to be medically examined before he can be employed, and many local authorities have fixed a maximum of five hours' work a day on school holidays, and a weekly maximum of 25 hours.

The *Education Act, 1944*, states that, if it appears to a local education authority that a school child (under 16) is being employed in such a manner as to be prejudicial to his health, or otherwise render him unfit to obtain the full benefit of his education, it (i.e. the authority) may prohibit the employer from employing the child or impose restrictions upon his employment of the child.

Agricultural work. The general law applies to this work as to all other work in that the lifting, carrying or moving anything so heavy as to be likely to cause a child injury is prohibited. Some local authorities have enacted bylaws prohibiting work involving heavy strain or work under the control of a gang master, and many provisions for safeguarding the child's health and welfare by requiring medical certificates to be obtained before employment may be undertaken.

Street trading. Persons under 17 are in general prohibited from street trading, but exceptions exist (e.g. where the young person is employed by parents).

Entertainment. This means generally appearing and performing on stage (as a singer, actor, etc.). Restrictions apply under 16, but local authority licenses give exceptions.

Going abroad. Restrictions apply to any person under 18 who may be sent abroad for the purpose of singing, playing, performing or being exhibited for profit. Exceptions are made in some cases where a licence is obtained.

General services for children and young persons

Deciding when or whether to intervene in a family is seldom easy: social workers are blamed for interfering, or they are blamed for not intervening soon enough. Certainly cases such as those of Maria Colwell, Wayne Brewer, Stephen Menheniott, Stephen Meurs, John Aukland, Lucie Gates, Kimberley Carlile, Jasmine Beckford, Tyra Henry and others have revealed problems of communication, bureaucracy, and over-emphasis on the importance of the natural family. But such decisions are always a matter of judgement and it is always easy to be wise after the event. The ideal and the broad trend of recent years has been to **prevent** the break up of the family and the bringing of children into care: the Seebohm Report, 1968 (see page 402), the recent and pending legislation and the work of voluntary bodies bear witness to this. But equally important is the general help and support which the State provides. These are summarised below, receiving fuller treatment in the other chapters.

Financial help to families

1 **Family benefits.** These are financial payments to parents in respect of children below certain age limits (see page 57).
2 **National insurance.** Unemployment, sickness and injury benefits, widowhood and industrial injury all attract grants of money or benefits payable by the State (see page 57).
3 **Income support.** These aim to bring the income of a person up to a defined level. The benefits, including Family Credit and the Social Fund are described in more detail on page 56.
4 War pensions and allowances. These are payable to widows and children of servicemen (see page 57).

Services for mothers and young children

1 **Maternity and child health services.** For details of ante-natal and post-natal care, clinics, health centres and hospitals, see page 168.
2 **Welfare foods service.** See page 168.

3 **Vaccination and immunisation.** See page 168.
4 **Nurseries, playgrounds and nursery schools.** See pages 172–3.

Services for schoolchildren

1 **School health services.** For this service, which includes medical and dental inspections under the School Health Service, see page 237.
2 **Clothing.** Provision is made to avoid children being ill-clad (see page 237).
3 **Transport.** The local education authority is required to provide transport for children in certain circumstances to attend school (see page 237).
4 **Education welfare service.** This service investigates non-attendance at school and refers cases in which families are in difficulty to social welfare agencies, including the educational psychologist and child guidance.
5 **School counselling.** Children and young persons at school may have personal problems. The schools and colleges appoint a teacher to act as a counsellor and adviser to those students in difficulties with such problems. This is sometimes known as 'pastoral care'.

Employment and training

The Departments of Employment and Education are responsible for a number of arrangements which seek to provide employment, careers guidance and training for school-leavers and young workers. (See Chapter 12.)

Youth services

Clubs and youth organisations. There is a wide variety of organisations available for young people from seven or eight to the age of 21. The object of the organisations is to provide leisure-time activities. So young children may join the Wolf Clubs or Brownies at seven or eight and then move on to join the Scout troops and Girl Guide companies. These are voluntary organisations, about half of which are sponsored by a church or chapel. Others are attached to schools or community centres.

Responsibility for youth service. This is shared in Britain by the Department of Education and Science (DES), the local education authorities (LEAs) and the wide range of voluntary organisations existing in Britain. The object of the three groups is to provide for the leisure-time activities of young people under 21, although many admit members over this age. Some organisations provide educational and religious as well as social and recreational activities, and an increasing number now offer service to the community (the town, city or village from which the organisation springs).

The DES (and equivalent departments in Scotland and Northern Ireland) provide grants in aid (money) to the administrative and training work of national voluntary youth organisations, and towards the cost of premises and equipment of youth clubs provided by voluntary bodies. LEAs cooperate with voluntary organisations in their areas: most give financial aid, lend premises and equipment; and most authorities employ youth organisers to help to promote and encourage youth work.

Charitable trusts (notably the King George Jubilee Trust) exist to give financial help for special projects. The greater part of the funds of the voluntary organisations is raised, however, by their own efforts.

The variety of organisations. The **Scout Association** was founded in 1908, and the **Girl Guides** in 1910, 'to develop character and good citizenship' in boys and girls. Total membership in Britain is more than 500,000 Scouts and about 700,000 Guides. The individual groups are run by leaders who give their spare time voluntarily to this work.

The **National Association of Boys' Clubs** has over 2,000 affiliated clubs and 165,000 members; and the **National Association of Youth Clubs** has some 3,350 affiliated clubs with 357,000 members whose ages range from 14 to 20.

The **Combined Cadet Force**, the **Army Cadet Force** and the **Air Training Corps** are pre-service organisations which combine social, educational and physical development with training for possible entry into the armed forces.

The **British Red Cross Society** and the **St John Ambulance Association and Brigade** youth sections train members in first aid and nursing. The **National Federation of Young Farmers' Clubs** and its Scottish counterpart encourage young people to appreciate the countryside and foster interest in agricultural subjects and rural crafts.

Voluntary service by young people to the community

All the above organisations assist the community on occasions, but recently there has been a notable trend for young people to combine together to give voluntary service to such as the elderly, the sick and the handicapped.

Voluntary service of this kind is promoted by bodies like Task Force, Community Service Volunteers (CSV) and the International Voluntary Service. In 1969 the Government established the Young Volunteer Force Foundation as an independent body to advise interested organisations in England and Wales on methods of involving young people in providing service to the community. The Foundation is grant-aided by the Government and employs teams of young people who are available on request to assist such bodies as local authorities, voluntary organisations and hospital boards in encouraging and promoting voluntary service. In Scotland, a similar organisation, **Enterprise Youth**, has been established.

Help to hospitals is given by the **Volunteer Emergency Service**, a group of young motor-cyclists who transport blood and drugs in answer to urgent calls for assistance. Young people also play an active part in fund raising for charitable organisations such as **Shelter**, which offers help to provide accommodation for the homeless, and **Oxfam** which assists in development in the poorer countries of the world and many local charities.

Some of the above organisations receive grants from the education departments of local authorities, and thousands of young people are doing voluntary work for the community. The opportunity is given to the young folk to 'run their own show in their own way' free from the local bureaucracy.

Other schemes and organisations

The **Outward Bound Trust** and **Operation Raleigh** promote character training through courses based on adventure and testing experience and maintains schools for young people. The **Duke of Edinburgh's Award Scheme** is operated by local authorities, schools, youth organisations, industrial companies and other bodies, and is designed to challenge boys and girls to reach certain standards of achievement in leisure-time activities. There are three awards: Bronze, Silver and Gold, for each of which young people must attempt activities in four out of five sections: service; interest; expeditions; and either physical activity or design for living. The **Youth Hostels Association** has a network of youth hostels for walkers and cyclists, and offers simple accommodation at a low charge. Thus young people can travel all over Britain at very reasonable cost, and improve their knowledge of both town and country. Many young people in their late teens go abroad without their parents, through voluntary service schemes to short work camps, or as independent travellers, especially to countries well provided with youth hostels and camping sites.

A pressure group which seeks to protect and promote the interests of young people in many different directions has been formed. Known as **Youthaid** it has emerged largely in response to the growing unemployment of young people (that this is the main worry of young people has been revealed or confirmed in the recent Thompson Report – see below). This reminds us that with 2 million unemployed, widespread domestic violence, 1½ million children living at or below the poverty line and an equal number living in single-parent families, the variety of specific services for children and young persons will be ineffective unless we help their parents. This implies a policy for dealing with some of the more fundamental problems of society including poverty, unemployment, and homelessness, together with a reallocation of resources within the health, education and environmental services.

The Thompson Report

The Thompson Report on the Youth Service in England (*Experience and Participation*, HMSO, October, 1982), whilst praising the flexibility and inventiveness of the mixed State and voluntary provision for youth, was largely critical. The Report drew attention to: (a) the very uneven nature of provision, (b) the lack of coordination within and between the two sectors and (c) their inadequate planning and management. But above all, (d) it criticised the failure of the youth service to fulfil what it saw as its primary function of promoting the personal and social development of young people. 'The fundamental purpose of the youth service is to provide programmes of personal development comprising . . . social and political education' and yet its links with the community were under-developed and young people themselves were insufficiently encouraged or allowed to organise their own activities.

The Report pointed out that a significant minority of young people felt outsiders in society and should be helped by the youth service to react positively and constructively through: (i) counselling and guidance, (ii) reducing the source of their alienation (e.g. unemployment) and (iii) developing their capacity to play an active part in changing their own conditions (including a programme of political education in an active, issue-based sense) and making a contribution to the economic and social life of their community.

Thus throughout the Report the education role of the youth service is emphasised, particularly in the field of 'social education'. To this end it recommends that LEAs' present optional power (under the *Education Act, 1944*) be converted into a mandatory duty to both secure and coordinate the provision for young people, and at national level a minister within the DES be appointed to coordinate all government work on youth affairs.

Questions

1   Under the *Children and Young Persons Act, 1969*, what is a 'child' and a 'young person'? When is a child deemed 'in need of care or control'? Who may start 'care proceedings'? What is the effect of a 'care order'? What is a 'supervision order' and 'intermediate treatment'?

2 What are the parental rights in regard to the child of a marriage?
3 What is meant by 'adoption' and what is legal effect? Who may adopt a child, and what courts have jurisdiction in this sphere?
4 What are (a) attendance centres and (b) detention centres?
5 What are borstal institutions? Who may be sent to borstal, and for what period?
6 What are the legal provisions regarding the fostering of children?
7 What is the law on cruelty and ill-treatment of children and young persons?
8 Describe the general rules regarding the employment of young persons.
9 Write an essay on the Youth Service, mentioning any organisations which specially cater for the interests of youths.
10 A group of young people wish 'to help the community' and they ask you to describe the official organisations which they may join. Advise the group.
11 The Family Rights Group is a pressure group which seeks to protect or promote the interests of families whose children go into care. Why should such a body be considered necessary?

9
Education

Introduction

What is education?

There is no general agreement about the meaning of education. Is it purely academic learning or is it a general 'learning for life'? Is it just a formal process or does it include what we learn from ordinary conversation, the television or general experience of life? Put briefly, education may be seen either as a formal process of training the intellect, or more broadly as the development of the all-round person, including intellectual, spiritual, moral, creative, emotional, even physical facets.

What is education for?

Why is education important or useful? Answers to these searching questions will vary:

1 For the individual such as you or me, education is important as a means of passing examinations *to get a job*.
2 Some may see education as a means of competing socially, for education and qualifications can give a person *status* in society.
3 Education may be important as a source of *self-satisfaction*, which comes from the sense of achievement gained through understanding, e.g. when an idea 'clicks' or makes sense after considerable thought. This is sometimes expressed as the 'joy of knowledge' or the 'pursuit of truth', and it can provide a strong motivation for many people.

You might ask yourself what you get, or got, out of education.

The functions of education

Here we turn to the importance of education to the community at large. Broadly, education has the following functions:

1   **Economic.** Briefly this means producing a labour force with the appropriate skills to supply the economic system. In a complex industrial society some basic *skills* such as the three Rs (reading, writing and arithmetic) are more or less essential for the general workforce. In addition there is the need for specific skills such as those of engineers, doctors, accountants, scientists.

In this respect the educational system is performing a selective or *sifting* function: people are graded according to ability and receive appropriate education and training. But it does raise the question of how vocational and work-oriented education should be.

2   **Political.** There are two aspects to this:

(a)   *Socialisation*, or the passing on or acceptance of the existing political system, its institutions, values and goals such as respect for the Queen or Parliament. In some countries this is done very explicitly, amounting perhaps to indoctrination, such as Marxist ideology in the USSR or the rewriting of the history books in Hitler's Germany. In Great Britain educational subjects like civics, history and British Government are obvious examples of socialisation processes, but so are school assemblies, discipline and even sports, since they all help to imbue a respect for authority and a belief in the validity of rules and procedures.

(b)   Providing political *leadership*. Again this illustrates the selective function whereby the education system sifts out those destined for high political office such as MPs, civil servants, cabinet ministers. A glance at the educational background of these political leaders will show many common features, especially public school and university experience.

3   **Integrative.** Here education introduces the individual to the structure and processes of society. This enables him to understand his world, to see its complex problems and to meet the inevitable changes. In short, it helps the individual to fit in and cope with life. This applies not just to technical or financial skills, but also to social skills such as how to *relate to people* or deal with public authorities.

4   **Stabilising.** This is closely related to the integrative function, for it implies the 'socialisation' of the individual or the *transmission of the culture* of society from one generation to the next. Culture here implies the whole way of life – bringing up children, attitudes to work, leisure pursuits, etc. All these cultural aspects form, explicity or implicitly, part of the school curriculum and imply a degree of conformism, the result of which is that society is sustained and its continued existence secured. This is not to say that education prevents change: it may even become the vehicle of social change as

when it transforms an ignorant backward society into a literate and progressive one.

Main features of education in 1800

Like the arrangements for health, there was no national system of education provision at this time. Education was supplied on a very piecemeal basis. But there are a number of features which were important then, and have had an enduring effect ever since.

Social class. Education provision followed class lines, both in terms of quality and quantity. Broadly there was a substantial supply for the upper and middle classes, through private tutors, or private schools and through grammar schools, which were usually endowed by their founders to provide some free places for worthy but not wealthy pupils. Such education could provide a stepping stone to Oxford or Cambridge Universities.

For the labouring classes, schooling was far less accessible. However, in the workhouse there were 'schools of industry' where the pauper children received a mixture of elementary teaching, training and work. These children might also receive some education in the factory to which they were often apprenticed. Such provision was required under the *Health of Apprentices Acts, 1801 and 1819*, though in practice not much was achieved. For those who could afford the charges there were fee-charging day schools, sometimes called 'common schools', but including also the endowed grammar schools. At very low charges were the Dame schools, usually run by spinsters with little teaching skill who for a few pence per week gave some elementary instruction together with child-minding service. Then there were charity schools which were free or with nominal charges. These included Sunday schools and day schools established by religious societies or by individuals like Mary Carpenter or Lord Shaftesbury whose schools were sometimes called 'ragged schools'. As we shall see, the most important of these charity schools were those founded by the Anglican, Alexander Bell, and the National Society (established in 1811), and those of the Nonconformist, Joseph Lancaster, and the British and Foreign Schools Society (established in 1808).

This is impressive in terms of individual initiative and social con-cern, but in practice working-class children still had very limited educational opportunities. The provision was not systematic, but very patchy. The quality was generally poor, physically and intellectually, and there was no compulsion with consequential loss of attendance since nearly all children were expected to go to work.

Narrow syllabuses characterised the schools at this time. For the working class it seemed that some basic instruction was appropriate, for example instruction in the '3 Rs' with the fourth 'R' of religion. A basic competence was all that was felt necessary, but including the ability to read the Bible. For the upper and middle classes education was very unfunctional, as befitted gentlemen, hence the emphasis on grammar, literature and classical studies. Girls' education was especially narrow in scope, and even more limited in supply. Thus the content of education was geared to the social structure; indeed it was intended to sustain and buttress the different rankings so that the people knew their station in society.

Limited state involvement. This was in line with the current philosophy of *laissez faire*. Not only did the Government not wish to get involved in educational provision, but there were powerful groups who felt their interests threatened by such State involvement and so they violently opposed any moves in that direction. Chief among these were the religious groups. Thus when in 1807 Samuel Whitbread introduced a Bill for a national system of elementary education it was rejected by the House of Lords mainly on the initiative of the Bishops who were firmly opposed to any form of religious instruction of an interdenominational nature.

The predominance of religion. The Church had for centuries held a pre-eminence in learning. The universities and the grammar schools were religious foundations, and so were most of the charity schools which were being established in the late eighteenth and early nineteenth centuries. One of the original purposes of such provision was to strengthen the nation's support for the Established Church particularly to 'combat Popery', as it was expressed in the seventeenth century. In the course and in the aftermath of the Industrial Revolution it was largely left to the Church to 'pick up the pieces', and education was one method of doing this.

On the negative side, however, the Church was antipathetic to State provision of education. There was also rivalry between the Anglican (the Church of England) and the nonconformist denominations which, in some areas, inhibited the provision of schools, and, more importantly, this delayed the creation of a national system of education.

State intervention and the growth of education provision

One of the main strands in the history of education is the changing emphasis from voluntary to State provision of schools. This really began in the second quarter of the nineteenth century, despite the opposition and the disputes over such questions as finance, inspection, supply of teachers and curriculum content. Here the Government stepped into education through the back door, i.e. by giving grants to organisations already providing education. This occurred in 1833, and the main beneficiaries were the two Church Schools Societies: the National Society, run by the Anglicans, and the British and Foreign Schools Society, run by Nonconformists. Both societies were already providing many schools in England and Wales, relying largely on the subscriptions from the public and the devotion of the Church and lay individuals. Both separately developed the 'monitorial' system of teaching by which monitors were first taught or instructed and then themselves gave instruction to other groups of pupils. It was effective up to a point, and it certainly economised on the use of scarce teachers. Those in favour of greater educational provision argued from a variety of standpoints:

(i)   The **moralists** argued that education would 'gentle the masses' (Owen); reduce the birth-rate (Malthus); or enable the masses to become less irreligious and better Christians (the Church).

(ii) The **humanitarians** argued that education was another 'collateral aid' which would help people to avoid poverty and recourse to the Poor Law. Many ratepayers supported this view.

(iii) The **educationalists** argued that education was good in itself, and should be promoted by the Government in the interests of the people themselves, i.e. they were in effect saying that education was a universal right.

(iv) The **economists** argued that an industrial society needs an educated labour force. George Birkbeck was a pioneer in this respect with his lectures to workers in Glasgow in 1800, leading to the creation of Mechanics' Institutes in the industrial areas of Great Britain in the 1820s and 1830s.

Following the defeat of several Educational Bills, the introduction of numerous petititions advocating a national system of education, and above all, the election of the new, reformed – and reformist – House of Commons, Parliament in 1833 voted £20,000 for building schools. It was a 50 per cent grant; so for each £1 spent by the school society, the Government gave a grant of £1 from the fund. In fact, the total was divided equally between the two Schools' Societies: the National Society and the British and Foreign Schools Society.

The scheme may be criticised on the grounds that the richer areas tended to get more money, and the overall amount was too small. But it was a start, and was repeated the following year. In 1939 it was raised to £30,000. The grant was now to be a regular annual subsidy, and a committee of the Privy Council was set up to supervise the administration. The secretary of this committee (late Sir James Kay-

Shuttleworth) appointed inspectors to advise and report on the grant-aided schools. He also improved teachers' pay, and introduced a system of teacher training (the 'pupil teacher'). Furthermore, he sought to broaden the curriculum as well as improve teaching methods, away from the monitorial system and towards a system based on the work of Pestalozzi which emphasised *interest* and *understanding* rather than on memory and repetition. By 1857 this Committee had become the Department of Education and was disbursing a grant of £500,000. However, there was still opposition to the wholesale provision of education:

(a) The Church was afraid of Government interference – the strings attached to grants – and some religious leaders started a move to drop State grants and become independent again.
(b) The Whig and Tory parties were suspicious of each other's motives for giving education grants.
(c) Industrialists were afraid of losing their supply of cheap labour.
(d) Many parents did not wish to lose their children's incomes. Opportunities for child employment were being restricted by Factory Acts of 1833 and 1847. These led in part to the half-and-half system in which children attended school for part of the day and then went to work. This system of 'half-timers' continued up to 1918.
(e) Taxpayers suggested that education was not succeeding in one of its declared aims: the reduction of crime.

Meanwhile the Great Exhibition of 1851 displayed Great Britain's industrial achievement and created an air of complacency.

The Newcastle Commission

In 1858 the Newcastle Commission inquired into the state of education and especially 'what measures, if any, are required for the extension of sound and cheap elementary instruction to all classes of people'. These terms of reference guided its recommendations, the most important of which was 'payment by results'. Under this, grants were payable to schools only where pupil attendances were of a minimum level, and where pupils passed tests of proficiency in the '3 Rs'. This system was adopted by the Government in 1862 (known as the 'revised code') and pleased those who were sceptical about education expenditure. As a result, education expenditure fell from £800,000 in 1862 to just over £600,000 in 1865. But this system tended to lower educational standards by distorting the curriculum and causing a return to mechanical and rote learning. Some claim it set back educational progress by many years by generating a dislike of school by pupils and a dislike of inspectors by teachers. Others say it damaged Great Britain's economy, because it stopped development of science teaching.

However, the Newcastle Commission (like most Royal Commissions) did provide much useful information. It revealed a poor picture of the state of English education with poor attendance and early leaving (over one third attended less than 100 days per annum, and few stayed at school after age 10). Teaching, especially in private schools, was often of poor quality. The report, in pressing for 'payment by results,' did improve attendances and above all it provided support for those who sought greater educational provision.

Church rivalry

Perhaps the greatest hindrance to wider educational provision was not so much financial consideration as the rivalry between the Church and the Non-conformists. On a number of occasions it had been suggested that more schools be provided from public funds, but the Church wanted denominational teaching, while the Nonconformists objected to their being taxed to finance teaching of Anglican doctrine.

However, in the 1860s it appeared that 40–50 per cent or more of children were still missing education, either through absenteeism or lack of school places. An inquiry in 1870 showed that there were 1.8 million school places available – about half the number required. Education leagues and societies pressed the new Minister, W. E. Forster, to legislate for a wider provision of schools. He adopted the policy of 'filling the gaps' and this was implemented in the *Education Act, 1870*, whose provisions we now consider.

The *Education Act, 1870*

The main provisions of this Act were the following:

1   The country was divided into school districts.
2   In those areas lacking sufficient schools, £6 million was allowed to enable voluntary organisations to provide, or expand, schools if they wished. Alternatively, *school boards* were to be created, through election.
3   School boards could levy rates and provide schools.
4   School boards could make attendance compulsory between the ages of 5 and 13.
5   School fees up to a maximum of 9*d*. per week to be charged, except for poor parents.
6   Board schools were to be non-denominational.
7   Voluntary schools could remain denominational, but would not receive rate aid, i.e. they would continue to receive Government

grants, but only if they accepted the 'conscience clause' which allowed parents to withdraw their children from denominational religious instruction lessons.

The reasons for the Act were briefly:

(a) The primary aim was to make elementary education available to *all* children. It was felt they had a right to have access to education.
(b) The political reason. The *Reform Act, 1867*, substantially extended the right to vote and it was felt that voters should be literate. ('We must educate our masters': Sir Robert Lowe.)
(c) Underlying this was the economic motive: to boost industrial efficiency and also help reduce some of the unemployment, especially of children.
(d) Other countries had developed more extensive systems of schooling. They provided an example and a threat.

Some criticisms of the Act. Important as the Act was it had its critics who argued:

(i) Education should be compulsory and free.
(ii) There was still no national system: there were two systems, the voluntary and the State, i.e. the 'dual system'.
(iii) Religious bodies disapproved of the lack of religious instruction.
(iv) Many schools were of poor quality, and payment by results still operated: it was diminished, but not finally abolished until 1897.

Achievements of the Act. The Act achieved a great deal. Many of the boards, e.g. the London School Board, were active and progressive, mainly by adding new subjects to the standard curriculum and giving prizes for regular attendance, and some 1 million additional school places were created between 1870 and 1880.

Many voluntary schools were created, too, with the Church of England and the Roman Catholics adding over 1 million places in the same period. By 1900 three fifths of all school places were in Church of England schools. However, other boards, especially in rural areas, were very slow moving, and some were too poor, even themselves illiterate, to do much. Over the next 25 years efforts were directed especially to making attendances more regular. Thus in 1876 and 1880 legislation required children to attend school up to the age of 10, and up to the age of 14 they were required to attend school half-time. However, a child could leave after 10 if he demonstrated his proficiency in the '3 Rs' or if he had made a minimum of attendances. In

1891 the minimum school leaving age was raised to 11 and in 1899 to 12, and from 1893 school boards were allowed to abolish fees.

With the growth of schools and the increase in education costs the Government felt it was time to examine the state of elementary education. Hence the **Cross Commission (1886–88)** was set up. This criticised the continued high rate of absenteeism and the narrowing effect of 'payment by results'. It recommended the expansion and improvement of teacher training and evening (continuation) classes, together with a tidying up of secondary education.

Secondary education in the nineteenth century

Apart from the private tutors, secondary education consisted of the endowed grammar schools, including those which developed boarding facilities and became 'public schools'.

As the middle class grew in the Industrial Revolution so they sought greater opportunities for the education of their children. Some of them imitated the educational methods of the aristocracy, i.e. private tuition and public schools, but others were critical of the narrow classical curiculum which existed both in the public schools and the grammar schools generally. Many were also critical of the idleness, corruption and 'fagging', and applauded the reforms introduced by such headmasters as James, Butler, Arnold and Thring who emphasised service to the community, Christian character and self-discipline, as well as some broadening of the curriculum. But such schools were limited in number and were perhaps too expensive for some. So, aided by the development of railways, many new schools – often modelled on the better public schools – were established in the nineteenth century (e.g. Marlborough, Clifton, Bath) and, in addition, a number of attempts were made to alter the terms of school endowments so as to modernise curricula, usually with little success.

The criticisms levelled at the public schools led to the **Clarendon Commission (1861–64)**. After investigating nine public schools it concluded that classical studies were still a desirable key element in the curriculum, but that there was a need to add depth to those studies and also add breadth by the introduction of subjects such as mathematics, science and English. There was no official action along these lines, but many of the schools took note.

The Taunton Commission (1864–68) was a very comprehensive inquiry into endowed schools and private schools, covering what we call 'secondary education', i.e. all those schools excluded from the Newcastle and Clarendon Commissions. It was very critical about standards and efficiency, and suggested a number of reforms which would have led to a national system of secondary education.

In many ways the Commission was too advanced for the time, and faced much opposition. The only immediate result was the *Endowed Schools Act, 1869*, which facilitated changes in endowments and thus permitted more school places for girls.

In the meantime the growth in the general public demand for secondary education opportunities was evident from the numbers staying at school beyond school leaving age, and the formation of upper classes or 'higher tops' in the elementary schools. Some of these classes came together into separate central or higher-grade schools, a number of which developed science classes so as to qualify for grants from the Science and Art Department, a government body established in 1852. It was this unplanned growth of secondary schools to which the **Cross Commission** drew attention, but it was divided over the question of whether to give approval to the higher-grade schools.

In 1894–95, the issue was reconsidered by another Royal Commission, the **Bryce Commission on Secondary Education**, partly as a result of yet another Commission, the Samuelson Commission on Technical Instruction, 1881–84, which said that Germany's industrial success was largely attributable to her secondary-school system. The Bryce Commission pointed to the chaotic state of educational administration due to the great variety of authorities and the overlapping of their functions, i.e. the school boards, higher-grade schools, endowed schools, private schools, the technical schools – all variously overseen by the Education Department, the Art and Science Department, Governors, the Charity Commission and local authorities. Thus it recommended:

1 A central department with a Minister of Education, to supervise elementary and secondary education.
2 Local authorities to become responsible for local education administration.

Both ideas had a lot of support, so that in 1899 the Board of Education was created, and under the *Education Act, 1902*, the local education authorities were created. Elementary education and secondary education were now linked together and provided a *national system* of education. The *Education Act, 1902*:

1 Abolished school boards and replaced them with local education authorities (LEAs).
2 Local education authorities were to provide rate aid for voluntary schools, and in return took some places on the boards of managers.
3 Timetable conscience clause (see page 219) was retained for voluntary schools aided by rate grants.

4   Local education authorities could provide for the training of teachers.

Reasons for the passing of the 1902 Act were:

1   To tidy up the local administration of schools.
2   To allow secondary schools to be provided by the State. (There had been doubts about the legality of the bodies responsible for elementary schools, i.e. the school boards, having the power to provide secondary education. In 1901 the Cockerton judgement decided that secondary classes in higher-grade (elementary) schools were illegal.)
3   To establish an organised system of elementary, secondary and technical education and thereby a ladder of opportunity to university level.
4   To help maintain the voluntary schools many of which were struggling financially.

Criticisms of the Act included:

1   Fees were charged for secondary schools, though LEAs did introduce some free scholarship places, and fees were not completely abolished in elementary schools.
2   Many nonconformists protested at the rate levy for the voluntary elementary schools, predominantly Anglican, and some wanted to abolish them by transferring them to LEAs.
3   The system was not so tidy because some small local authorities (called 'Part III authorities', i.e. boroughs and urban district councils) were allowed to provide elementary schools apart from the county councils and the county borough councils. Many *powers* of LEAs were not *duties*. The LEAs could, therefore, act at their own discretion.
4   Most secondary education was still provided by private or voluntary schools.
5   The Act seemed to emphasise that secondary education was something quite different from elementary, instead of seeing them as connected stages in the same process. As a result the Act did not create a truly national system, though it did provide its basis.
6   The Board of Education was not strengthened to give it adequate power over LEAs.

Development of the national system: 1902–44

In the last 40 years of the nineteenth century education policy was concerned mainly with increasing access to *elementary* education.

The next 40 years turned attention to *secondary* education. More secondary schools were provided, especially by LEAs. In 1901 the Board of Education increased its grants to LEAs providing secondary schools and also insisted on 25 per cent free scholarship places in them. LEAs, in fact, developed two kinds of secondary school:

1 Those which were modelled on the public and grammar model, with traditional curriculum and special emphasis on the study of Latin – that is, *secondary grammar* schools, which acted as a pathway to the universities and professions.
2 *Central* schools, which provided full-time general education up to 15 with the object of enabling pupils to enter a trade or industry, and having some commercial or industrial bias. Included here were some junior technical schools.

Those pupils leaving early or 'half-timing' up to 14 received attention in the *Education Act, 1918* (the Fisher Act), as part of the reconstruction plans after the First World War. The Act provided that:

(a) All elementary school fees be abolished, and school leaving age raised to 14. There were no loopholes, and 'half-timing' was to cease in 1922, and no employment of children under 12.
(b) Local authorities were required to provide secondary education for those pupils seeking it, i.e. those who stayed on after 14.
(c) Those who left at 14 were required to attend continuation classes up to 16, and later 18. The hours of attendance were to be fixed by the local authorities.
(d) School medical inspection and treatment was extended to local authority secondary schools.
(e) Local authorities were given powers to open nursery schools, and to pay maintenance grants to secondary scholarship pupils.

The 1922 'Geddes Axe' cut public expenditure and prevented implementation of many of these provisions. There was also opposition from employers to day continuation classes.

Educational theory and practice

Meanwhile, educational theory and practice were being influenced by three different developments:

1 **Educational psychology** was developing a quantitative approach. This was called 'psychometry', which attempted to measure mental abilities. Based on the pioneer work of Binet in France in the early 1900s, it was developed by Burt and Spearman and adopted by many LEAs as a means of selection for secondary education.

2 **Developmental psychology** and studies of child behaviour began to influence teaching methods, and moved them away slowly from regimented learning to a more child-centred approach, with greater emphasis on interest and pupil–teacher relationships.

3 **The concept of social equality** was becoming more important during this century, especially after the First World War. In the educational field the 'scholarship system' had been seen as a major step to equality. The demand for 'secondary education for all' was to grow in volume.

The Reports of the *Hadow Committee* of 1926 and 1931 reflected these influences. Among its recommendations were:

(i)   Elementary schools should be called 'primary schools', which should be divided into (1) infant and (2) junior departments, with senior departments where necessary. Emphasis was to be on activity and experience rather than the acquisition of facts.

(ii)   There should be secondary education for all, with the age of transfer from primary school to be 11–12. As far as possible this should take place in a separate school.

(iii) For those who did not seek the traditional secondary education, thereby staying on to 15 plus, there should be central or senior schools, to be called 'modern schools'. They could be selective or non-selective, and they would develop a curriculum which was broadly based and geared to the needs, interests and abilities of the pupils, with a substantial *practical* bias though not narrowly vocational.

(iv) The school leaving age should be raised to 15.

This was a very far-sighted report whose achievement was hindered by economic conditions, cuts in public spending and by laggard LEAs. Nevertheless, by 1939 some 69 per cent of urban and 22 per cent of rural elementary schools had been reorganised so that the children of secondary age were in separate secondary schools instead of the traditional elementary all-age school.

Secondary education received further consideration in the **Spens Report** of 1938. This committee examined the long-standing suggestion of a common secondary school for all, i.e. comprehensive. It concluded against the idea of this type of comprehensive school, mainly on grounds of probable size. It emphasised the need, however, for a third type of secondary school – the technical school.

The desirability of tripartite secondary education was reiterated in the **Norwood Committee Report** of 1943 which was investigating the curriculum of secondary schools. It suggested that the three types of school were to cater for three types of intelligence: (1) the academic; (2) the practical or applied; and (3) that which dealt more easily with 'concrete things than with ideas'. These views, later called 'the Norwood myth', are reminiscent of the Taunton Report, but they had more psychological foundation at that time and were a significant influence on both the education legislation and more especially the educational practice of the 1940s.

The *Education Act, 1944*

This was known as the Butler Act (after R. A. Butler, later Lord Butler), and resulted from the Second World War. The evacuation of families from the main cities to the remoter rural areas revealed low standards of life and behaviour, and led to a widespread feeling that this state of affairs ought to be remedied. Churchill had said that the advantages and privileges of the few should be shared by the many after the war, and Beveridge (see page 42) had declared that ignorance was a problem to be conquered if general welfare was to be improved. The demand for universal secondary education was at last to be fully implemented by the Act, the main features of which were:

1 The Board of Education was replaced by the more powerful Ministry of Education.
2 Part III Authorities (see page 222) were abolished (though LEAs would have Divisional Executives).
3 LEAs were required to reorganise into primary, secondary and further education.
4 Fees were abolished in the State secondary schools, and the leaving age was raised to 15 years, and later to 16 years.
5 Children were to be educated in accordance with 'their age, abilities and aptitudes' (the 3 As) and 'in accordance with the wishes of parents', but only if it did not threaten schools' efficiency and was not too costly.
6 The 'dual system' was retained, with voluntary schools being described as voluntary aided or voluntary controlled.
7 Religious instruction and worship was obligatory in all schools.
8 LEAs were required to provide nursery education where necessary.
9 County colleges were to be established for day-continuation education up to age 18.
10 LEAs' powers and duties were extended respecting education welfare services and awards for higher education.

Comment on the *Education Act, 1944*. It has been described as the greatest Education Act ever, and it provides the basis of our present education system. Nevertheless, it has been criticised as much for the way it has been implemented as for its actual content:

1   Although it did not actually mention selection and allocation to the separate secondary schools it has been taken to imply that. Most LEAs, therefore, operated the '11-plus' and the tripartite system. The 11-plus selection has been criticised as being inaccurate, too early and arbitrary; and that, as the Norwood Committee pointed out, it is impossible to decide what sort of education a child of 11 is best fitted for. In the 1970s, the work of Dr Burt – a pioneer of intelligence testing who emphasised the inheritance element – was found to be faulty if not fraudulent.

2   The tripartite system was criticised as based on a false division of abilities, and especially because of the lack of parity of esteem. The secondary modern schools have generally been seen as inferior and not, therefore, offering a truly *equal* opportunity for secondary education.

3   Nursery education has been neglected.

4   County colleges hardly developed, and day-continuation has tended to take the form of vocationally oriented day-release in technical colleges.

5   There have been continuous criticisms of poor school buildings, shortages of books, materials and teachers and large classes.

Expansion of education since 1944

The years since 1944 have seen expansion and development of the educational system on an unprecedented scale.

Teacher supply. Between 1945 and 1951 an emergency training scheme added over 30,000 qualified teachers to a force numbering under 200,000. By 1951 the annual output of trained teachers was double that of 1939. By 1970 it was over five times as large, despite the fact that from 1960 the two-year training course for non-graduates was lengthened to three years. Primary pupils per teacher or pupil–teacher ratio (PTR) fell from 28 (1966) to 23.6 (1978) and to 21.9 (1987). Secondary PTRs fell from 16.9 (1978) to 15.9 (1987).

School building programme. By 1970 more than 8,500 primary and secondary schools had been built, housing over one quarter of the 7½ million children in maintained schools. Many are attractive and some highly experimental.

Comprehensive schools. From the early 1950s the sharply segregated tripartite organisation of secondary education in grammar, modern and technical schools with which the country started in 1945 was growing less rigid as some of the new secondary modern schools developed 'grammar' courses and different types of schools amalgamated to form bilateral (i.e. grammar–modern under one roof) or comprehensive schools. In 1965 this movement was accelerated by a 'request' from the Government that all local education authorities plan the organisation of secondary education on comprehensive lines. Most LEAs complied but the *Education Act, 1976, required* them all to go comprehensive. This was repealed by the 1979 Act.

Methods and curricula. Innovations designed to extend and improve the quality of the education given in primary and secondary schools included the introduction of television services (1957), language laboratories and other audio-visual aids. Large-scale research and experiment into the teaching of various subjects, such as languages, mathematics and science, were undertaken. In 1965 a new external examination, leading to a Certificate of Secondary Education (CSE), was introduced, designed for children of middling intellectual ability. In 1986–8 the CSE and GCE examinations were replaced by the GCSE (see pages 246 and 254).

Schools council. This body was created in 1964 to assist and assess all curricular developments and to advise the Secretary of State (see page 242). In 1988 this was replaced by the School Examinations and Assessment Council and the National Curriculum Centre.

Further education. Massive increases in the numbers of students – full-time, 'sandwich' and part-time day – have occurred. The structure of technical education was rationalised, with colleges being graded on four levels, and new courses being introduced such as those arranged by the Business Technician and Education Council (BTEC).

Colleges of advanced technology (CATS). In 1966 ten of the top-level further education colleges were given university rank and called Colleges of Advanced Technology, subsequently becoming Universities. In addition a new top level institution was created – the **polytechnic**. There are now 30 of these. Following the James Report (1973) there has been a reorganisation of teacher training, with many Colleges of Education merging with the polytechnics and with universities. Some of the colleges are developing broader-based courses (including the two-year Diploma in Higher Education) and are designated Colleges or Institutions of Higher Education, of which there will eventually be 50.

This tremendous expansion and development was due to:

(i) A continuously increasing school population.
(ii) A firm trend towards staying longer at school.

(iii) An unprecedentedly large (and growing) demand for higher education, especially education of university level.

(iv) A growing realisation among the public that 'the future belongs to the higher educated nations' (Sir Winston Churchill, 1943).

A number of these tendencies are now clearly no longer operating. Graduate unemployment and perhaps the new, proposed loan scheme has diminished the appeal of university education, and the fall in the birthrate has cut the school building programme and the amount of teacher training since 1976: contraction has replaced expansion. Thus pupil numbers in primary schools show the following variation: early 1970s – 4.9 million; 1985 – 3.7 million; 1991 – 3.9 million. And secondary pupil numbers show the following variation: 1979 – 3.9 million; 1987 – 3.3 million; 1991 – 2.8 million (and remaining at around 3 million through the 1990s). School pupils (in the UK) increased by 2.4 million from 1961–76 and fell by 1.8 million from 1976–86.

The educational system of Great Britain

The educational system of any society is bound to reflect the values of that society. This follows from what we have said about the functions of education. For example, while in the nineteenth century and earlier twentieth century separate schools existed to cater for and maintain different strata of society, today our education system emphasises the *comprehensive* approach, which reflects the greater value which society now gives to equality. Education therefore both transmits the culture of society and it also forms part of that culture.

Today, there are about 11 million pupils and students in full-time education in Great Britain, and over 3.5 million part-time. Most full-time education takes place in 38,000 schools (with about 10 million pupils). Colleges and universities account for the remainder. The pattern of provision is summarised in Figure 8, and it can be seen that there are two broad groupings: the State sector and the independent (or non-statutory) sector. The statutory system is that part which is laid down by law in Education Acts. The *Education Act, 1944*, states that the system of public education must be organised in three stages, hence the diagram shows a three-fold division according to age into (1) primary, (2) secondary and (3) further and higher education.

Primary education

This normally begins at age five* and runs to age 11. In the State sector this occurs in primary schools, which are divided (perhaps

*It may be just before (the 'rising fives') or just after. Parents are required by law to see that their children receive efficient full-time education at school or elsewhere between the ages of 5 and 16 years.

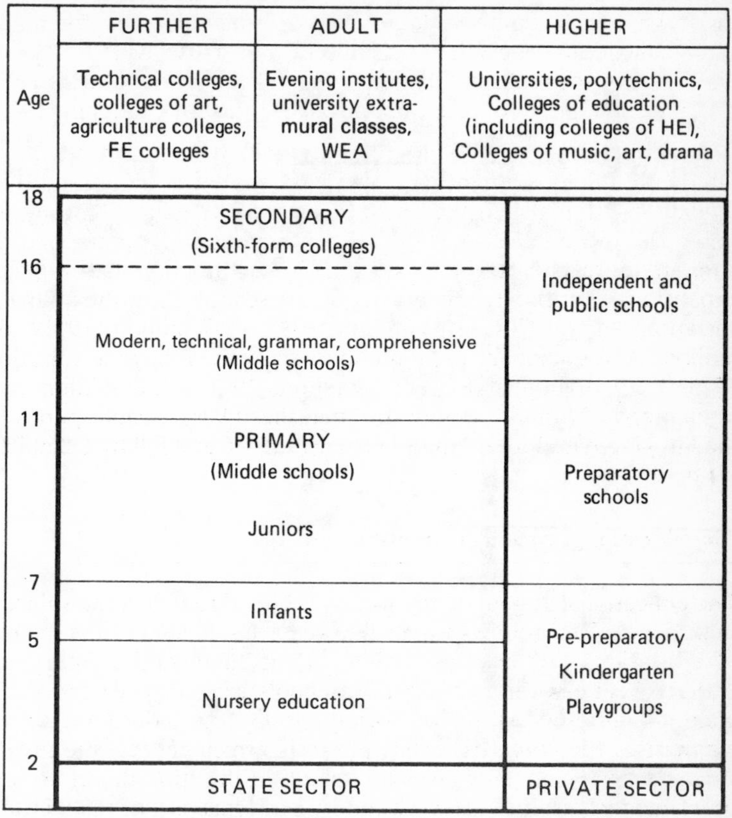

Age	FURTHER	ADULT	HIGHER
	Technical colleges, colleges of art, agriculture colleges, FE colleges	Evening institutes, university extra-mural classes, WEA	Universities, polytechnics, Colleges of education (including colleges of HE), Colleges of music, art, drama

Age	STATE SECTOR		PRIVATE SECTOR
18	SECONDARY (Sixth-form colleges)		Independent and public schools
16	Modern, technical, grammar, comprehensive (Middle schools)		
11	PRIMARY (Middle schools) Juniors		Preparatory schools
7	Infants		
5			Pre-preparatory Kindergarten Playgroups
	Nursery education		
2	STATE SECTOR		PRIVATE SECTOR

Figure 8   *Structure of education in England and Wales*
Note: Middle schools may be classed as primary or (more usually) secondary

physically separated) into **infants** and **juniors**, with the break at seven years. There are currently some 4½ million children at this level.

However, some children are given **nursery** education, sometimes called 'pre-school education'. This can occur anytime from age two, and may take place full-time or part-time in a separate nursery† school, or more usually, in nursery classes within the infants' school. Here children are provided with informal educational and play facilities. But in practice such provision is limited. Numbers are about 285,000 in nursery schools and 248,000 in infant classes. Since these represent only between 20–50 per cent of the different years in the age group (45 per cent overall in England), the result is that many

---

†Not to be confused with day nurseries which have similar but distinct functions and are run by the local authority social services departments, not the local education departments (see page 173). Day nurseries also charge fees.

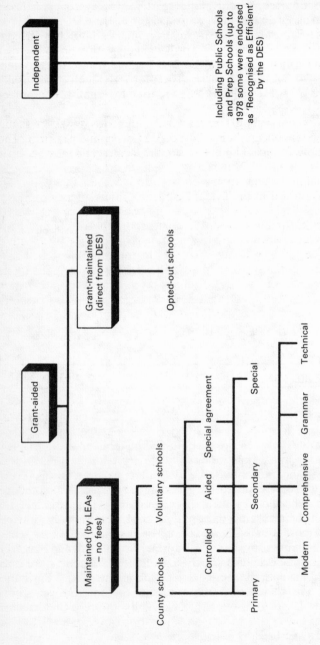

Figure 9　*Structure of schools in England and Wales*

parents turn to the private or voluntary sector in the form of independent nursery schools, kindergartens or playgroups. It is estimated that about 15,000 playgroups exist.

Since the *Education Act, 1964*, many primary schools have become what are known as **first schools**, providing education up to age of 10 years, from which pupils (currently 0.5 million) transfer to **middle schools** up to age 12–14 years. These arrangements have usually occurred as part of secondary reorganisation to establish 'comprehensive schools' (see page 232).

Primary schools vary in size from 300 pupils to as few as 25 (though many small schools are being closed as an economy measure). They contain pupils of mixed abilities from the locality and may be single-sex schools or mixed. This period of education is often seen as the most crucial in the educational process, and teachers themselves find substantial reward in the evident curiosity, interest and progress of the children. This area has also seen the most significant changes in educational techniques: from the nineteenth-century system of rote learning, silence in class and regimentation to what is called 'activity learning', learning by doing, discovery learning and the 'open classroom'. Some critics say such 'progressive' methods have gone too far – for example, the row at William Tyndale's School, Islington, London, in 1975/76 – and that some basic learning was being neglected. To a large extent the 'Great Debate' of 1977 was the result of misgivings about educational standards and recent reforms have reflected this (see page 252).

Secondary education

Since 1944 the pattern of secondary education is a mixture of grammar, technical and modern schools, the so-called 'tripartite' system. More recently we have seen the amalgamation of some of these separate types of school into multilateral or comprehensive schools.

Following the *Education Act, 1944*, not many technical schools were developed, with the result that after the age of 11 years children have been allocated to grammar and secondary modern schools on the basis of their progress in primary school, especially as measured by the '11-plus' tests. These consist of intelligence tests: 'verbal reasoning'; and perhaps a test of arithmetic and English. Together with teachers' assessments of progress and achievement, the 11-plus determined the path of transfer to secondary education, i.e. whether the pupils are allocated to the grammar or the technical schools (sometimes called the 'selective schools') or to secondary modern. The former have different objectives and orientations to the secondary moderns, especially of providing a more academic ('learning for learning's sake') approach to education, and of providing avenues to higher education or professional qualifications. Consequently they took the 'cream', i.e. the top 20–25 per cent of the secondary age range. The actual number transferring to selective schools in a particular area is, of course, determined by the number of such school places available in that area. Some LEAs have also transferred pupils at 13-plus.

However, since the 1960s the emergence of comprehensive schools has changed and continues to change this pattern of provision, so that today over 80 per cent of the 3.5 million secondary school pupils attend comprehensive schools. It is Labour Party policy to make this form of secondary schooling universal, though the Conservatives are pledged to maintaining some grammar schools and other selective schools.

Comprehensive schools. With some 3 million pupils, these schools vary in age range according to the particular form which has been adopted. There are at least six possibilities, ranging from the 11–18 age group (the all-through school which tends to be large with perhaps some 2,000 pupils) to the two-tier schools comprising junior lower (or middle) school and senior (or higher or upper) school with transfer at 13–14 years. Alternatively, there is the three-tier system with 'first schools' to age 8, 'middle schools' to age 12 and 'upper schools' for pupils aged 12 plus. All these schools, as the name implies, are non-selective and therefore contain the whole range of abilities.* The comprehensive system avoids the need for allocation at 11-plus and breaks down the barriers created by separate school-ing. As a result, the range of provision in comprehensive schools can be enormous in the areas of academic subjects, craft and social skills. There are, however, problems of size and questions about 'streaming' (see page 246). Under the *Education Act, 1980*, parents of secondary and primary pupils can express a preference in the choice of school for their children. The LEA must comply unless it would be prejudi-cial to efficient education or the economic use of resources. There is an appeals system for dissatisfied parents, and they must be well informed about the schools available (and their arrangements for exams, discipline, curriculum, etc.).

---

*There are some exceptions to this. First, many of the children with special educational needs formerly maladjusted and educationally sub-normal (ESN) are excluded (see page 234). Second, in some areas the comprehensive school is not truly comprehensive because some selective schools have been retained there and thus 'cream off' top pupils. Third, it may be the case that different comprehensive schools contain different ability ranges as a result of drawing pupils from different neighbour-hoods with different social backgrounds.

Grammar schools. With 100,000 pupils, 150 of these schools continue to exist (c.f. 1,180 in 1965) in those parts of Britain which have not 'gone comprehensive'. They provide for about 3 per cent of the secondary school population. Their pupils have been selected on the basis of the 11-plus and follow the academic education provided by mostly graduate teachers. They aim at GCSE qualifications and A levels as the basis for future usually professional careers.

Secondary modern schools. These used to provide for the majority of secondary school children, but owing to comprehensive reorganisation they now have only 200,000 pupils (in some 400 schools). They average about 500 pupils in size and most are mixed rather than single-sex schools. They provide for a wide range of abilities from borderline grammar pupils to those bordering on the educationally subnormal.

Generally speaking the secondary modern schools have been a disappointment, for instead of developing what many hoped would be new, experimental and exciting curricula, and a distinctive ethos or orientation, these schools either continued the old 'senior elementary' courses (though with better equipment) or they began to ape the selective schools by developing streams, the 'house system', prefects and team games. By and large, they have suffered (a) socially from a lack of public esteem and (b) educationally from a lack of resources, i.e. in terms of class sizes, proportion of graduate teachers, etc. (see the Newsom Report *Half Our Future* (1963).

Technical schools. Some of these were 'technical–commercial' schools. They number not more than a hundred and provide for about 1 per cent of secondary pupils. They sometimes form part of a local technical college. The aim was to give children of academic ability (i.e. who pass the 11-plus examination) a course which was industrial or commercial in orientation.

Voluntary schools. All the schools mentioned so far (primary and secondary) come within the 'maintained sector', i.e. LEAs are responsible for supporting them. Most of these schools (about 70 per cent) are wholly maintained and administered by LEAs. These are called 'county schools'. Alongside them and forming what is called the 'dual system' are 8,500 'voluntary' schools responsible for 30 per cent of maintained school pupils. Voluntary schools are mostly religious foundations, especially Church of England; they form a significant part of our educational heritage (see page 218). They take three forms: 1 **Voluntary controlled schools**, of which there are 3,500. In these, the LEA appoints the teachers and is responsible for the maintenance of the school buildings. The LEA also appoints two thirds of the governors of each school.* This managing body must be consulted on the appointment of the head teacher and the religious education teacher. 2 **Voluntary aided schools**, of which there are about 5,000. In these the voluntary body appoints two thirds of the governors who, together with the LEA, share responsibility for the maintenance of buildings. The LEA must approve the appointment of teachers, but the governors control religious education in the school. 3 **Special agreement schools**, created in 1936. They are few in number, i.e. about 100. Here responsibilities for building, staffing and management are shared between the LEA and the voluntary body.

Sixth-form colleges. These began to emerge in the mid-1960s as a means of concentrating scarce resources for examination courses, especially for GCE A-level subjects, instead of having them duplicated and spread thinly in separate grammar schools. There are about 100 such colleges each offering about 25 GCE A-level subjects, and they contain about 500 pupils who are technically still 'at school' though aged 16–19 years.

Many schools are reluctant to lose their sixth forms since it deprives them of older and abler pupils who can provide example, leadership and prestige. Nevertheless, many older pupils preferred to leave school and study in the local further education college or 'tech' (see page 238). Since 1970 there have developed a number of so-called **tertiary colleges**. These are strictly speaking part of the further education sector, rather than schools. They are something of a compromise between the sixth-form college and the further education college, in that they absorb all local sixth formers and yet also run many vocational courses such as full-time and part-time secretarial, child-care and craft courses. This can provide a useful flexibility for those who may well wish to change courses.

Special schools. There are about 2,000 of these (about 80 per cent owned and controlled by LEAs, 20 per cent by voluntary bodies plus a few private schools together with a number of hospital schools, with some 3,000 pupils). The special schools provide for pupils who suffer from mental or physical disabilities. There are about 200,000 such pupils handicapped by way of being blind, deaf, autistic, epileptic,

---

*All educational institutions have a managing or directing body of 'governors'. Their functions are to give some general direction to the school in regard to curriculum, structure and the appointment of staff, but usually under the firm guidance of the head teacher and within the general requirements of the LEA. Following the Taylor Report, 1977, under the *Education Acts, 1980* and *1986*, governing bodies now contain parents and teachers (elected by parents) in addition to members appointed by the LEA (and the Church in the case of voluntary schools). See also page 253.

delicate, educationally subnormal (ESN) or maladjusted. Under the *Education Act, 1981* (and following the 'Warnock Report', 1978), these categories of handicap are replaced by the wider term **special educational need** and apply to those children with educational difficulties however they are caused.

Where possible the LEAs are expected to provide special education for these disabled children in ordinary schools so that they may participate as far as possible in the normal life of the community, and about a third are so educated, the number having risen (from 10 per cent) following the Warnock Report and the 1981 Act. But often their disability makes this **integration** impracticable or undesirable, so special schools have been created. The schools have specially trained staff, smaller classes and perhaps residential facilities, e.g. boarding schools, perhaps situated in a hospital. In addition some children (about 4,000) stay at home and get home tuition. In spite of significant strides in the treatment and provision for these children many deficiencies remain. For example, owing to lack of suitable teachers not enough handicapped children attend ordinary schools (the Warnock Report recommended an expansion in the training of such teachers). There are currently some 14,000 ESN and maladjusted children for whom there are no vacancies in special schools.

The independent sector

So far we have looked at State schools. We now turn to the private sector which provides for 6 per cent of the school population.

Independent or private schools are so called because they are financially self-supporting, having for the most part been established through endowments of individuals or organisations such as the Church or a guild. There are more than 2,500 such schools with over ½ million pupils, and it is among these that most of the 'public schools' are to be found.

The term **public school** is not an official title. Its meaning is not entirely clear. Originally it referred to those schools which, being residential, could draw on the whole population for pupils. It may also have referred to those schools which, while charging fees, nevertheless acted in the 'public' interest by not seeking to make profits. Today it refers to those schools whose headmaster belongs to the Headmasters' Conference or whose governing bodies are admitted to membership of the Governing Bodies Association.

Originally there were nine such schools: those recognised by the Clarendon Commission of 1861 (see page 220). Now there are about 300, many with national and international reputations – Eton, Harrow, Rugby, Westminister, Winchester, etc. A number of the 'direct grant' schools (see below) came into this category and there are some maintained schools, but they are overwhelmingly fee-charging (some over £3,500 p.a.), financially independent, single-sex and residential, and they are entirely for secondary school age pupils. They have developed certain traditions, placing a special emphasis on character-building.

At the primary level are the **preparatory schools**. These take children (mainly boarding) from about 8 to 13, at which age they transfer to the public and other independent schools. The basis for this transfer is the Common Entrance Examination for which, therefore, the 'prep schools' prepare their pupils.

Being 'independent' does not mean that such schools are uncontrolled. Since 1957 all independent schools must register with the Department of Education and Science, and the schools can be inspected and, if necessary, can be closed. (Up to 1978 they could also volunteer to undergo a more rigorous inspection and acquire the appellation 'Recognised as Efficient'.)

Before 1978 another type of independent school existed in the form of the **direct grant school**. Some of these were special schools, but most (about 180) were single-sex grammar schools. They received some grant aid *direct* from the Department of Education and Science (DES) on the condition that the LEAs could take up a certain number of places (at least 25 per cent) at the school. (See also Grant Maintained Schools page 254.)

Because they were selective, direct grant schools had high records of performance and high academic reputations. They also tended to have favourable staffing ratios (i.e. fewer students per member of staff). Half of them were boarding schools. However, being selective, these schools clashed with the comprehensive principle and the Labour Government abolished them in 1978 (and most of them became entirely independent). However, under the *Education Act, 1980*, the Conservative government introduced a new arrangement: the **Assisted Places Scheme** 'for the purposes of enabling pupils who might otherwise not be able to do so to benefit from education at independent schools'. Thus selected bright youngsters from poorer homes have their school fees remitted (according to parental income, up to some £12,000 p.a.) by the 230 independent schools in the scheme, and the schools' lost fee revenue is reimbursed by the DES. There are currently some 33,200 places (from 13,000 in 1985) and 40 per cent have their fees remitted in full, at a cost of over £30 million a year.

Special educational services

Under the *Education Act, 1944*, the LEAs have a special *duty* to promote not only the mental, spiritual and moral development of children, but also their *physical* development. This implies that they provide healthy surroundings in their educational institutions: adequate lighting, ventilation, space, heating. The buildings must be clean and have adequate toilets, washing facilities, playing space and gymnasia. Most schools have playing fields and some have facilities such as camps and holidays abroad.

Meals and milk. There are regulations regarding the provision of school meals and refreshments. Up to 1979, LEAs were required to provide milk and lunches in schools under the *Education Act, 1944*. These need now, under the *Education Act, 1980*, no longer be provided except on grounds of ill health or poverty in which cases they are provided and free of charge. Any other provision is charged for and these charges have risen significantly in recent years. Under the *Social Security Act, 1986* schools may now only provide free meals to pupils from families on Income Support; previously they could include others.

Clothing. LEAs also have the power to provide clothing and school uniform, including physical education outfits, with or without charge. Alternatively, LEAs can given grants for this purpose, depending on parental income.

Medical inspections also take place, usually once or twice during a child's school life. About 15 per cent are found to need treatment for visual, audio or oral defects, and more than 50 per cent have dental defects.

Psychological help. Children may need psychological attention either at a Child Guidance Clinic or at a clinic of the Educational Psychological Service, particularly in cases of learning difficulties or perhaps excessive school absences – there are an estimated 140,000 truancies a day. These services are obviously important as part of the preventive health services, but staff shortages prevent their full provision. Education welfare officers (or social workers, some 3,000 in all) are likely to be most involved here, but could well be concerned with some of the other welfare services mentioned here.

Transport. If a child lives three or more miles from his school (two miles for infants) the LEA will either provide transport or will give grants.

Parents abroad or mobile. Where parents work abroad or where their employment causes them to move regularly, then the LEA will provide boarding education. This would also apply where home circumstances are unsatisfactory such as marriage breakdown.

Financial assistance may be paid by the LEA to enable children (currently about 30 per cent) to remain at school beyond the school-leaving age. These maintenance grants are based on parents' income, and similar grants may be made to enable children to participate in school activities such as camps, visits or school clubs. For students at universities and other institutions of higher education the educational financial awards (mandatory or discretionary grants) are regulated by the DES and the LEAs. The proposed (1989) 'top-up' loans are likely to involve financial institutions rather than education authorities.

Further and higher education

Further education in this chapter refers to the education provided for those above minimum school-leaving age (16) at an institution other than a school, i.e. at polytechnics, technical colleges, colleges of further education, art colleges, agricultural colleges, etc.

There are currently some 350,000 full-time students and 1½ million part-time students undergoing further education courses which are either *vocational* and geared to employment and training such as National Certificate or YTS courses, or *academic*, such as courses for the GCE Advanced level. Fees are charged, except for students under 18, but where a firm is sending its employees it can recoup the charge from an Industrial Training Board (see page 348).

Within further education is a category known as **adult education**, which generally refers to non-vocational education, ranging from the study of philosophy or economics to geology or natural history and to the more recreational studies such as art appreciation, yachting or needlework. There are about 2½ million students attending these classes, mostly in LEA colleges and evening institutes, but many classes are provided by the Workers' Educational Association (WEA), the universities' extra-mural departments and by certain residential colleges. The 1973 Russell Report advocated a continuation of the expansion of this area of education such that it would reach 4 million students by the 1980s. In practice, provision has decreased and tuition fees have been raised.

In recent years there has been a trend towards what is called **community education**, often based initially on a closer relationship between the youth service and adult education but leading to a removal of the barriers between the different stages of education, and regarding education as a continuous process which involves more voluntary and local group participation. In some areas it allows adults to join in school lessons.

Higher Education refers to education of an advanced nature, i.e. above GCE Advanced level or National Certificate, and therefore concerns the universities, polytechnics and colleges of higher education. Broadly the universities and polytechnics do research, while colleges do not.

There are over 500,000 full-time students in this sector as a result of the rapid expansion since the early 1960s – there were fewer than 200,000 such students in 1961. This expansion occurred through the foundation of new universities such as Aston, Bradford and Essex, so that there are now 46 universities (plus the private University of Buckingham and the Open University), and the creation of 30 polytechnics, many of which shed their lower level courses.

Universities are self-governing bodies which retain control of their courses and teaching in spite of their dependence on Government financial aid. The Government grants now amount to 55 per cent (compared to 80 per cent ten years ago) of the universities' income, are distributed as block grants (of over £1,000 million) through the *Universities Funding Council* (formerly the Universities Grants Committee), an advisory body appointed by the Secretary of State (DES) with members drawn from the academic and business fields. Parliament can investigate (through its Public Accounts Committee of MPs) the accounts of the universities to check the efficiency and administration of the grants, but it cannot question the broad policy or academic aspects of their usage.

About 45 per cent of the 260,000 university students (c.f. 300,000 in 1981) study arts or social sciences, and these tend to be oversubscribed in terms of places available, compared to science and technology where the figure is 40 per cent. The remainder are made up of those studying health, medicine, agriculture, architecture, planning, etc. A recent trend has been the broadening of studies, involving modules and interdisciplinary studies, but recent financial restrictions have led to a rationalisation of departments and faculties leading to some closure of departments or faculties and redundancies (in philosophy and architecture for example).

The universities of Great Britain are renowned throughout the world, and this reputation is achieved partly by the favourable ratio of staff to students (currently 1 to 8). More than 90 per cent of the students receive financial assistance towards paying for their tuition fees and for maintenance. The money comes from scholarships and awards by the universities themselves, from LEAs (who have a statutory duty to make awards to suitably qualified students), from industrial undertakings and from the DES and Research Councils (for post-graduate student grants).

The polytechnics. These were created in 1965 through the amalgamation of existing institutions such as colleges of commerce, art and technology. The number of full-time students currently attending polytechnics is over 200,000. The name implies 'many arts, many skills' so that courses range from the creative (e.g. painting, sculpture, music, architecture), the professional (e.g. law, accountancy, management), the community (teaching, social work), the humanities, and science and technology. Overall there is a strong bias to vocational education. (Similarly with the monotechnics which specialise in one interest, e.g. in agriculture or retail distribution.) The 'polys' provide a variety of types of course, including day-release and 'sandwich' courses as well as full-time courses, so that about half of the students are only part-timers.

About half of the polytechnic students follow degree courses (approved by the Council for National Academic Awards or CNAA). Others will be studying for various diplomas and certificates (such as those of the business and Technician Education Council, or BTEC, and ICSA). The administration and finance of the polytechnics was, until the *Education Reform Act, 1988*, the responsibility of the LEAs. They are now self-governing institutions (like the universities).

The LEAs had similar responsibilities for the colleges of higher education, of which there are about 150 with some 35,000 students. Twenty-eight of these have become autonomous alongside the polys. The colleges of education are the centres which train students to teach. To qualify as teachers the students must follow a three-year course of study; plus an extra year to gain the B.Ed. degree. Following a fall in the school population (and the 'James Report', 1973) a number of colleges have been closed and the nature of education courses changed, and these Institutes or Colleges of Higher Education (CHEs) now offer more general degree and professional courses. In 1981 a National Advisory Council was established for this LEA advanced further education sector (i.e. 'polys' and colleges of education) sector as a counterpart to the UGC. But under the 1988 Act this was replaced by the Polytechnics and Colleges Funding Council (PCFC) which parallels the UFC.

The universities on the one hand, and the polys and colleges of education on the other, present what is called the **binary system** of higher education. The division is not so much in the differing nature of their work, since they obviously overlap, but in the way they are organised: the universities are independent while the polys and colleges of education are maintained. One of the current policy issues concerns the wisdom of maintaining such a division as opposed to seeking to unify the whole area of higher education.

Other education provision

The Open University (OU). This started in 1971 and has some 90,000 students (from 30,000 in 1975 and 60,000 in 1980). This number is more than any other university or college in Britain. Originally referred to as 'the university of the air' (lectures and lessons are broadcast on radio and television), the OU requires no formal academic entry qualifications. It aims to give a second chance to those who missed educational opportunities earlier in life, but who cannot find the resources to study full-time. In this respect the OU is like other **correspondence colleges** or institutions (e.g. Wolsey Hall, National Extension College, Rapid Results and others) which collectively have some 500,000 registered students (including overseas students).

The Open University is 'open' in other ways; in particular it is open to unregistered students who may simply see or hear its programmes by accident or by design. In 1987 there began a similar **open college** or 'open tech' providing courses on a similar basis, but not up to degree level.

The BBC and IBA. Meanwhile the broadcasting authorities (BBC and IBA) produce a number of programmes geared to adult education, further education and to schools. In addition, many of their general broadcasts are of an educational and serious nature and obviously reach a very wide audience.

Newspapers. Great Britain has one of the highest readerships of daily newspapers in the world. There are hundreds of magazines and journals, books and audio-tapes. Articles and contributions in these publications are frequently educational and some are specialist, e.g. the *National Geographical Magazine, New Scientist, Community Care, Local Government Chronicle* and *The Economist*.

Miscellaneous. Formal training and educational courses are provided by the trade unions, the Co-operative Society, the armed forces, the Church and private firms and companies. Less formal though no less serious are the multitude of clubs and societies which exist in Great Britain. Some are recreational – e.g. stamp collecting, drama groups – others more learned – e.g. historical or archaeological societies – and the remainder somewhere in between – e.g. the Women's Institutes, Church discussion groups. Quite obviously there is no limit to education in its broadest sense, but we have necessarily concentrated on the formal aspects.

Policy-making and control

Our educational system is notable for its diversity: the universities are *autonomous* while other higher educational institutions are *controlled* by the LEAs. In the schools sector we have the 'dual system' alongside which is the private sector. Teachers have a great deal of professional freedom, and teaching methods range from the very informal and 'free' to the more orthodox and disciplined. The LEAs, who are responsible for most of the educational administration, vary in size, in resources and outlook.

The system has been described as 'the most decentralised and pragmatically organised in Europe'. Though underneath this appearance is 'a tightly-knit structure based on national controls' (Corbett, Open University). What are these controls and who makes policy?

The *Education Act, 1944*, enhanced the powers of the (then) Minister of Education (now Secretary of State). Previously he had 'superintended' education provision; now he is expected to 'promote it', and to do so he has, theoretically, powers to control and direct education authorities. In practice, he never uses his powers dictatorially, but he can exercise control and guidance by setting minimum standards of education provision, approving education building projects (new schools, polytechnics, etc.), determining the supply of teachers, their standards and their distribution (through the 'quota' system). Most of this guidance occurs through the issue of 'regulations' and 'circulars'.

The way the Secretary of State exercises his powers is influenced by Parliament, which can question and debate his actions, and by the LEAs themselves who are widely consulted. For example, the Association of Education Authorities or the teachers' unions (NUT, AMA and others) may be asked for their views on a policy proposal. Indeed, they themselves may initiate the proposals. In fact, the Secretary of State is required by law to appoint two Advisory Councils to advise him on matters of education policy. In practice, other advisory bodies have been created to perform similar, though perhaps more specialised, functions, e.g. the Secondary Examinations Council and under the 1988 Act, the Schools Examinations and Assessment Council and the National Curriculum Council advise on curriculum development (see page 254).

However, the Secretary of State does not determine the curriculum; he does not prescribe or censor books or teaching methods; he does not own or directly control an educational establishment. These aspects and rights rest with the LEAs and the teachers themselves. The Secretary of State can give guidance on such matters, especially through 500 or so of Her Majesty's Inspectors who periodically inspect schools and colleges. The HMIs cannot give orders, but they may criticise, commend and advise.

LEAs, i.e. the county councils and metropolitan district councils, plus the Inner London Education Authority, have the statutory duty 'so far as their powers extend, to contribute towards the spiritual, moral, mental and physical development of the community by securing that efficient education . . . shall be available to meet the needs of the population of their area'. They usually seek to do this through an Education Committee and an Education Department headed by a

Chief Education Officer. It is the LEA acting for the county council which in law employs teachers and ancillary staff, including specialist subject advisers or organisers, and the LEA's own inspectors.

Inevitably there is close contact between the Department of Education and Science and the LEAs, through approval of projects and schemes for reorganisation plans, through administrative circulars and by joint discussions. There is much informal contact too on queries and complaints. The upshot is that the Department of Education and Science exercises power through *influence* rather than through command; and policy matters are very much for local decision, many indeed with individual headteachers. It is partly because of this traditional local discretion in decision-making that so many protests arose over the Education Act, 1976, to *enforce* the abolition of the 11-plus examination throughout Britain. This was repealed in 1979.

Summary of main features of the educational system

1 Predominance of the State sector; more than 90 per cent of schoolchildren are in the State schools.
2 Decentralisation of administration of LEAs, and the freedom within the system (including 3 and 5 below).
3 Freedom of teachers from official direction (though see page 254).
4 Prominent part played by voluntary agencies, especially the Church (this illustrates the mixture of our system and the impact of history).
5 Academic autonomy of the universities.
6 System of financial support for students including mandatory awards.
7 Until recently it was an expanding system, due to population growth and a trend to staying on in education beyond the school-leaving age (16). But a fall in school population and a faltering economy is causing school closures and reductions in higher education places and education expenditure.

Issues and controversies in education today

The cost of education

The cost of providing an education service is enormous: currently over £17,100 million per annum *public* expenditure, i.e. exclusive of private education which is paid for privately and not out of Government sources. In 1984 the expenditure on education equalled that on defence and exceeded that on health, and overall it comprised nearly

14 per cent of Government expenditure. Today (1988) it is less than expenditure on defence (£18,600 million) and health and social services (£19,700 million), and constitutes only 10 per cent of Government spending (and 5 per cent of the Gross National Product, compared to 6.3 per cent in 1976 and 1 per cent in 1900). These relative reductions reflect the fall in the school population and Government policies to reduce State expenditure.

LEAs spend 85 per cent of the sum of £17,100 million. The remainder is spent by the DES (on grants to schools and inspections by the 526 inspectors – HMIs – in England and Wales) and by the universities, the latter receiving 55 per cent of their income from State grants (compared to 80 per cent five years ago).

How is it paid for? Mainly from general **taxation**; with local **rates** paying up to 40 per cent of LEA expenditure, and **charges** providing a small proportion – which means that all courses are subsidised whether they are 'free' or not. In recent years universities and polys have sought to undertake more business sponsorship and contract work.

Some suggestions: (i) It is argued that local authorities can no longer carry such a burden, and so it is suggested that the education service or its costs should be *transferred* from LEAs to the central Government, i.e. direct funding through a specific grant or central payment of teachers' salaries.

(ii) Should we consider *charges* as a way of financing education (and making parents more appreciative of the education service)? In recent years education fees (in FE and HE) and school meals charges have increased substantially, but attempts to charge for music lessons and school transport were defeated in 1981. Other ideas include free *'vouchers'* which parents can spend at any school and add to with their own money; and the notion of 'hiving off' more education to the private sector.

(iii) In the area of higher education (HE), it is suggested that students be given *loans* instead of grants, on the grounds that higher education is an investment, and loans can be repaid from the higher salaries which graduates and the well-qualified usually enjoy. This has now become much more likely with Government proposals (in a White Paper, November 1988) to freeze grants and provide top-up loans.

However, all this raises the question of whether education is a social service and therefore a *social right*. If it is so regarded, then charges will introduce (or reintroduce) a barrier which it has been a long-term aim to abolish. Also to what extent does education contribute to our economic well-being? In the interests of the economy, there may be a need for ever more educational provision, not just to eliminate slum schools or provide better teachers, laboratories, etc., but to provide extended or continuing educational opportunities to facilitate retraining and mobility of the labour force (see page 347), i.e. expenditure on education and training is preferable to unemployment payments.

(iv) Alternatively, we should seek more efficient expenditure in education. This is partly a matter of avoiding waste of manpower and resources. Is it right that there should be as many ancillary staff, administrative and support services as there are teachers? Are buildings and equipment used extensively enough? It is a matter of cost-effectiveness and better education management? Should meals cease to be an education function? Which sectors of education should receive priority? Should we devote more resources to, say, primary education, even at the expense of higher education? Further, does the education system waste much of the talent of the pupils who pass through it?

Equality of opportunity

This implies ease of access and the elimination of barriers such as money or favouritism. The idea of equality of educational opportunities has long been a dominant theme in our educational system and in many ways the history of education in Britain is itself the story of expanding opportunities through:

   (i)   The provision of schools where none existed.
  (ii)   The elimination of fees.
 (iii)   The introduction of compulsion.
  (iv)   The raising of the school-leaving age (ROSLA).
   (v)   Levelling standards among different kinds of schools.
  (vi)   Education welfare services and special education.
 (vii)   Expansion of further and higher education, plus grants.

Undoubtedly a great deal has been achieved in equalising educational opportunities by the removal of barriers. But some barriers remain:

1 *Varying quality among schools.* Equality of opportunity implies ease of access. But access to what? Schools can vary greatly in what they offer in terms of buildings, equipment and staffing. The Newsom Report (1963) drew attention to the seriously inadequate buildings and the higher teacher turnover in schools in slum areas of towns. The Plowden Report (1967) also drew attention to deprived areas and deprived groups, recommending that they should be given extra resources in order to achieve equality. This led to the creation of Educational Priority Areas (EPAs) which

received extra resources to enhance school facilities and attract additional teachers.

2   *Varying status.* Equality is not achieved simply through providing similar school buildings and staffing ratios. While secondary modern and secondary grammar schools were supposed to be separate but equal *in esteem*, merely selecting and providing for differing abilities and aptitudes, *in practice* secondary modern schools often came to be regarded as providing a second-class education for second-class employees and citizens; even though some developed examination courses such as the GCE and CSE (now to merge as the GCSE), they were seldom a first choice among parents.

3   *Selection.* Because of this development, selection at 11-plus came to be condemned, especially by middle-class parents who found that many of their children were going to secondary modern schools because grammar school places were limited and fees could no longer purchase a grammar school place as was the case before the Second World War. Besides, the percentage of grammar school places varied among LEAs and areas, and was partly determined by the birth-rate 10 years previously. Also the 11-plus tests were often shown to be an inaccurate guide to children's abilities (see page 226).

Comprehensive schools have been seen as a means of avoiding these difficulties, together with removing the stigma of 'failing' the 11-plus. They also have the positive merit of mixing those from different social backgrounds as well as those of differing abilities. But there are difficulties here. Some complain of some comprehensive schools being too big; others complain of the 'neighbourhood school' with students drawn from a catchment area which is predominantly of one social class.

Another criticism is that many comprehensive schools simply substituted internal selection for external selection, i.e. by **streaming** the pupils according to ability when they reach the comprehensive school. There is a great deal of dispute here about the efficiency of mixed-ability teaching as opposed to 'setting' and 'streaming'. One particular criticism of the latter, and indeed selection generally, is that it determines or strongly influences the expectations of both pupils and teachers and produces something of a self-fulfilling prophecy: initial success breeds success and high expectations, and initial failure breeds a sense of hopelessness, or at least places firm limits on ambition. A study in 1969 (J. Ford, *Social Class and the Comprehensive School*) showed that within comprehensive schools streaming reinforced the social-class influences on children's performances. Thus among children of equally high intelligence, those from working-class backgrounds had only a 50 per cent chance of entering the top or exam stream in the comprehensive school, and an even lower 20 per cent chance of entering the top stream of the grammar school, in comparison to middle-class children. This suggests that comprehensive schools as such will not achieve equality of opportunity. Schooling *can* make a difference to children's overall achievement (see M. Rutter, *Fifteen Hundred Hours*) but home background is of greater importance (see page 250).

The private sector

The private sector, which caters for about 6 per cent of schoolchildren, is criticised as buying privileged education, not just in superior facilities in and around the school, but also in social exclusiveness and pathways to prestigious higher education and occupations. These are among the criticisms made by the Public Schools Commission Reports of 1968 and 1970. Yet it can be argued that these schools save money for the State and provide an extra element of choice of parents. Furthermore, the high standards of the best of them provide something of a challenge or model for the State sector. While not all private schools provide a particularly good education, they may be chosen because they are small or local or perhaps they offer some special feature such as music or sport which is not readily available elsewhere. Besides, many parents will seek a boarding education for their children, because the parents regard it as desirable in itself or because their jobs (e.g. army) require them to move house, and boarding school places are very limited in the State sector.

Labour Governments look askance at the private sector as undermining the notion of equality of opportunity and as part of their policy Direct Grant Schools were phased out under the *Education Act, 1976*. (See page 227.)

The 16–19 age group

It has long been felt that this age group is neglected by the educational system. Many see it as a crucial age in relation to education, because:

1 They are formative years, being the threshold of adult life;
2 Education can reveal opportunities and broaden the outlook of those who left school early and started work. 'Many young people may change their vocational expectations or will develop them after 16 as they become more aware of their needs.' (Macfarlane Report 'Education for 16–19 Year Olds', 1980).
3 For those at work, education provision can allow them to keep up with those who stayed on in full-time education because they could afford to.

4   Modern industrial society needs a well-educated, up to date, adaptable work force.

Yet the majority (55 per cent) of pupils leave at the minimum school leaving age of 16 (though this is an improvement on the 63 per cent of 1975). And only a minority of these have access to further education (FE); 30 per cent of the 16–18 age group are in full-time education and only 15 per cent attend FE courses on day-release from work (and there are great variations in day-release among occupations). So apart from the unemployed, the majority of this age group receive no FE or training. Many therefore feel that the legislation of 1918 and 1944 should be fully implemented in this respect. A number of schemes have been suggested, including the universal payment of educational maintenance allowances. Superseding the Youth Opportunities Programme (YOPs) is the Government's ambitious Youth Training Scheme (YTS) for unemployed youngsters (see pages 350–1), together with the one-year full-time Certificate of Pre-Vocational Education (CPVE) course for 80,000 less academic youngsters (post-16) which aims to provide some work experience and prepare youngsters for the world of work.

Sex

There is a particularly striking differential between the sexes in access to education and training, for whereas 40 per cent of males of 16–18 are released by employers for FE, this is two and a half times the figure for females in that age group (and these are overwhelmingly concentrated in hairdressing). In the field of higher education, males used to significantly outnumber female students; but now the balance is 55 : 45 per cent. But in the school sector there is growing disquiet over the curriculum and equal opportunities. In 1988 a number of schools (in Swansea) were found guilty by the Equal Opportunities Commission of sexual discrimination. It found that girls were being hindered from taking craft lessons, and similarly, boys were being discouraged from taking cookery and needlework.

Pre-school education

It would appear that over the last 100 years opportunities for pre-school education have diminished rather than increased (Blackstone, *A Fair Start*, 1971) and despite the 1944 Act making nursery education compulsory the long awaited expansion did not occur. However, in recent years there has been an improvement for the proportion of 3–4 year-olds enjoying nursery education has risen to 45 per cent from 21 per cent in 1971 (though they are mainly the older children of the age group). About 15,000 voluntary playgroups help to fill the gap to some extent). The *advantages* of nursery education are:

1 Children develop mentally and socially and physically most rapidly and crucially in the first seven or eight years of life. (An estimate from the USA suggests that we gain 50 per cent of our intelligence by the age of four.) Consequently they will thrive with stimulus of organising play and interaction with other children and adults.
2 Many children are isolated at home because they have no brothers or sisters, and only one parent or they live in tower blocks.
3 Many more mothers are going out to work.
4 It provides a gradual loosening of 'apron strings' and a gentle introduction to the wider world, including primary schooling itself.

Consequently, in 1972 the Government published plans (in *A Framework for Expansion*) to more than double the pre-school places over a 10-year period. There has been some expansion, but economic circumstances have now forced most LEAs to freeze or reduce their nursery education provision, and under the *Education Act, 1980*, such provision ceased to be a duty for LEAs.

Higher and adult education

It is sometimes suggested that higher education has been over-expanded, and that we ought to reconsider our priorities and our expenditure in favour of, say, nursery and primary schools, on the grounds that this would be a better investment. In practice since 1981, Government expenditure cuts forced universities to reduce their student intake which jettisons the Robbins Report (1963) principle that higher education should be available to all those able and willing to pursue it – and at a time when the 18-plus population (and youth unemployment) was at its peak. Indeed a new principle has been enunciated by the chairman of the Universities Funding Council (UFC), Lord Chilver that students qualified to enter HE should also be willing to commit their own resources to pay for it. (Even today, only 14 per cent of the age group are in HE – well below the figures for Europe and USA.)

Adult education is usually the first victim of any education cuts, and it is often held to be a neglected area of the education system. The Russell Report (1973) pointed to much unmet need (e.g. over 50 per cent of adults had left school at or below the age of 14). In recent years provision has increased (partly a result of the ageing population), with enrolments standing at 2.65 million (including 1.2 in WEA and university classes). There has also been an increase in vocational subjects since 1981. Generally, courses comprise 23 per cent academic and commercial subjects, 35 per cent arts and physical and 26 per cent craft and domestic. But overall it only receives 0.5 per cent of the education budget.

In one particular aspect it is making important strides, in conjunction with FE; this is in **Access Courses**, which aim to enhance the opportunities for many older students who 'missed the boat' earlier, to qualify for entry to HE.

In the field of higher education itself, one particular issue is that of the 'binary system', i.e. where the universities on the one hand are self-governing and have their own special sphere of pure learning and research, and the polytechnics and colleges of education are LEA maintained until 1989 (see page 240) and geared more to the needs of industry, commerce and the professions. It is argued by some that the distinction and division in management and function have developed into a division and distinction of status, with the polytechnics receiving second-class acclaim, and, perhaps relatively, less favourable resources, leading on to the conclusion that they should merge and form 'poly-universities'.

Home background

The Robbins Report of 1963 showed that entrance to universities by students from non-manual (working) families was about six and a half times greater than for students from manual families; this was little different to the situation existing in 1930. Surprisingly there has been no change since though the proportion of working class 21-year-olds in higher education has improved from 3.2 per cent in 1963 to 6.9 per cent in 1985. Many other reports show the social class differential in favour of the middle class for entry to grammar schools, sixth forms and 'A' streams, and external examinations. These achievements could, of course, be due to superior innate ability. Indeed, there is some evidence to suggest that middle-class children score about 20 points higher than working-class children in measured IQ tests. But many would dispute these figures, and argue that IQ is evenly distributed throughout the population. Others would argue that the data may be technically correct, but only for the measures used, i.e. is measured IQ really 'intelligence', and may it not be influenced by environmental conditions, including upbringing or even early stimulus in the first five years? The whole issue has been further clouded following the 'Burt scandal' (see page 226).

There is much evidence of the impact of home background on education and other development (e.g. J. D. B. Douglas *Home and School*, K. Fogelman *Growing Up in Britain*). It can be shown that a child's performance at school is very much influenced by such things as size of family; position in family (eldest, youngest, etc.); education of parents and their attitude to education; quality of parental care. One particular aspect of this has to do with the development of language where it is suggested by Bernstein that the 'elaborated' language of middle-class children enables them to perform better at school than children with a more restricted code. Early leaving is also a particular feature of working-class children (about twice that of middle-class).

All in all the chances of receiving and responding to education are based very much according to social class. But can we *blame* the educational system for this? There are three views on this question:

(a) Those who would put the blame on the educational system say that we should get rid of such things as streaming and selection; that teachers should have a greater understanding of social processes and social problems (especially since teachers are mainly middle class); that school values which clash with those of working-class culture are not necessarily the right ones or the only valid ones.

(b) Others hold that the educational system is partly to blame, so that insofar as family and neighbourhood do not provide the milieu appropriate to scholastic success, that sufficient extra educational resources should be provided to compensate. Both of these views apply to the case of **racial disadvantage**. A number of recent reports (Parliament's Home Affairs Committee, 1981; Scarman Report, 1981) have pointed out the relative educational deprivation of areas of high immigrant population. The Rampton Report (1981) and the Swann Report (1985) attribute under-achievement in West Indian children to racism, negative teacher attitudes and an inappropriate curriculum. (A recent EEC report shows only 43,000 of the estimated ½ million children in the UK whose mother tongue is not English are taught at school in their own language.)

(c) Those who completely absolve the educational system from any blame for the apparent social class differential in educational achievement argue that if differences arise from the social background, then 'that's life; we cannot all be equal and we cannot all win prizes'.

Finally there is a view emerging that equality of educational opportunity should no longer be seen simply in terms of equality of *access*, but rather in terms of equality of *achievement*. Such a view suggests that the educational system should play its part where possible, but in the long run what is required is to equalise *life-chances* through a change in the structure of society, perhaps even to the extent of abolishing schools!

Standards, content and goals

In post-war years, education standards have greatly improved – at least in terms of examination achievement by pupils. One recent measure shows that today 74 per cent of 25–29-year-olds have educational qualifications at least equal to one CSE (see page 227) compared to only 42 per cent for the 50–59-year-old age group.

Since the 1970s economic problems combined with a deliberate policy of reducing State expenditure, have led to Government spending cuts. These are partly justified in education by falling school rolls. But in April 1982 a Government Inspectors' (HMI) report expressed fears at the consequences for education standards (reiterated in a report in May 1984).

However, education standards have been criticised for 20 years. Various factors (apart from expenditure) have been blamed: lack of discipline, poor teaching, comprehensive schools, 'free learning' methods, etc. The evidence is conflicting and inconclusive – especially as there is no universal agreement on the aims, content, or measure of education. Education must reflect society (as well as help change it). Thus schools should adjust to Britain's becoming a multiracial society and to women's greater equality. Although it is the formal curriculum which receives most attention, there are implications here for the 'hidden curriculum' i.e. what we learn unconsciously at school – values, achievements, rewards, patience, queuing, hierarchy, attitudes to authority, sex roles, etc. The Thompson Report (page 210) says, 'Schooling . . . is presented as a preparation for life and subsequent employment. For many it brings real opportunities, but for some disappointment and the stigma of failure. Moreover, some of the variations in school experience appear to mirror divisions in society itself, so that schooling comes to seem for some not the ladder of opportunity it was held up to be, but a foretaste of the frustrations which will be experienced later on. The experience of unemployment may be a test and a challenge, but it may equally produce a strong awareness of the futility of growing up into society's ideal person – well-educated and hardworking, when neither good education nor employment are real possibilities.'

In recent years Government education policy has had a number of (not entirely compatible) strands. The first is the orientation towards business. The DES has pointed out that LEAs have 'an inescapable duty to satisfy themselves that the work of the schools matches national needs'. They are urged to promote greater links (i) with business (through sponsorships, guest speakers from industry (or 'industrial tutors'), business members of governing bodies and business educational initiatives such as Shell's Education Service and Business in the Community), (ii) with the world of work (through work experience, link schemes and job shadowing) and (iii) to develop a more positive attitude towards technology (e.g. in 1980 a 4-year Microelectronics Education Programme was started). A further development has been the introduction in 1983 of the TVEI, i.e. Technical and Vocational Training Initiative (via the MSC) for those aged 14–18 who are less academically inclined. The teaching is more job-related, and aims to boost interest, motivation and sense of achievement – bearing in mind the high rates of truancy and that 100,000 leave school with no exam passes. Running parallel is the (1984) Certificate of Pre-Vocational Education (CPVE) which is awarded to an estimated 80,000 over-16-year-olds who follow (in schools or colleges) a one-year, full-time course of general education and vocational training as a preparation for adult life and work. The most recent development here is the establishment of 20 City Technology Colleges (CTCs) and City Colleges for the Technology of the Arts, financed by the Government and business (not LEAs) which aim to provide a model for the effective teaching of science, technology and business understanding. Outside the school sector, there is the YTS for 16–17-year-olds (see page 343) and a network of Regional Technology Centres which link HE institutions with business.

Some see this work-related focus as too narrowing and as sacrificing education for training. Others see it as misguided in view of the continuing high level of youth unemployment. A third view sees it as further Government centralisation (along with rate-capping of local authorities). Marxists go further and view it as another aspect of manipulation by capitalist employers (along with most school knowledge which they see as reflecting and sustaining bourgeois, middle class values). Thus we have a strong debate between those who criticise our education system as being too influenced by the past, dominated by 'the over-academic, decontextualised and useless', and those who condemn the trend towards 'vocationalisation' of education as materialistic, restrictive and divisive.

Second, the Government has sought to increase the power and influence of parents, and provide more opportunity for choice in education. Under the *Education Act, 1980,** parents became elected members of schools' governing bodies and under the 1986 Act, their representation was increased (subsequently to a majority position) thus giving them an important role in curriculum formation and the management of schools. The former Act also secured their right to a choice of school for their children, plus an appeals system (in so far as this is compatible with the efficient use of schools and the availability of resources. Under current legislation (see below) parents may now vote to transfer schools out of LEA control.

*This Act also abolished corporal punishment in schools.

Third is the policy of raising standards. This is to be achieved partly by a revised examination system. Apart from the introduction (1987) of AS-levels (which are intended to broaden sixth formers' studies by providing supplementary studies to their A-levels) the greatest change is the replacement of the GCE ('O' level) and CSE with the GCSE, which aims to 'promote more effectively worthwhile knowledge, understanding and skills'. But higher standards are to be achieved mainly by the *Education Reform Act, 1988* (popularly called the GERBIL, the Great Education Reform Bill). It is a reform of fundamental importance, and provides for:

(a) A national curriculum for all State schools (comprising 3 core subjects – English, maths, science – and 7 other foundation subjects).
(b) Assessment and testing at ages of 7, 11, 14 and 16.
(c) Increased public information on pupil performance and education services generally.
(d) Schools to admit pupils up to their capacity (rather than any limits imposed by the LEA).
(e) The delegation of budgets to individual colleges, secondary and larger primary schools, heads and governors (also known as local management of schools or LMS).
(f) All secondary and larger primary schools to be able to vote (via governors and parents) to opt out of LEA control and become autonomous institutions with direct funding from the DES (and known as 'grant-maintained schools').
(g) The establishment of City Technology Colleges (see page 253).

Many see this legislation as a liberating measure, providing opportunities for initiative and diversity. Others see it as a threat to liberty, with the imminent demise of LEAs and of teacher freedom in the classroom. It is estimated that about 50 schools will apply to opt for grant-maintained status in the first year of the scheme, though it may be that many of these will do so in order to avoid the threat of closure by LEAs concerned at low pupil rolls.

Questions

1 State the main provisions of, and reasons for, the following: the Education Acts of 1870, 1902, 1944, 1980 and 1986.
2 Discuss two of the following issues: (a) comprehensive schools, (b) nursery education, (c) the contraction of higher education or (d) equality of opportunity.
3 What are Educational Priority Areas? Why were they created? Are they justified?

4   To what extent does central government control education in Britain?
5   There are said to be 2 million illiterate and innumerate people in Britain, and leaders of industry have complained of the low standard of entrants to firms and companies. If you were Secretary of State for Education and Science how would you ensure that standards were improved to meet this criticism?
6   Discuss the place and function of (a) the polytechnics, and (b) the Open University in the educational system of Britain.

10
Housing

Introduction

Shelter, like food, is a basic human requirement. A lack of housing thus presents an obvious social problem. But housing itself presents some special problems because of its special characteristics; it is not an ordinary commodity, such as clothing or food.

Features of housing

The main special features of housing are:

1 It is very durable, and so normally has a long life.
2 It is fixed in location (apart from caravan homes).
3 It is expensive, and can absorb a large percentage of the householder's income.
4 It is usually rented, or bought on 'hire purchase' (i.e. by mortgage).
5 New supplies are only a small addition to the stock (about 2 per cent per annum).
6 Since it is a necessity, demand is relatively inelastic, i.e. a change in price does not have a marked effect on demand.

In addition there have developed certain 'special' attitudes to housing:

(a) The 'spiritual' attitude, i.e. people get very attached to their house as a home. It becomes more than just a commodity – four walls and a roof. It becomes something highly personal, charged with memories and attachments.
(b) The 'social service' attitude, i.e. the widely held view arising from past policies that housing, especially rented, should be low-priced. This has been called the 'housing illusion' (see W. Hagenbuch, *Social Economics*).
(c) The 'public health' attitude, i.e. the appreciation that the effects of bad housing are not confined to the inhabitants but can affect

the physical, mental and moral health of whole areas. Hence the considerable control developed by the public authorities in the nineteenth century.

Briefly, then, housing has become accepted as a social service because (a) it is a necessity, (b) expensive, (c) its provision is open to abuse and (d) bad housing can be a nuisance and a hazard to the health of the community.

History

Housing can be seen as one of our oldest social services, with provision for the homeless being incorporated in the Poor Law arrangements. Today housing policy is extensive, pervasive and important. It is important for the building industry, for the economy and above all for householders. Government action on mortgages, council housing, rents and slums are all taken for granted. But such policies are really quite new. In fact, a specific housing policy did not emerge until the nineteenth century, when, in the interests of public health, the State intervened in such matters as overcrowding, insanitary conditions, housing density and building regulations. The actual supply of houses was left to private and voluntary enterprise. The State was just seeking to develop a supervisory and regulatory role. Where landlords failed to keep their properties in good repair, local authorities could act in default, by closing them, demolishing them and replacing them (see *Housing Acts, 1868* and *1875*).

It is because these first council houses were designed to replace slums and rehouse slum dwellers that local authority housing has been left with something of a stigma. Indeed, the nineteenth-century legislation explictly stated the clientele in their titles: Artisans and Labourers' Dwellings Act, Labouring Classes Dwelling Houses Act, Housing of the Working Classes Act. The class distinction thus created between private and public housing was formally abolished in the *Housing Act, 1946*, but its spirit lingers on.

The following table illustrates the difference in the pattern of tenure and ownership between 1890 and 1980:

Tenure Pattern	1890	1970	1980
Private rented	90%	20%	13%
Owner-occupied	10%	50%	55%
Local authority	–	30%	32%

These figures show how the composition of our housing stock has changed during the twentieth century. The changes are rather striking, and there are many reasons for them:

1 New opportunities for investment have emerged so that capital funds have been attracted away from investment in houses to let and into such things as stocks and shareholdings.
2 Opportunities for owner-occupation have increased with the emergence of building societies, higher incomes and favourable interest rates.
3 Local authorities have been encouraged to provide accommodation to such an extent that they are now responsible for housing some 20 million people.
4 Legal restrictions on overcrowding and rents have reduced the profitability of private renting.

Thus, to explain our current range of housing provision we must take account of previous governments' housing policies.

Outline of housing policy

Before the Second World War. Legislation at the end of the nineteenth century allowed local authorities to provide lodging houses and houses to let as they saw necessary (i.e. not merely to replace slums). Not many councils made use of these powers, and it took the tragedy of the First World War to stimulate the large-scale provision of houses by local authorities. During the war house-building ceased, and in 1919 there was an estimated housing shortage of more than 600,000. Consequently the Government committed itself to a policy of 'homes fit for heroes to live in' by the *Housing Act, 1919*. This introduced **housing subsidies**, i.e. government grants to local authorities and private builders to supply low-cost houses for renting.

Over the next ten years these subsidies were frequently modified and redirected, especially with changes in government. Thus, for example, emphasis was shifted back and forth between local authorities and private builders as the main providers. Ultimately in the 1930s subsidies ceased for further new houses. Under the *Housing Act, 1930*, subsidies were to be paid to local authorities on the basis of the number of persons rehoused following slum clearance. Consequently, for the rest of the period the emphasis in the public sector was on **slum clearance**. The provision of additional new houses was left largely to private enterprise, which experienced a **building boom**, due to low interest rates, reduced building costs and a growing demand from those in employment and enjoying a rise in real incomes. As annual house-building expanded to a record figure of nearly 350,000 in the year 1937, this became the era of the suburb.

Meanwhile, in 1935, **overcrowding** was officially defined and made illegal. At the same time local authorities were empowered to survey their areas and, with some limited subsidy assistance, could provide

additional houses where necessary. However, while the surveys revealed about one third of a million dwellings as overcrowded (and
unofficial estimates put the figure nearer 1 million), only some 24,000
houses were built to replace overcrowded dwellings.

A further strand of housing policy was **rent control**. In 1915 rents
were frozen, except for new properties. By the early 1920s the
continued existence of rent control was being criticised as a deterrent
to private landlords and a hindrance to population mobility. Consequently a series of measures in the 1920s and 1930s loosened controls
and allowed de-control of middle- and upper-value properties.

All these developments took place against a background of a
steadily improving housing situation. In the inter-war period generally over 4 million houses were built. Of these more than 1 million
were provided by local authorities, and the rest by private enterprise.
Meanwhile the population rose by 4 million, and households by about
2¼ million. Consequently:

(a)   There was an approximate balance in the number of houses and
      families.
(b)   One in three households lived in modern dwellings, and one in
      ten lived in council houses.
(c)   Houses were built to higher standards, with more space and
      facilities.

But most houses went for sale, and thus to the middle- and upper-
working classes. Housebuilding was unevenly distributed and declining industrial depressed areas tended to be neglected. Among local
authorities housebuilding and slum clearance varied considerably,
and in 1939 some 4 million families were living in houses over 80
years old and 1 million families were living in slums.

After the Second World War. As a result of the war housebuilding
ceased, maintenance was suspended and about ¾ million houses
were destroyed or severely damaged. Altogether in 1945 about one
house in three needed some sort of attention. Consequently the
coalition Government established several housebuilding targets, and
had in the meantime frozen private rents at the 1939 level.

Under the *Housing Act, 1946*, the Labour Government (1945–51)
introduced general housing subsidies and placed emphasis for building almost completely upon local authorities and council houses to
let. However, a rapid rise in building costs, coupled with the economic crisis of 1947, led to a cut-back in the housebuilding programme,
but in 1949 local authorities were empowered to make grants for the
improvement or conversion of properties.

The Conservatives (1951–64) on entering office declared a national
housing shortage of about 1 million houses, a situation made worse
by the 'drift' of population to the south-east, which left empty many

properties in other areas. Consequently in 1952 the Government increased subsidies, reduced new housing standards and raised the permitted level of private house building. In 1956 the general housing subsidy was abolished, with subsidies being retained only for slum clearance and housing for the elderly. Yet, as a result of a substantial increase in household formation and increasing evidence of home-lessness and overcrowding during the later 1950s the Government reintroduced general subsidies in 1961. Meantime, the controversial *Rent Act, 1957*, decontrolled dwelling of £30 plus rateable value (£40 in London) and allowed other rent controls to cease with a change of tenant ('creeping decontrol').

Under the *Rent Act, 1965*, the Labour Government (1964–70) introduced rent regulation, based on 'fair rents' in respect of houses with a rateable value of up to £200. It also restructured the subsidy system such that individual local authorities' borrowing charges would be pegged to 4 per cent interest. At the same time (1967) the Option Mortgage Scheme was introduced in order to reduce (lower income) borrowers' mortgage interest charges by up to 2 per cent. The *Leasehold Reform Act, 1967*, sought to safeguard the tenure of many leaseholders. Meanwhile, since 1964 the newly established Housing Corporation had been helping to finance Housing Associations. Then the *Housing Improvement Act, 1969*, purported to make it easier to turn 'old houses into new homes' by encouraging moderni-sation and rehabilitation through increased grants to property own-ers.

The most controversial policy commitment of the decade was the *Housing Finance Act, 1972*, under which the Conservative Govern-ment (1970–74) sought to create a 'Fair Deal for Housing' by raising all rents, but at the same time providing universal rent aid or remission for those eligible. In the following year some *furnished* tenancies were brought into the fair rent category of regulation. The latter was extended under the Labour Government when in 1975 furnished tenancies acquired security of tenure. In the same year part of the *Housing Finance Act, 1972*, was repealed to allow local authorities to return, within reason, to fixing their own rents (being assisted in this by fresh housing subsidies). Meanwhile, under the *Housing Act, 1974*, local authorities are empowered to require or encourage, through generous grants, private housing improvements in newly created 'Housing Action Areas'. Finally, under the *Com-munity Land Act, 1975*, local authorities were empowered to acquire and release land for development. However, with a change of government in 1979, the Community Land Act was repealed (under the *Local Government, Planning and Land Act, 1980*) and the new decade began with the controversial *Housing Act, 1980* (see page 281).

Thus do we see that housing policy, somewhat in contrast to other social services, is subject to the ups and downs of the economy and the 'ins and outs' of party politics. This is partly due to the fact that the building industry is a significant element in the government's economic management and partly because housing is substantially within the private sector.

The nature of a housing policy

The need for a policy arises from the fact that the State now accepts that it has a commitment to see that people are decently housed. The degree of commitment can be gauged partly by crude measures such as the amount of government expenditure devoted to housing or by the quantity of legislation over a period dealing with housing.

Apart from overall commitment and degree of priority given to housing, housing policy is concerned with achieving certain objectives, not just an adequate overall supply of accommodation, but supply at the right price for people to afford, at an adequate standard and in the right place. It is easy to claim 'no shortage' when there exist lots of vacant properties, but it may be that these homes are unsuitable by way of price, location, standard or even style (e.g. high-rise flats which some people with young families find unsuitable and reject).

A third aspect of housing policy is the detailed forms it takes to achieve its objectives. Should housing policy take place, like the NHS, through universal State provision? Or like education in the nineteenth century, by ensuring that others provide a sufficiency? Or perhaps like traditional transport policy, by intervening in the private system through price-fixing? In practice recent housing policy assumes all three forms: with direct provision by local authorities; with grants and tax reliefs to landlords and owner-occupiers; and with rent regulation and subsidies. The validity of each, indeed all, of these methods is strongly argued and forms the major ingredient in arguments about housing policy.

The context of housing policy

Housing policy is concerned essentially with matching demand and supply of housing. Some of the elements which made up demand and supply are beyond control. Other elements are within the control of Government, or are at least subject to its influence. The main elements on the **demand** side are:

(i) The size and growth of the population.
(ii) The structure of the population: changing age and sex composition will significantly affect the rate of marriage and household formation.

(iii) Social trends, such as the stability of marriage, the mobility of the population, people's standards and expectations.

(iv) Economic trends: the growing affluence of the 1950s and 1960s not only raised people's expectations, but provided the means to increase the demand for housing. So has the growing availability of capital, with the rise of Building Societies and the spread of buying on credit. On the other hand, interest charges and taxation, such as rates, will reduce demand.

The main elements on the **supply** side are:

(i)   Houses provided by private builders for owner-occupation.
(ii) Landlords who let their properties for rent.
(iii) Local authorities who let or perhaps sell their houses to tenants.

The provision of new houses (or 'units of accommodation' to be more precise) will depend upon the capacity of the building industry, availability of land and supplies of capital. But overall, new building per annum adds only about 2 per cent to the total housing stock of the nation. In addition to new units of accommodation we must consider:

(iv) The utilisation of existing houses – for example, can a large house be made into several flats or can the interval during which houses stand empty be reduced?

(v)   The maintenance of dwellings: to what extent can we 'increase' overall supply by diminishing the number which fall into disrepair?

A further consideration in all this is the acceptable standard of housing. We could boost the supply of housing by reducing standards. On the other hand, people's standards or expectations are rising, which means that an acceptable house in 10 years' time will require more resources than a house that was acceptable 10 years ago. What is more, as we have seen, a house is not just a commodity, like a soap powder; it is individual, something personal, so that no two houses are in fact identical.

What is 'the housing problem'?

We all know there is a housing problem. In fact it has been a popular expression ever since the First World War when Lloyd George, as Prime Minister, promised 'homes fit for heroes to return to'. But what exactly does it mean? Obviously it means there are not enough houses and there are homeless people. But equally obviously, it means more than that, for a house is not a home unless it is in a fit condition and is satisfactory in other ways.

Briefly, the housing problem has many ingredients, many of which overlap:

(a) **Quantity** is the most obvious aspect: how many houses in relation to the demand, or, perhaps we should say, need? This is sometimes cynically called 'the numbers game', the implication being that we must take account of other aspects, such as the costs of housing. Abundant houses at high prices can still leave many homeless.

(b) **Quality** is another important aspect. Quality implies reasonable standards, and it can be argued that living in a slum is tantamount to being homeless. Having a roof over your head is not enough. Similarly, living in overcrowded surroundings is hardly being 'housed'. One difficulty with standards and measures of crowding is our changing perspective so that as we raise standards, so we increase the problem (like 'the poverty line'). A further aspect of quality is security of tenure. Being under the threat of eviction or dispossession is only marginally removed from the state of homelessness.

(c) **Location** is an important consideration, especially as transport becomes more expensive, less available or more time-consuming. The need to journey to work, or for leisure, can reduce the quality of life. Yet not everyone can live near his work; hence the suburbs, the congestion, traffic management and planning policies to disperse population, e.g. New Towns (see page 297). One of the current issues is the problem of the 'inner city', how the big cities and conurbations are 'sinking in the middle' like a soufflé as population moves to the suburbs, the overspill areas and the New Towns, leaving behind a legacy of decay, unemployment and despair.

(d) **Special groups.** So far we have looked at the housing problem in general terms. To this we must add the perspective of particular groups who may have specific housing needs or difficulties – for example, black immigrants, the elderly and low-income groups. What of the bad tenant? Should he be evicted for rent arrears? How should houses be allocated? How far should tenants be involved in local authority housing decision-making? In other words, there are the problems associated with housing management.

The housing problem, then, is a catch-all phrase which embraces a collection of problems. We now examine these and the policies to deal with them.

The present housing situation

Between 1945 and 1980 over 10 million houses were built in Great Britain, about half of which were provided by public authorities, the other half privately. Thus our current stock amounted to about 22 million dwellings. Of these about 80 per cent are houses and 20 per cent are flats; a small percentage of the population is housed in caravans, hotels and long-stay hospitals.

Over the same period of time, more than 1 million slums were cleared, which greatly reduced the number of unfit houses and led to the rehousing of more than 3 million people. Until recently, the rate of slum clearance was running at about 70,000 dwellings a year. At the same time some 3 million houses have been improved and

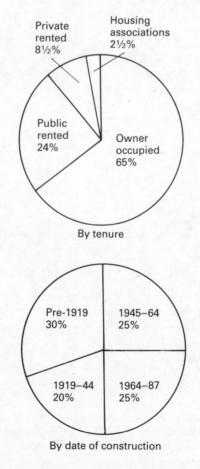

Figure 10   *Housing stock in Britain 1987 (= 22.5 million)*

the same time some 3 million houses have been improved with the aid of government grants, especially since 1969. Again the reduction in the number of dwellings lacking basic amenities (such as running water, indoor w.c.) has been substantial (see page 274).

So most families now live in their own homes, and half live in a post-war dwelling, including over 2 million people in New Towns. The general quality of housing is now higher than ever e.g. 70 per cent are now centrally heated (34 per cent in 1971); only 2 per cent lack sole use of bath or inside toilet (13 per cent in 1971). Overall, it is estimated that supply more than meets demand with a crude surplus of over £1 million dwellings over households (see page 278).

However, over 1 million are not available for occupation: some 250,000 are second homes, and many others are under or awaiting modernisation, repair or sale. Also many households (an estimated 800,000) are composite, with many potentially separate households being forced to live as part of other households (and so are concealed from the figures). Further, about a quarter of all our houses are over 80 years old. In 1981, the English House Condition Survey showed there still to be one million slums and 2½ million dwellings lacking essential amenities or in need of substantial repair (i.e. costing over £7,000 each) – thus amounting to one in six of all houses. The EHC Survey for 1986 shows an improvement, yet 10 per cent of houses need essential repairs of over £2,500 (5 per cent need over £4,000) and over 2 million have defective wiring creating fire hazards and ½ million lack basic amenities. Further, of the 2½ million improvement grants 1981–86, only 15 per cent went to houses in the worst condition, so that 200,000 houses are falling into serious disrepair each year. In addition, there are still many homeless persons (officially, in 1987, 120,000 households). Then there are those who live in overcrowded conditions; the estimates vary from 800,000 (the official figure) to 4 million people (Shelter figure). Many people may be said to be inadequately housed because they find the cost is a real hardship (see F. Allaun, *Heartbreak Housing*).

In the light of these figures, the Government and various authorities (e.g. D. Donnison, Dame Evelyn Sharpe) in 1970 suggested an annual supply of houses of 400,000 and 500,000 to provide for population and household growth, for replacement of old houses and for migration and redevelopment. (In 1977 the Government's revised figure was 300,000 – a figure reiterated by Shelter in 1983. The Housing Research Foundation in 1984 said 220,000 and in 1989 the National Housing Forum estimated 250,000 in *Housing Needs in the 1990s*.)

By 1967, the figure of 400,000 was actually achieved. The 1968 figure was an all-time record; but since then the rate of housebuilding has slumped (see Table 8), largely because of economic difficulties which have led to high interest rates and shortage of capital, and to cuts in public and private expenditure (see page 281). On the other

Table 8   Permanent dwellings completed (Britain)

Year	Number of dwellings	Year	Number of dwellings
1960	298,000	1977	303,000
1966	396,000	1978	280,000
1967	415,000	1979	242,000
1968	426,000	1980	232,000
1969	378,000	1981	198,000
1970	362,000	1982	171,000
1971	364,000	1983	179,000
1973	331,000	1984	203,000
1974	280,000	1985	189,000
1975	322,000	1986	198,000
1976	315,000	1987	203,000

Source: Annual Abstract of Statistics, HMSO and Building Societies Association.

hand, the building of numerous houses may in itself mean little if they are of the wrong type, such as tower blocks, or in the wrong place, say in New Towns, or of poor quality. (It was estimated in 1984 that £5,000 million was needed to replace much of the 'system built' housing of the 1960s and 70s owing to defects in materials, design and workmanship). Also, to concentrate on building new houses may divert attention from a policy of maintaining older houses or from a closer consideration of housing needs and priorities in the allocation of existing houses.

Housing policy, however, has long been criticised for its inconsistency; not only does it swing with the winds of party politics and changes of government but policies which run side by side can be contradictory (for example, raising building standards may increase costs and so homelessness for those who cannot afford better houses). We will, therefore, take a closer look at recent housing policies.

Aspects of current housing policy

Owner-occupation

Well over half the homes in this country are owner-occupied: about 65 per cent in 1989. In 1951 the figure was only 30 per cent and at the beginning of the century a mere 10 per cent; nearly half the increase is due to purchases by former tenants (especially private). Owner-occupation has a number of advantages, such as greater security and as a means of saving. Why, therefore, has it taken so long to increase and spread?

The main reasons have been the high cost of houses and the tradition of living in rented accommodation. However, during this century, private rented accommodation has substantially diminished (see page 257) and at the same time access to home-ownership has increased, partly through greater general affluence and partly as a result of deliberate government policies. These policies include:

1 **Low interest rates.** This was especially important in the 1930s and led to numerous suburban estates.

2 **Tax relief** on mortgage interest, a long-established system, currently costing (1989) an estimated £6,500 million a year (worth over £700 a year to the mortgagor). This has been criticised as inequitable on the grounds that the allowance increases with the value of the house and so the better off gain most as their higher *rate* of tax is eased. (In 1974 a limit of £30,000 was placed on the value to which relief would apply; this figure remains today, though £150,000 would be the true equivalent.)

   The option mortgage scheme was introduced in 1967 as a corollary to tax relief in that it provided for those who, because of low income and low or nil income tax liability, would not benefit from tax relief on mortgage interest. This scheme, therefore, provided mortgages at specially reduced interest rates up to 5 per cent reduction in 1982. About one fifth of mortgages took this form, and the scheme cost about £100 million per annum. It ceased in 1983 with MIRAS (mortgage interest relief at source).

4 In 1963 Schedule A (a tax on home ownership) was abolished.

5 **Rates** are another tax on property, and in 1966 rate rebates were introduced so that people on low incomes would pay reduced rates (in 1982 up to £5.50 p.w., £9 in London, reduction; limits ceased 1983). There is evidence of considerable ignorance and non-take-up of this facility (now in the form of housing benefit).

6 Government policies for land acquisition and development (e.g. the betterment levy, or the community land legislation) are justified in terms of stabilising land and also house prices.

7 **Sale of council houses** has long been a political party issue. The number of such houses which are sold thus tends to vary with the government in office, both centrally and locally.* Conservatives justify the sale of council houses on grounds of extending home-ownership which is inherently worthy, promoting maintenance and creating more of a 'social mix' on housing estates. The

---

*In 1967 and 1976 (Labour in office) sales were 2,000 and 3,000 respectively (including New Towns); in 1972 and 1980 (Conservatives in office) 46,000 and 85,000 were sold. See page 281.

Labour Party often opposes their sale on the grounds that it reduces the stock available to those who need to rent; that instead of selling these houses (at discounted prices) it would be more appropriate to help people to purchase on the private market; and that piecemeal sales create problems of housing administration and management. Thus some of the expansion of owner-occupation is at the expense of council housing, especially in recent years. But much more has been by withdrawals from the private rented sector.

Private rented accommodation

Traditionally this was the most important sector of housing, providing some 90 per cent of homes in the beginning of this century. By 1939 this figure had declined to 65 per cent, and today it stands at less than 15 per cent. In absolute terms it has fallen from 8.5 million houses in 1939 to under 2½ million today.

There are a number of reasons for this decline, such as slum clearance, the image of the 'wicked' landlord, or the sheer cost of building, which means that private renting can no longer appeal to the lower income groups. Most of the responsibility for the decline is laid at the door of rent control, and certainly rent restrictions have caused many landlords to sell off their properties. However, it is also true that the decline began before rent control was introduced in 1915, as funds began to be attracted away via building societies from houses to let to houses for owner-occupation.

Some people are not concerned about the diminution of the private sector, as they feel that there is something inherently wrong in profits from a market for necessities. Others are concerned at the decline, because it narrows choice in the housing market, and the private sector is, by tradition, not only cheap but varied and flexible. To prevent further reduction in supply of private rented accommodation, therefore, it has been suggested that landlords get tax concessions or more reasonable rent income.

Rent policy

The control of rents for private accommodation to let first came into existence in 1915, in an attempt to avoid financial hardship to tenants due to scarcity of housing and the inflation during the First World War. Rent controls were dismantled during the 1930s, but reimposed in 1939 on the outbreak of the Second World War. Rent increases were later allowed for new properties or to cover the cost of repair (under the *Housing Act, 1954*) but rent control was increasingly criticised as: (i) reducing the supply of rented accommodation; (ii) creating waste through under-occupation; and (iii) inhibiting the mobility of labour.

Consequently the controversial *Rent Act, 1957*, decontrolled houses with rateable value of £30 or more and allowed control to lapse on any house where there was a change of tenant (this was called **'creeping decontrol'**). Within 10 years the stock of 5 million 'controlled' houses was halved, mainly through 'creeping decontrol', which in places of severe shortage, e.g. London, was prompted by harassing and racketeering landlords ('Rachmanism', after a notorious character by the name of Rachman). In 1965 the Milner-Holland Committee (HMSO, Cmnd. 2605) reported on rented housing in London, and recommended greater safeguards for security of tenure and also the restoration of some form of rent restriction.

In the same year the *Rent Act, 1965*, therefore introduced **'regulated tenancies'** for properties with rateable value of up to £200 per annum (£400 in London). This meant that tenants were to be protected from intimidation, and eviction would now require a court order. These tenants were now to pay **'fair rents'**, i.e. rents which were agreed by landlord and tenant, perhaps with the help of a Rent Officer or a Rent Assessment Committee. In calculating a fair rent the scarcity element had to be set aside, i.e. the assumption was made that the supply of accommodation was in balance with the demand. The fair rent would take account of considerations such as location and state of repairs. Once agreed, the rent would remain fixed for three-yearly periods. Meanwhile, over 2 million 'controlled tenancies' remained in existence. When they changed tenants they fell into the regulated sector rather than 'creep' into decontrol altogether.

The concept of rent regulation was hailed as a great advance since it provided protection yet it avoided the rigidity of rent control. However, critics pointed to the continuing decline of the private rented sector, and others, observing the extent of rent increases, called the 1965 Act, a 'landlord's charter'. The Government was not sure and in 1969 set up a Committee to examine the workings of the *Rent Act, 1965* (which was reiterated and consolidated in 1968).

The result appeared in 1971 as the Francis Report. This concluded that the 'fair rents system' was working well and that it should in future incorporate the remaining controlled tenancies (about 1.5 million) and also furnished rented accommodation, though it was divided on the question of giving security of tenure to the latter, fearing it might reduce the supply of such accommodation. Subsequently the Government did bring furnished accommodation in the fair rents system (*Furnished Lettings Act, 1973*) and in 1974 they were given security of tenure.

Another form of private letting is **tied accommodation**, where the accommodation goes with the job; this embraces perhaps 1 million dwellings. Agriculture contains most of them, but other occupations include mining, the Armed Forces, forestry, catering and the Church. The most obvious problem with tied accommodation is lack of security of tenure: lose your job and you lose your house. There are other hazards such as the lowering of pay or job mobility. For employers it provides a useful means of attracting staff and consequently employers are anxious to retain the arrangement. The issue has been long argued, and in 1976 legislation provided a compromise (for agriculture). The 70,000 families living in tied cottages in England and Wales were to have security of tenure of the Rent Acts: they could only be removed if the dwelling was necessary for the running of the farm and they were provided with suitable alternative accommodation.

In the meantime the whole structure of rented accommodation, public and private, has been revised under the *Housing Finance Act, 1972*. Before we look at this we must consider the background to the local authority rented housing and subsidies.

Council housing

In the nineteenth century some local authorities had provided houses as replacements for slums they had cleared. After the *Housing of the Working Classes Act, 1890*, a few local authorities provided rented houses to meet local needs generally. But it was under the *Housing Act, 1919*, that council housing as we know it really started to develop. This Act was based on pre-war legislative plans and provided the main contribution to and the main ingredient in the Government's promise of 'homes fit for heroes'. Local authorities were now required to survey their areas and build houses to fill revealed shortages. Apart from the local authority contribution of the revenue from 1*d*. rate, the cost was to be met from central Government grants, or subsidies, and as a result rents could be kept low for the benefit of working-class tenants.

By 1921 some 170,000 houses had been provided under this arrangement (plus a further 40,000 houses built by private building firms who also began to receive grants). In that year, however, the scheme was proving unexpectedly costly for the Government, and subsidies for further building ceased. The housing shortage had not ceased, however, and in 1923 subsidies were revived. This time the subsidies went mainly to private builders, and the local authorities were only to provide houses where the private sector failed to. In the following year, with a change of government, subsidies were shifted back to local authorities (they were paid a fixed grant of £9 p.a. per house to run for 40 years). Within a few years the subsidy schemes were scaled down, and then stopped. By 1933, when subsidies ceased, about 2 million houses (private and local authority owned) had been built on the basis of subsidies. House provision was now to revert to normality, i.e. to private enterprise, although local authorities could continue to provide, without subsidies, if they wished.

Barely ten years later, in 1946, subsidies were revived, and local authorities alone were to receive them. The Second World War had recreated the situation of housing scarcity, and local authorities were seen by the Labour Government as the means of combining a 'housing drive' with a control on the public expenditure of scarce resources. The reality and generality of the shortage was revealed in the *Housing Act, 1946*, which declared that council houses were for *anyone* in need, not just the 'working class'.

By the mid-1950s it was felt that the housing situation had improved sufficiently for general housing subsidies to cease. Yet five years later, in 1961, they were reintroduced. This was largely due to the sustained growth in demand for housing, itself a consequence of the **growing population** and the rapid growth in household formation with the trend to **early marriage**. More recently, the problem arises from rising household formation due to more surviving elderly, more marriage, young people leaving home earlier and more family breakdown.

Criticism of subsidies. Subsidised council housing has long been criticised. Some criticisms are directed at the monotony of housing estates or the quality of the houses. Most criticisms concern the subsidies (whether they were drawn from local rates or from Government grants). Subsidies were said to be: 1. Costly in terms of public expenditure (£230 million in 1972–73). 2. Wasteful of resources because they artificially lower the price (i.e. rents) and distortedly expand demand. 3. Unfair, as among: (i) local authorities, since subsidies are paid to them regardless of their housing problem and circumstances; (ii) tenants, as not all local authorities were operating an income-based rebate system, while others charged uniformly low rents, regardless of the tenant's ability to pay,* and (iii) tax and ratepayers, who might be financing the subsidies for people who were better off than themselves.

On the basis of these criticisms the Government passed the *Housing Finance Act, 1972*; this met with a barrage of opposition. Some

---

*Being a council tenant, despite its apparent growth in popularity, has had serious disadvantages. The most serious was lack of legal security of tenure; but others may include lack of essential repairs and maintenance; living in tower blocks; lack of transfer opportunities; restrictions on such things as alterations, choice of house colour, keeping pets, sub-letting; secretiveness on the basis of the allocation points system. Obviously there are wide variations among local authorities: some are better landlords than others. One radical solution has proposed that tenants take over estates by forming cooperatives and purchasing the properties from councils. But see page 281.

local authorities actually refused to implement the Act; for example, the Clay Cross UDC which ultimately led to legal action in the Courts. The Act dealt with both council and private rented accommodation, and aimed at a 'fair deal' for tenants, landlords and taxpayers. Under the Act:

(a) Existing general subsidies were to cease and rents (public and private, and including the 1.3 million 'controlled' tenancies) were to rise to the 'fair' rent level, as under existing rent regulation arrangements (see page 264),

(b) New subsidies were to be directed to (i) tenants who had difficulty paying the rent; on the basis of a means test they would get a cash **allowance** (if a private tenant) or a rent **rebate** (if a council tenant) and (ii) to local authorities with the worst (e.g. slum) housing problems. (In 1981 50 per cent of council tenants either received rebates or had rent paid by Supplementary Benefits. Since 1983 those on Income Support Benefit receive local authority Housing Benefit instead, see page 63.)

The implementation of the new arrangements was to be phased over three years. But it got caught up with the Government's counter-inflation policy, and in 1974, with a change of government, there was a full stop. Then, under the *Housing, Rents and Subsidies Act, 1975*: (a) General subsidies were reintroduced. (b) Local authorites were freed to determine their own rents: these had, therefore, no longer to be 'fair' rents, but were to be a 'reasonable' balance between the interests of the ratepayers and tenants. (c) All local authorities had to operate a rent rebate scheme.

What the new Labour Government of 1974 objected to was the substantial rise in rents, the 'profiteering' which was a consequence of these higher council rents and the loss of local authority autonomy. Yet in 1975 the Minister himself admitted that housing finance was 'a dog's breakfast' and a thorough review was set in motion, which was completed in 1977 as the Housing Policy Green Paper. It was evident that rents would have to rise: by 1975 rents were meeting only 57 per cent of council house costs, compared to 77 per cent a few years earlier. It was proposed that they would in future rise to keep in line with earnings (which assumed that the existing level and pattern was satisfactory). In fact by 1980, they had fallen to 49 per cent, but rose to 62 per cent after rents more than doubled in the period 1979–82. They have continued to rise since; and while many are cushioned by Housing Benefit (rebate), others are perhaps thereby induced to buy – see page 281. In addition, under the *Housing Act, 1980*, controlled rents were converted to regulated rents (see pages 269 and 281).

Slum clearance

This is the longest established aspect of government housing policy, starting as it did in the mid-nineteenth century. After the First World War emphasis was placed on building new houses, and it was not until the 1930s that slum clearance resumed as the dominant policy.

The pattern repeated itself after the Second World War so that the emphasis on slum clearance re-emerged in the mid-1950s. Through the past 20 years the average rate of clearance or closure has been 60,000 to under 50,000 houses p.a. in recent years (21,500 in 1986). This is substantially below the pre-war figure (90,000 in 1938) and currently leaves about 1 million dwellings unfit for habitation (see page 274).

Part of the problem is cost, public expenditure and the state of the economy. (In 1973 a White Paper 'Widening the Choice: The Next Steps in Housing', rashly declared that all sums would be cleared in a decade.) Another part of the problem is social rather than economic: slum clearance in the form of comprehensive redevelopment is disruptive of communities. Consequently, since the early 1970s, wholesale clearance has been scaled down and replaced by conservation and rehabilitation.

House improvement

Improvement provides a constructive alternative to slum clearance for it seeks to safeguard and enhance our stock of over 22 million dwellings. Only about 2 per cent per annum is added by new building, so it makes sense to look after the 98 per cent we already have. Apart from preventing an outflow (of perhaps 100,000 per annum), improvement or 'rehabilitation' is quicker and cheaper than rebuilding, and it can help preserve *existing* communities – though this is not always so: there is the problem of what has been called 'gentrification', where certain run-down areas of cities are improved, become fashionable and popular, and are taken over by middle-class dwellers.

Public grants to offset part of the cost of housing improvements began in 1926 and were extended by the post-war housing legislation of 1949 and 1954. Grants from both central and local funds were paid at the discretion of local authorities. The policy was not very successful because: (i) Many local authorities were reluctant to make grants. (ii) Many house owners were ignorant of their rights or wanted a 'quiet life', especially the elderly. (iii) Many landlords lacked incentive in view of the limitations on rents. (iv) Many tenants feared increases in rent.

In 1959 the 'standard' grants (i.e. payable as of right) became available for improvements involving installation of basic amenities e.g. a bath, a w.c. or hot water; and in 1964 an element of compulsion to improve was introduced. But progress was still limited until 1969. At this point the Government in an effort to cut spending switched its housing policy from building new to improving old houses. Under the *Housing Improvement Act, 1969*: (a) Local authorities were required periodically to review their areas and identify dwellings which need to be repaired and improved, including their own houses. Both standard and discretionary grants were payable, on more generous and flexible terms, and loans provided for those with difficulty raising the initial capital. (b) Local authorities were to persuade and encourage owners to improve their properties (as a last resort they could use compulsion or take over properties). (c) Councils were to direct their main efforts to the improvement of whole areas rather than individual houses. In these (c), called **General Improvement Areas**, grants were paid at the rate of 65 per cent (i.e. above the usual 50 per cent). Since 1974 grants are generally known as **renovation** grants. Individual grants may be 'intermediate' (mandatory, for basic amenities, paid at 75 per cent, or at 90 per cent in **Housing Action Areas**, where housing is worst); 'improvement'; 'repair' (both discretionary); or 'special' (mandatory, e.g. fire escapes, adaptations for disabled).

Success of the policy. This particular aspect of housing policy has experienced a fair measure of success. There has been a substantial increase in grants since 1970. In the period 1970–75 there were as many grants as in the whole of the post-war period up to 1969. They fell back to about 200,000 p.a. for the 1980s (cf. 400,000 in 1973). The results are to be seen in the decline in substandard dwellings:

Dwellings in England and Wales	*1971*	*1981*
Unfit for habitation	1,244,000	1,160,000
Lacking one or more basic amenities	2,866,000	900,000
Lacking sole use of one or more basic amenities	2,753,000	1,350,000

Criticisms of the policy. It has been said that it is no more than a short-term policy, for the houses will ultimately have to be replaced. It is argued that:

1　In the long run it may not be cheaper than redevelopment.
2　Those in greatest need (tenants of private landlords) derived least benefit, since 80 per cent of grants go to owner-occupiers and local authorities.
3　Where improvement has occurred in the private rented sector it has often been followed by a change of tenure, i.e. sold for owner-occupation.

As a result of these and other criticisms, the Government in 1974 attempted to prevent abuse of the system by denying grants for improving second homes or for owner-occupied homes above a certain rateable value (£225, or £400 in London), and certain conditions were imposed, such as that for a five-year period the tenure will not change. There was some further increase in house improvement as the Government in 1977 began to divert resources from New Town development to stem the decline of the inner cities (see page 302). But while the Government has succeeded in stimulating awareness and demand for renovation grants (with grants rising from £90 million to £900 million 1979–84), it has now drastically cut back on funds. Councils are refusing grants and there are ½ million on their grant waiting lists. (See pages 283–4.)

Homelessness

To admit that there are people living without 'a roof over their heads' is perhaps the greatest indictment of Britain's housing policy. It is the equivalent of finding illiteracy in our educated society or allowing people to die of starvation despite elaborate social security arrangements. Yet there are 120,000 homeless households (over 250,000 people, and including 50,000 teenagers in London alone). This is the number accepted by local housing authorities in 1986 (c.f. 29,000 in 1980) as homeless under the *Housing (Homeless Persons) Act, 1977* (consolidated in the *Housing Act, 1985*). Under this law local housing authorities must provide help or advice, and for those in 'priority need' (i.e. those with families, or single people who are pregnant, disabled or elderly) they must provide accommodation.

However, double this number actually *apply* for such accommodation but are refused it. (A number of local housing authorities have been criticised for evading their responsibilities and turning applicants away by using the Act's 'escape clause' whereby a local authority is not obliged to offer accommodation to anyone deemed to be 'intentionally' homeless.) There are also those who do not make an application. In fact Shelter (a pressure group aiding the homeless) has suggested that there are perhaps 3 million homeless on the basis of counting also those who are **inadequately housed** (e.g. in 1986 it was officially estimated that 4 per cent of households – that is over 80,000 – were living in overcrowded conditions below 'the bedroom standard'. See also the data on housing conditions above. Whatever the accepted definition and the precise number, it is evident that during the 1960s and early 1970s the number was growing. This is due to: (a) An increase in the rate of household formation (with earlier marriage and better survival of the elderly). (b) A continued decline in the private rented sector, especially at the low-rent end. (c) The great rise in the cost of homes and mortgages.

Who are the homeless? They are overwhelmingly young and either single (an estimated 100,000) or with young families. In addition, they tend to have one or more of the following characteristics: (i) low incomes; (ii) marital breakdown/separation; (iii) eviction by land-lord; (iv) migrant; (v) ex-hospital patient; (vi) ex-offender, especially after a custodial sentence. About 40 per cent become homeless when parents, relatives or friends are no longer able or willing to accommo-date them; 20 per cent is the result of marriage or partnership breakup and 14 per cent a consequence of mortgage or rent arrears.

Provision for the homeless. This is undertaken by three agencies:

(a) **Central government** – through the Department of Social Secur-ity. Under the *National Assistance Act, 1948*, the DSS provides accommodation in hostels or 'Reception Centres' (sometimes called 'the Spike') for those of 'an unsettled way of life', i.e. tramps or vagrants.

(b) **Voluntary organisations** are especially important here. Many are charitable and derive from religious foundations such as the Salvation Army or the St Mungo Trust, and may seek to provide shelter for particular categories of homeless, e.g. the Langley House Trust provides for homeless ex-offenders. There are other housing associations (about 2,650) which not only provide for the homeless but also create permanent accommodation for renting or for co-ownership.*

(c) **Local authorities** (i.e. the Welfare or Social Services Depart-ments) under the *National Assistance Act, 1948*, were *required* to 'provide temporary accommodation for persons in urgent need'. Initially this was interpreted as mainly applicable to those who lost their homes through fire or flood, but it soon came to include others, e.g. those made homeless through eviction. Paradoxically, a Local Authority Housing Department could legally evict a family who would then become the responsibility of the Welfare Department of the same authority. However, local authorities did not accept all comers, since the amount of temporary accommodation they have is limited. They, there-fore, laid down certain conditions before approving applications – for example, married couples had to have children or must have been currently resident in the district. Some people criti-cised these criteria because so many were thereby turned away. Others were critical of the actual provisions as being deterrent. Some local authorities just took the children 'into care'; in

*The purpose of the **Housing Corporation**, set up in 1964, was to encourage the growth of housing associations through the provision of finance. Many are also aided by funds from local authorities.

others husbands were not admitted to the hostels with their families. Families often had to share facilities and live communally in overcrowded conditions; and they often had to vacate the premises during the day time.

Since the public outcry of the later 1960s, especially following the television play 'Cathy Come Home' in 1966, many of these conditions were improved, and some local authorities began providing alternative 'family unit' accommodation in substandard council property. Many councils also came to terms with the considerable number of those who 'squatted' in empty properties. A few local authorities provide **Family Rehabilitation Units** which, as well as providing short-term accommodation, seek also to guide less competent families to a more organised way of life, and thus avoid indebtedness, rent arrears and homelessness. Another aspect of preventive work has been the development of **Housing Advisory and Aid Centres**. These may be local authority sponsored or may be voluntary, e.g. SHAC (Shelter Housing Aid Centre), and give information and advice on tenancy rights, clearance or improvement regulations, and some provide financial help.

In 1977, the *Housing (Homeless Persons) Act, 1977*, has sought to improve the situation by transferring responsibility for the homeless from the Social Services Departments to Housing Departments of local authorities, who had greater access to accommodation. And yet, the shortage continued such that councils resorted to housing homeless people in bed-and-breakfast hotels, which is not only costly (at over £30 per night), but inimical to family life if sustained for any length of time. There are currently 10,000 homeless families (mainly – 70 per cent – in London) living in such accommodation (eight times the figure for 1981).

Empty houses. The census of 1971 showed there to be some 675,000 empty dwellings in England and Wales. Today in Britain there is an estimated 1 million, of which 120,000 are council properties (including 28,000 houses which have been empty for over a year). So why are there homeless people and why is there a housing problem? Partly it is because these houses are 'legitimately' empty, being in the process of changing hands or under repair or improvement. Another part of the explanation is that many unoccupied properties exist in areas where there is a housing surplus – for example, East Suffolk and Cornwall had an estimated 7 per cent of empty houses in 1971, and North Yorkshire 5 per cent. Each of these lies in an area of overall 'surplus' (see Figure 11). So for homeless people, many vacant houses are just in the wrong place, even if they could afford to occupy them.

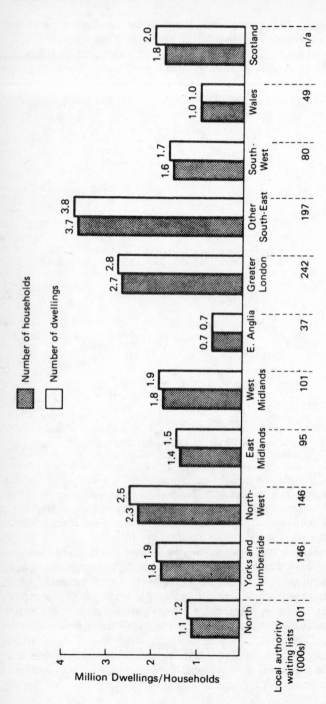

Figure 11 *Dwellings and housing need by region in Britain, 1980*
Source: Build Homes, Build Hope, Shelter, 1981

Housing need. The Department of the Environment makes an estimate of 'potential households' in need of dwellings: that is, all
married couples, other multi-person households and single-person
households in the population, with an allowance for those people
sharing housing by choice. This measure is only approximate and
cannot be taken as an exact indicator of housing need. Figure 11
shows estimates of housing need (measured as potential households,
plus 4 per cent for vacancies and second homes) by region in
comparison with the number of dwellings. Although the number of
dwellings in some regions exceeds the estimated need, this does not
mean that there is a surplus throughout the area: there may be
surplus houses in the countryside and a shortage in the towns, for
example. Council house waiting lists are an indicator (though imper-
fect) of local housing need.

Municipalisation. Nevertheless, there are many properties lying
empty, perhaps for the sole purpose of being sold later at a profit as
property values rise. It has long been advocated by some that such
properties be requisitioned or penally taxed. In the *Housing Act,
1974*, local authorities were encouraged to buy such houses where
there exists a serious shortage of housing, and especially in Housing
Action Areas. In 1974–75 some 23,000 houses were acquired by local
authorities, but cuts in public expenditure and rising repair costs have
restricted this (although the 'improvement for sale' scheme provides
Government funds for councils to buy, restore and sell run-down
properties). Meanwhile, squatters may take things into their own
hands and occupy empty (including council) properties. In 1979 the
Government halted this by tightening the laws on squatting.

Second homes. These account for some of the empty properties.
There are some 200,000 'second homes' in England and Wales,
excluding caravans. It is estimated that by the end of the century 10
per cent of families will own a second home. This gives some
credence to the view that the poor are living at relatively poorer
standards compared to the middle- and upper-income groups than 10
or 20 years ago.

It is too sweeping to demand that none shall have two homes while
some have none; but the existence of such empty properties does give
rise to ill-feeling where there are long waiting lists for local authority
houses or where agricultural communities are concerned to stop the
drifting away of the rural young. In response the Government in 1974
stopped tax allowances and improvement grants for second homes.
(One consequence of the young villagers being squeezed out of their
communities by second-home owners and soaring prices has been
sporadic fire-bombing and arson attacks on property. A more positive response is a joint scheme by the Government, the Housing

Corporation and the Rural Development Commission to finance small developments of homes at affordable prices and rents for young local people.)

Housing 'fit'. As there are empty dwellings, so there are empty rooms. Yet elsewhere there may be serious overcrowding: the 1971 census showed that nearly 4 per cent of people in private households were statutorily over-crowded (i.e. at more than 1½ persons per room). In 1980, 4 per cent of households were below the official 'bedroom standard'.

The reasons for the coexistence of overcrowding and under-occupation have to do with housing costs and what different people can afford, as well as people's inertia and attachment. But another important reason is lack of *variety* in housing: it appears that the present stock of housing is out of balance with household needs. The 1971 census showed the poor fit between household sizes and house-hold spaces: although there were 8 million one- or two-person households, only about 2.3 million one-, two- or three-room units of accommodation existed. For example, there are many elderly indi-viduals or couples who occupy and under-use houses which are larger than they need. In general there has been an over-concentration on building three-bedroomed houses, which are inappropriate or waste-ful for the one- or two-person households who now form 50 per cent of all households.

There is evidence that things are changing for the better: local authorities, for example, are responding to the subsidy inducement to build more appropriate homes for the elderly. In the meantime, since we cannot normally put rooms on wheels,* we perhaps can encourage people to take in lodgers or tenants to move by the aid of financial assistance. Thus in 1982 a **National Mobility Office** was introduced. By causing local housing and New Town authorities to set aside a small proportion of their lettings, the scheme enables tenants of those authorities who have a definite need (e.g. to take up a job or be near a relative) to move between properties in the same area or even between county areas. There is also a national **Tenants Exchange Scheme** to enable public sector tenants to exchange homes through-

---

*Apart from caravans, of course. But despite their advantages of cheapness, mobility, lack of stairs, etc., they are unsuitable for many people, especially those with young families. In addition, excessive site and connection charges, poor conditions and insecure tenure have often reduced the attractiveness of the caravan as a source of shelter. Nevertheless, the number of caravan dwellers has grown from 95,000 in 1951 to about 150,000 today in England and Wales, a figure which includes some 40,000 gypsies. The plight of the latter group has been recently recognised in the *Caravan Sites Act, 1968,* and the *Mobile Homes Act, 1975,* attempts to improve conditions for caravan dwellers generally.

out England and Wales. Both schemes are computer-based for speed (and under the former, there were some 7,000 moves during 1981– 82).

Housing Act, 1980

This important Act implemented a number of Conservative promises when in opposition: indeed they may have attracted the support of many voters in the 1979 and subsequent elections. Often referred to as the 'Tenants Charter' it:

(a) Required local housing authorities to sell council (and New Town) houses to those tenants who wished to buy. The selling price must be reduced by 33 to 50 per cent (60 per cent, or even 70 per cent for flats, under the *Housing and Building Control Act, 1984*) (according to length of tenure). Local authorities may also provide 100 per cent mortgages to facilitate such purchases.

(b) Gave council house tenants (i) security of tenure (plus one family successor); (ii) the right to sub-let and improve their homes; (iii) mandatory information about tenancy conditions, allocations and transfer rules, together with the right to be consulted about relevant housing matters. Housing subsidies were placed on a 'deficit' basis whereby central government grants vary with local (recognised) housing costs and local (rate) contributions to housing.

(c) Provided for private tenants that (i) controlled tenancies become regulated; (ii) registered ('fair') rents could be reviewed after two years (instead of three as before); (iii) a new 'shorthold' tenancy was created to provide secure and fair-rent tenancies for fixed periods (of 1 to 5 years); (v) a new 'assured' tenancy allowed new dwellings to be let outside the Rent Acts provisions (with the possibility of this being extended to improve *existing* tenancies).

Having declared that the 'supply of housing and demand are in better balance' and that 'problems have become increasingly specific and local' the government has radically reduced public expenditure on housing by reducing housing subsidies and Housing Investment Programmes (or HIPs) which are central approvals of local authority housing expenditure plans, viz, HIPs for England (£m):

1978/9	1980/81	1983/84	1986/87	1988/89
5,300	3,350	2,200	1,600	1,150

Thus, housing in 1988 accounts for 5 per cent of public (State) expenditure compared to 10 per cent in 1975. Sales of council and other State-owned houses and flats in the period 1979–88 have amounted to 1 million which is well over the sales for the whole period 1945–79. Meanwhile, council house rents have more than doubled since 1979. In 1981 the Parker Morris housing standard and the 'cost yardstick' (both affecting the quality of council housing) were abolished. In addition housebuilding and repairs have fallen dramatically, consequently a shortage of 800,000 dwellings has been estimated (e.g. by Shelter and by the Association of Metropolitan Authorities). All local authority spending is being closely monitored and controlled by the government (through HIPs and the Rate Support Grant) but the government has urged local housing authorities to provide extra housing by using their capital receipts from council house sales, and above all, it is relying on an expansion in private housebuilding (as it did in the 1930s). Council house sales are attracting the better-off tenants in the better (semi-detached) properties rather than the poorer tenants and flat-dwellers. Council housing is becoming residual: it seems to be reverting to its original (1919) role of (stigmatised?) welfare – providing for the poor, the disabled and the elderly. Meanwhile, the council house waiting lists have risen to a massive 1.4 million.

Housing Act, 1988

This Act has been described as 'potentially the most radical departure in housing policy since the end of the First World War' (1918), certainly as far as local authorities are concerned. It provides for:

(a) new private-sector lettings to be 'assured' tenancies i.e. with security of tenure but no rent control;

(b) 'tenants' choice', whereby council tenants can opt out of local authority tenure to that of a new landlord. If tenants vote* in favour of this, the council will sell the properties to the new landlord (most of whom are expected to be Housing Associations, but could be building societies, co-ops or private firms). The new landlords are expected (after vetting by the Housing Corporation, and under the guidance of a code of conduct) to behave 'socially' (i.e. over management, repairs and rents) and not seek to exploit the situation, since the new tenancies will be assured (as above);

(c) the appointment of Housing Action Trusts (HATs) to take over

---

*Voting involves the 'negative voting procedure' whereby those who abstain, or just don't bother, will be counted as in favour of the switch.

the worst council estates, improve them over a five-year period and then pass them on to new landlords. Twenty are planned so far.

The Government's aims are (i) to break up what it sees as the monopoly and inflexibility of local housing authorities, (ii) to institute better management and stock utilisation (with an estimated 50 per cent of council flats empty) and repair (with an estimated £19 billion worth in the council sector) and (iii) to improve, through higher rents, the supply of private lettings (including many of the 650,000 vacant properties) and thus also improve people's (labour) mobility. However, one authoritative inquiry in 1988 reported that housing councils do a good job and Housing Associations are by no means perfect. And many tenants are concerned about their weakened rights to succession, under the new tenancies, and the increased risk of eviction and possession (e.g. for arrears) and are campaigning or 'No' votes. Meanwhile some local authorities, in anticipation of the change, are themselves selling their estates (to keep them whole) to Housing Associations or council-sponsored companies.

The Government has also introduced plans for, or intimated, further changes. These include (a) plans to assist (with £28 million) and require councils to refurbish some 10,000 of their estimated 28,000 long-term empty properties – the aim is to remove the need for so much temporary bed-and-breakfast accommodation for the homeless; (b) plans to extend local initiatives by allowing all housing authorities to give 'portable discounts' of up to £10,000 each to council house tenants as inducement to move out into private owner-occupation – thus vacating council properties; (c) council tenants may have their rents converted into mortgage payments, so that in time they will have bought their houses from the council; (d) councils will no longer be permitted to transfer money from the General Rate Fund to subsidise their council house rents (these transfers currently contribute about 8 per cent to councils' housing income; (e) grants for repairs and improvement are to become means-tested for those who apply.

Conclusion

Housing standards have apparently improved over the last 30 years: there are fewer slums; there is less overcrowding; houses are in better condition; and they contain more modern amenities. In the 1920s and 1930s many people stayed out of doors as much as possible to avoid the discomfort of the home. Since the 1950s pubs and cinemas have been closing down as people have become more home-centred in their leisure hours.

Yet the problems remain: we still have slums, overcrowding, homelessness and squatters. These are the obvious problems; but there are others which are less obvious, such as the lack of community in the new estates which replaced the city slums; or the tedium of long journeys to work from the new houses in the suburbs. How many people are distressed by the strain of paying for their accommodation? (Some 20 per cent, or 1 million, council tenants are in rent arrears and nearly 12,000 home-owners had their homes re-possessed in the first six months of 1988 compared to 2,500 for the whole of 1979*.) And how many are really contented with quality or tenure of their dwelling? (A 1978 survey showed that 10 per cent of the population are dissatisfied with their accommodation or areas.) Is the 'bed-sit', the tower block, the tied cottage just what they wanted? Like 'felt poverty' (see page 35), there is no doubt a great deal of dissatisfaction below the surface, and the mere quantity of houses is no adequate measure.

Yet numbers *are* important: at the root of the problem is the relationship or balance of supply and demand (or rather 'need', currently estimated at 240,000–300,000 a year (see page 265). The housing problem is usually stated in terms of a shortage of houses, and to produce more via housing targets (of 300,000 p.a., etc.) seems obviously desirable. Many young people simply despair of owning a house in view of the massive increase in house prices in recent years (at 14 per cent p.a.). Perhaps, as we say with the health services, it may be as effective to utilise better the existing resources, especially since new annual supply adds only 2 per cent to existing stock of houses. Britain has a massive stock maintenance problem, partly due to the high percentage of aged houses. But also due to rapid-build policies, using non-traditional prefabricated materials (system-building) which are now having to be repaired or demolished – at an estimated cost of £10 billion. (The high-rise method was partly due to the 'green belt' requirements of planners – see page 000. Even more, the total cost of houses needing repair in the public and private sectors amounts to £19 and £27.5 billion respectively (though the National Housing Forum believes it is £82 billion). And the total cost of those houses (in England) needing repairs in excess of £7,000 rose from 860,000 in 1971 to 1 million in 1981, so we are not even keeping up with the problem of deteriorating housing.

---

*Amounting to £240 million. This is partly due to rising rents and unemployment, and it was hoped that the new Housing Benefits system would help deal with the problem. In fact it seems to have made it worse partly because of cuts in the levels of benefit (with rent and rates rebates amounting to £4,000 million p.a. and partly because of its hasty implementation and muddled administration (see *Sunday Times*, 11 September 1983)).

Housing policies have brought housing a long way during this century, though some would argue that the policies have often been a hindrance rather than a help. Indeed, this lack of agreement has bedevilled housing policy in contrast to most other social services. This lack of consistency – 'a housing policy of "ad-hockery" and crisis management' as the Minister himself in 1974 called it – occurs not just because of the 'ins and outs' of party government, but also because housing is used as an important element in economic regulation and so has suffered from 'stop-go' economic policies. 'The fact is that during the past 12 months housing policy has exhibited a volatility that makes sensible planning of building and grant-giving impossible' (*The Times*, November 1983). In addition, however, there are in-built conflicts and contradictions, actual and potential, in so many aspects of housing policy. For example, to prohibit overcrowding can lead to more homelessness; to give fixed tenure or rents to tenants may reduce the supply by landlords of tenancies; and 'a policy of housing those in most urgent need may conflict with a policy of replacing the worst houses' (D. Donnison, *The Government of Housing*).

Housing problems will emerge regardless of current policies, as buildings age, as population changes in structure and as population migrates. But in particular they will arise because, like health, the demand for housing is infinite as society continually aspires to better standards. Thus what is acceptable in housing today will be unacceptable in 30 years' time.

Questions

1 What was the structure of Britain's housing tenure in 1900?
2 Explain the significance of the *Housing Act, 1919*.
3 What do you understand by 'the housing problem' facing government?
4 Outline the main provisions of the following Housing Acts: (a) 1930, (b) 1946, (c) 1957, (d) 1965, (e) 1969, (f) 1972, (g) 1980, (h) 1988.
5 Distinguish between 'redevelopment' and 'rehabilitation'.
6 Who are the 'homeless'?
7 Distinguish between (a) rent allowances, (b) rent rebates and (c) rate rebates.
8 Distinguish between 'controlled' and 'regulated' tenancies.
9 What is the pattern of housing tenure in your local area?
10 What is the size of your local authority's housing waiting list?

11
Environmental planning

History

Man has always concerned himself with the home, village or town in which he lived and the classical architecture of Rome and Ancient Greece reminds us that our classical forebears managed to combine beauty and grace with utility and efficiency.

From the eighteenth century Britain suffered from the combined effects of the Industrial Revolution and massive population growth, which left a legacy of urban squalor in abundance. As manufacture increased there was an influx of workers to the industrial towns and houses were built rapidly and haphazardly, with little attention to the fundamental well-being of the workers. Ultimately, Britain's high density (currently about 600 persons per square mile) required measures to create a balance between the competing claims made on the environment by such considerations as housing, transport, industry and the need for open spaces.

The growth of the towns in the nineteenth century produced **public health** problems. The urban areas were insanitary and the Government was forced to act in the interest of public safety.

The Public Health Acts of 1848 and 1875 were passed to ensure proper sewerage and sanitation, and to prevent the spread of disease and squalor arising from the insanitary housing conditions. The *Public Health Act, 1875*, empowered the Local Government Board (acting for the Government) to permit sanitary authorities throughout the country to make building bylaws to ensure that buildings were sanitary, exposed adequately to air and moderately to light. The emphasis was on health.

The *London Building Act, 1894*, ensured that the local authorities could enforce the public control of (a) the formation and widening of streets, (b) the lines of buildings and frontage and (c) the extent of open space around buildings. Town planning was a logical extension of the control of certain minimum standards of housing, the type of housing, width of streets and the lines or limits of frontages to those streets.

Meanwhile, certain **private experiments** in the planning of towns (not just streets and houses) had been made at Bournville, near Birmingham, in 1876, and at Port Sunlight in 1887. Both were completed on the initiative of private individuals. The Cadbury family, the chocolate manufacturers, of Birmingham and others (Lever Bros. at Port Sunlight) were concerned that their employees should have suitable houses and a good environment.

The *Housing, Town Planning, etc., Act, 1909*. The first Act which *permitted* local authorities (after obtaining permission of the Local Government Board) to prepare town planning schemes with the general object of 'securing proper sanitary conditions, amenity and convenience' was the *Housing, Town Planning, etc., Act, 1909*. The Act was restrictive and vague, and, in fact, very few local authorities took advantage of it.

The *Housing, Town Planning, etc. Act, 1919*. The First World War prevented development during that time of crisis. However, after the war, the *Town Planning Act, 1919*, made the preparation of planning schemes *obligatory* on all borough and urban districts of or above 20,000 population. The 1919 Act also enabled local authorities to build an increased number of working-class houses. The local authorities were subsidised by the Government to build houses for the many who could not afford to buy one. Thus began the nation-wide growth of the council-house estates familiar to all. The Act laid down standards, e.g. three-bedroomed house, with kitchen, bath and garden. All such houses had to be built to a prescribed density (12 to the acre). Development usually took place on the virgin land on the edges of towns. Municipal estates grew alongside suburbs or beyond them.

The *Town and Country Planning Act, 1932*, extended the planning powers of local authorities to any type of land, built-up or developed, and introduced a zoning plan, i.e. land was zoned for particular uses: residential, industrial and so on.

The urban and district councils to whom powers were given by the Government were frequently small and weak, and were inactive in using the powers they had. The introduction of large-scale planning improvements were costly, and because the improvements involved increasing the rates the councils were reluctant to embark on expensive projects. Where, however, a landowner wanted to develop his own land for housing or industrial use the private developer made application to the local authority. Permission would rarely be refused since the local authority would otherwise be depriving itself of rate income from the new householders or the occupiers of the industrial buildings erected by the private developer.

The Ministry of Health (then responsible for planning) had no powers of initiation (this being left to local authorities) and no power to grant financial aid to local authorities for planning. The Ministry's function was to regulate and ensure that local authorities did not treat property-owners unfairly where their property was acquired by local authorities for planning, road widening, etc.

Housebuilding between 1930 and 1940 was carried on either by private builders or by local authorities who wished to extend council houses in their areas. During the ten years some 2,700,000 houses were built in England and Wales, and by the outbreak of the Second World War in 1939 one third of all the houses in England and Wales had been built since 1918.

London presented special problems. There was a natural increase of population and an increase by migration from outside. Greater London, as it was called, comprised all the London Boroughs within the Metropolitan area.

Depressed areas. Outside London there were depressed areas where there was great unemployment. In 1934 the unemployment rate in Greater London was 9.6 per cent of insured workers. In Workington the proportion was 36.3 per cent; in Gateshead 44.2 per cent; and in Jarrow 67.8 per cent. From the 1930s to the outbreak of the war there was economic depression.

Certain areas in the country were regarded as 'depressed areas', notably the North-East Coast, West Cumberland, South Wales and the industrial areas around Glasgow. The *Special Areas Act, 1934,* was passed to 'initiate, organise, prosecute and assist measures designed to facilitate the economic development and social improvement of the Special Areas'. A Commissioner for England and Wales and a Commissioner for Scotland were appointed to spend, or approve spending of, money for the purposes mentioned. Some £21 million were spent by 1938, which enabled 123 factories in the Special Areas to be opened between 1937 and 1938; 372 were opened in the London area. If new factories were excluded from London, as some were, it did not follow that they would spring up elsewhere in a depressed area.

National planning. The Barlow Report ('Report of the Royal Commission on the Distribution of the Industrial Population', Cmnd. 6153, HMSO, 1940) is a landmark. Its terms of reference were:

to inquire into the causes which have influenced the present geographical distribution of the industrial population in Great Britain, and the probable direction of any change in the distribution in future; to consider what social, economic or strategic disadvantages arise from the concentration of industries or of the industrial population in large towns or in particular areas of the country; and to report what remedial measures if any should be taken in the national interest.

The Report noted that the problem of planning had not been

undertaken from a *national standpoint*. 'There is no duty imposed on any authority or Government department to view the country as a whole and to consider the problems of industrial, commercial and urban growth in the light of the needs of the entire population.' Remedial measures had to be considered to be in the national interest.

The Report noted the advantages of concentration of industry in certain areas: proximity to markets; reduction of transport costs; and availability of a supply of suitable labour. But these were accompanied by serious disadvantages such as heavy charges on account of high site values, loss of time through street traffic congestion and the risk of adverse effects and efficiency due to long and fatiguing journeys to and from work. London presented the largest problem.

All the members of the commission were unanimous in condemning the existing situation and the inadequacy of both policy and machinery for dealing with it. All agreed that a far more positive role for government was required and that control should be exercised over new factory building at least in London and the Home Counties; that dispersal from larger urban concentrations was desirable; and that measures should be taken to anticipate regional economic depression. The question was: How is this to be done?

The Second World War then broke out, and the attention of the nation was concentrated on the immediate task of the defeat of the enemy.

The Uthwatt Committee. Meanwhile in 1941 the Uthwatt Committee on Compensation and Betterment and the Scott Committee on Land Utilisation in Rural Areas were set up. Compensation for land acquired by a local authority or the central Government is always a difficult problem. Thus, when a house is acquired by a local authority to enable a road-widening scheme to go through there may well be a dispute as to the amount claimed by the owner and the amount offered by the local authority. The question is solved either by agreement, or if no agreement is arrived at then by arbitration or by recourse to the Lands Tribunal. Betterment arises when, for example, a local authority develops land or provides a road, street-lighting or other amenity as a result of which a private land-owner finds that his premises have risen in value. What should be charged to him for the betterment in value?

After the Second World War and the 'Beveridge Report' (1942) the time was ripe for a fresh look and a new approach to planning. Many cities lay in ruins and had to be rebuilt, and there were many homecoming service personnel who wanted a house and work.

Within two years of the end of the war the *Town and Country Planning Act, 1947*, was passed which laid down the foundation from which the modern approach to planning has emerged. The 1947 Act created a new ministry: the Ministry of Town and Country Planning, with special responsibilities for the tasks ahead.

The modern system of land planning is contained in the *Town and Country Planning Act, 1971* (England and Wales), and the *Town and Country Planning Act, 1972* (applying to Scotland). Both are consolidating statutes. The *Local Government, Planning and Land Act, 1980*, revised the division of (overlapping) planning responsibilities of the County and District authorities (see below).

Planning today

Central government control

The central Government department with overall responsibility for planning is the Department of the Environment (created in 1970), which is headed by a Secretary of State. He is assisted by two senior ministers: (i) the Minister for Local Government and Environmental Services and (ii) the Minister for Housing and Construction. The Secretary of State for Wales is responsible for town and country planning and its associated problems in Wales, and the Secretary of State for Scotland is the responsible Minister for Scotland.

Local government control

England. This has 45 large councils. (Up to 1986 there were also six metropolitan county councils.) Within the 45 large counties are some 296 smaller district (borough or city) councils.

Wales. There are 8 county authorities and 37 district authorities. Some 25 of these district authorities have additional status as city councils (two) or borough councils.

Scotland has 9 regional authorities divided into 53 districts.

Northern Ireland. There are some 26 district councils who are responsible to the Department of Housing, Local Government and Planning.

Greater London. Greater London is administered by 32 London boroughs and the City of London, which are responsible for the broad range of local authority functions. (The GLC was abolished in 1986 – see page 25.)

Broadly, therefore, we have a responsible Secretary of State for the Environment (served by a Minister for Local Government) and we have county councils, below which lie the district councils. Thus there is a three-tier responsibility.

Development plans

All planning authorities must prepare plans setting out their proposals and objectives for the development of their areas and submit them for ministerial approval.

Development plans consist of a series of documents and plans and maps which show a local planning authority's main objectives for land use in its area for a period of 20 years ahead. The plans set out the guide for future land use. Some will show areas for various uses: residential, industrial, shopping or business, public buildings, parks, open spaces and the proposals for roads. Some areas will be designated for comprehensive development; some will show **green belts**, i.e. areas around a town or urban area which will remain unchanged (see *Which*, August 1989). These amount to 4.5 m. acres or 15 per cent of the country (2.7 m.) created since 1968. Except in special circumstances no new building or change of use other than for strictly rural purposes is allowed. The aim of the green belt policy is to prevent urban and industrial sprawl, though in 1983–4 the Government published plans to loosen controls to allow house building (using perhaps 5,000 acres p.a.).

Whereas in the past the local authorities were concerned with the prevention of undesirable development, the present requirement is for *positive planning* for the creation of a pleasant environment.

The development plans for positive development can only be prepared on the basis of a detailed survey of the particular county area, in particular its physical and economic characteristics, communications, transport system, traffic and other important considerations. These development plans are made up of two parts: 1 **Structure plans,** prepared by county councils (regional authorities in Scotland). 2 **Local plans,** prepared by district councils, which must conform with the structure plans. In the Metropolitan areas **unitary plans** form a combination of the two (as there is no upper tier county council).

The structure plans require Ministerial approval and have to conform with the regional proposals (see later) of a strategic kind for the region as a whole. Local plans are adopted by the planning authorities (i.e. the county councils and the district councils) without being subject to Ministerial approval unless the Secretary of State 'calls in' a plan for his own decision. Both structure and local plans are under continuous review. For example, a new industry may develop in an area which could upset a plan previously laid down. The local authority would then have to alter its plans accordingly.

Objections by the public

In a democratic society we must take account of the objections by members of the public particularly affected (for example, when houses are to be acquired by the local authority). Where a new development on a big scale is proposed many people will want to be heard. Some may approve; some may violently object to the scheme.

A local planning authority must, therefore, give adequate notice and publicity to the contents of its planning survey and to the matters proposed in the structure plan. Interested members of the public can then make representations about the proposals to the authority (county council) before the structure plans are drawn up. The authority must taken these comments into account in drawing up the structure plan.

Once the plan is made, copies must be made available for **public inspection**. Obviously, unless the public know what is happening they will not be able to register objections. Objections to the structure plans may be made to the Secretary of State (the DoE for England; the Secretary of State for Wales; and the Secretary of State for Scotland).

The local planning authority must inform the Secretary of State of the steps taken to publicise (a) the survey, (b) the proposals for the structure plan and (c) the representations made by individuals or the public about the proposals. If the Secretary of State is satisfied that the local authority has done enough to ensure public involvement, he may return the plan to the local authority to take further action. In short, the Secretary of State may give the approval to go ahead. But he may, under the *Town and Country Planning (Amendment) Act, 1972*, provide for an examination in public (by a small panel under an independent chairman) of issues important to the Secretary of State's consideration of the plan. Naturally, the Minister must take national interests into account which may not be present in the minds of local inhabitants in their proposals.

The above applies to structure plans (for counties). Local plans (made by a district council) are dealt with similarly, and here again local objectors must be given a chance to be heard at a local public inquiry or other hearing. This sort of inquiry is held by an inspector appointed by the Secretary of State. He hears the views of objectors and the local planning authority and reports independently to the Secretary of State.

Control of development

Planning involves control over the use of land by its owners. One may imagine that because one owns land one can build on it or, say, erect a garage. But this is not so; consent is required from the local authority before one starts. There is usually much heart-searching about this, and an ambitious private landowner may feel very frustrated by what he regards as the dilatory narrow-minded attitude of the local council.

What is 'development'? Development includes most forms of construction, engineering and mining and any **material change in the use of land or existing buildings.** So, to take a simple example, to change one's private house into offices for a business would amount to a change of use and thus require permission. An application must be made to the council with the plan of what one proposed to do. They must now determine whether to approve or disapprove. Small alterations may be approved by a local planning officer employed by the local authority, while bigger developments will be reserved for consideration by the local planning committee, who go through the applications, inspect the plans and approve or disapprove.

The authority, when determining an application, must keep in mind the provisions of (a) the structure plan and (b) the local plan, as well as (c) other relevant considerations, such as the effect of the proposal on road safety, the appearance of the surroundings or public services such as drainage and water supply. These are difficult decisions; for example, with a Georgian crescent composed of fine old buildings, the local authority would scarcely be likely to approve the building of a modern house in the middle. To do so would spoil the shape and character of the road and the crescent and detract from the beauty of the locality.

If proposals for development do not accord with the local authority's plan, the authority *may* give its consent if it believes that they do not involve substantial departure from the plan or affect the whole of the neighbourhood. In case of other departures from the plan, the authority must, if it proposes to permit the development, give public notice of the application, asking for representations from the public. The local authority must then send a copy of the application to the appropriate Minister. If the Minister considers that the matter is a minor one and purely local he may not intervene. If, however, he considers otherwise he may 'call in' the application and make his own decison (altering the proposals, if need be) or direct that planning permission be refused. Otherwise he may leave it for decision by the local planning authority.

When a person makes an application for planning permission the local planning authority can (1) refuse its consent, (2) grant unconditional permission or (3) grant consent, subject to such conditions as it thinks fit. In the case of (1) or (3), the applicant may **appeal** to the Minister responsible against the refusal or the conditions attached to a grant of permission. (If the authority is thought to be acting *ultra vires* – i.e. outside its powers – an applicant may apply to a court of law.) The Minister has legal power to decide all appeals, but (in England and Wales) he may transfer certain kinds of appeal (those concerned with local issues) to an inspector. The latter decides on the Minister's behalf. Some 75 per cent of appeals are decided in this way. In either case, a local or **public inquiry** may be held.

Now let us suppose a private developer caries out a development of his property without permission of the local planning authority. In such cases the local planning authority may serve an 'enforcement' notice which specifies the steps which the planning authority require to be taken to remedy the breach of development control. This can order the developer to remove a building. Those who refuse to comply with the enforcement notice may be prosecuted.

Public opinion and planning

Current legislation recognises the need to take into account public opinion about development proposals. It provides:

1 Registers of all planning applications to be open for public inspections.
2 Proposals of certain kinds to be advertised locally.
3 Local inquiries into planning appeals and applications 'called in' for decision by the Minister are normally held in *public*, and members of the public may there express views about the proposed development.

Also, where a development scheme is of **national or regional importance**, or of a very scientific or technical nature, the Ministers responsible may decide to set up a **planning inquiry commission** to carry out investigations and hold inquiries locally. Thus the siting of a major airport to cope with increasing air traffic would almost certainly cause many local people to object (as at the current Hinkley and Sizewell nuclear power inquiries), though some may approve. Ultimately, of course, the Minister has to decide after weighing all the factors. This, as everyone knows, e.g. having regard to the pressure on Heathrow and Gatwick airports in London, is a difficult problem.

Compulsory purchase and compensation

Clearly, if local authorities want to build new housing estates, new roads and public open spaces the authorities may find it necessary to compel a private owner of the land to sell it to them. The legislation of 1947, as extended in 1968, has given the local authorities wide powers to secure land in town and country for the creation of what are called **action areas** (i.e. areas planned for comprehensive development, redevelopment or improvement). Where local authorities propose the comprehensive reconstruction of commercial and civic centres in towns and cities and to replan other areas of large cities and towns to provide better living conditions for a growing population, the authorities must acquire land compulsorily where a private owner refuses to sell.

Where land is compulsorily acquired the further question arises as to the amount of compensation to be paid to the former owner. The general rule is that the owner should be compensated in accordance with the market value of his land. A compensation code in England and Wales is laid down in the *Land Compensation Acts* of 1961 and 1973.

Where a local authority wishes to purchase, for example, a considerable number of houses in a particular area, the public will be informed and plans will be prepared. Any owner of a house in that district will find that he will not be able to sell his house to another private purchaser because of the prospect that the local authority at some time in the future will act on its plan. In such cases we say that an area is affected with **planning 'blight'**. In some circumstances a private owner adversely affected can require the local authority to buy the land in advance on compulsory purchase terms.

A complete picture of Britain's land usage is emerging from the recent comprehensive government survey which resembles the Domesday Book of 1086.

Regional planning

From the 1920s, and particularly during the economic depression of the early 1930s, it has been evident that certain older industrial areas were in decline. There was large-scale unemployment. Special steps were taken by the *Special Areas (Development and Improvement) Act, 1934*, which declared certain areas to be in need of Government assistance (by way of loans and grants to industrialists setting up new works).

This policy has been continued (under the *Industry Act, 1972* and *1975*) in order to reduce the imbalance between different regions due to their differing fortunes: decline, de-industrialisation and unemployment in some contrasting with the growth and optimism of those others where newer expanding industries are located. To try to redress the growing imbalance the Government has sought to limit industrial and commercial growth in some areas and promote it in others. The latter have been designated as **assisted areas** or **areas of expansion** and fall into three categories: (a) special development areas, (b) development areas, (c) intermediate areas (in descending order of priority or economic plight). Altogether, these assisted areas cover 25 per cent of the working population (40 per cent before the 1979–80 review). See Figure 12. State aid amounted to £700 m. in 1983.

In these areas firms receive aid in the form of (i) regional development grants (22 per cent or 15 per cent) towards the capital cost of

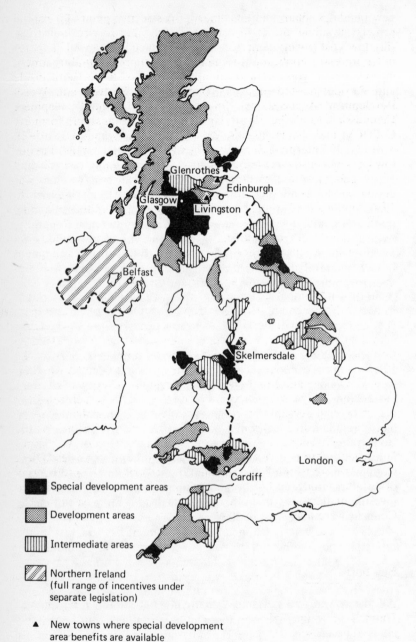

Special development areas

Development areas

Intermediate areas

Northern Ireland
(full range of incentives under
separate legislation)

▲ New towns where special development
area benefits are available

Figure 12   *Development areas in the UK*

new buildings, plant and machinery, (ii) selective grants for capital projects, training and (unusually) for office and service industries, (iii) low cost government factories, (iv) special financial help for microprocessor application, tourism, etc., (v) preferential treatment in government contract allocations. Similar assistance (both inside and outside assisted areas) is given by the Scottish and Welsh **Development Agencies**, and for rural areas, by the **Development Commission** (and the Rural Development Commission, formerly CoSIRA) and the Highlands and Islands Development Board. In 1981–84, 25 **Enterprise Zones** were created in problem areas of major towns; here, businesses are subject to looser planning controls and enjoy generous tax, rates and capital allowances. Another was announced for Sunderland in 1988 with the closure of its shipyard. In 1986 'simplified planning zones' were created to reduce planning restrictions and delays to encourage firms to set up. Generally, outside the development areas, the rationing of permits (industrial development certificates) restricted industrial and office development (and these were lifted in 1982). And the Government itself has dispersed some of its own offices to the assisted areas.

In 1964 a national and regional planning framework was established with the creation of the Department of Economic Affairs (DEA) (wound up in 1969). England was divided into eight regions, with Scotland and Wales treated as single units. **Economic Planning Councils (EPCs)** and **Boards (EPBs)** were set up in each reigon. The EPCs comprised about 30 part-time members, appointed for their wide knowledge and experience of their regions. They were **advisory** in function, and were assisted in this by the Boards, which consisted of senior civil servants representing relevant Government departments (agriculture, transport, employment, etc.). The task of the Boards was to coordinate the economic planning work of the various ministries and to help formulate regional plans and strategies. These strategies were to provide a regional framework for the preparation of local planning authorities' development plans and a guide to investment decisions in both the public and private sectors. The Councils were abolished in 1980.

New towns

All the towns and cities of Britain grew from small beginnings. Hamlets grew into villages which grew into towns and eventually cities. The reasons for growth were various: some were based on convenient routes, some were seaports, some were founded on industries such as coal and iron. People moved from the country to the towns for work during the Industrial Revolution, and as prosperity increased more and more people were drawn to the centres which provided the essentials for living: food, shelter and work.

As we have noted elsewhere, industrialisation brought many problems. One of these we see today is overcrowding; and some cities have just become too big. The building of new towns is one of the most striking planning achievements in Britain. New towns can: (1) Ease overcrowding in cities; (2) Provide conditions for industrial expansion and regional growth; (3) Provide opportunities for people to live fuller and more satisfying lives.

Short history

Ebenezer Howard in the 1890s was a moving spirit. He reacted against the overcrowding in the industrial towns and advocated the growth of new self-contained communities in the countryside where housing, jobs and necessary facilities could be provided. Two towns – Letchworth (1903) and Welwyn Garden City (1920) – were established on these lines.

Various Government Reports were produced in 1940, 1944 and 1945, and in the following year the *New Towns Act, 1946*, was passed. This provided for the creation of the new towns which have been built since the Second World War. The present legislation is contained in the New Towns Acts of 1965 and 1968 which together provide authority for the Government through its ministries to designate any area of land as a site for a New Town. Since 1946 thirty-three New Towns have been created (though Runcorn and Warrington Corporations have recently merged and Stonehouse was prematurely halted in 1976). In addition two local authorities have sponsored New Towns – Cramlington and Killingworth – in the North East. Many have now reached their population targets and are therefore completed. The distribution of new towns in Britain (see Figure 13) is as follows: England and Wales – 22; Scotland – 5; Northern Ireland – 4. Of these we may note that 11 towns are situated within a radius of about 80 miles of London. These were built to relieve the housing problems in the London area. Others are near large cities with similar difficulties.

How the towns are created

In so important a matter the Government must give the initiative. Thus the responsibility is exercised by the Secretary of State for the Environment (England), the Secretary of State for Scotland, the Secretary of State for Wales and the Northern Ireland Housing Executive.

The first step in the creation of a new town is the appointment of a **Development Corporation** responsible for the development of the

NEW TOWNS

•••••• National Boundaries

Miles
0 20 40 60 80 100

0   40   80   120
Kilometres

N

SCOTLAND

Glenrothes

Cumbernauld

East Kilbride

Irvine

Livingstone

Stonehouse

Ballymena

Londonderry

Antrim

NORTHERN
IRELAND

Craigavon

Washington

Peterlee

Aycliffe

Central Lancashire
New Town

Skelmersdale

Warrington

Runcorn

ENGLAND

Telford

Peterborough

Corby

Newtown

Redditch

Northampton

WALES

Milton Keynes

Stevenage

Welwyn Garden
City

Harlow

Cwmbran

Basildon

Hemel Hempstead

Hatfield

Bracknell

Crawley

Figure 13   *New towns in the UK*

town. The Development Corporation is composed of members drawn from all walks of life and who have some contribution to make or have special knowledge of the locality. The membership includes representatives of local authorities. The Corporation appoints its own staff similar to those found in existing local authorities: chief executive, finance officer, engineers, architects and the like.

A 'master plan' is drawn up in consultation with the Minister, any interested government department and the local authorities of the area. Residents too are given an opportunity to state views, and, if necessary, a public inquiry is held. Once the plan is agreed, the Development Corporation draws up detailed proposals for the different parts of the town, based on the master plan. All this is again done with the approval of the Minister and after consultation with the local planning authorities.

Land and buildings are acquired by purchase or by compulsory measures. Using Treasury loans (which have to be repaid with interest) the Development Corporation then proceeds to build houses, offices, factories (which are then rented out) and provides roads, sewers, water and 'mains services' – electricity, gas, telephones – which have to be arranged.

Once a new town is substantially completed, the Development Corporation is dissolved and its assets are handed over to the **Commission for the New Towns** or (for the housing assets) to local authorities. This has happened in the cases of Crawley, Hemel Hempstead, Hatfield and Welwyn for example. The overall target is a population of some 2½ million. Most of England's new towns are now reaching completion and the larger urban/city areas are tending to lose population to the suburbs. So the new town experience may be over. However, 'rural' or small-scale (and essentially private development) new towns are beginning to appear, especially in the South, where they have to confront problems of planning permission in green belt areas (see page 291).

Facts and figures

Since the late 1940s more than 1 million people have moved into the New Towns of Britain, which now have a total population of over 2 million. Approximately ½ million new houses and flats have been built, with over 1,000 schools and more than 6,000 new shops. Health centres, libraries, law courts, police stations, bus depots have all been provided together with parks, youth clubs and churches. Many other features which go to make up a town are catered for, such as arts centres, dance halls, sports facilities and other means of recreation. Altogether they have amassed over £6,000 million worth of saleable assets.

Expansion of existing towns

To build a New Town entirely from scratch is very costly at a time of economic stringency. An alternative policy is the planned expansion (under the *Town Development Act, 1952*) of an **existing town**. Peterborough, Northampton and Warrington are examples of towns which have been selected for expansion. The advantage of the growth of existing towns is that they already have an experienced administrative organisation, i.e. local authority, staff and resources, which can work alongside the Development Corporation. Such towns already have public services, shopping centres and other facilities, and contain established industries. Renewal of outworn areas here can be undertaken more effectively and economically.

More than 70 towns submitted expansion schemes, of which about a half are related to London. Where large cities have 'overspill' problems voluntary agreements have been made by the authorities in the cities with the authorities in towns near by to accept people and industry from the cities to strengthen their economic basis. For example, Swindon in 1951 had a population of 69,000, and a planned population of 241,000. Thus it aimed to attract the 'overspill' from London since it is within reasonable distance of the centre of London and has the land upon which new factories or offices can be built, and new houses provided for those who choose to move. Similar arrangements have been made in regard to the cities of Birmingham, Bristol, Liverpool, Manchester, Newcastle and Wolverhampton.

There was thus a conscious plan by the Government to tackle the problem of overcrowding in the cities and to encourage the growth of existing towns where the inhabitants can be catered for so that they may live and work in more congenial and convenient locations. However, in 1979 the Government announced that town expansion schemes were to be curbed – owing to the slow-down in population growth and the fear of attracting too many away from the inner areas of the conurbations, especially London.

Criticisms of new towns

Despite the widespread praise of New Towns a number of criticisms have emerged. These include the following:

1 Farmers and rural conservationists regret the loss of agricultural land.
2 The New Towns were accused of being boring, soulless and unimaginative, lacking charm, character and neighbourliness (dubbed the 'new town blues').
3 Councillors in these areas claimed that their democratic powers as local leaders were usurped by the Development Corporations.

4   Councillors and businessmen who seek to sustain the economic
    life of depressed industrial towns argue that the New Towns have
    undeserved privileges.

In the late 1970s, the Government scaled down the target population of some of the New Towns, and in 1980 it announced that the
New Towns Commission and the remaining Development Corporations were to be dissolved by the early 1990s. (*The New Towns and
Urban Development Corporations Act, 1985* provides for the dissolu-
tion of the New Towns Commission.) In the meantime, New Town
(alongside local authority) housebuilding has been curbed and house
sales are being further encouraged (including the provision to pick a
new landlord – see page 282). Similarly the New Towns Commission
is urged to sell its commercial assets. Any further New Town expansion is to derive from private capital investment which the Corporations are able to attract (though this may well prove difficult where
housing is not available).

The reasons for this recent policy towards the New Towns are: (i)
the Government's desire to reduce public expenditure; (ii) the substantial fall in national and regional population growth and forecasts;
(iii) the continuous loss of population from the inner areas of the
conurbations (which is held to be due, at least in part, to the New
Towns and town development policies of the past). The Government
therefore has sought to stem the population dispersal by ending the
New Towns programme and focusing more attention on the urban aid
programme (though some, such as the Towns and Country Planning
Association, argue the two policies should be seen as complementary
rather than as rival alternatives).

Urban renewal, urban aid and the inner city

Allied to the new towns scheme is the newer concept of what is
termed 'urban renewal'. There are or were slum dwellings in most of
the older cities and towns. Since the Second World War all local
authorities have worked to demolish these and to build new houses or
flats either in the same area or elsewhere (see page 273). Sometimes
whole residential areas have to be cleared, sometimes derelict land
has to be reclaimed for this purpose. The problem of planning the use
of land which has been cleared or reclaimed is then posed. See page
290.

Many towns have 'town centre maps' which explain the broad
strategy and development of the town centre as a whole, with the
plans for roads, traffic circulation and car parks. Again the planning
authorities have to bear in mind a host of considerations. Research
has been undertaken at various establishments so that the authorities

can benefit by the new knowledge which is available (including the work of the Community Development Projects: see below).

Government grants are available to support the use of the powers, policies and techniques of urban renewal. Moreover, the Ministers responsible make available to the local authorities guidance in the form of notes and memoranda to assist them in their enterprises. Historic towns we may wish to preserve, for example, so that a roadway around the town rather than through it might be the best solution. The heavy investment of the large commercial companies, supermarkets, etc. and the property development companies have been useful here. But the quality of city centre developments has varied widely, and an unfortunate side-effect has been that high land and building costs have often raised rents to levels which have forced small family and specialist shops out of the city centres, which is a loss to the community.

Government attempts to help the more deprived urban communities began in 1969 as a specific policy (i.e. apart from the more general support by way of planning, slum clearance, improvement, Rate Support Grant, housing subsidies, etc.). Thus under the *Local Government Grants (Social Need) Act, 1969*, the Home Secretary was empowered to dispense grants to help local authorities to provide extra help to areas 'of special social need'. In introducing the **Urban Aid Programme** the Home Secretary (James Callaghan) said that the aim was 'to provide for the care of our citizens who live in the poorest overcrowded parts of our cities and towns. It is intended to arrest . . . and reverse the downward spiral which afflicts so many of these areas. There is a deadly quagmire of need and poverty'.

Under the Act, local authorities (and voluntary groups) submitted projects which would help relieve urban deprivation. These were to be small scale but quick acting, and if approved, they were eligible for a 75 per cent Government grant. Many ideas were put into practice including, for example: holidays for the handicapped or deprived children, adventure playgrounds, day nurseries, day centres for the disabled or elderly and language classes for immigrants. Thus, in effect, the schemes made extra **social** provision and sought to facilitate community development. It is a further example of 'positive discrimination' (like EPAs – see page 245).

Expenditure did not amount to more than some £5 million p.a. in the first years. In the meantime, the Home Office had set up 12 'Community Development Projects' (CDPs) in various urban areas. These action–research projects aimed to both provide and stimulate local activities which would help counter the deprived and demoralising conditions of those areas, and also undertake research into the causes and nature of the social problems together with finding ways of meeting more effectively those communities' needs. After producing some very critical and radical reports, the CDPs came to an end in the mid-1970s. But in the meantime (1972–77) the Government had established a number of Inner Area Studies which recommended that more attention should be given to the **economic** regeneration of the inner cities.

Consequently, in the *Inner Urban Areas Act, 1978*, the Government undertook a 10-year plan to give 'the inner areas an explicit priority in social and economic policy' in order to combat 'mounting social bitterness and an increasing sense of alienation'. Under this Act:

(a) expenditure was to rise from £36 million (1977) to £145 million (1980);
(b) seven **partnership** areas were designated with local government–central government joint committees whose function was to coordinate and guide public sector activities in those urban areas, and provide loans and grants for the establishment of business enterprises or for the enhancement of the environment (e.g. improvement grants);
(c) 15 'programme authorities' were designated in other local authority areas; they had similar but lesser problems and powers;
(d) 20-plus other areas became 'designated authorities' with similar but again lesser powers.

Following the urban riots (in Brixton, Toxteth and Moss Side) and the Scarman Report in 1981, the urban programme was boosted to £270 million (£348 million in 1984, though central Rate Support Grants to local authorities have been reduced). For two particular dockland areas (Liverpool and London) the Government has created **Urban Development Corporations** which have been given substantial powers to develop those areas, e.g. the Liverpool Garden Festival, 1984. In 1987 a further eight UDCs were created, and a number of mini-UDCs. Another recent development in this policy area is the establishment of Enterprise Zones (see page 000). Some **Partnership Enterprise Zones** (PEZs) are also being identified, to bring together private and public funding for inner city regeneration schemes. A group of private construction companies have formed their own UDC, called **British Urban Development**; it aims to develop inner city wastelands (of which there is an estimated 150,000 acres) and make a profit from it. The church has also set up an urban fund to help with urban regeneration.

Of potentially equal or greater importance is the Government's recent policy of speeding up and urging greater flexibility in planning decisions, particularly as they affect industry and commerce. Local planning authorities have been asked to 'pick out for priority handling those aplications which will contribute most to national and local economic activity' (Circular 22/80). The Government is particularly keen to encourage the formation and expansion of small-scale businesses.

In emphasising the economic costs of the planning system in preventing, restricting or delaying development, the Government urged that local planning authorities insist on having sound and clearcut reasons for planning application refusals – particularly when it is realised that the annual value of development passing through the planning system is of the order of £10 million. Whilst the planning system seeks to balance the protection of the natural and the built environment with the pressures of economic and social change and has undoubtedly brought great and lasting benefits, the system does have a price. Care must be taken to ensure that the price is not out of all proportion to the benefits. As with other social services, difficult choices have to be made and in each of the countless decisions many compromises have to be struck to balance the long- and short-term interests of the community.

In 1988 the Government announced further plans for the inner cities in a programme called 'Action for Cities'. It sees the priorities for action as the promotion of new businesses, the improvement of training and job potential and the improvement of the urban environment. This is designed to change the face of cities over a decade. It builds on existing programmes such as the Enterprise Allowance Scheme, the Small Firms Service (which offers business advice), the Loans Guarantee Scheme, Training for Enterprise, the Youth Training Scheme, Community Programme, Restart and the work of the City Action Teams and Task Forces (which were set up in 1986 and, through co-ordinating different Departments' programmes locally, aim to involve private firms and local authorities in development programmes. In addition, there will be 12 **Compacts** or agreements between employers and local schools, which will guarantee jobs and training for school-leavers provided they reach agreed standards of achievement. City grants will replace existing urban development and regeneration grants to the businesses, and be easier to obtain. (Another contribution will come from the **City Technology Colleges**; see page 253.) Meanwhile a host of private companies are contributing to the effort, many through the **Business in the Community** (BiC) scheme.

It is clear that the urban regeneration/inner city policy is an accumulation of schemes and initiatives. It appears unco-ordinated and complex and confusing. This is partly because the urban problem itself is complex, and requires the attention of so many agencies – private, voluntary, local authority – and a number of Government departments. The range of cost of the policy is indicated in Table 9 which focuses on the key elements only.

Table 9

Estimated expenditure in inner cities	*1988/89*
Estate Action, involving tenants in management and improvement of their homes. Housing capital expenditure by local authorities...............................	£140m
Funding for housing associations through Housing Corporation and local authorities (£50m)....................	£450m
Training and programmes to encourage enterprise, including small firms support (DoE and MSC).............	£1,100m
Support for business, including Regional Selective Assistance, investment and innovation grants for small firms, and English Estates.......................................	£200m
Derelict land reclamation...	£25m
Urban Programme including urban development and urban regeneration grants..	£314m
Urban development corporations..............................	£203m
Task forces and city action teams.............................	£21m
Roads (DoT programme and grant-supported local authority roads)...	£250m
Scotland, Wales, Scottish Development Agency, Urban Programme, UDC, housing associations, MSC............	£300m
Total:	£3,003m

Source: The Times, 8 March 1988.

Some of the success of these efforts is to be witnessed in the regeneration of places as far apart as Glasgow, South Wales and London.

Historic buildings and monuments

There is a wealth of historic buildings and monuments in Britain. If these are allowed to decay they will be lost for ever, and we shall all be the poorer.

The first legislation which acknowledged the need for the State to take care of **monuments** was the *Ancient Monuments Act, 1882*, which attempted, with the cooperation and goodwill of the owners, to preserve monuments. The term 'monument' is defined widely and may include any building or structure made or occupied by man at any time. The Department of the Environment is responsible for the care and preservation of prehistoric settlements, Roman walls, Norman castles and Gothic abbeys. An owner of a scheduled monument (i.e. one on the list of the Department of the Environment) must give the Department three months' notice if he wishes to repair, alter, demolish or do any work affecting it. The Department exercises oversight over these monuments, of which 12,000 are protected in Britain. The Department is advised by Ancient Monument Boards (AMBs) set up for England, Scotland and Wales.

The Department of the Environment may make **preservation orders** which prohibit *any* work on a monument without the written consent of the Secretary of State. Further, the Department may become 'guardian' of a monument whereby it becomes permanently responsible for preservation, maintenance and management. Some 800 monuments are in the charge of the Department.

Historic buildings, like monuments, need care and preservation. There are nearly half a million buildings which are listed as of special architectural or historical interest (400,000 in England, over 35,000 in Scotland and 10,600 in Wales). The *Historic Buildings and Ancient Monuments Act, 1953*, gives the Department power to make grants for the preservation of these buildings. It is, moreover, an offence to demolish or alter the character of any 'listed' building without special consent from the local planning authority or the appropriate Secretary of State. Where consent is given to demolish a building either because it is in the way of a new road or is falling into a state of disrepair or collapsed, the Royal Commission on Historical Monuments is given the opportunity to photograph it and so record it for posterity.

The work of compiling lists of historic buildings is undertaken by the local authority for the Minister. If, however, a building is not listed, a local authority may nevertheless serve an emergency 'building preservation notice' to protect that building.

The Secretary of State for the Environment (and the appropriate Ministers for Scotland and Wales) may make grants and loans for the repair and maintenance of buildings, or groups of buildings, of outstanding interest, and local authorities may make grants and loans for *any* building of architectural or historic interest even if it is not listed. More than 4,000 buildings in Great Britain have received grants and loans totalling about £16 million. Moreover, local planning authorities have designated for special protection some 4,000 'conservation areas' of special architectural or historic interest, e.g. Bath, Chester, Chichester and York; each is a historic town with many famous buildings, and each is trying to preserve its historic features in the face of increasing motor traffic.

The Secretaries of State for the Environment, Wales and Scotland are advised by the **Historic Buildings Council (HBC)**, whose members have special skill and interest in regard to historic buildings, and on any grants and loans which the central Government may propose to make for the preservation, repair and maintenance of historic buildings. In 1984 the **Historic Buildings and Monuments Commission** was established through the amalgamation of the AMB and the HBC for England. It has a staff of 1,000, and a budget of £54 million.

We shall refer later to amenity societies, but it should be noted that within most towns and cities there are civic societies who are immediately concerned with their own locality, while the National Trust, the Ancient Monuments Society, the Society for the Protection of Ancient Buildings, the Victorian Society and others are primarily concerned with problems of preservation from a national standpoint.

The coast

Local planning authorities adjoining the sea are responsible for planning the land use of the coast. They must produce development plans (a) to safeguard the coast's natural attractions, (b) to provide facilities for recreation and holiday-makers and (c) to improve the amenities generally.

The **Countryside Commission** set up under the *Countryside Act, 1968,* has a wide range of advisory and executive functions relating to the whole of the countryside and coast. Scotland has a separate Commission with similar responsibilities to that of England and Wales. Jointly with local authorities, the Commission has identified nearly 800 miles of protected or 'heritage' coastline. And in 1965 the National Trust established 'Enterprise Neptune' to raise funds to buy and protect coasts. It was re-launched in 1985 and has raised £11 million (though its target of 900 miles will require an estimated £31 million).

The Countryside Commission

The Commission encourages the provision and development of facilities for open-air recreation in the countryside. These include the provision by local authorities and private individuals of:

1 Country parks within easy reach of towns.
2 Establishment of camping sites and picnic areas.
3 The use of reservoirs, canals and other waterways for bathing, sailing and other activities.

In Britain there are some 200 country parks and 240 picnic sites approved by the Government. Grants are made to local authorities for schemes approved by the Commission which advises the Secretary of State.

National parks

The *National Parks and Access to the Countryside Act, 1949*, enables the Countryside Commission to select national parks and 'areas of outstanding natural beauty' and to make proposals for the creation of long-distance footpaths and bridleways. Ten national parks have been established:

1	Northumberland	6	Snowdonia
2	The Lake District	7	The Brecon Beacons
3	The Yorkshire Dales	8	The Pembrokeshire Coast
4	The North York Moors	9	Exmoor
5	The Peak District	10	Dartmoor

Covering 5,258 square miles (9 per cent of the area of England and Wales) and containing a quarter of a million people, they are run by separate committees. Although the bulk of the land remains in private hands it is subject to close development control.

There are no national parks in Scotland, but there are five national park direction areas which are subject to special planning control under the Secretary of State for Scotland. These are:

Loch Lomond–Trossachs
Glen Affric–Glen Cannich–Strath Farrar
Ben Nevis–Glen Coe–Black Mount
The Cairngorms
Loch Torridon–Loch Maree–Little Loch Broom

Over 98 per cent of the land in Scotland has been designated as countryside within the jurisdiction of the Countryside Commission for Scotland.

Forest parks

There are seven forest parks in Great Britain. These are under the care of the Forestry Commission and constitute some of the finest portions of the country. They are:

1	Argyll	5	Forest of Dean and Wye Valley Woods
2	Glen Trool	6	Snowdonia
3	Glen More	7	Border Forest
4	Queen Elizabeth Forest Park		

In addition there are five forest parks in N. Ireland and five forest drives.

Local footpaths and open country

Local authorities have a duty to prepare maps showing public **rights of way** (an estimated 135,000 miles). These must be kept free of obstructions and must not be permanently disturbed. Local authorities also have a duty to provide signposts. They may create paths and ways, and may close or divert existing ones to secure a more efficient use of land. They may also convert minor roads into footpaths and bridleways. 'Open country' under the *Countryside Act, 1949*, includes mountains, moors, heaths, downs, cliffs and foreshores, woodlands, rivers and canals and their banks. Local authorities can secure access to these by means of agreements, and where these cannot be obtained local authorities may acquire land or make orders for public access. The *Commons Registration Act, 1965*, provides for the registration of all commons and village greens, and under the *Countryside Act, 1968*, local authorities can provide facilities for enjoyment of such lands to which the public has access.

Nature conservation

There are some 350 national nature reserves, and 130 are run by local authorities. There are 5,300 sites of special scientific interest (SSSIs) in Great Britain, designated because of their flora, fauna or geological or physiological features. Local planning authorities must consult the Nature Conservancy Council before granting planning permission for development affecting the sites. *The Wildlife and Countryside Act, 1981* has increased the power of central and local authorities in this field, and has the active support of many voluntary naturalist and conservation groups (see page 313) though farmers are often unhappy with the restrictions or compensation arrangements it applies. Another contentious area is forestry, where it is felt that excessive conversion of moorland to the growing of conifers (often for tax benefit purposes) can endanger ecological environments.

Land reclamation

Many areas of Britain have been spoilt by coal mines, industrial tips and abandoned factories. Government policy is to reclaim such derelict land (amounting to 113,000 acres in England) and local authorities are given responsibility for this task, e.g. the six metropolitan counties contain a massive 128 km^2 of derelict land (more than the size of Liverpool). They are empowered to acquire, clean up and carry out renovation, for which they get 100 per cent grants. The sites may then be used for agriculture, housing or open spaces, e.g. planted with trees, converted into parks or filled with water for recreation purposes.

Under the *Derelict Land Act, 1982* public and private bodies may receive grants for such land reclamation; and up to 1987 some 26,000 acres had been so restored (at a cost of £390 million).

Other environmental policies

Throughout planning literature and planning debates we meet the word 'amenities'. Sir William Holford in *Preserving Amenities* (Central Electricity Generating Board, 1959) wrote:

> . . . amenity is not a single quality, it is a whole catalogue of values. It includes the beauty that an artist sees and an architect designs for; it is the pleasant and familiar scene that history has evolved; in certain circumstances it is even utility – the right thing in the right place – shelter, warmth, light, clean air, domestic service . . . and comfort stations.

Some of the amenities of a place may be affected by:

Tree preservation. A local authority has powers to prevent a private owner from felling any tree by issuing the owner with a tree preservation order. Where a tree dies or is removed or destroyed the local authority may require the owner to replace it by another tree. Woodlands and trees can thus be preserved or replaced 'in the interests of amenity'.

Outdoor advertising. Advertisement hoardings erected in open country can be a serious eyesore. Over a third of England and Wales is now subject to 'special control', i.e. areas which are designated for 'special protection on grounds of amenity'.

Litter. The *Litter Act, 1958*, makes it an offence to leave litter on lands to which the public has free access. The legislation may be enforced by a local authority or police, but the general attack on the problem of litter is through exhortation and education. The *Dangerous Litter Act, 1971*, and the *Deposit of Poisonous Waste Act, 1972*, are acts which introduce more stringent controls to prevent dangerous litter and the illegal dumping of poisonous waste materials. Where offences are detected prosecutions may be undertaken by the local authority acting for the public.

Clean air. The *Clean Air Act, 1956*, enables local authorities to declare 'smoke control areas' within which emission of smoke from chimneys constitutes an offence. Over half the premises in the conurbations are covered by smoke control orders, the effect of which is that our air is purer and the fogs and smogs have been much reduced. In central London since 1962 winter sunshine has increased by 70 per cent.

Noise. The *Noise Abatement Act, 1960*, and the *Public Health (Recurring Nuisances) Act, 1969*, are the two main acts which empower local authorities to control the emission of noise within their areas. Once detected, the person making the noise (usually by the use of machinery) may be served with a notice requiring the noise to be abated. If the author of the noise refuses to comply suitable legal action may be taken in the courts to secure compliance.

Control of pollution. Responsibility for the control of pollution is shared by various Government departments, local and water authorities (who have powers under *The Control of Pollution Act, 1974*) and statutory agencies. Local authorities must provide for the proper disposal of waste, often with advice from the Inspectorate of Pollution. (The Nuclear Industry Radioactive Waste Executive (Nirex) is responsible for proper disposal here.) Industry cooperates and voluntary bodies help to focus public interest. A standing **Royal Commission on Environmental Pollution** advises the Government and publishes reports. It has recently (Tenth Report, 1984) criticised Government delays in responding to its reports, and stated that 'the control of pollution is not "an optional extra". It is a fundamental component of national economic and social policy, and has many international implications.' Its reports have expressed concern and made recommendations on various issues: straw burning, acid rain/dust, petrol fumes, discharge of radioactive waste, sewage contamination and cleanliness of beaches and river estuaries. While **acid rain** causes an estimated £200 million loss of agricultural output through soil pollution, it seems that farmers too are guilty of chemical pollution through the use of fertilisers and pesticides (which affects animal and plant life and gets into rivers). There is some evidence that we are managing to reduce many forms of environmental pollution (e.g. coal smoke down 80 per cent in 20 years, lead from petrol down 20 per cent since 1973). Farmers are being encouraged (with subsidies) to set aside land and leave it fallow (especially in what are called 'environmentally sensitive areas'), and 72 per cent of Britain's beaches now meet EEC quality standards (compared to 62 per cent in 1987) – though they are not necessarily the most important ones.

Indeed, in many ways Britain has a long way to go to escape its reputation as the 'dirty man of Europe'. For example, there are only five inspectors (of pollution) to supervise the use of 5,600 hazardous waste dumps. Further, there is evidence that perhaps one in five of the Water Authorities, who are responsible for ensuring the quality of water supply, are actually guilty of pollution by allowing excessive sewage to flow into rivers and coastal waters. And while river quality improved in the years 1958–80, it has not done so since (and may have deteriorated).

In 1988 the Prime Minister expressed grave concern about the environment, and focused her attention on issues of international importance – acid rain due to excessive 'raw' fumes from industrial production, the destruction of the earth's protective shield of ozone (due to the use of man-made gases, or 'CFCs') and the potentially disastrous consequence of a warming of the Earth caused by the 'greenhouse effect' (again caused by the production of gases). Action here will be costly – but so will inaction.

Amenity societies

In addition to the official bodies, i.e. the central Government, the local authorities and the Countryside Commission, there are numerous voluntary organisations to which the public may belong whose aim is to protect the heritage which is ours. There is the **Town and Country Planning Association** (founded in 1899) and the **Civic Trust** (founded in 1957), the latter encouraging interest in architecture and planning. Of the 1,000 amenity societies we may mention the Council for the Protection of Rural England, the Council for the Preservation of Rural Scotland and the Ulster Society for the Preservation of the Countryside. There is also the Georgian Group, the Victorian Society and the Pilgrim Trust. The **Committee for Environmental Conservation** acts as a liaison body and is concerned with broader questions of amenity than those covered by individual societies. Another important pressure group is SAVE (Save Britain's Heritage). All such groups seek to protect the heritage of a good environment, e.g. Friends of the Earth recently reported on the excessive and virtually uncontrolled use of pesticides by farmers.

Much attention is focused on the plight of urban areas. But rural communities face their own and similar problems, such as the lack of suitable housing (see page 000) or education (with the closure of small schools) and, perhaps above all, unemployment. In these respects, much help and advice is given by the 38 **Rural Community Councils** (or councils of community services or voluntary service). They are sponsored by the Rural Development Commission, and are affiliated to the charity **Action with Communities in Rural England (ACRE)**.

The National Trust

This was formed in 1895 by Octavia Hill, Sir Robert Hunter and Canon Rawnsley, to preserve as much as possible the history and beauty of the country for the people. The Trust was incorporated in 1907 to ensure the preservation of lands and buildings of historic interest or natural beauty for public access and benefit. It is a charity, independent of the State, and relies on the voluntary support of individuals for working funds. Other sources of income are from rents, admission fees (7 m. visits in 1983, ten times 1953, e.g. to historic houses and premises), legacies and gifts, and from the annual subscriptions of the 500,000 members. The trust is now the largest private landowner and third overall to the Crown and the Forestry Commission. It protects nearly 500,000 acres, much of it in the Lake District, Snowdonia, the Peak District and other National Parks. Where a private owner of a historic house or home cannot afford the upkeep or has fears that estate duty will be too burdensome for his successors, he may transfer ownership to the National Trust so that the public may enjoy the buildings, gardens and furniture. Thus is the heritage preserved for all.

Questions

1   Give a short history of town planning.
2   Planning is distributed among: the Minister, the regional/county council and the district council. What part does each play in the process?
3   What are structure plans and local plans? What arrangements exist for public inspection or participation in forming these plans?
4   What is 'development' so far as the Planning Acts are concerned?
5   What are the New Towns? What were the reasons for their creation?
6   How would you assess the achievements of the New Towns?
7   What do you understand by 'urban renewal'?
8   What is the Countryside Commission and what is its function?
9   Write what you know of (a) land reclamation, (b) tree preservation orders and (c) the control of outdoor advertising.
10   What legislation ensures (a) clean air and (b) the control of noise?
11   Name some of the more important amenity societies in the UK and describe the foundation and function of the National Trust.
12   Why is there a conflict of interest among farmers, housebuilders and conservationists?
13   Describe and comment on inner city policy since 1968.

12
Employment

Introduction

We have already touched upon the changes in the way of living brought about during the last two hundred years as Britain ceased to be a predominantly agricultural community and became an industrial society. There were developments in health (page 74), education (page 215), welfare and social security (page 36). The Industrial Revolution witnessed a movement of people from the country to the towns and cities, which became important mainly because they were the centres of industry in coal, iron, steel, cotton, wool and machinery. The conditions of work in factories and mines were often deplorable; women and children were used as cheap sources of labour.

In the nineteenth century Britain became the greatest industrial nation in the world, with a vast empire and territories overseas from which primary products were drawn. With these and other states we traded as an industrialised country.

In the twentieth century, after two world wars, Britain found itself drained of material and spiritual resources. Today it is no longer a superpower and has to ensure defence by means of alliances and treaties such as membership of NATO, and favourable trading conditions by joining the European Economic Community (EEC). Notwithstanding these alliances and trade associations we are reminded that the world does not owe Britain a living, and we have to compete in trade with other developed and developing industrial countries to expand and control our economy.

The *laissez-faire* policy of the nineteenth century has been replaced by increasing State control; the nationalisation of important basic industries, e.g. coal, electricity, gas, steel and railways; positive control of the conditions of work in factories and offices, and in the siting of new factories, workshops, etc. We have now what is termed a 'mixed economy'; partly state-owned and partly private industry, the ownership vesting in one or more individuals (as in a partnership) or in a company which may be a private company or a public company ('plc') in which members of the public may be shareholders.

In recent years Britain has faced two major problems: unemployment and the control of inflation. The importance of both can scarcely be exaggerated. This chapter does not seek to analyse why we have unemployment or how inflation may be brought under control.

The importance of employment

There are two aspects of employment: (a) economic and (b) social.

(a)   **Economic.** Most people need to work for a living, to provide for their own personal wants and those of their family and dependants. Formerly men went to work to provide the food, clothing and home for their wife and family, and women traditionally stayed at home to rear the family. During the present century the pattern of employment has changed and women make up a large section of the total work force, so that today they contribute largely to the family income. The law has ensured equal pay and the *Sex Discrimination Act, 1975* (see page 31), ensures equal entitlement to available jobs. Although work and the types of employment have changed by the use of machinery and applied technology, nevertheless people still need to work. It is part of the natural law, in the opinion of some, and it is one of the Human Rights (Universal Declaration of Human Rights, UN No. 2 (1949), approved by the General Assembly of the UN, Paris, December 10, 1948).

(b)   **Social.** Because man is a social being, his work intimately affects his social standing. We may consider the following:

Table 10   Manpower in Britain 1965–86 (thousands)

Year	Employees in employment*	Employers and self-employed	Unemployed†	Armed Forces	Total working population
1965	23,080	1,702	299	423	25,504
1970	22,471	1,895	555	372	25,293
1975	22,707	1,925	866	336	25,834
1979	22,920	1,886	1,344	314	26,464
1980	22,621	2,037	1,891	332	26,881
1982	20,964	2,118	3,066	323	26,471
1984	21,238	2,496	2,999	326	27,090
1986	21,594	2,627	3,180	322	27,772

Source: Britain 1988, HMSO.
  *Part-time workers are counted as units.
  †Excluding adult students.

(i)   *Time spent at work*. The greater part of our lives is spent in work. A worker usually enters work at 16 and continues until retirement, usually at 65 (men) or 60 (women). The average person must, therefore, think hard as to what he proposes to devote his energies during his lifetime.

(ii) *Rewards*. In a materialist society there is a clear relationship between the rewards obtained from work and the life-style the worker adopts. This is observed in the emergent countries of Africa and South America, and in the advanced industrial societies of Europe and North America.

Table 11   Distribution of civil employment in Britain (%)

		1971	1982
Manufacturing	Food, drink and tobacco	3.2	2.8
	Chemicals and allied industries	2.0	1.9
	Metals, engineering and allied industries	17.5	12.9
	Textiles, clothing and footwear	4.3	2.7
	Other manufacturing industries	6.5	5.7
Other Production	Agriculture, forestry and fishing	3.1	2.6
	Mining and quarrying	1.7	1.4
	Construction	6.6	6.2
	Gas, electricity and water	1.6	1.4
	Transport and communication	6.8	6.5
Service	Distributive trades	12.9	13.0
	Professional, financial, scientific and miscellaneous services	27.1	35.9
Public Administration	National and local government service	6.3	6.5
		100.0	100.0

Employees in employment	1980		1986	
Males	13.1m	58%	11.9m	55%
Females	9.4m	42%	9.7m	45%
	22.5m	100%	21.6m	100%

The *Sex Discrimination Act, 1975* (see page 000) applies and forbids discrimination against women in opportunities for employment. There is, of course, no even distribution, and we find that there are few women who are managers and few personal secretaries are men. Women are chiefly employed in the food, drink and tobacco industries; the manufacture of electrical goods, textiles and clothing; transport and communication; the distributive trades; the financial, professional, scientific and miscellaneous services; and public administration.
Source: Britain 1983, and 1988, HMSO.

(iii) *Prestige*. The work one does frequently attracts prestige. Those successful in their work usually receive promotion and honour as they move up the latter of success, as it is sometimes called.

(iv) *Psychological aspect*. Some employments give a sense of purpose in life. Men and women have devoted themselves to science, medicine, art, music, for example, because of an ideal, a sense of purpose, and found the psychological satisfaction more valuable than the material rewards. We cannot all be outstanding in our respective fields, but every person is aware of the personal satisfaction in doing a job well. On the other hand, everyone knows that repetitive and dull work in a factory and the pursuit of efficiency can lead to stress and psychosomatic illness found in advanced countries the world over.

How the state intervenes

State intervention in employment has a long though checkered history in Britain, dating from various mediaeval regulations over labourers' wages and apprenticeship. The responsibilities of modern governments are much broader and more consistent. They include the following:

1 The provision of employment services.
2 The alleviation of unemployment.
3 The regulation of the terms and conditions of employment.
4 The improvement of industrial relations.
5 The provision of training services.
6 The promotion of regional development and labour mobility.
7 The safeguarding of the health and safety of workpeople.

These are all examined in more detail in the following pages. In the pursuit of these tasks, government departments operate by various means – advice, memoranda, notices, visits by inspectors and, finally, the courts may be invoked if individuals or groups fail to comply with the law.

History

The Government did not intervene in the working conditions of the people until moved to do so by parliamentarians who agitated for reform. The first *Factory Act, 1802*, applied only to cotton and woollen mills, and was aimed chiefly to prevent the cruel ill-treatment of 'pauper apprentices'. The Justices of the Peace were ordered to appoint two 'visitors' for their district – one a magistrate and one a clergyman – who were empowered to enter mills and see that the owners complied with the Act. The inspection system was a failure, and a further *Factory Act, 1833*, allowed for the appointment of official inspectors of the central Government. Lord Shaftesbury (1801–85) was the moving spirit behind this legislation. The Act forbade the employment of children under 9; allowed children from 9 to 14 to be worked for nine hours a day only; children from 14 to 18 were not permitted to work for more than 12 hours a day; and night work was forbidden for those under 18.

Further Factory Acts were passed in 1847, 1850 and 1853 which applied to both factories and mills to secure a 10-hour day for all employees in the textile industry. Between 1864 and 1878 the Factory Acts increased control over factories and mines (inspectors for these were appointed in 1850) to ensure better safety and conditions which were more humane.

From these beginnings the controls have increased by means of legislation enforced by inspectors appointed by the central Government. As new machinery and tools were invented and new chemicals were discovered and produced, new hazards arose. New diseases became associated with a new industry, so legislation was passed to prevent or minimise the harmful results. A product may be beneficial for commercial or industrial purposes, e.g. lead, cyanide or asbestos, but its production and working can be highly damaging to health and life of workers engaged in production over long periods. In the last hundred years there has been increasing involvement by the Government, and its agencies, in industry and commerce to protect those unable to protect themselves.

Safety and conditions of employment

Employers have a duty at common law to: (a) take reasonable care of their employees and (b) provide a safe system of working. Employees have a duty of care towards each other.

The provision of a 'safe system of working' includes the provision or employment of competent fellow employees, since the safety of one employee may well depend on the care and skill of another – for example, a competent signalman on the railway is a necessity, since other fellow employees are at risk if he is incompetent.

Space does not permit the inclusion here of all the common law duties applicable to employers and employees. The following is some of the important legislation operating now.

The Government departments with general responsibility for ensuring safe working conditions are:

1   Department of Employment
2   Department of Trade and Industry
3   Department of Agriculture and Fisheries
4   Department of Health and Social Security
5   Department of Transport

This list is not exhaustive. Thus the Home Office is responsible for general control of the police service, whose task it is to ensure that goods vehicles and private vehicles are safe and comply with the law as to construction and use under the *Road Traffic Act, 1972*. The Civil Aviation Authority is responsible for ensuring the safe operation of civil aircraft and safe working conditions of the staff. Other Ministeries and authorities have comparable duties which are distributed widely.

The economic aspect of industrial safety is very important. Recent research has shown that 32,400,000 accidents involving damage occur each year, and that in Britain alone the annual cost exceeds £1,000 million (Tye-Pearson Accident Ratio Study: 1974–75, quoted in *The Times*, May 14, 1976).

The *main* statutes concerned with safety and health at work are:

1   *Factories Act, 1961*
2   *Factories, Offices, Shops and Railway Premises Act, 1963*
3   *Health and Safety at Work, etc., Act, 1974*

In addition there are the *Mines and Quarries Act, 1854*, the *Agriculture (Poisonous Substances) Act, 1952*, the *Agriculture (Safety, Health and Welfare Provisions) Act, 1956*, and other statutes.

Responsibility for enforcement was formerly distributed among several government departments. Now the *Health and Safety at Work, etc., Act, 1974*, has set up a **Health and Safety Commission**, which consists of representatives of both sides of industry (i.e. employers and employees through their representative institutions, the CBI and the TUC) and local authorities. The Commission takes over the responsibility for developing policies in the health and safety field from government departments.

The Health and Safety Executive is a separate statutory body appointed by the Commission which works in accordance with directions and guidance given by the Commission. The Executive consists of inspectors who enforce legal requirements in addition to providing an advisory service to both sides of industry. The major inspectors in the health and safety field have been brought within the Executive instead of being scattered among several government departments. The inspectors of the Executive may:

(a) Issue a **Prohibition Notice**. In effect this will require an employer to cease any activity giving rise to a risk.

(b) Issue an **Improvement Notice.** This requires the person contravening a provision of the Act to remedy the fault within a specified time. There are 150–200 such notices a year.

(c) Prosecute any person contravening a relevant statutory provision.

(d) Seize, render harmless or destroy *any* substance or article the inspector considers to be the cause of imminent danger or serious personal injury.

Proceedings by way of prosecution may be taken in a Magistrates' Court (Sheriff's Court in Scotland) or in a Crown Court. Local authorities, under the Commission's guidance, enforce the legislation in some areas of employment, including many covered by health and safety legislation for the first time. In general these are 'non-industrial activities'.

The Health and Safety Commission has been given the task of approving **Codes of Practice** for various industries or types of employment, which are drawn up and approved only after full consultation with employers, workers and experts, laying down standards in working conditions and operations required in particular areas of employment. Such codes are not law but failure to meet the require-

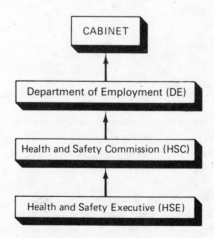

The HSE includes HM Inspector of Factories, HM Inspectors of Mines and Quarries, HM Inspectors of Nuclear Installations, and local authorities and other enforcement agencies

Figure 14 *Government health and safety agencies*

ments in the code is evidence in criminal proceedings that an employer has breached his legal duty of care towards his employees.

The *Fire Precautions Act, 1971*, which applies to many premises not previously subject to control – e.g. hotels and boarding houses – lays down standards which are enforced by the fire authorities (under the local authorities). The Act imposes on owners of premises the duty to obtain **fire certificates** showing that the premises conform to the standards laid down in the Act.

The Acts and regulations referred to above apply to about 250,000 industrial premises (factories, warehouses, shipyards, docks and construction sites) which fall under the *Factories Act, 1961* (a consolidating Act); about 750,000 premises are subject to the *Offices, Shops and Railways Premises Act, 1963*. The Act and regulations are designed to secure the health, safety and welfare of employees, and deal with such matters as fencing machinery, precautions against fire and special risks, safe conditions of premises, cleanliness, lighting, temperature and ventilation.

Anyone intending to employ other people in industrial or commercial premises to which the Acts apply has to notify the enforcing authority of his intention before he begins to employ people. Every fatal accident and every accident causing more than three days' incapacity must be reported. Certain dangerous occurrences must, under the Factories Act, be notified for investigation by the inspectors under the Act.

In Britain today four people will be killed at work every ordinary working day, 900 die a year from industrial diseases and more than 3,000 injured seriously enough to lose three or more days from work. Apart from the human pain and misery, these deaths and injuries cost industry hundreds of millions of pounds in lost production and over £3 million a week in industrial injury benefits. Part of the problem is insufficient factory inspectors: their numbers have fallen from 760 in 1980 to 540 in 1989 (and the target figure at their inception, in 1974, was 1,050).

The Employment Medical Advisory Service (EMAS). This service was established in 1973, under the *Employment Medical Services Act, 1972*. It is, therefore, a statutory body and acts as the medical arm of the Health and Safety Commission. EMAS performs the following functions: 1   Advises on the effects of a particular job on health. 2   Undertakes medical examinations to protect employees against hazardous substances. 3   Studies the medical requirements for different kinds of work, especially in relation to disabled persons.

EMAS has a special responsibility for the health of young people at work. It carries out medical and other surveys related to work but it does *not* provide medical treatment. EMAS aims to be the focus for the development of industrial medicine in Britain. The service is staffed by 100 doctors (full- or part-time) who specialise in occupational medicine. The doctors are based in the main industrial centres, but there is a Chief Employment Medical Adviser who, with a small headquarters staff, is based in London.

The *Employment Protection (Consolidation) Act, 1978*

This superseded previous legislation in providing safeguards for employees in their terms of employment. Under this legislation, employers must give employees written information on their terms and conditions of employment, the disciplinary rules which are applicable and the grievance procedure. Termination of employment is also regulated and there are arrangements for redundancy payments (see page 63). The law also covers unfair dismissal (which varies with length of employment) and a number of maternity rights for female employees (including certain rights to re-employment after confinement). There is concern that the proposals in the *Employment Bill, 1988*, to relax the regulations governing the employment of young people and their working hours may increase accidents. In 1985 the under 21s lost the protection of the **Wages Councils** which set minimum wages.

Industrial relations

History of trade unions

The system of industrial relations in this country is based mainly on the organisation of employers and workers into (1) employers' associations and (2) trade unions. The relationship between these two powerful groups and their relationship with the Government is vital to the future of this country.

The history of the growth of trade unions covers two hundred years. Originally workers in the industrial towns and the country labourers were very poorly paid. Sometimes they had to resort to poor relief (see page 5) to supplement their earnings. When they fell sick there was little provision for them except the friendly societies which were later formed (see page 10).

In the course of time workers combined to try to bargain with employers to obtain a living wage. The workers knew there was and is strength in numbers. Fearing that this combination of workers would result in bloody revolution similar to that in France (1789–92) some attempt was made to increase the poor rate. At the same time Parliament passed the *Combination Acts, 1799* and *1800*, which forbade all workers to combine for the purpose of obtaining higher wages, shorter hours or for securing any other regulation, under a penalty of three months' imprisonment or two months' hard labour. The *Combination Act, 1799*, stated that disputes about wages and allied matters in the cotton mills were to be decided by the arbitration of a representative of the workers and a representative of the employers.

In 1812 the Act was repealed, and the Government resumed its policy of *laissez faire* and 'freedom of contract', which broadly meant that workers and employers were free to lay down and determine their own conditions of service by mutual agreement. In disputes the law would be applied in the courts to which each party had access. There were many ups and downs, however, and the law, particularly the law of conspiracy, was applied harshly. Conspiracy was committed when two or more persons combined together to do an unlawful act or to do a lawful act in an unlawful manner. So, if *A, B, C* and *D* (workers) agreed together to withdraw labour from *X* (employer) in breach of contract, this amounted to conspiracy and was punishable.

The workers became incensed against that sort of law and Parliament was forced to amend its legislation to accord with more humane standards. The memory of these injustices and the harsh treatment of some of the early trade unionists – such as the Tolpuddle Martyrs who were convicted at Dorchester Assizes and sent to Australia as convicts – is recalled today by those orators who hope to inspire and encourage others who seek to protest and better their lot.

Originally trade unions were formed among the skilled craftsmen, but they have now spread to include general labourers and unskilled workers. Today trade unionism has increased among clerical, supervisory, technical and administrative workers. The qualification for membership of some unions is based on *occupation*. For example, a trade union may recruit clerical workers or general engineers wherever they are employed. In a number of unions recruitment is based on an *industry* irrespective of the particular occupation of the individual. Sometimes qualification for membership is based on a combination of occupation *and* an industry.

In 1980 the membership of British trade unions was 13.3 million, but it fell to under 12 million in 1984 and 9 million today. There are 453 unions, but nearly 80 per cent of members were in the 27 largest unions with a membership of 100,000 or more, while less than 1 per cent were in the 263 smaller unions with under 1,000 members each. Collectively, the trade unions have assets worth over £250 million and an annual income of some £200,000 million (mainly from subscriptions, which, individually, amount to only 0.3 per cent of the average earnings). Expenditure on services and administration is substantial (about £200,000 million p.a.) though expenditure on disputes amounts to only about £10 million p.a.

The Trades Union Congress (TUC)

The TUC was founded in 1868 and is a voluntary association of trade unions, the representatives of which meet annually to consider matters of common concern to their members. The TUC elects a General Council to keep watch on all industrial movements, legislation affecting labour and all matters concerning the trade union movement.

The TUC maintains systematic relations with the Government and government departments, with the Confederation of British Industry (CBI) and with numerous other bodies. The traditional interests of all trade unions have been the pay of the workers and the conditions of work and welfare of their members. These general aims remain the same today.

Employers' associations

Most employers in Britain are members of employers' organisations wholly or partly concerned with labour questions. The primary aims of such organisations are to help to establish suitable terms and conditions of employment, including a sound wage structure and proper standards of safety, health and welfare; to promote good relations with employees; the efficient use of manpower; and to provide means of settling any disputes which may arise.

The main national body representing employers is the **Confederation of British Industry (CBI).** It acts as a national point of reference for all who seek the views of industry and management, and it advises the Government on all aspects of government policy which affect the interests of industry and business, both at home and abroad. Membership of the CBI represents some 300,000 companies and over 150 trade associations and employers' organisations. There is a national council of 400 members which meets monthly, and there are regional councils in England, Scotland, Wales and Northern Ireland.

Trade disputes and conciliation

History

Industrial disputes occur daily; they have many causes. Some are trivial; others culminate in the withdrawal of labour or 'strikes'. An industrial dispute in a large or vital industry can be costly to individual workers, to companies or corporations and to the country at large.

To ensure industrial peace and harmony the Government passed the *Conciliation Act, 1896*, and the *Industrial Courts Act, 1919*. Under the latter Act, the Minister had powers to provide independent conciliation and arbitration as a means of assisting the two sides to resolve the dispute. These legislative powers supplemented the particular industry's own machinery or method of settling disputes. There was no legal obligation on the parties in an industry or factory to notify the Minister for settlement by the means provided by the *Industrial Courts Act, 1919*. What the Government hoped was that both sides would get together and thrash out the problem together and solve it in their own way. Only when that was not possible did the Government intervene to try to settle the matter by conciliation and, subsequently, if the parties agreed, by arbitration. Where both sides (i.e. workers and employers) agreed, disputes might therefore be referred to voluntary arbitration. This might take the form of (a) a single arbitrator, (b) an *ad hoc* board of arbitration of (c) the Industrial Arbitration Board. The latter was a permanent tribunal established under the 1919 Act, and was presided over by an independent person appointed by the Minister. This person was usually assisted by one member representing employers and one representing workers.

Sometimes the Minister will set up a *Court of Inquiry* to investigate a dispute. The Court's report is submitted to Parliament, and although its recommendations are not binding on the parties, they are often the basis for further negotiation for a settlement.

Industrial disputes in the UK are mainly confined to coal-mining, transport, shipbuilding and motor vehicle production. These are important industries and the strikes have been costly to the nation. However, the vast majority of plants in manufacturing industry are free of such disputes. In all industry and services, annual strike losses in the period 1969–79 amounted to 13 million days a year (equivalent to under half a day per employee). In 1981 just 4.2 million days were lost through strikes and in 1986 it was down to just 1.9 million – the lowest since 1941. Most disputes are about pay, or in recent years the threat of redundancy (e.g. the coalminers' strike in 1984) and the impact of new technology. (In 1982, the UK lost 250 working days per 1,000 workers, c.f. 133 France, 13 Japan, 1 W. Germany, 1,108 Italy, 548 Canada and 518 Ireland.)

Current legislation

The legal control of trade unions and the legal enforcement of collective agreements made by trade unions with employers are current problems facing Britain. The traditional attitude of the trade unions has been one of 'free collective bargaining'. This usually meant that the representative organisation of the workers, the trade union, would try to secure the maximum pay for its members, but that any agreement which it made with its employer would not be legally enforceable in a court of law. The arguments, for or against, cannot be dealt with here.

The *Industrial Relations Act, 1971*, a Conservative measure, was resisted by the trade unions on the main issue of legal control of the trade unions and their collective agreements. Sir Harold Wilson, former Labour Prime Minister, has described the breakdown of the 1971 Act as a 'confrontation' with the Government, and his administration repealed the Act and passed the *Trade Union and Labour Relations Act, 1974*. This Act lays down, among other things, that collective agreements will be presumed *not* to be intended to be legally enforceable *unless* they are in writing and contain a provision to that effect. The 1974 Act regulates the status of trade unions and employers' associations, and gives rights to employees who are 'unfairly dismissed' from their employment.

The *Employment Act, 1980* reformed industrial relations by enabling the Government to make funds available to encourage the wider use of secret union ballots and to produce codes of practice to promote better industrial relations (e.g. a maximum of six pickets at a works entrance). It limits lawful picketing to the pickets' own place of work and restricts the scope for 'secondary' action such as blacking and sympathetic strikes. It provides greater protection (including compensation) for the individual (with a deeply held personal conviction against trade unionism) in relation to the 'closed shop' (or Union Membership Agreement). (It also makes a number of changes in the Employment Protection legislation, especially to help small firms, e.g. regarding unfair dismissal regulations – see page 329.) The *Employment Act, 1982*, is more radical and outlaws a number of trade union actions, namely secondary strikes (i.e. against third-party firms not in dispute); 'blacking' non-union firms; disputes arising from contracts between firms specifying union labour only or arising from inter-union disputes; disputes concerning political or overseas issues. Compensation is payable (by unions or employers) to non-members dismissed under a closed shop agreement unless it has been agreed by an 80 per cent majority (which must be thus renewed every 5 years). Consequently, trade unions lose a number of immunities which have existed since 1906; trade union funds are at risk for damages by employers, and the big unions could be liable for up to £250,000. (In 1983, the National Graphical Association was fined heavily for calling a strike among newspaper printers as it was secondary action to the Eddie Shah dispute.)

The *Trade Union Act, 1984*, goes further and will require unions to (i) hold elections for their officials, (ii) hold ballots before taking strike action, and (iii) review their keeping of a political fund (i.e. collecting a political levy from members as part of their union subscription, the money being used to support subsequent political activity, especially donations to the Labour Party. Members can 'contract out', i.e. refuse to pay the levy and the unions have promised the Government to make this easier for members to do).

The *Employment Act, 1988* strengthens the law against the closed shop and enables union members to restrain their union from calling on them to take industrial action without the support of a proper ballot. In addition, unions are required to conduct postal ballots for the election of their leaders (assisted by Government funds).

This legislation has been hailed as a 'cause for general rejoicing' which could produce a 'decade of jobs and prosperity' (*Economist* 6.2.82). But the trade unions have declared it a savage attack on basic trade union rights and working-class power.

The Employment Protection Act, 1975. This is an important statute with wide-ranging provisions. It is relevant to the question of industrial relations in that it establishes: (1) the Advisory, Conciliation and Arbitration Service (ACAS); and (2) the Central Arbitration Committee (CAC).

(1) **The Advisory, Conciliation and Arbitration Service (ACAS)** was set up by the Government as an *independent* organisation under the management of a Council appointed following consultations with the TUC and the CBI. The Council comprises nine members (three from the TUC, three from the CBI and three independent experts in industrial relations), and a Chairman. The council has a Secretary and a Chief Conciliation Officer and eight regional offices. The main **functions** of ACAS are: (a) Conciliation in industrial disputes. (b) Provision of arbitration services. (c) Advisory and information services to industry. (d) Longer-term investigations for the improvement of collective bargaining. ACAS operates on the principle that where two sides quarrel, let us say *A* and *B*, and the dispute is costly to both, then it is wise for some third person, *C*, to intervene to try to see things independently and to attempt a reconciliation. Work can then be restarted and the breach healed. One requirement is that both *A* and *B* should have faith in *C*'s independence and fairness.

So far, ACAS enjoys the goodwill and cooperation extended to it by employers and trade unions. This is attributable to three factors: firstly the service is *independent* (i.e. it is not seen as an agent of a government department); secondly, the service operates by *voluntary* means (i.e. there is no compulsion or direction by the government or ACAS to accept the service offered); thirdly there is a recognition among employers and trade unions that on occasions the intervention of a conciliator can help to bring about a settlement in a dispute.

Note that employers and workers should try to reach a settlement through their own arrangements which they may have already set up and which they have trusted. If there is a breakdown then ACAS may be invited to come in and help. Generally ACAS sets about its work by: 1   Listening to and talking to each party to the dispute, at first separately and then jointly. 2   Providing a calm atmosphere and patient understanding of difficulties. 3   Trying to identify the areas of *agreement*; and separating these from the items of disagreement. 4   Acting as intermediary for conveying suggestions between each side. 5   Ensuring that there is no formal commitment. People's attitudes then tend to become less rigid, and the parties can see for themselves how a settlement is reached. 6   Where a settlement is reached by the parties themselves ACAS withdraws.

In 1986, ACAS was called in to 1,500 disputes and responded to 270,000 inquiries and requests for advice. Few of these disputes became known to the general public, and most of the work of ACAS is removed from the glare of publicity. To put the function of ACAS graphically, where a strike occurs ACAS operates a 'fire-fighting' operation, trying to extinguish the blaze. ACAS operates its 'fire prevention' role by advising companies, unions and employees how to improve industrial relations, so avoiding a greater disaster later on.

Unfair dismissals from employment are remediable by statute (*Employment Protection Act, 1975*). Where these dismissals occur ACAS may give advice in cases of alleged infringement of individual rights, and may conciliate between the employee and employer. More than 1,000 such cases a year are referred by industrial tribunals to ACAS so that it can try to obtain a settlement. Moreover, about 60 per cent of all cases of unfair dismissal are resolved between the parties without the need for a hearing by a tribunal.

But what if no settlement is reached? Although ACAS tries its best to reach a settlement voluntarily there is recourse to statutory procedures, e.g. arbitration. We must now turn to the Central Arbitration Committee.

(2) **The Central Arbitration Committee (CAC).** We have already referred to the need for arbitration in industrial disputes. The most common dispute which causes the greatest disquiet is a wage claim. One group of workers may assert that its members are underpaid and that the employers, whether the State, a national corporation, company or otherwise, do not pay sufficiently high wages in comparison with other similar workers. The settlement of this type of dispute is frequently difficult.

It is helpful, therefore, that where an arbitrator or an arbitration board is appointed each side gives an undertaking to abide by the finding of the arbitrator or board. Note, there is no compulsion about this, but unless there is some final award a dispute can endure for some time. Usually the arbitration proceedings conclude the matter – at least for the time being.

The CAC's function is to take over the work of the Industrial Arbitration Board (referred to on page 328) set up under previous legislation, i.e. the *Industrial Courts Act, 1919*. The CAC has other additional functions: for example, to hear and determine a complaint where an independent trade union requests recognition under the *Trade Union and Labour Relations Act, 1974*, and is not so recognised by an employer. The CAC is empowered to make an award incorporating terms and conditions.

The Employment Appeals Tribunal. The *Employment Protection Act, 1975*, set up this Tribunal, which began operating in 1976 in London. It is staffed by three judges, who sit singly with an assessor or assessors (i.e. lay members representing both sides of industry). The Tribunal hears appeals on points of law or principle from decisions of tribunals set up under various acts, e.g. *Redundancy Payments Acts, 1965, 1969, Equal Pay Act, 1970, Contracts of Employment Act, 1972, Trade Union and Labour Relations Act, 1974, Employment Protection Act, 1975*, Appeals from the Certification Officer. Formerly, appeals on points of law in claims and actions under the industrial legislation went to the High Court.

In England and Wales there are 27 permanent **Industrial Tribunals** hearing disputes (mainly over unfair dismissal). In 1986/7 they received 40,000 applications of which they heard 14,000 – over one-third were successful.

Influencing the demand and supply of employment

In 1984 Britain experienced two main problems: unemployment (3 million) and inflation. They are inter-related. Most developed countries in the world are experiencing unemployment due to a world recession of trade; and most face inflation. Since the Second World War governments have sought to deal with both problems by regulating or 'managing' the economy. The theory behind such actions comes from the economist J. M. Keynes (1883–1946) who showed how government budgeting could influence (increase or decrease) 'aggregate demand' in the economy and so affect economic growth (the GDP), employment and prices.

The present (Conservative) government, on entering office (May, 1979) stated that inflation was the major problem and that long-term economic growth and full employment could only be assured when inflation is overcome. Thus in the short-term it might be necessary to endure an increase in unemployment. Consequently the government adopted a 'monetarist' approach to economic policy – both by (a) seeking to reduce taxation and to encourage industrial investment by private firms, and (b) by aiming to control the money supply, especially through reductions in State expenditure (in order to cut government borrowing – the Public Sector Borrowing Requirement or PSBR – which inflates the nation's money supply). Hence we have experienced substantial reductions in actual or planned expenditures on State activities and social services (especially housing – see page 281).

Inflation has fallen from over 20 per cent to between 5 and 6 per cent (1989). But some would argue that the cost has been too high in terms of unemployment. Thus, from a figure of 1.5 million in 1977, unemployment today – compounded by the large increase in school-leavers following the 'birth bulge' of the early 1960s and by the introduction of new technology, which is creating additional redundancies – stands at about 2½ million or 10 per cent. (It is perhaps 3 million if non-registered workers, especially displaced women employees, are included.) Of these a third are under 25. Moreover, 40 per cent have been unemployed for over a year. The impact of such unemployment on living standards, health, family stability and personal identity is well documented (see page 112) and may have implications for such things as work-sharing, a re-fashioning of the 'work ethic' and more time for leisure.

The Labour Opposition has proposed a massive reflation of the economy through increases in State expenditure and the control of imports, together with some 'agreement' with the trade unions over wage increases. But the present Government is afraid that such a move would revive unacceptable rates of inflation.

Government measures

Although the State has failed to fulfil the commitment to the maintenance of high and stable levels of employment (inaugurated by the White Paper *Employment Policy*, 1944) recent governments have introduced a number of policies to reduce or spread the burden of unemployment. Most of these have been based on the assumption that high unemployment would be a passing phase, and so aimed to keep people temporarily occupied until the recession passed and the economy started to grow again and the nation could return to full employment. In practice, these **job creation** programmes or **special employment measures** have become longer term. The measures include:

1 A **Temporary Short-time Working Compensation Scheme** to encourage employers (through employment subsidies) to use short-term working as an alternative to redundancies. This involved 175,000 workers in 1982.

2   A **Youth Opportunities Programme** (YOPs) to provide a range of training and work experience to unemployed 16–18-year-olds (see page 343). It was replaced by the **Youth Training Scheme** in 1983 (see page 343).

3   A **Special Temporary Employment Programme** (STEP) to provide worthwhile temporary jobs for adults in development and urban stress areas (see pages 295 and 302). This was replaced in 1982 by the **Community Enterprise Programme** (or **CP**), for those adults unemployed over 12 months. In 1986 it provided some 106,000 paid jobs, each a year long and of 'community benefit'. This is an especially important form of work creation since the longer a person is unemployed the more difficult it is, and the more hopeless it seems, to get a job.

4   A **Job Release Scheme** to encourage older workers to retire early and release jobs for the younger unemployed. This involved 60,000 in 1982 and a third of a million 1977–87. (The scheme was abolished in 1988.)

5   A **Job Introduction Scheme** whereby employers receive a grant for employing disabled workers for a trial period of 6 weeks.

6   A **Training Opportunities Scheme** (TOPS) – see page 350. It involved 70,000 in May, 1982, and some ½ million over the year 1980–81.

7   A **Training in Industry Scheme** provides grants to firms to encourage training. It covered 35,000 in March, 1982.

8   An **Enterprise Allowance Scheme** under which unemployed people (60,000 in 1986, rising to 110,000 in 1988/9) are given a weekly allowance (£40 per week) to help them start their own business. Applicants must have been unemployed for 13 weeks, and be able to raise £1,000. The scheme is over-subscribed (with applications at over 600 a week) and there is a 15 week waiting list.

9   In 1982 the government announced a grant-aided scheme for **job-splitting** (for which an employer could receive £750). See page 358.

10   A **Jobstart Allowance** (£20) is payable to the long-term unemployed who take a low paid job (under £80 a week).

11   **Restart** is a programme of interviews and courses to help long-term unemployed find and apply for vacancies.

12   **Jobsearch** promotes many of these programmes by providing funds for travel to job interviews.

13   The **New Workers Scheme** makes payments to employers who take on young people full-time in their first year of employment.

Many of these schemes incorporate some training, and all these (plus private) measures help to mitigate some of the efforts of unemployment. Where jobs are available, occupational placement can provide a vital service.

Occupational placement

Jobcentres (employment exchanges)

These were first created by the *Labour Exchanges Act, 1909*. The function of Labour Exchanges, as they were called, was to reduce unemployment by informing those who were unemployed where jobs were available. Sometimes an employer wanted workers who were unaware that vacancies existed locally. The Labour Exchange acted, therefore, as a link or centre where those without work might find it and those who were without workers could find them.

The Board of Trade was the government department responsible for running the Labour Exchanges, and the staff were civil servants. In 1917 the Exchanges were placed under the responsibility of the Ministry of Labour. The Ministry now responsible is the Department of Employment.

In addition to finding jobs for the unemployed, Labour Exchanges, now called Employment Exchanges, paid out unemployment relief (sometimes called the 'dole'). Such amounts were paid out weekly to the unemployed from government funds. As noted elsewhere (see page 288), an economic crisis occurred in the 1930s when over 2 million people were unemployed. That crisis lasted almost until the outbreak of the Second World War.

The old Employment Exchanges were tatty and rather run-down places. In 1973 they were given a new 'image', fitted out with decent furniture, made more attractive and sited at convenient places in towns and cities. They were given a new name: **Jobcentre** and were separated from the unemployment benefit offices of the same Department. The staff became 'Employment Advisers' or Counsellors (formerly they were clerical officers) and sometimes the unemployed are now called 'jobseekers'. All this tends to preserve the dignity and self-respect of those who are without work. Phrases like 'Labour Exchange', and the 'dole' and the 'unemployed' had unpleasant overtones and are reminiscent of the 1920s and 1930s.

With 2½ million out of work (1988) the Department of Employment faces heavy responsibilities in fitting the unemployed into available work (it placed 2 m. in 1987) and ensuring that payment is made to those out of work so that they can survive. The *Employment and Training Act, 1973*, is an important statute. It set up the **Manpower Services Commission (MSC)** together with two subsidiary agencies which subsequently (in 1978) became Divisions within the MSC known as the Employment Services Division (responsible for Employment Exchanges or Jobcentres, and thus for placing people in employment); and the Training Services Division (responsible for the encouragement and provision of training). In addition, a Special Programmes Division was created with responsibility for running the newly established Youth Opportunities Scheme and other special programmes. However, in 1988 the MSC, briefly re-named the Training Commission, was abolished and the Department of Employment Group became responsible for all these programmes (though training is being substantially devolved to the private business sector; see below).

Using the service. Jobs available are put on cards and displayed. These days video display systems (such as SUPERVAC) are being used. If a jobseeker sees a job that suits him he tells the receptionist who will telephone the employer to make an appointment for interview. In 1984 the Government announced plans (over 4 years) to reduce Jobcentres from 995 to 350; to create **Jobshops** (self-service, no advisers) and set up 500 small **Jobpoints** (in Post Offices, libraries, etc.) equipped with computers and a small staff. **Jobclubs** have also been set up to provide coaching in job-seeking techniques; they provide facilities for writing applications as well as giving support and motivation, and are thus similar to **Restart**. In 1988 the latter was used (in some cases on a mobile basis, visiting housing estates) to give more extended interviews to the long-term unemployed to see if they were making sufficient effort to find work, in view of the large number of job vacancies (an estimated 153,000 in London alone, including unskilled work).

Professional, scientific, technical and managerial appointments are dealt with by a special service called the **Professional and Executive Recruitment Service (PER).** This service is described in more detail on page 337.

Getting help from employment advisers. All types of persons may go to Jobcentres to discuss job opportunities. An adviser may be able to suggest a job which has not occurred to the applicant. Some people cannot work normal hours, perhaps through family commitments. Such persons can be helped because there may be work available at the times wanted. Alternatively, Jobcentre advisers may be able to assist with knowledge of facilities such as day nurseries and playgroups where children may be cared for, or homes for the elderly or infirm unemployed: home help services, day units and 'meals on wheels' may be available for such persons.

Taking a job in another area. Where a person is unemployed or threatened with redundancy the Jobcentre can help under its **Employment Transfer Scheme.** The Jobcentre can look for or assist in looking for and obtaining a job in another area, beyond travelling distance from home. *Grants and allowances* are available to cover travelling, lodgings and moving house. If a person finds himself in this position he can either settle permanently in a new area or work there until a job to suit him becomes available nearer his home.

If an applicant lives in one of the Development or Intermediate Areas (where jobs are scarce and where the Government wants to encourage development of industry – see page 288) before transferring under the scheme, then additional benefits may be available. Grants may also be possible if an applicant for a job is prepared to improve his job prospects by taking training course run under the **Training Opportunities Scheme** (**TOPs**) – see page 350 – or other training scheme. All this facilitates labour mobility.

Special categories

(a) Nursing

A special job-finding and advisory service exists for nurses and midwives and for those wanting to enter this type of work. Advice is available for those wanting to train as a State Registered Nurse or a State Enrolled Nurse. Refresher courses are available for those who wish to return to nursing after interruption of a career. Jobcentres can use the knowledge and guidance of professional nursing consultants employed for this purpose.

(b) Commercial occupations

All Jobcentres deal with those qualified for or seeking work in shops and offices. In the large cities there are specialist offices, and in London PER (see page 337) runs a separate section for highly qualified personal assistances, bookkeepers and shorthand typists.

(c) Hotel and catering

Information and advice about opportunities for jobs in hotels and catering, including seasonal and part-time work, are available at all Jobcentres. Again in the large centres such as London, Glasgow and several other cities, there are also a number of employment offices dealing with the more skilled posts in hotel and catering.

(d) The disabled

Here we shall take the term disablement to mean incapacity for normal work arising from accident, disease, war injury and other factors.

The first national scheme to help the disabled began in 1914 under the authority of the Ministry of Labour which worked in cooperation with the Ministry of Health. Its object was rehabilitation and training of war casualties arising out of the First World War.

The Second World War inspired further employment services for the disabled. At that time of crisis the country was short of manpower for defence, and there was a need for all persons, including the disabled, to be trained for suitable work for the war effort. Where persons were injured in the war or while engaged in the factories producing guns, aircraft, tanks, ammunition, etc., there was evident need to train or retrain those so incapacitated.

The present services are based on the *Disabled Persons (Employment) Acts, 1944 and 1958*. The first Act was based on the Tomlinson Committee Report of 1943, and the 1958 Act was based on the Piercy Committee Report of 1956. The effect of both Acts is to ensure that the disabled, whose incapacity arises from whatever cause, may be trained for employment in society to which they may contribute their skill and work. Under the *Chronically Sick and Disabled Persons Act, 1970*, local authorities must seek out the disabled in their areas and make known to them the services available for them. A *register* of the disabled in an area is kept at the local Employment Office or Jobcentre.

Under the 1944 Act, the **quota** system was established to ensure the employment of a satisfactory proportion of disabled people as part of the regular workforce. Under this scheme all employers of 20 or more workers are obliged to recruit at least 3 per cent of employees from the special list of disabled people registered for employment; employers may receive £45 p.e. towards wages under the Job Introduction Scheme. In addition the Act authorised the **designation** of certain occupations as being reserved exclusively for registered disabled people (e.g. car parks and lift attendance).

About 600 specialist **Disablement Resettlement Officers** are attached to Employment Offices or Jobcentres. In touch with local employers (and guided by local advisory committees) they give advice to the disabled on jobs and training, and may loan or give grants for special equipment which the disabled can use to work at home (even to set up their own businesses). Similarly employers may receive grants for equipment or to adapt premises for disabled employees. In addition to the 'Job Introduction Scheme' the Government has launched (1979) the 'Fit For Work' Scheme under which employers receive awards for pursuing positive policies on the employment of disabled people (e.g. adapting premises, providing equal training or career opportunities). There are special services for the **blind** and some Employment Offices have Blind Resettlement Officers attached to cater for the visually handicapped in the area. In 1983 overall 70,000 were placed in jobs by Jobcentres. In 1988 the Disabled Graduates' Career Information Service was established.

For those who cannot return to normal working life (being unemployable by the private firm) the only course open is to build workplaces where these severely handicapped may be specially provided for. Such **sheltered workshops** may be provided by (i) Remploy

Ltd, which is a non-profit-making company supported by government grants. It has some 94 factories and about 8,750 disabled employees working under protected conditions. (ii) Certain charities make similar provision, the best known of which are the Blind Workshops. These too are aided from public funds. (iii) Local authorities may also provide sheltered employment and like the others enable the disabled to perform real industrial work and receive real wages. (iv) Sheltered Industrial Groups provide employment alongside able-bodied workers.

(e) **HM forces**

Many Service personnel leave the Forces quite young or in middle life. They then may become unemployed. Some map out what they want to do on retirement; some do not. Where a person has left or is about to leave HM Forces the Jobcentre will help him to find a job.

Responsibility for the resettlement of men and women leaving the Armed Services lies with the **Forces Resettlement Service**. This advises officers and other ranks before release of the available training and employment opportunities. The Occupational Guidance Service at a Jobcentre is also able to give Service personnel further help in deciding on civilian careers. Two training schemes are run specially for Forces personnel; courses for potential supervisors and business appreciation courses. Arrangements may also be made for serving personnel to be attached for a short period to civilian employers to gain experience of a particular job or understand the workings of an organisation.

(f) **Professional and executive recruitment service (PER)**

This Government agency provides a service for those qualified academically or by experience for professional, administrative, managerial, executive, technical and scientific appointments. PER provides the service an applicant will require. It operates throughout industry, commerce and the public sector. Those with a minimum of two GCE A-levels may start at trainee position, or be available for middle management and technical positions, to the senior levels of employment. There are 36 PER offices throughout the country, and in London there is a specialist branch for PER executive secretaries, i.e.highly qualified secretaries and personal assistants. It organises three-day 'self-presentation courses' for people who are unemployed or about to be made redundant which are designed to improve job-finding techniques. The courses are held at many centres by consultants from various professional institutions. The courses are free, and PER meets the cost of certain out-of-pocket expenses. Employers are charged a fee. And in recent years PER has been made more cost-effective and now breaks-even. However, in 1988 it was sold off (i.e. privatised).

(g) Female employment

Many inequalities formerly applied to women in regard to employment. Pay, opportunities for promotion, training facilities, education were all fields where discrimination was common. Discrimination continues today although there are many women's groups who work to redress the balance. The law has set out in explicit terms in two important statutes that there shall be equality and no discrimination. These Acts are the *Equal Pay Act, 1970*, and the *Sex Discrimination Act, 1975*. Both Acts came into force on December 29, 1975.

The *Equal Pay Act, 1970*, ensures equal treatment in respect of pay and other terms of employment. Where men and women are doing the same, or broadly the same, work, they shall therefore be paid equally for that work.

The *Sex Discrimination Act, 1975* makes it unlawful to treat anyone, on the grounds of sex, less favourably than a person of the opposite sex is, or would be, treated in the same circumstances. Discriminatory advertising – for example, where anyone uses advertisements giving descriptions implying the sex of the jobholder, such as 'foreman' or 'waiter', without making it clear in some way that both men and woman may apply – is now an offence. Legal action *may* be taken by the Equal Opportunities Commission (see below).

Where a person is discriminated against in employment he or she may take legal action before an industrial tribunal. If the person's income or capital is small application may be made for legal aid and assistance under the *Legal Aid Act, 1974*. This 'assistance' will be given by a solicitor and may include drafting letters in addition to oral advice as to legal rights and how to sue. A person who is discriminated against may present his or her own case to an industrial tribunal hearing, or a lawyer may be engaged to act for him or her; or a trade union official or other person may present the case. Conciliation officers of the Department of Employment may arrange to settle the matter without recourse to legal proceedings, which are taken only after the matter causing complaint cannot be settled by negotiation.

The Equal Opportunities Commission (EOC) was created by the *Sex Discrimination Act, 1975*, and came into being in June 1975. Its chairman is Baroness Platt, Conservative County Councillor for Essex. The staff consists of 400 persons. The function of the EOC is to: help complainants who allege discrimination; investigate abuses; to issue 'non-discrimination notices'; to force practices to be stopped if these notices are not complied with; to apply to the courts for an injunction and to grant a declaration of rights; to bring proceedings in respect of discriminatory advertisements or instructions or pressure to discriminate; to review the working of the *Sex Discrimination Act, 1975*, and the *Equal Pay Act, 1970*.

Where discrimination is proved legal proceedings *may* be brought for damages. If the question is one of discrimination in *employment* the case will go to an *industrial tribunal* which *may* award compensation to the complainant, in the same way as a successful case for 'unfair dismissal' under the *Trade Union and Labour Relations Act, 1974*, and the *Employment Protection Act, 1975*. The tribunal may also make a 'Declaration of Rights' and recommend a particular course of action in a particular company, industry or corporation.

As examples of the under-representation of women, and therefore discrimination against women, we may quote the case of the two Houses of Parliament: both in the Lords and in the Commons there is great imbalance between the sexes (only 4 per cent female MPs). Women are under-represented in trade unions generally (forming only about one third of the membership); in 62 unions there are only 71 full-time women officials as against 2,259 male officials. Glaring instances are seen in the professions and other categories of work which remain male-dominated (e.g. women form only 5 per cent of barristers, 7 per cent dentists, 9 per cent administrative civil servants, 2 per cent technicians).

(h) Ex-prisoners

Those who have been unfortunate enough to be sent to prison for crimes are faced with very great difficulties on their release. They need to be re-established in their homes, if they have any to go to, and reconciled with their families. A further difficulty is that any person convicted may well find that he has no job to go to. His previous employer may have had to discharge him and does not want to re-engage him on release.

For those serving long terms of imprisonment there are opportunities to engage in prison industries while in custody to gain a training and experience which will fit him to get and retain a job on discharge. Pre-release courses are conducted in all prisons, and prisoners are sometimes allowed leave towards the end of their sentences to enable them to preserve links with families and friends, and to make new contacts with people, including employers, who may be able to assist them on release.

The **National Association for the Care and Resettlement of Offenders (NACRO)** assists in finding hostels for those having no home to go to and in finding work with suitable employers.

Any prisoner may take advantage of the facilities available at Jobcentres or Employment Offices and, with other workless persons, will be assisted by advisers and resettlement officers of the Employment Service.

At a time of large-scale unemployment it is doubly difficult for ex-prisoners to obtain once more a footing in society, with a home or hostel and a suitable job. If society rejects prisoners they will obviously become desperate and sometimes return to crime.

One great difficulty always faces an ex-prisoner. How much of his past should he reveal to a prospective employer? If he tells all, he may be rejected; if he conceals his past he faces the prospect of unemployment should his new employer subsequently find out the truth concerning his past. It is a dilemma which is not easily solved.

The *Rehabilitation of Offenders Act, 1974*, enables an individual who has suffered his punishment for a 'spent conviction' (as defined in the Act) to make a fresh start. By s. 4(3) a convicted person is under no obligation to disclose a spent conviction and such conviction 'shall not be a proper ground for dismissing or excluding a person from any office, profession, occupation or employment'. Thus if an employer asks for details of past convictions this is deemed not to include a spent conviction.

The 1974 Act does not provide any sanction for refusing employment. As regards dismissal it would appear that (a) a summary dismissal on discovery of a spent conviction would be wrongful, and (b) dismissal for this reason would not come within 'conduct' nor 'other substantial reason', and it would, therefore, be unfair under the *Trade Union and Labour Relations Act, 1974*.

(i) Youth employment

This subject is important for two reasons: (1) the transition from school to work is an important event in any person's life; and (2) the choice of a first job is specially important, hence the need for guidance.

In former times, when jobs were scarce one entered whatever employment was available locally. So much depended on the economic life of the country; where one lived; what education and training one had received; family tradition; and other factors. Often there was little choice at all. Parents usually influenced their children and assumed the function of adviser directly or indirectly.

History. The *Education (Choice of Employment) Act, 1910*, gave local education authorities *powers* to establish vocational guidance for school leavers. Of the 162 local education authorities at that time some 132 assumed the duties. Those authorities which did not operate a vocational guidance scheme could adopt a scheme operated by the Board of Trade.

In 1945 the Ince Committee on the Juvenile Employment Service recommended administrative unification at national level, i.e. the Ministry of Labour was made the responsible government department and had power to delegate responsibility to the Central Youth National Executive, staffed from both the Ministry of Education and the Ministry of Labour. The *Employment and Training Act, 1948*, implemented the scheme.

The present scheme derives from the *Employment and Training Act, 1973*. A number of bodies play a role:

1 In practically all of the secondary schools there are school **careers teachers** who are nominated to advise school-leavers on jobs or professions. This service is additional to or supplements the Careers Officers described below. The schoolteacher responsible for careers must know or obtain information about a wide variety of careers or jobs. In the further education colleges a lecturer may be appointed with similar functions. Advice is also given to those who wish to proceed to polytechnics or universities about the need for the requisite academic qualifications.

2 Careers Officers are appointed by local education authorities and there are now Careers Officers in most cities and towns. The functions of Careers Officers are to: (i) contact young people to introduce them to employment and training opportunities and advise them on suitable vacancies at the appropriate time; (ii) liaise with schools and colleges and to assist careers teachers (as at (i) above); (iii) contact employers regularly to obtain knowledge of the current employment situation and occupations available; (iv) maintain a service by the circulation, exchange and distribution of information both to employers and schools and school leavers; and (v) liaise with Employment Office or Jobcentre. The Careers Service therefore provides an *advisory* service for everyone in education, and a *placing* service when they leave it. A **Careers Officer** interviews each applicant, obtains a confidential report from his school and advises the youth on the best course to pursue. Parents can attend interviews with the school-leaver if they so wish. After placement, the Careers Officer maintains contact through interviews after the youth enters employment so that he may talk over any difficulties he may have. If dissatisfied with his job, the youth may be found another.

3 Thus young people who have left education can continue to use the **Careers Service** but, alternatively, they can seek help and advice from Job centres or Employment Officers in the ordinary way.

Criticisms and problems. The administrative criticism which may be made is that there is duplication and overlapping of functions, for example, by schools career teacher, the Careers Officer (appointed by the local authority) and the Employment Service of the Jobcentre.

The only justification is that it is better that the wisest advice and guidance is plentifully available so that manpower is not wasted by fitting 'square pegs in round holes'. However, schools career teachers whose whole lives have been spent in academic institutions may have little idea of the life, careers, work and the difficulties found on the shop floor or in the offices of various professions or industries. Moreover, many of them 'drift' into the role of career guidance rather than aspire to the post through strong interest and conviction. 'Despite improvements in careers teaching and guidance over the past decade, many of these young people have a poorly developed idea of their job prospects or career future and are ill-equipped to make the transition from school to work.' ('Outlook on Training', MSC 1980.) In FE colleges, careers guidance is largely confined to full-time students only; careers officers often attend infrequently, and they may be given few facilities (HMI Report, 1983).

No amount of advice and guidance is going to avail if there is large-scale unemployment. So the primary requirement is the creation of a situation where industry (private or public) can flourish and progress so that the labour available can be absorbed. There are many problems facing the Government, and unemployment is one of the most serious.

Job-creation programme for unemployed school-leavers

In recent years unemployment has affected the young school-leaver acutely. Many students leave school at 16 only to find that there are no jobs to go to. They therefore join the official queue of the unemployed and receive Income Support paid by Giro cheque (as from September in the year of leaving). The Government has become specially concerned with these teenagers for obvious reasons: many are likely to drift and fall into cynicism and disillusionment due to enforced idleness for which they are being paid. The following options are now open to teenagers: 1   Return to school to obtain more education. 2   Enrol at a further education college to learn a craft or skill, such as shorthand-typewriting, building crafts, engineering crafts. 3   Undertake a training course organised by the Job-centre (Employment Office) or the Careers Service. 4   Enrol in a Job Creation or a Youth Training Scheme.

It is with No. 4 that we are here concerned. In 1975, the Government made a £30 million grant (later increased) to help teenagers in performing work in the **Job Creation Programme**. The first step in the scheme (which is administered by the Manpower Services Commission or MSC) was to devise a **project** which may be sponsored by local authorities, charities, voluntary organisations or similar bodies. The unemployed youths perform the work and complete the project, and they are paid wages which come from the MSC (i.e. funded by the Government). In some cases payment is made for materials, equipment and administration. The projects might include tidying the streets, clearing beaches, washing graffiti from walls and other worthwhile environmental jobs. In 1976, a £19 million **Work Experience Programme**, designed to help young people aged 16–19 who were finding difficulty in obtaining jobs, was launched by the MSC. In addition **recruitment subsidies** were paid to firms who employed youngsters who had been unemployed for 6 months or more.

These schemes were in effect superseded by the **Youth Opportunities Programme (YOPs)** which began in 1977 and followed the Holland Committee Report which proposed an end to all the separate and temporary schemes to reduce teenage unemployment and the introduction in their place of one integrated plan to secure work, training or education for all up to 18 years of age. Consequently the YOPs programme incorporated the following schemes: (a) courses to prepare young people for work through employment induction courses, short industrial courses, remedial and preparatory courses; (b) work experience schemes – on employers' premises (WEEP), training, workshops, community service, etc. Courses varied from a few weeks to a year in length. In the period 1981–82 some ½ million entered the YOP programme. In addition the **Unified Vocational Preparation** scheme provided off the job training and education for some 18,000 young people who have just entered employment. The **Community Industry Scheme** (not to be confused with the Community Programme for adults, see page 332) provides temporary employment in a supervised environment for disadvantaged young people. The **Young Workers Scheme** (started 1982) was designed to encourage employers to keep on youngsters in full-time jobs after completing their 6 months YOP placement. Employers receive grants which vary inversely with the 17-year-olds' earnings, since it is argued that high wages have priced many youngsters out of jobs, and high redundancy payments make it more economic for firms to retain older workers than hire young ones. It ceased in 1988.

All this is now largely superseded by the **Youth Training Scheme (YTS)** introduced by the MSC in 1983. It provides a year's broadly-based training for all 16-year-old school-leavers, unemployed 17-year-olds and the disabled up to 21. In 1985 it was extended to two years, and in 1988 it was made virtually compulsory in that 16 and 17 year-olds lost entitlement to Income Support and must rely on the YTS allowance. As well as work experience (which YOP provided) youngsters get education and at least 13 weeks off the job training. Those who are employed get wages; others receive an allowance (£29.50 p.w. in the first year, £35 in the second). Most trainees (75 per cent) are with firms (which receive grants per trainee) under what is called 'Mode A'. The others come under 'Mode B', run by local authorities and voluntary bodies. While many employers subsequently keep their trainees on, many others do not, so they join the dole queue. As a result many critics suggest the scheme is just a form of cheap labour, or it makes things worse by raising expectations among the young. But YTS does not just aim for training: it seeks to provide personal development, life skills, guidance, support and motivation (see page 350).

(j) Immigrant workers

After the 1950s considerable numbers of people from Commonwealth countries in the West Indies, Asia and Africa entered Britain to take up employment with the intention of settling permanently here. It is estimated that black Commonwealth immigrants and their families number some 2.2 million, i.e. about 4 per cent of the UK population (and 40 per cent were born here). The number grows though the Home Office operates a quota system now, usually allowing not more than 5,000 persons with their families to enter the UK annually. Some 60 per cent have settled in Greater London and the West Midlands, including Birmingham.

Because of the discrimination exerted against the newcomers Parliament passed the *Race Relations Act, 1965*, and the *Race Relations Act, 1968*. The Acts made it an offence to discriminate on grounds of colour, race, ethnic or national origin. The **Race Relations Board** was set up under the 1968 Act to supervise the working of the Acts, and the **Community Relations Commission** was set up to coordinate on a national basis the measures adopted to secure harmonious community relations, and to advise the Home Secretary on any matter referred to the commission by him.

The *Race Relations Act, 1976*, repealed the previous Acts of 1965 and 1968, and consolidated the law. It abolished the Race Relations Board and the Community Relations Commission, and set up the new **Commission for Racial Equality**, the first chairman being Mr David Lane, former Conservative MP. The Commission comprises 8 to 15 individuals appointed by the Secretary of State on a full-time or part-time basis.

The Commission for Racial Equality has powers of investigation and enforcement similar to those of the Equal Opportunities Commission established under the *Sex Discrimination Act, 1975*. The Commission identifies and deals with discriminatory practices by industries, firms and institutions; it is empowered to issue non-discrimination notices and bring legal proceedings against those who persistently break the law. The Home Secretary stated (*The Times*, June 14, 1977): 'The Government is convinced that it is right to put discrimination on the same footing as other forms of civil wrong and to make redress available to victims of discrimination by direct access to the courts and industrial tribunals.' An individual who alleges discrimination, and is able to prove this to the satisfaction of a court or tribunal, may be awarded compensation or damages.

Whereas in 1967 less than a quarter of the black population in Britain was born in this country today about two out of five have been born here and the time is not far off when most of the black population would be British-born. Although there has been a strengthening of the law, the most effective means of defeating discrimination and racial prejudice are by public education and debate rather than prosecution. All political parties are committed to the principle of equal rights for all citizens in the interests of future racial harmony.

In the 1950s large numbers of immigrant workers from the Caribbean, Pakistan and India were encouraged to come to this country to take the many jobs then available. The position now is much different, and stringent controls on immigration are imposed. For the few who are permitted to enter the country, a **work permit** (issued by the Department of Employment) is needed. The prospective employee applies for a work permit for a specific job for a fixed initial period not exceeding 12 months in the first instance.

In general, Commonwealth citizens and foreign nationals (other than nationals of the EEC countries) are eligible for permits on the same terms. However, some Commonwealth citizens and others may be admitted for fixed periods of training 'on the job' arranged in advance if such persons hold trainee permits issued by the Department of Employment. But important new categories are introduced under the *British Nationality Act, 1981* (operative from January, 1983).

(k) **European Community workers**

The EEC regulations, now enforced in Britain, establish the rights of workers to move freely between member states for the purposes of employment. Workers entering another member state are entitled to be treated in the same way as nationals of that state as regards facilities of the national employment services, pay and working conditions, trade union rights, vocational training and retraining facilities, access to housing and property, and insurance and industrial injury benefits. Workers who wish to remain in the UK for longer than an initial period of six months are expected to apply for a residence permit. If they are in permanent employment the residence permit is valid for five years. If the employment is temporary (i.e. expected to be of less than one year's duration) the permit is valid for the expected duration of the employment. As a result of the *(European Communities (Amendment) Act, 1986,* Britain will become subject to the single European market in 1992 and continental workers will be freer to obtain work here.

Britain, as a member of the OECD, paticipates with 13 European countries in arrangements for assisting nationals of the countries concerned to obtain employment in other member countries.

(1) Private employment agencies

In addition to the official Employment Offices or Jobcentres provided by the State, there exist private employment agencies. These usually specialise in a particular kind of employment, e.g. shorthand typists, who are registered and placed with an employer seeking such services. The private agency charges a fee for the placement. A glance at newspapers will reveal the names of the private agencies (e.g. Brook Street Bureau, Alfred Marks, etc.) and the specialist workers whom they seek to attract, such as managers, engineers, salesmen and so on.

To ensure that the public are protected against exploitation, all such agencies are now licensed with the Department of Employment and inspected to ensure efficient service (under the *Employment and Training Act, 1973*). The fact of their existence shows that the agencies continue to make a profit and that they fulfil a public need outside the services given by the Government Employment Offices and Jobcentres.

Training

Most people achieve a better performance and skill if they have been properly trained. All advanced industrial societies must train their workforce in the new knowledge, materials and machinery which emerge year by year. Electronics, atomic energy, computers, offshore oil exploration and telecommunications are some examples of man's advance. In a sophisticated world the newcomers and those already employed must be trained to use the new techniques and machinery. Training is equally necessary in the field of social services and public administration. There are four broad sectors of training: (1) by private firms or companies of their own staff; (2) in further education colleges and polytechnics; (3) private training establishments; (4) government establishments. However, in 1982, the MSC launched the 'Open Tech' Programme whereby training packages or kits can be used by trainees at work, at home or at college as time and flexibility suit.

1 Private firms and companies

Modern industrialists ensure that efficient training is given to staff. A company producing specialist goods knows what kind and quality of goods it wants, and how best to produce them. It sets up its own training school to ensure the best techniques are learned.

Some companies who were forward-looking gave day-release to young employees at their own privately-owned schools long before day-release schemes became part of the further education system (see page 238). The primary object was to stimulate young people to learn something about society and their function and role in the company employing them.

2 Further education colleges and polytechnics

There are some 700 colleges of further education in Britain. These provide education at GCSE and 'A' level, and beyond, and at the same time provide training in a wide variety of skills such as brick-laying and building, engineering, mechanical and electrical and other types, shorthand-typing, clerical, hotel and catering, business studies, social work, public administration and many other subjects.

The polytechnics number 30. These provide higher education to degree level, and at the same time have departments geared to business and industry from whom they draw many students. Some of these attend full-time, some part-time and some attend sandwich-courses in association with local industry or a commercial undertaking.

The further education colleges and polytechnics expanded after the Second World War, and now have the buildings, staff and equipment to ensure successful training and education.

3 Private training establishments

These are privately owned and exist for students who prefer to train for a particular career or job outside the colleges or other educational and training establishments controlled or run by the local authorities or central Government. Thus, there are secretarial colleges which train students for careers as private secretaries or shorthand typists; colleges for the training of journalists, interpreters and a host of other employments, usually of a specialist kind. Students must, of course, pay for their tuition or training. They may take the public examinations such as GCSE or professional examinations or courses offered by the Royal Society of Arts and similar bodies.

4 Government training provision

Although the main responsibility for carrying out industrial and commercial training lies with individual employers (as part of their investment to aid efficiency) the Government has developed a comprehensive strategy to help to improve the supply of trained manpower needed by the economy, to provide opportunities for individuals to acquire new skills, and to improve the efficiency and effectiveness of training generally. Responsibility for this rests with the Department of Employment (formerly the MSC) and takes three main forms: (a) Training in Industry; (b) Training Opportunities Scheme (TOPS); (c) Other Direct Training Services to Industry. These are examined in some detail below.

(a) Training in industry. The framework of training in industry and commerce is mainly based on the *Industrial Training Act, 1964* (as amended by the *Employment and Training Acts, 1973* and *1981*).

The Industrial Training Boards, set up under the 1964 Act, number 23 plus a training committee for the foundry industry (they were reduced from 27 in 1974 see also page 349). Some 12 million employees (or about 60 per cent) of those employed in industry and commerce are covered by these training boards. The Training Services Division of the Department of Employment (DE) exercises control over the activities of the training boards. Among the largest are the Construction Industry Training Board, the Engineering Industry Training Board and the Hotel and Catering Industry Training Board.

Under the *Employment and Training Act, 1973*, there was a significant change in financial responsibility with the individual boards becoming financed by Government grant (about £50 million in 1980–81) to cover (a) operating expenses, (b) advisory services and (c) grants for certain key training activities. In addition to the Treasury grant (i.e. grant from public funds) the training boards have power to raise *levies* (i.e. payments) imposed on firms and companies to finance training activities. The levy rate normally is limited to 1 per cent of an employer's payroll. The training boards' plans and budgets are agreed with the DE for periods of five years. The main functions of the boards are: (a) to give *direct* help and assistance to firms to develop their training plans, and (b) to improve the *quality* of their training. The boards employ more than 2,000 advisory staff for these purposes.

Large companies can set up training courses for their employees, or a particular section, and claim back from the board (to which they pay the levy) the expense incurred in running the course. Small companies or firms may employ only very few staff who require training. They may, however, get together with other small firms and the training board can set up a course of training for them. The board in effect sponsors what are called 'group training schemes'. By these means small companies (who may be producing very valuable products of a specialised kind) can benefit equally with large companies and take advantage of the facilities and organisation of the training board.

The Department of Employment exists to coordinate training generally in industry and commerce, and to assist by way of information, experience and facilities to ensure that employees are better equipped for their work by being better trained. This applies equally to the working population who are outside the statutory ITB sector.

Sectors not covered by the statutory Industrial Training Boards are:
1 Nationalised industries (coal, the Post Office, British Rail, gas, electricity and water); 2 Public service (education, health services, Civil Service and local government); 3 Private sector (banking, insurance and finance; other industry and commerce).

These categories represent 40 per cent of the working population. Some of these industries and services run their own training schemes efficiently; some do not. An important objective of the DE is to establish relationships with numerous organisations in this sector to assess training needs, expertise and facilities, and to determine how best the DE might contribute to improving training standards or, as a whole.

In 1979 the MSC instituted a review of the *Employment and Training Act, 1973*. The report 'Outlook on Training' (1980) raised a number of critical questions about (i) the relationship between the MSC and the ITBs (and the latter's dual responsibility to both their industry and the MSC); (ii) the central controls exercised by the civil service over the staff of the Industrial Training Boards; (iii) the problems of public funding created by the rigid system of Parliamentary accountability.

In addition, the new (Conservative) Government was especially concerned about excessive public (State) expenditure, and has sought economies in all sectors of State activity. Thus apart from certain reductions in the training and MSC budgets, the Government, under the *Employment and Training Act, 1981*, has: (a) abolished 16 statutory Industrial Training Boards, (b) withdrawn funds from the remaining ITBs, together with its controls over their staff appointments and conditions of service.

Thus the Government aims to restore greater responsibility to industry which will thus operate over a wider field in the way it has been operating in 40 per cent of the training field, i.e. on a voluntary training basis, with or without training boards. It is believed that this will be cheaper, more cost-effective and less bureaucratic as well as making the system more adaptable and responsive to changing needs. And many firms are happy not to pay levies for ITBs to supervise training they can adequately carry out themselves. However, the statutory basis for ITBs will continue to exist for certain key areas, and for 'speculative' training (i.e. for future uncertain skill needs). Thus the public involvement in future is to 'supplement not substitute for industry's own training efforts'.

(b) Training Opportunities Scheme (TOPS). This scheme is intended to supplement the training given by industry by providing opportunities for those who wish to train for a skill, to re-train or to up-date existing skills. The scheme also provides some preparatory courses in basic skill prior to employment or further TOPS training. Applicants must normally be 19 or over and have been away from full-time education for two years, though these requirements may be waived, especially for disabled persons who can follow ordinary TOPS training courses or have specially designed courses.

Much TOPS training is carried out at 68 **Skillcentres** (plus 20 annexes). They are State-owned and administered by Training Services Division staff. Courses usually last 6–12 months.

Training under the TOPS scheme is also given at some 700 **Colleges** of Further Education or at Polytechnics, Universities, Business Schools and on employers' premises. Four residential training colleges, run by voluntary organisations with Government financial aid, cater for severely disabled people who can be trained (e.g. St Loyes College, Exeter).

Overall there are some 500 different courses, ranging from bricklaying to management, from typing to electronics. Skillcentre courses concentrate on engineering, construction and automotive trades, while the colleges tend to specialise in clerical and commercial, management, technician and other skills. In recent years particular attention has been given to computer training and electronics engineering courses biased towards micro-electronics and microprocessor applications. TOPS trainees are paid allowances which vary according to the number of dependents and former earnings, and there may be travelling and lodgings allowances. Some 70,000 adults were trained under TOPS in 1980–81, but demand exceeds available places and applicants often have to wait for a place.

Skillcentres have been made to become more financially self-supporting by cutting back on State-funded TOPs courses and increasing fee-charging (or 'sponsored') training for businesses. This will reduce the amount of 'speculative' training, which just adds to the general stock rather than meets specific demand.

In 1981, the Government published plans for a massive **Youth Training Scheme (YTS).** It replaced YOPS and cost £1,000 million p.a. Outlined in a White Paper 'A New Training Initiative' Cmnd. 8455, HMSO, 1981) the programme aims to: (i) guarantee a full year's foundation training for all those leaving school at 16 without jobs; (ii) extend the scheme when possible to the older unemployed school-leaver (and whenever possible, to those in work); (iii) increase (grant) incentives for employers to provide more and better training for young employees; (iv) develop an 'Open Tech' programme to make technical training more accessible to those who have the necessary ability (see page 241); (v) increase opportunities for vocationally relevant courses for those staying on in full-time education.

In 1985, the two-year scheme was announced, and trainees who are not in employment receive weekly allowances (of £27.50 in the first year and £35 in the second). From 1988, the unemployed under-18s are virtually obliged to join the scheme as they will no longer be entitled to Income Support. However, the scheme does guarantee a job after training (and about 75 per cent of YTS trainees currently do find employment or go on to further training or education). There are about 435,000 currently (1989) on the scheme. At its inception the Minister described the scheme as, 'The most far-reaching proposals for industrial training ever put before Parliament'. Increasingly the YTS results in qualifications which are recognised by the National Council for Vocational Qualifications (NCVQ), set up in 1986 to reform and rationalise vocational qualifications. It covers all occupations and recognises awards on a basis of demonstrated competence.

Meanwhile, we have seen the introduction of the **Cetificate of Pre-Vocational Education (CPVE)**, a one-year, full-time education-cum-training course for those over 16. And the experimental schemes for the **Technical and Vocational Education Initiative (TVEI)** is now extended to all LEAs. (For CPVE and TVEI, see page 253).

(c) Other direct training services to industry. The Department of Employment (DE) provides a number of other services here. The **Training Within Industry** scheme is intended to develop the skills of supervisors in developing leadership, instructing and communicating, improving methods and improving safety practices. Special courses are also available for supervisors employed in offices. Courses in international trade procedures (export documentation, etc.) are available for staff employed in export/import offices. For **training instructors** courses in instructional techniques are available to skill-centre staff and industrial and commercial firms at the DE's two instructor training colleges and at three instructor training units attached to skillcentres. In-plant courses are also available. Thus as new needs arise, the DE devises courses to meet demand. Similarly with new legislation, e.g. the *Health and Safety at Work Act, 1974*, led to courses for safety officers.

Employers are able to apply for **Sponsored Training** for their employees for refresher and up-grading training at skillcentres. The courses are usually of short duration and are designed specifically by the DE to meet the needs of the employer. The costs are shared with the DE providing the training and the employer meeting the employees' wages. There is also a complementary **Mobile Instructor Service** for firms. Under this the DE provides a small team of instructors with wide industrial experience to visit firms and provide 'in-plant' (rather than 'off-the-job') training. The service is available for firms with specific projects: when the firm's particular project ceases, the service is withdrawn. The service is normally paid for (at cost).

Training for the disabled

Instead of returning to work after an absence (particularly following a long illness) it may be necessary to undergo a course of rehabilitation. This is not training as such: more an orientation or 'flexing' of mind and muscle. Thus the aim of rehabilitation is to help the disabled to adjust to and prepare for normal working conditions; it may also be used to determine the type of work or training which is most suitable.

Such provision occurs in **Employment Rehabilitation Centres (ERCs** – formerly Industrial Rehabilitation Units) of which there are 27, provided by the DE with a capacity of over 2,500 places. There is also some grant-aided provision by voluntary agencies and local authorities. Some are residential or have hostel/lodging attachments; others are within daily travelling distance. They are staffed by doctors, occupational psychologists and therapists, social workers, DROs and craft instructors and supervisors. (See *Residential Training for Disabled*, MSC.)

Courses are free and maintenance and travelling allowances are payable. Courses are mainly about 7–9 weeks long, but may vary from 2–26 weeks since individual needs are bound to vary. Some of the disabled may go on to TOPS courses at college, work or skillcentres.

EEC social fund

The purpose of the European Social Fund is to provide cash grants to help improve employment opportunities for the working population of the Common Market. Theoretically it is available to help ease problems of redundancy, migrant workers, the unemployed and the physically or mentally disabled who need rehabilitation, etc. In practice, funds are concentrated on vocational training, especially for young people (i.e. YTS). Applications (which must be submitted via the Government) must give details of the project and must be sponsored by a public authority which is prepared to help financially: the Social Fund will then (if approved) provide an equal contribution. In 1983 Britain received over £320 million in this way.

Training loans

In 1988 the Government introduced a scheme whereby people who want to improve their career prospects by taking training courses (lasting up to a year) can apply for a **Career Development Loan** of up to 80 per cent of the cost of the course (which must be vocational). The money will come from the banks, but the Government will pay the interest.

Employment training scheme

This was introduced in 1988 as 'the largest and most imaginative training programme ever seen in Britain'. Basically it amalgamated two existing schemes, – the Job Training Scheme (launched in 1987) and the Community Programme. It thus applies only to adults (since YTS effectively covers those up to 18). Up to 600,000 trainees a year are anticipated. Trainees will receive their social security benefits plus an allowance (of £10 p.w.). Employers are expected to play a prominent part in the scheme, (through Local Employer Networks or LENs) including taking on (with others such as voluntary organisations) the role of acting as **training agent** (to assess and provide guidance) and **training manager** (to provide or arrange the actual training, which should lead to a vocational qualification). (Agents and managers receive fees for this.) Each trainee is entitled to spend at least 40 per cent of their programme on directed training (including practical training with the employer). The programme is designed to give long-term unemployed people the skills and confidence to take up the vacancies which are emerging. The Minister (Norman Fowler) explained the purpose as 'training the workers without jobs to do the jobs without workers'.

Part of the motivation is the growing shortage of young recruits to the workforce and the fact that half of the long-term unemployed are under 35; re-training is important to British industry, especially if we are to meet European competition after 1992 (see page 345). (It is estimated that British industry devotes only 0.15 per cent of total wage costs to training, in other countries, it is ten or even twenty times that much.) The same reasoning underlies the Government's White Paper of December 1988 *Employment for the 1990s*, with growing concern that skill shortages are limiting output (reported in up to one-third of businesses). The proposal are that:

1   Employers will take over a greater share of the responsibility and cost of training.
2   Training both for the employed and (under the Employment Training Scheme, as above) for the unemployed will be decentralised to local **Training and Enterprise Councils** (TECs), which will be employer-dominated; these councils will analyse local labour market conditions and training requirements, and promote and direct private and public sector investment in training, vocational education and enterprise activities designed to strengthen the local skill base; they will sub-contract these activities to local providers (in the same way as the Department of Employment's (DE) Training Agency now contracts with training managers and agents; see above).

3   A National Training Task Force of 12 members (eight from business) will assist the DE in establishing the TECs.
4   At national level, the main authority concerned with training promotion will be the Training Agency of the DE. (There is also a Skills Training Agency but this may be hived off or dissolved, just as the Wages Councils (see page 465) may be.)
5   The seven Industrial Training Boards (see page 348) are to lose their statutory basis and become fully supported by employers in their own sectors.
6   YTS is to continue, but more emphasis is to be placed on qualifications, and employers are expected to assume a fuller share of the costs.
7   In 1989, the Training Agency is to launch a £1.4 billion programme **Business Growth through Training** which will provide support and coordination of services to small firms, the self-employed and training organisations.
8   TVEI is to continue its extended application (see page 253) and the programme of work-related Further Education will continue to respond rapidly to the changing needs of employers.

For those who are working, training is also encouraged through local **Training Access Points (TAPs)** and the up-dating courses organised by the DES through the **Professional, Industrial and Commercial Updating Programme (PICKUP)** which coordinates refresher courses in universities, polytechnics and colleges. The target is 2 million (or one in ten) over the four years to 1992.

Employment services: problems and criticisms

1   The Employment (and Careers) Services suffer from a rather poor public **image**, despite the changes introduced under the 1973 legislation. Jobcentres and careers offices still tend to be seen as places of 'last resort' for those who cannot find employment on their own initiative, and many of Britain's 55,000 employers still prefer to find their staff privately.

2   **Private** employment agencies still flourish. Despite control (under the *Employment Agencies Act, 1973* – see page 346) there is evidence of some malpractices, e.g. enticement by inducing personnel to change their jobs frequently so as to increase the agencies' job turnover and thus their profits.

3   We have mentioned some of the problems surrounding the employment of young people (see page 341) including the overlapping administration and the often amateur of part-time approach to

careers and life skills education. But the **careers service** is trying to operate in a background of heavy youth unemployment about which there is little it can do.

4 The disabled, the aged and immigrants tend to suffer disproportionately in times of unemployment. Their unemployment rate is double or more that of the general working population. For the **disabled** the quota system's effectiveness has been called in question (the proportion of employers not meeting their quota rose from 38 per cent in 1960 to 61 per cent in 1976). But there are problems in the voluntary nature of registration: many are not on the register (the current figure is 130,000) and so in many areas there are insufficient disabled people to fill vacancies. In July, 1981, the MSC recommended the abandonment of the quota scheme as unworkable and replacing it with a statutory duty requiring employers to take reasonable steps to promote equality of employment opportunity for disabled people. In addition there should be more enlightenment and voluntary cooperation by employers.

For the **aged**, it seems all too obvious to require or encourage them to retire early in order to make way for other, younger workers. If the terms are right, many no doubt welcome the chance to cease the working life. But for many others retirement is worse than unemployment in its psychological impact. Post-war Government policies here seem to vary according to the state of the manpower market: in the 1950s it considered raising the retirement age; up to 1988 it effectively reduced it, under the Job Release Scheme (see page 332).

The high level of unemployment among ethnic minorities is due to prejudice by workers, trade unions and employers. However, another cause of the problem is that many work in occupations which are disappearing, such as manual work.

5 Women do not have the same training and employment opportunities as men, despite legal requirements (see page 338). The 1978 Report of the Equal Opportunities Commission showed that **women** on average still earn less than two thirds of the weekly wage rate of men (but see page 174). Part of the problem arises from the fact that the *Equal Pay Act, 1970*, only applies to the relatively small number of women who could compare their jobs with those of men employed by the same employer.

6 There is the problem of **confusion** which is due to the plethora of employment, training and education schemes of recent years. The host of changing programmes, schemes, courses, initials and acronyms bewilder many members of the working and non-working population, employers, education and training instructors, and even staff of employment offices who are giving advice and guidance.

7   Then there is the problem of **liaison**. Many of the training and employment programmes fall under the general control of the Department of Employment, and the Further Education colleges under the local control of Local Education Authorities and the general control of the Department of Education and Science. It has been argued that there should be closer integration between the Department of Employment and the colleges, freer use of information, techniques and existing buildings, and accommodations and equipment could be more efficiently used. Departmentalism at central and local government level and within colleges or Departments themselves is both costly and imprudent. Training is often looked at too narrowly. For example, should Skillcentres be responsible for placement (finding jobs) as well as training? Should the wide range of job subsidies paid to employers be overhauled and integrated with company taxation and National Insurance to give a simpler and more direct encouragement to firms to take on labour?

8   There have been criticisms of **waste and inefficiency**. In November, 1976, the Department of Employment and the MSC were criticised by the Federation of Personnel Services for wasting money: it was claimed that State spending was ten times that of private employment agencies on helping the unemployed but was filling fewer job vacancies. It also claimed that Jobcentres were overstaffed and over costly to run (though the cost of placing a person has fallen from £79 to £70 and the number of people found work per Jobcentre employee has increased from 150 to 250, 1980–84).

A Comptroller and Auditor General's Report (1977) found 27 per cent of those taking part in Government training schemes were dropping out before completing the course (which, at least, raised questions of the MSC's selection methods). His Report in 1978 drew attention to muddles and irregularities in job-creation projects sponsored by voluntary bodies. Youthaid (1978) criticised the appointment of civil servants with inadequate knowledge to staff area programme teams.

In 1977 a study for the Policy Studies Institute showed that 30 per cent of those leaving Skillcentres were failing to obtain jobs in their new trade and another 30 per cent only remained in their trade for a short time. Further, the chances of these trainees finding work within three months, using their new skills, has declined from 68 per cent to 25 per cent, 1978–82. In 1980 a Parliamentary Committee criticised the operations of the MSC; it urged that it spend more to help the long-term unemployed instead of the provision of Jobcentres on expensive sites (though it did praise the MSC's YOPS programme).

The various criticisms have led to a review of MSC procedures. Coupled with cuts in State spending, it has also led to cuts in some employment and training programmes (estimated in 1981 to cost

£4,000 m. overall, half borne by the State) to reduce wasteful expenditure and to produce a 'slimmer and fitter service more closely geared to the areas where they could make the most effective contribution'.

9 There has been a great deal of employment **legislation** in recent years, including the following Acts: *Redundancy Payments, 1965–68; Equal Pay, 1970; Health and Safety at Work, 1974; Employment Protection, 1975; Sex Discrimination, 1975; Race Relations, 1976.* Much of this has been passed in the interests of the working population, but it creates problems for employers – so much so that some employers (especially small) have become reluctant to take on staff. And more generally, health and safety and anti-pollution measures are costly and time-consuming to implement and raise production costs. Some ask whether we pay too highly for the benefits of this legislation in higher prices, fewer sales (at home and abroad) and greater redundancies, though recent legislation (e.g. the *Employment Act, 1989*) and other deregulation (e.g. the Government's 'Lifting the Burden' policy) has reversed this considerably.

10 Ultimately the state of the nation's employment and the extent of unemployment depend on the condition of the **nation's economy**. A depressed economy which leads to mass unemployment can be only marginally affected by the employment services, and these can be as good as we can afford. Consequently, the various schemes outlined above have been described as palliatives, tinkering and a means of massaging the statistics for political ends.

Is Britain condemned to a future of heavy unemployment as a result of (a) depressed world trade, (b) our inability to compete, (c) new technology displacing labour, (d) Government policies (e.g. high interest and foreign exchange rates) which add to the economy's depression? Or is it possible to do something to fundamentally improve the situation now rather than wait for an upturn in the economy?

The Government argues that Britain's problem in the past has been partly **over-employment**: that employers and trade unions have caused production to be inefficient through overmanning. And that the present situation, at least in part, is part of a deliberate policy to 'shake out' excess labour, to produce a slimmer and fitter productive system. (And yet, paradoxically, it seems that in various subsidised ways employers are being pressed or induced to take on unemployed workers they perhaps do not really want or need). However, notwithstanding the money supply and PSBR, there seems some considerable scope for a Keynesian approach: for increased public expenditure through investment projects which would benefit society, the economy and employment, e.g. the environment, inner cities, housing, public health, roads, sewerage.

In the meantime, pending improved economic growth and the expansion of aggregate employment opportunities, *job-sharing* needs to be pursued more fully. In a sense it exists already in that 3 million have no work while 22 million have plenty. We are paying some £12,000 million a year for that unemployment. Might it be better instead of paying taxes to finance unemployment benefits (at £5,000 p.a. for each unemployed person) to reduce the average working week or year? Or to subsidise employers to create jobs? Or provide older workers with decent early retirement incomes and part-time pre-retirement work? The Government's job-splitting scheme, which offered (1983–84) employers £750 towards the costs of dividing a full-time job into several part-time jobs was modest start in this direction.

With our economy so depressed, it seems harsh for the Minister (Norman Tebbit) to tell the unemployed to 'get on yer bike' – to search for work. It is reminiscent of the 1834 Poor Law Commission (see page 7). And yet there *are* job vacancies and employers complain of shortages of skilled manpower (e.g. in microtechnology and robotics) and even unskilled (e.g. an estimated 50,000 in London alone). Hence the importance of appropriate training. Thus, in a White Paper *Training for Jobs*, February 1984, it is proposed to transfer a quarter of the £800 m. spent each year by LEAs on work-related Further Education to the DE, where it is felt 'training will be more closely directed towards the skills needed by employers'. As a result, the number of adults trained under MSC courses would be doubled to over 250,000 a year. The new Employment Training programme will provide a massive boost and be supported by others (such as PICKUP; see page 210).

In regard to the young unemployed, the Thompson Report (see page 210) said, 'The point we make here is that the largest growing group of long-term unemployed is in the 18–25 age-group, and relatively little is being done for them. The possibility of being unemployed, or the actual experience of unemployment is without doubt the chief worry of the majority of young people today. Throughout his or her conscious life, work will have been held up as the essential badge of adulthood. It stands for the end of dependence and the beginnings of real responsibility and freedom. It brings with it financial means, status, and the chance to choose within a range of opportunities. It also combines in itself many of the kinds of experience which are requisite for personal development. Its absence is the more keenly felt; and it is meaningless to say to the youngster who has no employment that the "work ethic" is over-valued in our society.'

At the time, there were suggestions about introducing military service for the young or cutting their wage rates to price them back into work. But times have changed and young employees are becoming short in supply, with almost 1 million fewer 16–19-year-olds in 2025 (see Appendix 3, page 472) than there are today (because of past birth rates). Their bargaining power may improve and they can be more selective about the job they do.

Being able to *choose* one's job is important for everyone, for there are jobs and jobs: some are more satisfying than others. Having a job may not be everything, so that the figures for successful Jobcentre placements may not tell the full story. There is evidence to suggest that *over one third* of the working population are seriously dissatisfied with their jobs. The unemployed may be just the tip of an iceberg, just as those in absolute poverty are among the deprived.

Questions

1   Describe the special provisions available for the disabled to obtain employment.
2   Describe the structure and functions of the Manpower Services Commission.
3   What are (a) Employment Rehabilitation Centres and (b) sheltered workshops?
4   Explain and comment on the provisions of the *Employment Acts, 1980, 1982*.
5   One of the most crucial problems today is the large number of school-leavers without jobs. What action has the Government taken here?
6   'To pay young people on leaving school to do nothing is plain stupid. There is much work to be done, and youths should do community work of some kind before they become entitled to payment.' What are the problems involved in adopting this policy?
7   'Today people must learn to change jobs three or four times in their lives, and they must be mobile.' How far has the Government recognised this and what provisions exist for change and mobility in employment?
8   *A* has been sent to prison for one year. What services will be available for him on release to obtain a job?
9   What are the main provisions of the *Health and Safety at Work, etc., Act, 1974*? Who enforces the Act and how is this task performed?
10   Find out the size and structure of unemployment in your locality. How does it compare with the national pattern?

13
The treatment of offenders

Criminal courts today

The courts in which criminal cases are tried are:

(i)   The House of Lords
(ii) The Court of Appeal (Criminal Division)
(iii) Crown Courts
(iv) Magistrates' Courts

The composition and jurisdiction of these various courts are now examined in outline.

The House of Lords

This court hears appeals from the Court of Appeal (Criminal Division). It is the highest appeal court in the entire legal system and its importance need hardly be stressed. Either the prosecutor or the defendant may appeal, but an important requirement is that leave of the Court of Appeal (Criminal Division) or the House of Lords must be obtained on the grounds that the case involves **a point of law of general public importance**. This requirement prevents any frivolous or minor cases going to the final court.

Composition. The court is composed of the Lord Chancellor, the Lords of Appeal in Ordinary (11) and other peers who have held 'high judicial office'. The quorum is three, and each judge delivers a separate judgement, the verdict being by a majority.

Court of Appeal (Criminal Division)

The *Criminal Appeal Act, 1966*, provides that the Court of Appeal shall consist of two divisions: one exercising civil jurisdiction and one criminal.

Composition. The court is composed of the Lord Chief Justice and the Lord Justices of Appeal. The Lord Chief Justice, or, in his absence, the Master of the Rolls, may require any judge of the Queen's Bench Division (one of the three divisions of the High Court) to sit. A quorum of three is necessary, and only one judgement is delivered except where the presiding judge permits separate verdicts to be pronounced on a question of law.

Jurisdiction. The court hears appeals from Crown Courts (described below). It may dismiss or allow the appeal and may order that any conviction recorded in a lower court shall be quashed. The court may order a new trial, but it may not on hearing an appeal increase the sentence against which the appeal is being made. For example, let us suppose that a person has been sentenced to five years' imprisonment in a Crown Court and wishes to appeal to the Court of Appeal (Criminal Division). After hearing the appeal the court may think that the appellant should be sentenced to 10 years' imprisonment. But it will not be able to increase the original sentence. Formerly the Court of Appeal (Criminal Division) had this power, but it was found in practice that convicted persons were less likely to appeal (however justified they might feel their case to be) if they ran the risk of an increase in the sentence. The number of appeals in recent years has increased as a result.

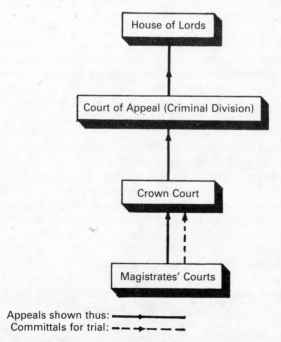

Figure 15 *Structure of the criminal courts*

Crown Courts

These courts are the successors of the former Courts of Assize and
Courts of Quarter Sessions which had existed for many centuries.
The *Courts Act, 1971*, abolished Assizes and Quarter Sessions and
established Crown Courts. In general terms, the Crown Court has
taken over all *first instance* business (i.e. where someone is tried the
first time for an alleged offence) and all appeal business formerly
exercised by the Court of Quarter Sessions. So, the Crown Court has
therefore both original jurisdiction (i.e. first instance jurisdiction)
and appellate jurisdiction in respect of appeals from persons convicted at Magistrates' Courts.

Jurisdiction. The Crown Court is responsible for trials on indictment.
(An indictment is merely a document which sets out the crime(s) with
which a person is charged. Any offence punishable with three
months' imprisonment or more is 'indictable', i.e. the accused may
claim trial in a Crown Court). The Court also sentences offenders
committed for sentence by Magistrates' Courts, e.g. where the
Magistrates' Court finds the accused guilty but has insufficient powers
adequately to deal with the defendant. Finally the Crown Court acts
as an appeal court to hear appeals from Magistrates' Courts.
    The court is served by the following judges:

1   **A High Court Judge**, a puisne judge of the QBD. He is similar to
    that of his predecessor sitting as an Assize Court Judge, who was
    also a judge of the QBD. The judge is appointed to one of six
    circuits.
2   **A Circuit Judge** appointed by the Crown to serve in (1) a Crown
    Court and (2) a County Court (Civil). He must be a barrister of 10
    years' standing or a person who has held the office of a recorder
    for three years. He retires at 72, but may be allowed to extend his
    period of office till 75 years.
3   **A Recorder**, who is a part-time judge of the Crown Court. He is
    appointed for a fixed term. Appointments are made from persons
    of high professional standing who are prepared to commit them-
    selves to not less than one month's work on the bench each year.
    The new style recorders operating part-time will enable the Lord
    Chancellor to assess their suitability for appointment to Circuit
    judgeships or to the High Court Bench.

    At the Lord Chancellor's request a Court of Appeal judge can sit in
a Crown Court. All trials in the Crown Court take place before a
jury.
    The Crown Court has about 90 centres, each chosen as far as
practicable to be within travelling distance of the whole population.

There are six circuits:

1 South-eastern (with London as its administrative centre)
2 Midland and Oxford (Birmingham)
3 North-eastern (Leeds)
4 Wales and Chester (Cardiff)
5 Western (Bristol)
6 Northern (Manchester)

On each of these circuits the town where the judges sit are classified in three types:

1st tier centres, where High Court judges and Circuit judges deal with criminal cases, and High Court judges also take civil business.

2nd tier centres, dealing only with criminal business, but served by both High Court and Circuit Judges.

3rd tier centres, served only by Circuit Judges and Recorders who deal only with criminal cases.

How business is distributed. The distribution of business in the Crown Court is determined by directions from the Lord Chief Justice, with the agreement of the Lord Chancellor. The general rule is that the higher the status of the judge the more serious will be the cases he tries.

A High Court judge will always try the offences of murder and treason. Offences normally tried by a High Court judge include manslaughter and rape. The vast majority of indictable offences can be tried by any judge of the Crown Court, Circuit Judge or Recorder. Offences such as wounding and theft may be tried either on indictment or summarily, but in the more serious cases, are almost always tried before a Circuit Judge or Recorder.

Lay magistrates have a role to play in the Crown Court. A Circuit Judge or Recorder sits with between two and four magistrates for appeals and committals for sentence from Magistrates' Courts, and *may* sit with magistrates to try the less important cases on indictment. For the more serious cases a High Court judge sits alone.

In the City of London, where the Crown Court is known as the Central Criminal Court, or more commonly the Old Bailey, the Lord Mayor and aldermen can sit with any judge in any type of case.

Magistrates' Courts

The first justices were appointed in 1327 as 'conservators of the peace'. For more than six hundred years their successors, now known as Justices of the Peace, or magistrates, have performed the duties of enforcing the common law and statute law and of preserving locally the public peace and good order.

During the past fifty years Parliament has burdened Magistrates' Courts with enforcing increasing amounts of legislation, much of it highly complex. Magistrates' Courts (or Courts of Petty Sessions as they are sometimes called) today exercise wider jurisdiction and deal with more cases than any other court in the English legal system. Over 98 per cent of all criminal prosecutions in England and Wales are dealt with by magistrates. They also deal with a wide variety of civil cases (e.g. undefended divorce) and perform administrative duties, particularly licensing matters, such as the licensing of hotels, etc., for the sale of intoxicating liquor.

There are two kinds of Justices of the Peace: (i) County Justices and (ii) Stipendiary Magistrates.

(i)   **County Justices** are appointed by the Lord Chancellor on the recommendation of the Lord Lieutenant of the county assisted by an advisory committee. The justices have jurisdiction throughout the county. The important features of these magistrates are that they are unpaid (though they may receive out-of-pocket expenses when adjudicating) and they are laymen. They number 22,000 in England and Wales. Because of the importance of the work falling to magistrates, it is now ordained that all magistrates appointed after January 1, 1966, must undergo basic training in the duties of their office. They must understand the meaning of 'acting judicially', elementary legal procedure and sentencing policy, so as to preserve the highest standards of efficient judicial administration.

(ii)   **Stipendiary Magistrates** are full-time paid magistrates. They are appointed by the Lord Chancellor and must be barristers or solicitors of at least seven years' standing. Stipendiary Magistrates can do alone any act which requires two or more lay Justices sitting in petty sessions. There are some 39 Stipendiary Magistrates appointed for the Metropolitan Area, which includes the City of London and the County of London, the latter being divided into court areas. These magistrates are known as Metroplitan Magistrates. Outside London certain important cities (11 in all) appoint their own Stipendiary Magistrate.

The Clerk to the Justices is the official attached to each Magistrates' Court who advises the Justices on points of law and procedure, makes a record of evidence and prepares depositions (i.e. statements sworn on oath in the presence of an accused person) made by witnesses in those cases sent forward for trial at a Crown Court. He also performs the administrative work of the court such as preparing informations, summonses and warrants granted by the magistrates, and collecting fines which have been imposed.

The *Justices of the Peace Act, 1949*, provides that a clerk must be a barrister or solicitor of at least five years' standing. The Act also provides for the setting up in the counties of committees to supervise the administrative work of the Magistrates' Courts.

A clerk to the Justices must not retire with the Justices to consider their verdict. Such matters must be for justices alone.

Jurisdiction of Magistrates' Courts. The jurisdiction of these courts falls under three main headings: (a) as a court of trial; (b) as a court of preliminary investigation; and (c) miscellaneous.

(a) **Court of trial.** The jurisdiction is exercised by from two to seven Justices, and the maximum punishment that they may impose for any one offence is six months' imprisonment or a fine of £2,000 (£10,000 in special cases). A single Justice in petty sessions may try trivial cases such as simple drunkenness. Criminal offences can be divided into three classes:

(i) Indictable offences, i.e. those triable on indictment at a Crown Court. All offences punishable with three months' imprisonment or more are indictable. The magistrates must ask any person accused of such an offence whether he wishes to be tried on indictment or to be tried summarily (see below). An indictment is simply the document used in jury trials which names the offence(s) with which an accused person is charged.

(ii) Offences triable summarily, i.e. there and then in a Magistrates' Court. Offences which can only be tried summarily include riding a pedal cycle at night without lights, begging in a public place and being found drunk and incapable on the highway.

(iii) Indictable offences triable summarily in the Magistrates' Court if the accused so elects. Let us take by way of example a case where the accused is alleged to have stolen a penknife. Since theft is an indictable offence (it is punishable by seven years' imprisonment) the accused may claim trial by jury. Accordingly, the magistrates before whom he appears for the first time will offer him the choice of either trial at a Crown Court (i.e. on indictment) or trial by the magistrates. If he chooses to be tried at a Crown Court, the magistrates will sit as a court of preliminary investigation (see below).

The agenda of a typical Magistrates' Court reveals a wide variety of offences: petty theft, wilful damage, common assault, drunkenness, driving a motorcar without a driving licence, driving without insurance, failing to obey traffic signs, parking offences, driving without due care and attention, and similar road traffic offences. Some offenders will be dealt with then and there (even though they qualify for trial by a Crown Court), while defendants who elect for trial by jury will be committed for trial if the proescution makes out a *prima facie* case in respect of each. (A *prima facie* case is one which appears 'at first sight' or 'from first impression' to be an offence.)

(b) **Court of Preliminary Investigation.** In this capacity the Magistrates' Court is called upon to determine whether an accused person, who is brought before it by means of a summons or by arrest, shall be committed to stand trial at a Crown Court. If the offence is serious – for example, murder or manslaughter – the accused has no option; if it is a case such as theft, the accused may elect for trial by jury when the Clerk to the Justices reads out the charge. The prosecution calls its witnesses and produces exhibits (gun, knife or other articles). The evidence of the prosecution witnesses is taken down in writing in the presence of the accused, and the document (called a deposition) is signed by the witness (called a deponent) and by the Justice present at the hearing. After all the evidence for the prosecution is heard, the accused is charged with the alleged offence. He may plead 'guilty' or 'not guilty'; he may give evidence himself and call witnesses in his support, or he may reserve his defence until the actual trial. Usually an accused reserves his defence.

After hearing the evidence the magistrates decide whether the prosecution has made out a *prima facie* case. If it has, the accused and the witnesses who have given evidence are bound over to attend the trial at a Crown Court. These proceedings are known as **committal proceedings**, and although they may be taken before one Justice, in practice two or more lay magistrates usually preside over this important step in the judicial process.

If the prosecution has not made out a *prima facie* case against the accused, the magistrates must release him. When an accused is committed for trial he may be either **remanded in custody** (i.e. to a prison to await trial) or **remanded on bail** (i.e. liberated from the Magistrates' Court on condition that he turns up at the trial at a Crown Court at a later date when his case will be heard).

The *Criminal Justice Act, 1967*, provides that in certain circumstances an accused person may be committed for trial on *written* evidence alone instead of oral evidence taken down in the form of depositions. This Act also restricts the publication of reports of committal proceedings to purely formal matters, i.e. the identity of the court and magistrates, the names of the parties and the nature of the charges. The object is to avoid prejudicing the accused by pre-trial publicity.

(c) **Miscellaneous jurisdiction.** In addition to the foregoing duties, the magistrates perform administrative functions in regard to liquor licensing (approving applicants and premises), betting houses, theatre and cinematograph licensing, and have a limited jurisdiction in regard to civil debts (e.g. unpaid income tax where the amount is under £30). Other important duties include: (i) making matrimonial orders for separation and maintenance of spouses; (ii) affiliation orders; (iii) consent to marriage (for example, where a young girl of 17 wishes to marry but her parents oppose her proposed marriage); (iv) guardianship of infants; (v) adoption of children; (vi) orders under the *Mental Health Act, 1959*; and (vii) orders in regard to children and young persons in need of care, protection or control.

Juvenile Courts. Certain magistrates attached to a petty-sessional division form a special panel to deal with offences committed by children (i.e. persons under 14) and young persons (i.e. over 14 and under 17). The Juvenile Court is formed by three lay Justices, one of whom must be a woman. All such Justices retire at 65 years of age. A Stipendiary Magistrate may sit in this court. The Juvenile Court sits separately from the adult court. If it cannot sit in a different room it must sit on a different day. Proceedings in Juvenile Courts are shielded from publicity. The press must not disclose the identity of the child or young person unless the court, in exceptional cases, permits. Where a child or young person is charged jointly with an adult the case is dealt with in an adult court, i.e. the usual Magistrates' Court.

Appeals from Magistrates' Courts are organised as follows: (a) Where the defendant wishes to appeal against (i) conviction and/or (ii) sentence, appeal lies to the Crown Court. (b) Where the defendant (or prosecution) wishes to appeal against conviction or sentence on a point of law, a special form of appeal lies to the Divisional Court of Queen's Bench by way of 'case stated'. (c) Appeals concerning separation and maintenance orders, affiliation orders, adoption and consent to marry lie to the Family Division of the High Court.

National Prosecution Service. In 1986 independent State prosecutors (like those in Scotland) took over the conduct of all prosecutions from the police. The service is headed by the Director of Public Prosecutions, under the supervision of the Attorney General.

Central Criminal Court

This famous court, known as the Old Bailey, was set up in 1834. It exercises the criminal jurisdiction of a Crown Court and hears cases on indictment committed from the City of London and the Greater London area. In addition, the Central Criminal Court may try any crime committed at sea. Proceedings may be removed into the Central Criminal Court from a provincial court if there is a risk that strong local feelings might otherwise prejudice the accused's case. The Court is very busy – mainly because crime has increased in recent years – and is in almost continuous session. Officially it is held at least 12 times a year.

Composition. The judges of the court are the Lord Chancellor; the judges of the Queen's Bench Division; the Lord Mayor, aldermen, Recorder and Common Serjeant of the City of London; and the judges of the City of London Court. In practice, the judges are those of the Queen's Bench Division and judges appointed by commission.

The nature of a crime

Definition of crime

Two definitions serve to bring the concept of crime into focus. These are:

> A crime is an unlawful act or default which is an offence against the public and renders the person guilty of the act liable to legal punishment. (Halsbury, *Laws of England*)

> Crimes are wrongs whose sanction is punitive, and is remissible by the Crown, if at all. (Professor Kenny)

The main distinction between a **civil wrong**, such as a tort and a **crime** lies in the object of the proceedings. Whereas the object of proceedings in a crime is punishable, that of proceedings in tort is damages – or money equivalent to the wrong done to the plaintiff.

The next distinction is that crimes are offences against the State. Accordingly proceedings against a culprit are taken in the name of the Crown. Hence cases in the Crown Courts are cited: *R.* v. *Jones* or *R.* v. *Smith*. (*R = Regina*, Latin 'Queen', or *Rex*, Latin 'King'). In tort or similar wrongs the action is cited as *Brown* v. *Smith*, where Brown is the plaintiff and Smith is the defendant. These two persons are the only ones concerned. The State or the public are not concerned whether proceedings are started or not or whether Brown or Smith gets the verdict. In summary criminal proceedings in Magistrates' Courts the prosecution is usually brought in the name of an Inspector (or other officer) of the Police who acts as representative of the State and may prosecute an alleged offender. Sometimes the solicitors attached to the local authority undertake the prosecution for the police, and sometimes in the event of serious offences the prosecution may be taken by the Director of Public Prosecutions on behalf of the police. He acts on behalf of the Crown since we have said that the Crown is the 'injured' party (the offence is against the Crown which represents the State or the public).

Classification of crimes

(a) **Crimes and offences.** Strictly all crimes are offences against the law. Therefore all crimes are offences. Riding a pedal cycle at night without a light is a criminal offence, or a crime, yet we do not look upon this as such. In general, we use the word 'crime' to denote those offences against the law of a serious kind, usually triable before a judge and jury in a Crown Court, such as: murder, manslaughter, burglary, theft, rape, bigamy, arson, perjury. The word 'offence' is commonly applied to those less serious offences ordinarily triable before a Magistrates' Court, e.g. parking offences, driving a motor-car without a current driving licence or insurance certificate and similar acts.

(b) **Indictable and summary offences.** On page 362 we noted that certain crimes are triable on indictment before a judge and jury (e.g. in a Crown Court), and that certain other offences, known as summary offences, are triable in a Magistrates' Court by the Justices who sit without a jury.

This again is a broad division only. Some crimes are indictable (i.e. triable before a judge and jury in a Crown Court), but they may, with the accused's consent, be tried by a Magistrates' Court. For example, simple theft and driving a motorcar without due care and attention on a highway may be tried by (a) a Crown Court on indictment or (b) a Magistrates' Court, depending on the election of the accused. An accused person liable to three months' imprisonment or more, if convicted, may claim trial before a jury as of right, i.e. by a Crown Court. All such offences are indictable.

(c) **Arrestable offences.** The *Criminal Law Act, 1967*, fundamentally altered the classification of crimes. Before that Act the classification was: (i) treason, (ii) felonies and (iii) misdemeanours.

Treason is the most serious crime against the State, still punishable by death. It is in a separate category of its own. Felonies were those serious crimes declared by law to be felonies, e.g. murder, rape, theft, burglary and so on. Misdemeanours were all other crimes. This classification was unsatisfactory because some misdemeanours, which were considered as less serious, were in fact much more harmful than some felonies. The distinction is now of historic interest and need not detain us.

Arrestable offence now means:

(i) An offence for which the sentence is fixed by law (i.e. the judge has no discretion as to penalty on a finding of guilt).
(ii) An offence for which a person may be sentenced to five years' imprisonment on *first* conviction.

There are few offences under (i). Murder was formerly punishable only by death; the judge had no discretion. The death penalty for murder has now been abolished. The following are the main arrestable offences under (ii):

Assault causing bodily harm
Assault with intent to rob
Indecent assault on girl under 13
Armed assault
Burglary
Conspiracy to murder
Causing death by dangerous or reckless driving
Drug offences
Using explosives with intent to cause grievous bodily harm, or causing injury by using explosives
Obtaining money or property by deceit
Possessing firearms while committing another offence

Possessing firearms with intent to endanger life
Using firearms to resist arrest
Assisting prisoners to escape
Manslaughter
Murder
Piracy
Rape
Theft
Treason
Wounding causing bodily harm
Wounding with intent to murder or maim

All these are examples of offences which are punishable with imprisonment for five years or more. Some, such as murder, manslaughter, piracy and rape, are punishable with life imprisonment.

Other offences (non-arrestable offences). There are offences for which there is no power of arrest either by a police officer or a private citizen. A police officer has a much wider power of arrest than that of a citizen. An example of 'other offence' is riding a pedal cycle without a red rear-light during the night time. No power of arrest exists here. The defendant, if detected, may be stopped and reported for summons before a Magistrates' Court where the offender is then dealt with. There are many offences of this kind and they are too numerous to catalogue.

The essentials of a crime

The maxim of the Common Law is *Actus non fecit reum nisi mens sit rea* (the act does not make a person guilty unless the mind is guilty). In other words, the mere doing of an act will not constitute guilt unless there is a guilty mind. So there are two aspects to be considered: (a) a guilty act (*actus reus*) and (b) guilty intent (*mens rea*).

(a)   **Guilty conduct.** This may consist in a criminal act or an omission or default. Shooting, wounding, breaking into premises, stealing goods, forging £5 notes are common examples of guilty action. As to default or omission to act, the general rule is that a person is not liable to the criminal law for the harmful results of his omission of default, unless he is under a legal obligation to take action in the circumstances in which he is placed, as where a parent leaves a baby to starve to death.

(b) **Guilty intent.** The mental attitude which at Common Law is an essential element of every crime is often summarised by the expression *mens rea*. This phrase does not, however, denote any single mental condition, for the mental factor may assume various forms varying from a specific intent to commit an illegal act to mere negligence in certain crimes. Thus the mental element in murder is 'malice aforethought', i.e. some evil intent to do harm to another without just cause or excuse. Where however, a £5 note is forged the required element is described as 'intent to defraud' or 'intent to deceive' (*Forgery Act, 1913*). Some statutes prescribe that a particular offence must be done 'knowingly', 'wilfully' or 'maliciously'. The prosecution must prove in these kinds of cases that the defendant had the particular intent laid down in the statute to secure a conviction.

There are certain statutory exceptions to the above rule where no intent or element of *mens rea* need be proved. These offences are known as absolute offences, i.e. not requiring *mens rea*. They are rare and the only reason they are included or retained is that it would be impracticable otherwise to enforce the law. The general rule is that *mens rea* must be proved.

Other aspects of intent. Relevant here are two important common law principles that every man is presumed (i) to intend the natural consequences of his acts, and (ii) to be innocent until the contrary is proved.

As to (i) this means, for example, that if A throws a brick into B's shop window the law presumes that A intended to break the window (that is the natural consequence of so doing), and if X shoots at Y with a gun the law presumes that X intended to kill or at least injure or maim Y.

As to (ii), this is one of the cardinal principles of English law. It is the duty of the prosecution to prove the guilt of the accused person. That duty rests on the prosecution throughout the trial. If at the end of the trial the jury are in reasonable doubt the accused is entitled to be acquitted. Thus the general rule, therefore, is that the prosecution must prove the guilt of the accused **beyond reasonable doubt.** Qualifying this is the rule or principle that in determining whether a person has committed an offence, a court or jury shall (a) not be bound in law to infer that he intended or foresaw a result of his action by reason only of its being a natural or probable consequence of that action, but (b) shall decide whether he did intend or foresee that result by reference to all the evidence, drawing such inferences from the evidence as appear proper in the circumstances (*Criminal Justice Act, 1967*, s. 8).

All this information as to the courts, judges and magistracy, jurisdiction exercised, the description of the various kinds of crime, and what we mean by the technical expressions found in common use by those who have the task of deciding what sentence to impose, will help us to grasp more surely what follows. What we have in this country is a legal system which is one of the most respected in the world, a judiciary which is independent of the State, lawyers who also enjoy independence of the State and a body of law which seeks to protect the right of the individual to ensure that he has a fair trial. We have a system of appeal courts which can be used by those who consider themselves to be wrongly convicted or too severely treated by the judge or magistrates who have sentenced him. The treatment of offenders starts from the moment the offender is detected and either summoned before the courts or arrested and brought to a police station and charged with an offence.

It is of the utmost importance that the accused person be fairly treated by the police at the outset. The police are subject to rules and regulations which ensure that any confession or statement which an accused person makes shall be made voluntarily, i.e. freely and without constraint or by fear of force or hope of advantage. Moreover, where the police arrest a person and charge him, the police must allow him bail, or if they do not do so must bring him before a magistrate within 24 hours of the arrest. This means bringing him before a Magistrates' Court where the JP (there may be two or more) may grant bail or remand the accused person into custody, e.g. where the police have not completed their inquiries into the offence. These procedural matters are mentioned here only to put the main facts before the beginner in the social services so that he will more clearly appreciate the fact that the machinery which operates in this country is as fair as it is possible to make it and that the prosecution does not receive undue advantage over the accused once the trial begins and is carried through. *The Police and Criminal Evidence Act, 1984*, introduced important changes here (e.g. by extending the 24 hour limit to 96).

Measuring crime

The main source of information of the extent and nature of crime is the annual publication of the Home Office's Criminal Statistics. However, these figures can be very misleading since, firstly, an unknown number of crimes go unreported. Secondly, there may be no distinction between serious and less serious crimes (e.g. theft of 50 pence). Thirdly, one must be aware of legal and other developments, e.g. the spread of telephones may lead to more crime reporting; so does the new law allowing anonymity in rape cases. The apparent massive rise in crime may be overstated.

Punishment and other orders of a Criminal Court

The Purpose of Punishment is fivefold:
  (i) **Retribution.** This means paying the culprit back, demonstrating that crime does not pay, and that the Rule of Law must be upheld.
 (ii) **Prevention.** The public must be protected. Imprisonment or detention prevents the offender from committing more crimes.
(iii) **Reform.** Imprisonment, probation, fine or other treatment seeks to reform the culprit, to make him 'go straight'.
 (iv) **Deterrence.** The punishment should deter the culprit and deter others inclined to crime, thus encouraging a healthy respect for law.
  (v) **Reparation.** Some punishments require offenders to help make amends (e.g. community service).

There is much argument about penology (the science of punishment), the kinds of punishment which should be applied and the effect of each. We shall refer to these matters briefly later. The chief aims of the penal system in Britain are to *deter* the potential law-breaker and to *reform* the convicted offender. The element of deterrence is intended to lie in the fear of detection, public trial and the possibility of punishment rather than in the severity of the punishment itself. The treatment of offenders is today based increasingly on the knowledge that the public has a responsibility not merely to punish or reject the offender, but to **rehabilitate him**, i.e. to fit him back into society as a citizen with self-respect, and guard him from relapse into crime. But it is extraordinarily difficult to deter and punish while aiming to reform. There is an inherent antithesis in the two aims of punishment and reform. We are often reformed by kindness and loving care and may be made much worse by harsh and unthinking punishment which may in the end make us more vindictive to those who impose the punishment in the name of society.

One of the chief problems facing Britain in this field, in common with other modern industrial nations, is contending with the marked increase in the number of offenders since the Second World War. The material prosperity which one might have supposed would lead to a reduction in crime has been accompanied by an increase. So poverty as such is not the root cause of the rise in crime. But there is evidence that the poor and unemployed get into trouble with the law because of their money problems; that they act out of desperation or cannot *afford* to live within the law. Some JPs are sympathetic and show leniency, e.g. in 1984 only 6 per cent of offenders in Bradford were jailed, c.f. 32 per cent in Oxford. We have to approach the problem with care; there is no simple cause and there is no simple cure. We shall refer to the matter of research later. This section is concerned with treatment of offenders and we now turn to the kinds of punishment which may be imposed.

Kinds of punishment

The early penal methods adopted in Britain were based on the principles of retribution and deterrence. From the fifteenth century onwards deterrence grew in importance, the belief being that the spread of crime could only be halted if the offenders were treated with ferocity. In the eighteenth century there were more than 160 capital offences, called felonies. These ranged from simple theft to murder, so that to steal a chicken or a sheep involved death to the offender. As an alternative one might be transported, mainly to Australia. The other kinds of punishments for other offences (called misdemeanours) were flogging, fines and the use of the pillory and the stocks.

During the early part of the nineteenth century there was a movement of reform inspired by humanitarian spirits (Jeremy Bentham, Sir Charles Romilly, Elizabeth Fry and many others). From 1830 onwards the police service was formed – first in London (the Metropolitan Police), then the cities and boroughs followed suit with their forces and finally the counties constituted their forces – all based on the experience of the Metropolitan Police whose main function was the prevention and detection of crime and the prosecution of offenders before the courts of law. The emphasis in the police has always been to prevent crime – by patrols and the like – so far as possible, and in detecting those who had committed crimes. Those duties remain to this day.

The kinds of punishment now imposable may be classified as (a) custodial, (b) semi-custodial and (c) other forms.

Custodial	*Semi-custodial*	*Other forms*
Imprisonment	Borstal	Absolute discharge
Hospital order	Detention centres	Conditional discharge
	Community homes	Binding over
	Attendance centres	Probation order
	Care orders	Fine
		Compensation order
		Bankruptcy
		Supervision order
		Suspended sentence
		Deferred sentence
		Community service order
		Deprivation of property
		Disqualification from driving
		Day training centres

The punishment of death is the supreme penalty and is reserved for a few offences only: treason, piracy on the high seas and setting fire to HM shipyards. Treason is the most serious offence in the criminal calendar, and the death penalty remains. Whether this form of penalty would be carried out is doubtful having regard to the fact that the sentence of death by hanging for the offence of murder has been abolished by the *Murder (Abolition of Death Penalty) Act, 1965*. The question of the reintroduction of the death penalty for such offences as terrorism by hi-jacking – for example, where one or two gunmen may hold two or three hundred passengers on a plane as hostages or commit other heinous offences – is still a live issue among politicians. How far does one yield to violent threats?

Clearly the type of punishment or order which may be made by a court will vary with the type of offender. There are, of course, other factors which may weigh in the mind of the court. Thus the offender who is convicted may be 30 years of age, with two or more previous convictions and sentences ranging from two or three or more years' imprisonment who is pursuing crime as his habitual mode of living. Imprisonment may be the only appropriate sentence having regard to the court's duty to protect the community from, let us say, persistent attacks on old women or young girls, or offences of robbery or burglary. On the other hand, the offender may be a man of 45 or more who has led an honest life. His offence may be shoplifting following a nervous breakdown. The appropriate sentence in this case may be an absolute or conditional discharge; this is a minimal order, appropriate to the offence and the kind of offender. Then again the court (usually a Juvenile Court) may have to consider how best to treat a lad of 16 who has committed vandalism, or defrauded his employers of a mere 10p. The offender may be a woman of 70 who has all her life been engaged in fraud or stealing from lodgings; she may be a housewife with four children who has little money from her husband, and steals from the local supermarket to provide food for her children; she may be a girl of 16 who comes from a broken home, leaves her local town, goes to London and there engages in theft or fraud. There are many kinds of persons who are 'offenders': priests, doctors, teachers, police officers, dustmen or door-keepers. And they are of all ages. The court must, therefore, in deciding the appropriate penalty or order which it makes, have regard to sex, age, mode of life, and the antecedents or history of each of the offenders and then decide in the light of the facts of the case what sentence to award.

It is important, therefore, to bear in mind the wide varieties of men, women, young persons and children who fall into the category of offender. And if we consider the spectrum of society that forms the category of 'offender' we can readily see the need to provide different kinds of imprisonment. Some may be sentenced to secure prisons, some may be sentenced to open prisons where the offender may be allowed a relative freedom.

Custodial punishment

Imprisonment. An adult offender is committed to one of HM Prisons, of which there are various kinds, some 'open' and some 'closed' prisons. Broadmoor Mental Hospital is allocated for those suffering from insanity or those sentenced to be detained 'during HM pleasure'. We have abolished flogging, 'penal servitude' and 'imprisonment with hard labour'.

Most statutes lay down maximum punishments for particular offences. Robbery (*Theft Act, 1968*) and arson (*Criminal Damage Act, 1971*) are punishable by imprisonment for life. (There are currently about 1,500 life prisoners compared to 176 in 1958.) A Crown Court may award any sentence imposable by law from imprisonment (or death) to absolute discharge. A Magistrates' Court may not sentence a person to more than six months' imprisonment for any one offence.

Hospital order. This order may be made by a court where it is found that the offender is suffering from mental illness or severe abnormality, subnormality or psychopathic disorder. The power is exercisable when a person is convicted on indictment of any offence, or, in the case of Magistrates' Courts, if he is convicted of an offence punishable on summary conviction with imprisonment. A Court may also make an order without first convicting him, if satisfied that the accused did the act charged.

Before making a hospital order a court must be satisfied on the evidence of two doctors (one must have special experience in the diagnosis or treatment of mental disorder) that the offender is suffering from mental illness such that it warrants detention in hospital for medical treatment. The purpose of the order is to enable an offender to be compulsorily detained, or placed under guardianship for as long as is necessary in his and the public's interest. Cases are reviewed from time to time by the managers of the hospital, and appeal against detention may be made to the Mental Heath Review Tribunal. (See page 164.)

Semi-custodial punishment

Borstal. These institutions (so named because the first institution was at Borstal, in Kent) are for the training of young offenders over 15 and under 21 who are convicted of an offence punishable with imprisonment where the court is of the opinion having regard to the circumstances of the offence and the offender's character and previous conduct, that it is expedient that he should be detained for training for not less than six months. A sentence of borstal training may not be passed on a person under 17 on the date of his conviction unless the court considers that no other method of dealing with him is appropriate. A sentence of borstal training may only be passed by a Crown Court, and may not exceed three years. The emphasis in borstal training is on remedial and educational treatment based on close study of the individual. The training seeks the all-round development of character and capacities – moral, mental, physical and vocational. Release from a borstal sentence is followed by a period of supervision by the probation and after-care service for up to two years from the date of release. The date of release of each person is decided by the Home Secretary.

Note: **Youth Custody Centres** have now replaced Borstals. (See page 391.)

Detention centres. A person over 14 and under 21 found guilty of an offence punishable by imprisonment if he were an adult, may be sent to a detention centre for up to three months. Thereafter he will be subject to supervision for one year. The object of detention centres is to give a 'short, sharp shock'. The regime is rigorous and provides training and education, though the maximum term of detention restricts the possibility of serious training. Since 1980 a few of these have been nominated to provide especially tough treatment. (See page 200.)

Community homes. These are regulated and approved by the Home Secretary, and are planned and provided on a regional basis. The homes are administered by the local authorities and vary in the form of treatment and accommodation which they provide and the degree of restriction which they impose on the inmates. The community homes are used for children (i.e. 10–14) and young persons (14–17) for the purpose of remand, correction or care, in cases of serious offence. Those homes providing education are known as CHEs or, in Scotland, List D schools. (See pages 189, 194 and 198.)

Care orders. These orders are made by a court 'committing the offender to the care of a local authority' (under the *Children and Young Persons Act, 1969.* See page 198). Orders may be made where a child or young person is in need of care, protection or control, or has committed a criminal offence. The child or young person is committed to the care of a local authority who may place him in a community home or a foster home, or he may be made subject to a hospital order or a guardianship order.

Other forms of punishment

Absolute discharge. This order may be made by a court where it finds the accused guilty, but, having regard to all the circumstances, thinks it inexpedient to inflict any punishment or to impose a probation order.

Conditional discharge. This is similar to the above except that the offender is discharged subject to the condition that he does not commit another offence. If he does, he will be liable to be sentenced for the original offence. The condition cannot remain in force for more than three years.

Binding over. The offender is found guilty, but the court requires him to enter into a recognisance to keep the peace and to be of good behaviour. Binding over is a form of preventive justice. If the offender then commits another offence he is liable to forfeit the sum named in the recognisance (or bond) he has already entered into.

Probation order. An order may be made requiring the offender to be placed under the supervision of a probation officer for a specified period (not more than three years). A probation order may be made subject to conditions designed to ensure that the offence is not repeated. If the conditions are broken or a further offence committed during the period of the probation, the probationer may be recalled for sentence on the original charge.

Fine. This is the imposition of the payment of a sum of money to the court for an offence committed. Certain statutes lay down the maximum which may be imposed. JPs may not impose fines over £2,000 (except in special cases).

Compensation order. A court may order a person convicted of an offence to pay compensation 'for any personal injury, loss or damage resulting from that offence or from any other offence which is taken into consideration by the court in determining sentence'. The maximum compensation awardable in a Magistrates' Court is £2,000 for each offence (from 1984). Where civil proceedings are taken subsequently in respect of the same damage the amount awarded by the Criminal Court will be taken into consideration and the award of damages adjusted.

Bankruptcy. A court may make a criminal bankruptcy order where, as a result of an offence of which a person has been convicted, either standing alone or with other relevant offences, loss or damage (not personal injury) has been suffered by persons whose identity is known to the court and the loss or damage exceeds £15,000. A criminal bankruptcy has the effect of an 'act of bankruptcy' under the *Bankruptcy Act, 1914*. The Official Petitioner (i.e. the Director of Public Prosecutions) initiates the proceedings. The object of the order is to prevent fraudsmen from enjoying their ill-gotten gains when released from prison sentence(s) (*Criminal Justice Act, 1972*).

Supervision order. This may be made by a court after trying a juvenile or after 'care proceedings' – for example, where he is being ill-treated or neglected, or his health impaired, or he is exposed to moral danger, or beyond the control of parent or guardian or not receiving full-time education (if of school age), or guilty of an offence other than homicide – sometimes known as the 'offence condition'.

Suspended sentence. Any court which passes a sentence of imprisonment for a term of not more than two years may order that the sentence be suspended for a period to be specified in the order (though of not less than one nor more than two years). The general effect is that the sentence remains in suspense during the period named. If during that time the person concerned commits an offence punishable with imprisonment the original sentence may be imposed. (*Criminal Justice Act, 1967*, as amended).

Deferred sentence. This enables a court to defer sentence for up to six months in order to have regard to the conduct of the person charged after conviction, including reparation, and to any change in circumstances (*Criminal Justice Act, 1972*).

Community service order. A person over 16 (see page 391) may be required to perform community service of not more than 240 hours of unpaid work, usually at week-ends. There are certain conditions. Thus the offender must consent to the order (or CSO), and the service must be fulfilled within 12 months. The community service intended will be work involving repairing footpaths, slag heaps, nature reserves, churchyards, beaches, canals, children's adventure playgrounds, work in hospitals and so on. The community service must not interfere with religious observance, his normal work or education (*Criminal Justice Act, 1972*). (See page 386.)

Deprivation of property. Where a person is convicted of an offence punishable with not less than two years' imprisonment, and the court is satisfied that any property in his possession or control on arrest has been used for committing any offence, or was intended to be used for that purpose, it may deprive him of any rights he may have in the property, which shall be taken into, or remain in, the possession of the police. A motor vehicle, therefore, may be confiscated under this section (s. 23, *Criminal Justice Act, 1972*).

Disqualification from driving a motor vehicle. Where a person is convicted on indictment of an offence punishable with not less than two years' imprisonment a Crown Court may, if satisfied that a vehicle was used by the defendant or anyone else for committing the offence, disqualify him for such period as the court thinks fit. A Magistrates' Court may not exercise this power (*Criminal Justice Act, 1972*, s. 24).

Day training centres. There are over 60 such day centres. They provide an alternative to prison for adult petty, especially persistent offenders. They provide intensive supervision and social education as a condition of a probation order.

Research into punishment

Research into causes of crime and the treatment of offenders is carried out by the Home Office Research Unit which liaises with universities. Criminology has grown in importance and interest, and considerable research is undertaken in the universities, chiefly at Cambridge which has its own Institute of Criminology, and at Edinburgh and Glasgow. The main interest is investigating the forms of institutional treatment and the criteria of successful treatment, the probation system, and other forms of supervision and control.

Prisons

Britain's 135 prison units divide into:

1 **Local prisons** which are closed prisons and are the only ones to which the courts can commit prisoners direct. They therefore receive all categories of prisoner, together with those on remand and awaiting trial.
2 **Other closed prisons** which take the longer term prisoners and those requiring greater security. Among these are the 'training prisons' which are supposed to seek to implement Rule 1 of the prison department which holds that the purpose of prison treatment and training is to 'encourage and assist prisoners to lead a good and useful life'.
3 **Open prisons** are an important development and 'represent one of the most successful applications of the principle of the individualisation of penalties with a view to social readjustment' (UN Congress on the Prevention of Crime and the Treatment of Offenders 1955). The value is that they provide the best conditions for the rehabilitation of the offender. These conditions serve to encourage prisoners in self-respect and self-responsibility which are much more likely to be achieved in the more humane

atmosphere prevailing than in the depressing conditions of a closed prison.

The allocation of prisoners to these prisons depends on factors such as age, type of offender, kind of offence committed, length of sentence and similar factors. The allocation of prisoners who have committed the most serious offences or who for some other reason require the highest degree of security is made by the Home Office. Otherwise allocation is carried out by the local prisons, which have review boards comprising the governor and members of his staff, including the welfare officer. Two essentials must be borne in mind: the prisoner's needs and quick relief of the constant pressure on accommodation in local prisons resulting from the increase in crime generally since the Second World War.

Administration. The Home Secretary and the Secretary of State for Scotland are responsible for questions relating to the treatment of offenders, for collecting statistics and other information in the operation of the penal system, and for appraising the methods of treatment and bringing those to the notice of the Courts. The Home Secretary is responsible for prisons and borstals in England and Wales, and the Secretary of State for Scotland is responsible for these institutions in Scotland. The Home Secretary is supported by a staff of experts – the Director General of the Prison Service, with assistant directors, and the governors of prisons and borstals.

Prisons are supervised by Visiting Committees and Boards of Visitors. The Visiting Committees are appointed by magistrates from among their number, and the Boards of Visitors are appointed by the Home Secretary from interested and suitable people. These two bodies supervise the prisons and have free access at any time. They deal with disciplinary matters and misbehaviour by prisoners, and they can hear complaints by prisoners against ill-treatment or conditions and similar matters. The bodies report annually to the Home Secretary. In addition there is an official Home Office Inspectorate of Prisons (since 1980).

The prison service. Each prison has a Governor at its head. He has overall responsibility. Below him are various grades of officers and staff. Governors are responsible for security, good order and discipline, the control of prison staff, developing prison activities, vocational training, education and recreation for prisoners.

Each prison has its complement of specialist staff: medical officers, psychiatrists, psychologists, chaplains, social workers, nurses, instructors and clerical staff. These staff are civil servants, and they number some 11,000 men and 2,000 women in England and Wales. In

Scotland there are 1,200 staff, and in Northern Ireland there are approximately 290 men and women prison officers.

Prisoners sentenced for serious offences involving sex or violence or with a history of serious offences are excluded from open prisons, as are those suffering from medical or mental disability. However, those sentenced to long periods may, after careful study of their cases, be transferred from closed prisons to open prisons. Prisoners found unsuitable for open prisons may be returned to closed prisons.

Women's prisons. There are closed and open prisons available for women prisoners. But by the very nature of things special care is needed. Women generally seem to be less capable of withstanding the stresses of close confinement than men. Many women prisoners are highly disturbed, and it is found in practice that they are best dealt with in small establishments. Domestic training is provided in mother and baby units for all women who have babies with them in prison or have been sentenced for neglect of children or cruelty to them.

Work in prisons. Work should be an essential element in the training of a fit prisoner. It should fill much of each weekday, teach him a trade and accustom him to the idea of working hard, consistently and efficiently for the same number of hours and under the same conditions as obtain outside. But this is not always possible, particularly in short-stay cases and the rapid turnover of prison population. Subject to conduct prisoners are allowed a small amount of pocket money to spend in the prison shop. The amount varies according to the job the prisoner is doing, his skill and industry. Production workers are, where possible, paid at piece rates.

Discharge and after-care. A grant of a sum of money (depending on the means of the individual prisoner) is payable to all adult prisoners serving sentences of over three months. Every person discharged from a prison service establishment receives a travel warrant (or fares) for the journey to his destination. Clothing is provided on discharge to ensure that the individual prisoner is adequately clothed on release. Where a prisoner is released on licence he must comply with the terms of the licence, to be of good behaviour or to submit to after-care of a probation officer. Otherwise a prisoner need not accept any form of after-care.

Remission of sentence. Every prisoner sentenced for a term of more than one month is eligible for release after serving *two thirds* (in 1981 the Government considered reducing this to one third) of this sentence, provided this does not result in his serving less than 31 days. The early release is subject to good conduct and industry. Provided therefore a prisoner does not commit a specific offence against prison discipline he may expect to be released after serving only two thirds of the sentence. Persons serving a sentence of life imprisonment may not claim remission under this condition, though they may be released on **licence** by the Home Secretary. The latter consults the Lord Chief Justice and the trial judge if he is available, and ensures that the Parole Board have recommended release. Decisions to release prisoners serving life sentences are reached only after careful consideration of the circumstances of the offence, the offender's record and his fitness to take his place in society again. Life prisoners so released are subject to recall for the rest of their lives.

Parole is release from detention in prison before the period of sentence is expired. During the period of parole the released person must conform to any conditions laid down in his licence. The Review Committee attached to each prison is made up of the governor, a prison visitor, an independent member, a JP and a probation officer. The committee recommends to the Home Secretary who may order release of any person considered suitable. Entitlement to parole depends on the type of offence committed, behaviour in prison, and the prisoner's release plans – for example, his accommodation, hostel, return to wife, and, if possible, work.

An example will show how the scheme works: *A* is sentenced to three year's imprisonment. He is entitled to one year's remission for good behaviour, but he may also be released *on parole* after serving one year only. Should he commit an offence or a breach of condition of his release whilst on parole he will be recalled to prison or other place of detention. (In 1980 about half (i.e. 5,000) of those serving sentences were released on parole. Of these less than 10 per cent were recalled after being convicted of a further offence.)

The probation and after-care service

Probation has been defined as 'the submission of an offender while at liberty to a special period of supervision by a local caseworker who is an officer of the court' e.g. *X* is convicted in the local Magistrates Court of theft, and because it is his first offence is fined £5 and placed on probation for one year. The probation officer supervises *X* during the year of the probation order made by the court.

Probation officers were originally appointed to ensure that the probation orders were observed, but their duties have increased to cover the aftercare service of those released from places of imprisonment or detention, and the service is now named the Probation and After-Care Service. The *Powers of Criminal Courts Act, 1973*, para 8(1), Schedule 3, gives a description of the duties and responsibilities.

It states:

> It shall be the duty of probation officers to supervise the probationers and other persons placed under their supervision and to advise, assist and befriend them, to enquire, in accordance with any directions of the court, into the circumstances or home surroundings of any person with a view to assisting the court in determining the most suitable method of dealing with his case, to advise, assist and befriend, in such cases and in such manner as prescribed, persons who have been released from custody and to perform such other duties as may be prescribed or may be imposed by any enactment or instrument.

Organisation. The Home Secretary is responsible to Parliament and is also responsible for the standard of the service in England and Wales. The Home Office guides and stimulates the work and it has a special probation and after-care department to deal with this.

There are 56 probation and after-care areas in England and Wales. Each of these is administerd by a probation and after-care committee composed of local magistrates and coopted members with legal and specialist interests. The areas vary widely in nature and size. Some are rural and some are in the large cities, towns and conurbations; some are areas with problems of deprivation and high unemployment, and some contain large immigrant groups.

Probation officers are appointed by the committees and work within the particular areas as members of small teams under the leadership of a senior probation officer. He may have a small case load of his own, but he has the main task of running the district for which he is responsible and giving support to and supervising the team. Some members of the team may have special responsibilities, e.g. liaison with a local probation hostel, care of homeless men, borstal after-care, the supervision of probation students entering the profession or the training of voluntary associates. Each team meets regularly for discussion. Some probation officers are employed to do social work in prisons; others run day-training centres, schemes of community service by offenders and other special projects.

Qualifications. A person seeking entry to the Probation and After-Care Service as a qualified Probation Officer must hold the Certificate of Qualification in Social Work (CQSW) from the Central Council for Education and Training in Social Work (see page 400). This is the basic professional qualification for all fields of social work. The minimum age of entry is 22 years. Older candidates with experience in other walks of life are accepted, and, of course, although we have referred exclusively to male probation officers, there are many females among the 6,500 officers in the service.

Nature of the job. Crime has no single cause, and there is no simple remedy (see pages 387 and 389). Often behind the crime itself lies a social or emotional breakdown. The probation officer is a social worker who, like his forerunner, the Court Missionary (see page 396), is concerned with the offender whom he supervises, advises, assists and befriends. The basis of his work, therefore, lies in the *personal relationship* which the probation officer tries to establish. Through this he endeavours to build trust, and show that he is someone who cares, but who is not afraid to set clear limits.

The probation officer must be sympathetic to the personal pressures and circumstances often associated with offending behaviour, but he must also be able to use his authority as a probation officer to exercise effective control when necessary. He must also be able to win the confidence of people who may be seriously at odds with society, and he must be able to judge the kind of help needed in a particular case. In particular he must seek out ways of making that help available by exploring new methods of work and using the resources of the community, e.g. education, employment, industrial training, physical training, sport and accommodation.

Supervision of offenders remains the major activity, and the basic skills of the probation officer are those of the social caseworker. Group work, community work or outdoor pursuits and projects are various ways of helping particular offenders. The probation officer may provide these within his own service or enlist the help of other agencies locally or nationally. Extensive use is now made of voluntary associates, i.e. people who give up spare time as volunteers in the community who can actively demonstrate the concern of the wider community to help an offender.

Probation as a court order is now confined to offenders over 17, but the service continues to supervise the majority of juveniles placed under a supervision order (see page 198) awarded by a court following an offence.

About one third of the Probation and After-Care Service's case-load consists of people released from detention centre, borstal or prison who are subject to supervision under a **licence** or on a voluntary basis. Parole (i.e. release) from prison or detention before the expiration of the full term of custody, has been a growing responsibility for the Probation and After-Care Service from 1968 onwards. Probation officers participate in the selection process of those considered eligible for release on parole, and they submit reports to the Parole Board attached to prisons. However, the after-care role is now to be scaled down (see page 386).

Some probation officers also work as welfare officers in prisons. Their task is to help prisoners with problems which may arise during imprisonment, to promote understanding of social work in the prison regime and to assist with resettlement plans on the release of prisoners.

Recent developments in the probation service include the management of probation hostels, bail hostels and day-training centres (see page 380). **Probation hostels** are placed which provide some supervision and where the residents (who are on probation) can be helped with their personal problems, learn acceptable social behaviour and acquire the habit of regular work in the community. A variant of these is the **probation home**, which is similar except that the residents are employed on the premises, at least for the earlier part of their stay. Until recently probation hostels and homes catered only for young offenders under 21. Now a large programme has been started to provide probation hostels for adult offenders as an alternative to imprisonment. The wardens are usually probation officers.

Community service (see page 379) is regarded as the most exciting and constructive addition to penal treatment introduced in modern times. The court may order an adult who is convicted of an offence punishable by imprisonment to carry out a community task in his spare time for a total of not less than 40 and not more than 240 hours within a 12-month period. An order may not be made unless the offender consents. The court is also required to consider a report by a probation officer on the offender and his circumstances and to be satisfied that he is suitable to carry out work under an order and that arrangements can be made for him to do so. If an offender fails to carry out his work, he may be returned to the court which may fine him or deal with him in any way which was open to the judge or magistrate when the original order was made. The probation service assists by arranging the tasks, which may include painting, decorating and gardening for old or disabled people, teaching spastic children to swim, building adventure playgrounds, assisting in youth clubs, footpath clearance, providing help in hospitals, looking after children in a family centre while the mothers are visiting husbands in prison. There were 35,000 such orders in 1986.

We have referred elsewhere to the increasing numbers seeking divorce or separation. The probation service undertakes **matrimonial conciliation**, and where there is a dispute as to custody of the child or children the probation service is called upon to undertake a social inquiry if the court feels that an understanding of social background may help in their deliberations. Consequently the probation service has developed a marriage counselling function. However, in 1984, the Government announced limits on the matrimonial and after-care work of the probation service so it can concentrate more on supervising offenders and CSOs, and perhaps reparation work: see page 392.

So the task of a probation officer is difficult and complex requiring many skills, an understanding of the individual and society itself, an ability to make clear and comprehensive reports. They must also be able to give evidence satisfactory in court so that the judge or magistrates may be assisted by their findings. They must be able to liaise with other services, and have a pretty clear knowledge of what the central and local government department, plus the voluntary agencies, do and if need be enlist their support. At the same time s/he is *an officer of the court* and friend and adviser of the offender.

> Often great patience is required to wear away the barriers of resentment and suspicion behind which many vulnerable and unhappy people barricade themselves. The probation officer must be ready to receive upon himself the grudges that bewildered folk feel against life and society, yet, despite his sympathy, he has, as an officer of the court, a commission from society to represent it and its authority to his client. It is necessary to resolve the conflicts within this if one is contemplating a career in probation (*The Probation and After-Care Service in a Changing Society*, COI publication)

Most people are concerned about our inability to check the growth of crime in what is reputed to be a civilised society. There is little an individual can do alone, but the Probation and After-Care Service is avowedly one group of people attempting to tackle delinquency in an objective but compassionate, constructive and purposeful way. It currently supervises some 150,000 offenders a year (with about 30 per cent of them serving under one year).

Criminology

Criminology is the study of the causation, correction and prevention of criminal behaviour. This is a relatively new science, but its importance in the treatment of offenders is great. Today we have sociologists, psychiatrists, psychologists, lawyers, police officials, prison administrators, parole and probation officers and others who specialise in some aspects of criminology. For the judge or magistrate it is obvious that if an offender is convicted the judge or magistrate will have to determine the sentence of the court. He will want to know the antecedents or history of the offender, whether married or single, how many children he has, where he works, whether he keeps a job long, whether he has previous convictions and whether all convictions are for the same class of offence, e.g. burglary. His age, health, mental capacity and personal characteristics will weigh in the mind of the judge before sentence. Every person who puts himself in the position of a judge must realise the extreme difficulty in passing that sentence which will be most beneficial for both the offender and the society whose interests must be considered.

We have on page 374 already discussed the treatment of criminals in the past. In the early nineteenth century Cesare Lombroso considered that the so-called criminal type had peculiarities of physical appearance, particularly skull deformities which were said to be a throwback to primitive man. However, in the early twentieth century Charles Goring overthrew Lombroso's theory of physical traits by establishing that there were as many criminal physical traits among English university students as among English convicts. Some early researchers or thinkers in the field ascribed criminal actions to poverty or heredity. These facile theories have been overthrown. Today, for example, in the materialistic age when no one is poor (in the early nineteenth-century sense) crime has reached new heights.

William Healy (an American psychiatrist) has stated that crime results from many factors together. He pursued research into any deviation from normality in health, personality, school record, home or other conditions. Sir Cyril Burt in England pursued the same line of inquiry into delinquency in London. Sheldon and Eleanor Glueck (American researchers) measured several hundred attributes in 500 delinquents and in a matched sample of non-delinquents in Boston, Mass. They found that delinquents differed from non-delinquents in more often being impulsive, aggressive, hostile, poor learners in school and of mesophormic (i.e. husky type) body-build, with inconsistent, discordant or criminal parents. Edwin H. Sutherland (*Principles of Criminology*, 1939) viewed crime as the normally learned behaviour of persons who are exposed so much earlier, more intensely, more frequently or longer to pro-criminal behaviour that its influences outweigh those of anti-criminal (or loosely more 'normal') behaviour. Broken homes, retardation in school, high delinquency neighbourhoods, idleness or other factors were noted as predisposing factors.

Sufficient has been noted above to indicate the complexity of the problem, without even touching on why forgers are forgers – what is called 'whitecollar crime' – or indeed the existence of highly organised crime by gangs or sophisticated syndicates who rob banks or engage in international crime, or the more recent phenomenon of hijacking or political terrorism. So from the petty theft in the local supermarket, or the vandalism on the trains going to the football match, to the involved company fraud involving millions or the bribery in Government contracts, there are many gradations. The causes of crime are manifold and therefore need the most careful study. Such is the problem of causation, but one which is ever present in the fixing of the most appropriate sentence or order to be meted out to the offender.

Side by side with the causes we have to place research into the effectiveness or otherwise of the various penal remedies enumerated on p. 374. How effective or successful are these? What factors affect the likelihood of reconviction? The Home Office Research Unit has shown that the older the offender the less likely he is, generally speaking, to be reconvicted. Thus, more than 50 per cent of offenders under 14 at their first offence were reconvicted within five years, compared with 30 per cent of first offenders aged 21–29, and only 9 per cent of first offenders aged 40 or over. Similarly *all* offenders aged

8–11 who had two previous offences were reconvicted, compared with only just over 40 per cent of such offenders aged 30 and over. Again, the more offences an offender had already committed, the more likely he is to be reconvicted within a given period.

The evaluation of sentences

Some progress has been made towards evaluating sentences by means of comparative studies, and the consistency of the results is encouraging. To study reconviction rates is, of course, to assess the effectiveness of sentences from one point of view only; some kinds of sentence may have fewer disadvantages for society even though they do not give better relative reconviction rates. Moreover, until more information about offenders' social circumstances has been obtained for all kinds of offender, so that the assessment of expectation can be made more complete, the results of research should be treated with a good deal of reserve. Some significant points emerge from the figures discussed in the preceding paragraphs (*The Sentence of the Court. A Handbook for Courts on the Treatment of Offenders*, HMSO, 1969).

1 **Fines**, particularly the heavier ones, appear to be among the most 'successful' penalties for almost all types of offender.
2 **Discharges,** too, seem to have good results, particularly when used for juvenile offenders (for whom the fact of being caught and appearing before the court would often be a sufficient deterrent).
3 **Probation.** Again the relative 'success' of probation (claimed to be 75 per cent) is interesting. Although first offenders convicted of breaking and entering tended to be reconvicted more often than other first offenders, it was found that when they were put on probation the reconviction rate was lower than for other offences. This was true of all age groups.
4 **Custody.** This appears to be relatively unsuccessful. Over 80 per cent of those from Borstal institutions have offended within 2 years of their release; and 75 per cent of boys (14–16) after leaving Detention Centres.

An interesting experiment in USA known as 'mediation' involves first-time offenders going back to meet their 'victims' (of say, burglary) and discussing the incident and talking it through. (See also page 392.)

In the final paragraph of the *Handbook* we find that the research is somewhat limited. The report states: 'The social circumstances of offenders have not, in any case, so far been specifically allowed for in the researches completed (though adverse environmental conditions have, of course, been covered to the extent that they are reflected in the offender's past criminal record). Inevitably the extent to which the various sentences are used differs from court to court.'

So the judicial machine is not perfect, since one is more likely to be punished by fine in one court than in another, or more likely to be sent to prison by one court than another, e.g. see page 373. To offset this difference of treatment among courts, the practice has been instituted of holding meetings of magistrates and judges to consider sentences from hypothetical cases. This will go some way to ensure uniformity of treatment.

5   **Imprisonment.** It costs over £10,000 p.a. to hold someone in prison. Imprisonment (whether in open or closed prison) may be the only means of protecting society from the most hardened or habitual criminal or one who is insane. But we saw (page 373) that one of the aims of the treatment of offenders is reform. Yet if we ask whether the average prisoner (if there is such a being) is reformed by imprisonment we may be sceptical. A prisoner in constant association with others who are 'worse' than he is – more violent, coarse, unstable, aggressive, crafty, deceitful and so on – will himself be affected by the group. This is a well-known fact; associate with those better than yourself and you somehow become better; associate with those worse, and the challenge to maintain a modest self-respect, let alone an improvement, is more difficult. Recent research into institutions representing the entire range of Swedish penal methods found that the negative influences on the inmates (criminalisation, drug addiction, institutionalisation, stigmatisation, alienation) outweighed any positive effects. The negative effects were found equally in all types of institution; these effects increased with length of custody; young inmates were affected as much as adults, women as much as men. In every such institution there was found to be a strong criminal sub-culture, and seemed to confirm E. Goffman's theory of the negative effect of 'total institutions' of whatever kind. Even the most therapeutically orientated seemed to have failed to create a climate in which the inmates felt more helped than harmed. The uncertainties of the indeterminate sentences was felt to be an additional and unjust punishment. Overall positive treatment in institutions seems to be largely ineffective and that institutions are more likely to increase than to decrease criminal tendencies.

The problem in Britain is compounded by old buildings, staff shortages and severe **overcrowding**. In 1981 the prison population reached a record figure of 45,000 and 50,000 by 1988 and resulted in 4,900 prisoners living three to a cell and 11,000 living two to a cell – cells suitable for one person. In some cases inmates are locked up for 22 hours or more each day, including some on **remand**, i.e. unconvicted prisoners awaiting trial, one third of whom subsequently do not receive a prison sentence. (Of the 5,600 – half are of school age – on remand in 1982, 100 had been there over a year, though the average is 41 days. The Government has now begun to introduce a statutory time limits (i.e. trial deadlines) as in Scotland where trial must be held within 110 days, or 40 for minor offences.)

There have been prison riots; a pressure group (PROP) has formed to promote prisoners' rights; prison staff have taken industrial action; prison governors have referred to some prisons as 'festering slums' and 'penal dustbins'. The director of NACRO has said, 'Keeping prisoners in such conditions can neither reduce nor prevent crime. It can only increase it by putting back into society . . . prisoners who are more embittered and less able to cope than when they went in.'

HM Chief Inspector of Prisons has described the conditions as 'degrading and brutalising' (Report, 1981) and recommended a reduction in the prison population by 7,000. Suggestions for reducing numbers include that by 'Justice' to de-criminalise many offences by converting them into 'contraventions'. Another suggestion is to give shorter sentences generally. Thirdly is the view of those (e.g. the May Committee, 1979) who argue for more non-custodial sentencing (e.g. for problem drinkers or mentally disordered), for more weekend dententioning and for greater access to bail for those remanded in custody. The Government has agreed to these, and in 1988 produced some further ideas for treating offenders in the community, including curfews and house arrest, compensation and electronic 'tagging' (to keep some surveillance on the offender).

However, such a community-based penal policy relies on the active involvement of the public and 'on a patient approach drawing on the healthy concept of the unitary nature of society which, whenever possible, must resolve within itself the problems which it generates'. (G. Bevis, Chief Probation Officer, Cheshire.) Furthermore, judges and magistrates object strongly to being guided or directed on sentencing, especially when it occurs by way of odd remarks or speeches by the Home Secretary. Perhaps Parliament should lay down clearer guidelines.

The *Criminal Justice Act, 1982*. This seeks to reduce the prison population, and it introduces some important changes in the treatment of juvenile offenders. Under it: (a) Borstal and prison for under 21 year olds is to be replaced by 'youth custody'; custodial sentences for 17–21 year olds are to be for determinate periods. (b) Detention centre sentences can run from 3 weeks (minimum) to 4 months (maximum). (c) Magistrates have the power to pass 'residential care orders' for second or persistent offenders. (d) Community service orders are extended to 16 year olds. (e) Parents can be held more responsible for their children's fines. (f) Powers to impose partially suspended sentences are extended. (g) Prison sentences are removed for certain offences (vagrancy, soliciting) or sentences are reduced (fine defaulters). (h) Appeals against refusal of bail become subject to legal-aid. (i) Time spent on remand is deductible from detention centre sentences. (j) Supervision orders can have additional conditions attached (e.g. banning attendance at football matches). (k) Curfews can be imposed on offenders aged 12–20.

Many of these measures are costly and will take time to implement. Many are also controversial: it is claimed that they might increase the prison population (e.g. where a previously suspended sentence now becomes only partially suspended). And already there is evidence of an increase (50%) in custodial sentencing, when the general philosophy over 15 years has been towards community treatment for the young offender. There is evidence too that the so-called new 'short, sharp, shock' regime of the detention centres has been a failure, with high reconviction rates (or 'recidivism') among their young offenders. More successful seems to be the work of the Juvenile Bureaux which exist in parts of the UK (see below).

Victims of crime. It is often said that the State and voluntary groups give more attention to the offender than to the innocent victim. Yet, while there may be apparently 'soft treatment' by the courts and plenty of groups campaigning for offenders (e.g. the Howard League, the Prison Reform Trust, etc.), there are increasingly local voluntary groups to help those who suffer from criminal offences. Such **Victims Support Schemes** give advice and comfort in often very fraught situations and often help victims to make claims to the Criminal Injuries Compensation Board. There are 350 such schemes with 8,000 volunteers (and in 1986 they advised over 250,000 crime victims). Another development, emerging cautiously and somewhat informally, are the reparation and conciliation (of offender and victim) schemes; these are often initiated by the probation service and Juvenile Bureaux (involving police, probation, teachers, social workers, etc.) These provide some recompense for the victim (as well as perhaps shame the offender).

Statutory provision exists in the form of the Criminal Injuries Compensation Board, which has a limit on compensation of £400. In view of this limit, JPs have been trying to give regard to victims of crime by imposing compensation orders (see page 378).

The best way to deal with crime is to prevent it happening; that is easier said than done, and involves a fundamental examination of social and economic policies. But a more immediate policy which is currently being implemented is the 'Neighbourhood Watch' scheme, where local people are organised to work closely with the police in alerting them to suspicious behaviour. These have mushroomed in recent years to some 60,000 today (with considerable beneficial effects according to the Home Secretary in 1988).

Meanwhile offending continues to occur, and its treatment places great difficulties on the Government, the judiciary and society itself. At the centre of the problem lies the discordance among the five original aims and philosophy of punishment or treatment – reformation, deterrence, prevention, retribution, compensation. In particular, that which will deter will not reform; and that which will reform will not deter. Such is the dilemma of criminology and those responsible for determining our penal policies.

Questions

1 State the composition and powers of Crown, Magistates' and Juvenile Courts.
2 What is meant by (a) an indictable offence and (b) a summary offence?
3 Give examples of (a) custodial, (b) semi-custodial and (c) other punishments.
4 Describe the nature and kinds of work performed by a probation officer.
5 'A society can be judged by the way it treats its prisoners.' Discuss.
6 Some thinkers describe young delinquents as 'deprived' and blame the environment and home; other thinkers describe them as 'depraved' and attach little importance to environment and home. How do we reconcile these views?
7 Describe (a) care, (b) supervision and (c) community service orders.
8 In 1989 the Lord Chief Justice doubled the prison sentence imposed on an offender by the Crown Court, on the grounds that it was too lenient. Comment on this development in our penal system.

14
The social work profession

Definitions

Social work has been described as 'the newest profession'. It was born in the slums of London in the late nineteenth century, though it had existed fitfully before that. But what is 'social work'? And what is a 'social worker'? The answers to these questions are by no means simple or clear. A few definitions may serve as a useful introduction:

1 A service is 'social' if its aim is the enhancement of the individual or the community, either through personal action or by collective effort. Thus, social work involves helping people 'to adjust to changed circumstances, to accept stressful circumstances which cannot be altered, to improve poor personal or family relationships, or to regain confidence and self-respect' (F. Mitchell, *The Social Workers*, BBC, 1965).

2 'Social work is concerned with all those social relationships which may result in problems of mutual adjustment between the individual and his environment. The contribution of social workers in this broad field of social relationships is made through their experience of working with people, their knowledge of community resources and their ability to mobilise these resources to deal with the needs of the community' ('Report of the Expert Group on the Development of National Social Service Programmes', UN, 1959).

3 Social caseworkers in Europe are primarily required to fulfil one or other or a combination of the following functions: (a) To determine eligibility for financial assistance and to give it humanely in consideration of individual needs within the general framework of regulations. (b) To administer some particular part of a public welfare programme in which provision is made for a personal service. (c) To interpret complex legal enactments to the client and to enable him to get those services and facilities to which he may be entitled. (d) To make arrangements on behalf of the client, calling upon the aid of public and private agencies and combining various services to produce the desired result. (e) To

recruit, orient and direct volunteers, who may be the persons directly responsible, for example for supervision of probationers or foster home placement. (f) In recent years and, to a limited extent, to render a service to individuals which is concerned not only with environmental changes but also with helping the person to achieve some release from his personal problems and from the pressure of his family and social relationships (E. Younghusband, *Social Work and Social Change* 1962).

4   A Social worker is one who is particularly skilled at understanding and helping individuals or groups who are experiencing conditions of stress and strain which they cannot meet themselves' (E. Younghusband, op.cit.).

Origins of social work

From the beginning, social work has been interwoven with poverty and deprivation. Extreme poverty has diminished 'but this revealed other persistent social and personal need. Social work remained concerned with deprivation in all its manifestations, with misfits and the "undeserving" and those who for different reasons could not cope with the circumstances of their lives. Its constant aim has been to discover how to help such people, though it has had very different ideas from time to time about how to do so' (E. Younghusband, *The Youngest Profession*, IPC, 1981).

Through the nineteenth century, social provision relied substantially on the family and the informal community. However, where this failed or was weak, there was the State poor law, the Church and some employers' welfare provision. To avoid the poor law, some workers set up self-help organisations, and among these were **friendly societies**. These societies offered friendship and limited comforts in times of distress to members, who paid a sum to join. When a member faced a crisis (sickness, injury, death) regular payments were made to him to tide him or his dependants over the crisis.

Alongside the mutual aid offered to its members by the friendly society, there grew up numerous **charities** to meet every conceivable social need. There were many private benefactors. It became a Victorian fashion, and a Christian duty, to do something for the poor and needy.

By the middle of the nineteenth century the help provided by charitable means was chaotic. Private benevolence, charities and friendly societies existed as a patchwork. To bring order into this state of affairs the Society for Organising Charitable Relief and Repressing Mendicity (begging) was established in 1869. This later became the **Charity Organisation Society** (COS – today known as the Family Welfare Association). The coordination of all charity work and social work was beyond the capacity of the COS but it made its mark.

What it did was to employ **methods** of attack on the social problems of the day. Their main method became known as 'casework'. In short this means a **disciplined, organised and consistent** means of dealing with individuals in need. Records of work with individuals or families were kept. These were discussed, progress was monitored and certain deductions were drawn (about character, motivation, appropriate forms of help, etc.). Attempts were made to draw up a set of rules (or code), and to pass on techniques through training.

Similar work was being developed by **Octavia Hill** in the area of housing improvement. She bought up blocks of dilapidated houses, repaired them and let them out, under a system of enlightened, reformist management which combined rent collecting with casework and community development. She sought to encourage the tenants to become independent.

A third source of inspiration to the development of social work lay in the **university settlement** movement. This began with the establishment of Toynbee Hall in the East End of London by Canon Barnett in 1884. The aim was 'to bring the life of the university to bear on the life of the poor' by persuading members of the university to live and work in a poor area. Here they studied social conditions, conducted classes and led clubs, and tried to introduce certain reforms.

However, the first groups of social workers to be developed on anything like a national basis were the **probation** workers and the hospital almoners. In the later nineteenth century enlightened magistrates were concerned as to the harmful effects of imprisonment on young persons and the first offender. Accordingly they began to impose only token sentences, remanding the offender to the custody of his parents or his master for more careful supervision, and by binding over the offender conditional upon his good behaviour. After conviction, a missionary attached to the court was required to 'advise, assist and befriend' the offender and generally help him to lead a good and honest life. From these humble beginnings, the Probation Service sprang.

The word 'almoner' originally meant an official distributor of alms. The first **almoner** to be appointed in the role of medical social worker was Mary Stewart who, in 1895, was allocated a dingy corner of the out-patients department of the London Royal Free Hospital. Her duties were 'to prevent the abuse of the hospital by persons able to pay for medical treatment'. However, she had more positive aims and tried to create a social service based on the application of casework principles to the special needs and problems of hospital patients. Almoning became established subsequently as a recognised branch of social work, and eventually almoners were appointed to most other general hospitals.

Social services and social work 1900 to 1939

At the beginning of the twentieth century the idea was emerging that social services should not be regarded as a form of charity but rather as a natural benefit available to the citizens of the civilised state, ranking equally with defence, justice and law and order. Individualism was giving way to collective provision. Socialist ideas and the evidence of social surveys were beginning to make an impact. Thus Parliament passed a number of important social policy laws (in the era known as 'the Liberal Reforms') and forming in effect the first phase of the Welfare State. The most important of these dealt with National Insurance (1911), Housing subsidies (1919) and slum clearance (1930), Maternity and Child Welfare (1918) and Old Age Pensions (1908). Other important Acts covered school meals (1906) and medical inspections (1907), Juvenile Courts (1908), Probation (1907), Youth Employment (1910) and Adult Employment Exchanges (1909) and Minimum Wages Boards (1909). In the 1920s welfare services were established for the physically and mentally disabled, largely through government grants to local authorities and voluntary organisations. Meanwhile, *private* employers increased their own welfare services (e.g. appointing medical staff in their factories). **Social work** continued in the limited areas of probation, hospitals and university settlements. It developed further during this period in voluntary organisations concerned with family welfare (mainly centred on financial aid), moral welfare groups (especially the church concerned with unmarried mothers) and societies for handicapped children. Youth clubs were developing, and clubs and centres (providing a basis for social groupwork) were set up for the unemployed in the 1930s.

Some training was given to workers in the NSPCC and Barnardo's, and a training board was established for probation workers (these latter also received the first government training grants). The other important development was in the field of mental health where psychiatric social workers began to receive education and training based on psychological ideas from the USA, especially concerning such concepts as personality and motivation, and stressing the importance of family relationships.

Social services and social work 1940 to today

The outbreak of war (1939) revealed weaknesses and defects in Britain's social provision. The evacuation of women and children from the cities to the country showed many city dwellers to be poor, dirty and ill-provided. There were considerable inequalities in the medical services of town and country. When young men joined the

Services, many were below the physical and intellectual standard required.

Housebuilding ceased and air raids caused devastation and further depleted the available accommodation. As a result, by the end of the war (1945) there was a grave shortage of housing.

Notwithstanding the prosecution of the war, the Government found time to plan better and more comprehensive services to meet the needs of servicemen and families. Most of the legislation passed from 1940 onwards formed the basis of our present social services or Welfare State. These have all been dealt with in detail in earlier chapters. Here we provide a résumé:

1   Social Security including Child Benefits (1945), National Insurance for pensions, sickness and unemployment (1946), Supplementary Benefits (1948) with various modifications and extensions since.
2   Health Services (1946) providing universal and free services for medical and mental disorders as well as some preventive measures.
3   Education following the 1944 Act, also providing a universal and free service up to 15 (later 16), with opportunities for further and higher education, and a range of education welfare provisions.
4   Personal Social Services or welfare services (1948) for individuals and families in general and special groups in particular, such as physically handicapped, elderly, deprived children and the mentally disordered.
5   Housing (1946) at reduced cost through subsidies and (later) rent and rate rebates and security of tenure.

Apart from these 'big 5', other important services established include environmental planning, employment and training and the treatment of offenders.

Social work. As we have seen, a number of these services were introduced or enhanced as a result of the Second World War. This also had a significant impact on the development of social work. The Government established resettlement centres for ex-prisoners of war. But it was a total war and it affected civilians as well as troops.

The evacuation, the blitz, the loss of relations created distress and shock and the value of social workers, skilled in human relations, became widely recognised. Social workers were needed 'because they knew about people and about distress, because they could help to bring the wide array of statutory and voluntary agencies to bear on the several needs of a particular individual at a particularly urgent point in time, and because they were qualified to report in practical terms on the way in which one service reacted on another and on the people needing help' (R. Titmuss, *Problems of Social Policy*, Longman, 1950).

Thus social casework was acknowledged as an important development in the relationship of the public with public services. By the end of the war, 70 local authorities had appointed social workers in addition to those in the Ministry of Health and mental health social workers (helping with war neuroses). Further there were those in various voluntary organisations including the newly-formed Citizens Advice Bureaux, and the Family Service Units dealing with problem families.

Social workers began to be employed in large numbers in local authorities, especially in the child care service (following the 'Curtis Report', 1945) though many of those appointed in health and welfare services were unqualified.

Training content. There has been a training 'explosion' since the 1950s, stimulated in part by the payment of grants. The continuing emphasis has been on psychology since it had become clear that despite the elimination of much poverty and bad housing, many complex factors existed to cause or contribute to social and personal distress. Thus whilst training courses dealt with concepts such as human emotions, drives, defence mechanisms, attachment and loss, identity and self-awareness, skills were being developed in such areas as family therapy, behaviour modification and crisis intervention.

Sociology was also making an important contribution to training. It provided insights into the impact of class, environment, deviance, work roles, marriage and family patterns and child rearing practices. This led to a recognition of community social work (helping local groups to work together) and to some developments in the so-called 'integrated method' which sought to combine client-centred casework with group work (e.g. in day centres for the handicapped or elderly) and community social work (e.g. working with and for neighbourhoods or New Town communities).

Clearly, social work had transformed its old attitudes: it had become far less moralistic and judgemental. There was greater toleration and acceptance of clients' ways. Clients were allowed greater self-determination and the old distinctions between the 'deserving and undeserving' and concepts like 'moral fibre' were no longer acceptable.

Increasingly it was felt that separate and specialised training was both costly and inappropriate. It was becoming obvious that there was much common ground in the theory and practice of the different fields of social work, and the clients too had much in common whether they turned up as 'social casualties' in hospital, in court or on the local authority's doorstep. Thus there began to develop the 'generic' course in applied social studies, aiming to meet client needs rather than to reflect the then administrative structures (see *Seebohm Committee Report*, page 401).

Training structure. Education and training in social work had been pioneered by the probation service and by the Institute of Almoners which issued certificates to successful candidates. Under the post-war expansion of social work various systems of training existed and there were three national councils for training in social work (all responsible to Ministers): (1) the Central Training Council in Child Care; (2) the Council for Training in Social Work; (3) the Advisory Council for Probation and After-Care. There were also other national training bodies in this field such as the National Nurseries Examination Board and the Training Council for Teachers of the Mentally Handicapped.

In 1971 the **Central Council for Education and Training in Social Work** (CCETSW) was set up and superseded the various training bodies, and it was immediately faced with the problem of bringing over 120 different courses up to a common minimum standard set by the new **Certificate of Qualification in Social Work** (CQSW) which is now accepted by employing authorities throughout the UK for employment and salary purposes.

The CCETSW is an independent body with statutory authority to promote training in all fields of social work, and it represents employers, educational institutions and professional associations. The Council approves courses run by universities, polytechnics and FE colleges; it appoints assessors and awards students who successfully complete a recognised course. Training for the CQSW normally takes two years, or one year for certain students who have previously obtained relevant degrees or diplomas. (The minimum qualifying age is 22). Training courses generally include such subjects as psychology, human socialisation, sociology, criminology, social services and social work method. Some courses also include management topics (such as budgeting, communications, monitoring, cost-effectiveness). In addition, supervised field-work experience (or 'placement') is necessary to equip the trainee social worker with basic theoretical knowledge and practical ability. Some 4,000 qualify each year (though an estimated 5,000 are needed).

Outside of 'mainstream' social work, other trained staff are needed (social work assistants, home help and volunteer organisers, day-care staff, etc.). For them, in 1976 there began training courses for the **Certificate in Social Service** (CSS). It involves for some 1,000 p.a. in-service training, usually on a day-release basis. For the residential social worker, there is the **Certificate in Residential Social Work** (CRSW) and for others, including care staff, there is the **In-Service Certificate** (ISC, 4,000 p.a.). For school-leaver trainees, there is the 2-year full-time **Preliminary Certificate in Social Care** (PCSC, 1,700 p.a.). Since 1983 (i.e. following the *Mental Health Act*), because of concern about their powers over mental patients, those social workers involved have had to become specifically qualified through special training: see page 164. Youth workers study for the **Diploma in Youth and Community Work**.

In 1984, the Parsloe Report recommended that the CQSW and the CSS be merged, but contain two levels. Building on this, CCETSW's *Care for Tomorrow* (1987) provided a fundamental training reform package. It would have cost £40 million and involved a series of levels (corresponding to those set down nationally by NVQ) up to entry to the final qualification, the **Qualifying Diploma in Social Work (QDSW)** which itself would normally take three years. In 1988 this was rejected by the Government, which offered instead some £1 million for the purpose of improving training course planning and coordination between colleges and employers and additional support for specialist areas such as child abuse and mental disorder. (The rejection was a blow to CCETSW after its long (six years) research, negotiation and planning. But not everyone agreed with the proposals: see for example Professor Pinker, *New Society*, 18 March 1988.)

Is social work a profession? 'Although it is debatable whether social work can truly be described as a profession equivalent in status to medicine and law, it is nevertheless an occupation demanding thought, organisation, discipline and self-control, and its practitioners have ample justification to reject the description of "well intentioned do-gooders" which is sometimes applied to them.' (J. Haines, *The Nature of Social Work*.)

Social work does have a claim to professional status because (i) it has a Council (CCETSW) which validates and monitors education and training courses; (ii) it has its own influential associations – the British Association of Social Workers (BASW) and the Social Care Association (SCA), previously the Residential Care Association; (iii) it has its own qualifications (CQSW, CRSW, CSS, ICSC) awarded to those who successfully complete training, and which is nationally recognised and widely commended; (iv) it has developed a code of ethics and conduct; and (v) it has its own methodology – the 'social work process' – and is even considered a science by some. Social work is neither woolly-minded humanitarianism nor official interference; nor is the social worker a 'universal aunt'.

The Seebohm Report

The *Report of the Committee on Local Authority and Allied Personal Social Services* or Seebohm Report, (1968), recommended that specialisation in social work should be radically altered; that the then separate groups of social welfare officers, medical and psychiatric social workers, child-care officers and mental welfare offices should drop their distinctions and become generic (i.e. general) social workers. This would enable the social worker to bring to the family or individual in need of social care a more comprehensive approach, instead of the partial, symptom-centred approach. Thus a family with multiple problems of, say, an alcoholic father, delinquent son, school truanting daughter and a mentally ill or exhausted mother could be visited by a single comprehensively trained worker rather than by a succession of specialist social workers.

The outcome of the Seebohm Report was the *Local Authority Social Services Act, 1970*. This abolished local authority children's departments and welfare departments and created instead personal social services departments (SSDs) under chief officers called Directors of Social Services. The area of administration was divided into districts, each having its own team of social workers with a district office: some have local or 'patch' structures.

Similar developments occurred in Scotland, but there they went further in that their new social work departments (SWDs) incorporated probation too (while many English local authorities have retained education welfare services in their education departments). Whilst in Britain generally, in 1974, the medical and psychiatric social workers, while retaining their places in hospitals, were brought into the local authority social worker structure in order to promote a more community-based approach to medical and especially psychiatric social work.

Many people would argue that social work became a recognised profession with the passing of the *Local Authority Social Services Act, 1970*, which enacted many recommendations of the Seebohm Report. This is enhanced by the 'Griffiths response': see page 416.

However, the new departments (variously known as SSDs, PSS or LASS) have faced many problems. First they had to establish themselves as entirely new structures and with over 200,000 employees in

Table 12   Personal Social Services Staff (whole-time equivalents) 1985

Social Services Managers		5,000
Senior Social Workers	4,500	
Social Workers	19,800	24,300
Home Helps		54,700
Day Nursery Staff		9,200
Adult Training Centre Staff		9,000
Staff in Homes for Mentally Disordered		9,500
Staff in Residential Homes for the Elderly and Physically Disabled		57,500
		169,200

Note: Excluding care assistants and staff in children homes.
Source: Health and Personal Social Services Statistics, 1987, (HMSO)

all, management problems have arisen: there are criticisms of bureaucracy and delayed decisions, and the larger departments may have given rise to greater unionisation. The new SSDs have also had to face the organisational upheaval created by the reform of local government in 1974 (1975 in Scotland) and the lesser problems of the reorganisations of the NHS (1974 and 1982). Further, there have been increasing demands placed on SSDs by new Government legislation (some 60–70 Acts since 1972 including the *Access to Personal Files Act, 1987*) and by demographic change (especially the increase in the elderly). Finally, they have had to cope with spending cuts and reductions in expansion plans since 1975.

Social work today

It is easy to assume that when basic income, health and welfare provision has been made, there is no further need for social work – indeed many social workers feared that the Beveridge Welfare State would make them redundant. However, we have found that people need advice about what services are available, where to find them and how to use them. Further, when an attempt is made to meet this need,it becomes apparant that those in need of the advice often need help with personal problems which have arisen out of their material difficulties, and may even lie at the root of them. We have become increasingly aware of the influence which family and group relations can have on people's physical, mental and social well-being. Thus we have witnessed a massive expansion in numbers and types of professional social workers concerned with helping people to deal with their personal problems.

The range of social work is vast. Many people claim to be 'social workers' – teachers, doctors, police officers, clergymen, youth leaders. Indeed it is claimed that anyone with a warm, compassionate heart can lay claim to the title – even the milkman or postman is described as in the front line of social work (especially in regard to old people living alone).

Such a definition, however, is too wide for our purpose. Essentially we take the professional social worker to be the 25,000 or so social workers employed by local authorities in their social service or social work departments. These are commonly known as 'caseworkers' or 'fieldworkers'. Three-quarters of them are professionally qualified. In addition we could add the 50,000-plus residential care workers (in children's and old people's homes, etc.) only 15 per cent of whom are qualified. Thirdly, there are the 8,000 day-care workers: of those who are qualified at all (30 per cent) nearly all are qualified in areas other than social work (e.g. nursing). In addition there are some 13,000 workers in voluntary organisations (e.g. NSPCC or the National Children's Home): 60 per cent of their field workers are qualified.

Although they are servants of the magistrates' court and therefore, cannot be classed as social workers as such, it may be legitimate to regard the 6,000 Probation and After-Care Officers as social workers in the broad sense of the word, bearing in mind the nature of their work (and 10 per cent of them are seconded to prison welfare work). In addition, others may be included such as para-medical groups – occupational therapists or speech therapists, and other professional groups, such as careers officers and certain employment officers (e.g. DROs). It is very much a matter of opinion as to whether we should include such groups as school/college counsellors, youth (problem) advisors or Marriage Guidance counsellors, etc. as these are largely part-time roles.

It is clear then that the area of social work is wide and not clearly delineated. This is partly because the tasks of the social workers are many and varied (they are themselves the result of the history, tradition, legislation and the expectations of society regarding the kind of care which should be provided). Consequently, they may well overlap with the roles of other professional groups, especially since social workers do not have a monopoly of concern for people with problems: clearly many other groups and individuals play a part (just as alongside the 'school teacher' are many other people or organisations who guide, instruct and 'teach' children).

The basic roles of social workers can be described as (i) the assessment and arranging of social care, and (ii) counselling, i.e. face-to-face communication between clients and social workers, in which the latter are helping clients to tolerate (e.g. permanent handicap) or change some aspect of themselves or of the world they live in. These responsibilities arise because individuals cannot provide adequately for themselves. Other, 'indirect', social work is also called for, including such things as recruiting and briefing volunteers, advising residential care staff, etc.

Social work services are available to all, regardless of age, sex or class. But in practice most problems seem to arise from fairly well-established areas, namely, old age, physical handicap, mental disorder, low income and family relationships.

In meeting the various problems, social work is commonly classified into: (i) **casework** or fieldwork (dealing with individual clients or families); (ii) **group work** (with several clients together where they have similar or common problems); and (iii) **community work** (which implies working with local or neighbourhood groups and organisations, or perhaps helping to create them and sustain them, e.g. tenants' groups or community relations associations). In practice individual social workers often engage in all three forms of social work, though some do specialise. Equally a particular client may be involved in all three at various times.

Qualities needed for social work. It has been suggested that certain values lie at the heart of formal social work. These include; (a) respect for all persons, (b) compassion; (c) understanding, (d) sympathy; (e) and a sense of justice or fairness. Whilst these are not unique to social work, they do impose certain obligations or requirements on social workers themselves. First, they need to understand their own personalities, attitudes and prejudices and the ways these may influence their response to clients. They thus need to see each client in the light of his individual characteristics and circumstances, uninfluenced by stereotypes, myths or hearsay.

Secondly, they must have courage and resilience to cope with conflicts and dilemmas (e.g. facing parents where a child goes into care, or where a lack of resources (training places residential accommodation, equipment, activities, etc.) conflicts with what is seen as in the best interests of the client).

Thirdly, they have to respect the clients' rights to confidentiality and (excepting legal restraints) to self-determination, though this may often prove frustrating or difficult to reconcile with recognised norms of behaviour (sometimes pejoratively labelled as 'middle class').

Consequently certain **skills** are called for including (i) skills in human relationships; (ii) skills in analysis (i.e. assessing people, analysing situations, evaluating effects of action taken); (iii) skills in effectiveness (carrying out action which has been planned). These skills further require or presuppose knowledge of two kinds: (a) practical information for immediate use (e.g. on available social services); (b) knowledge which provides insight into human behaviour, organisations and communities. Hence the course content of social work training (see page 399).

Problems and criticisms

A host of problems face social work today. We only have space here to briefly indicate some of these.

1 *Insufficient resources* exist, both for social services in general and for social work services in particular. The Barclay Committee (see page 407) found that 'everywhere there is evidence of unmet need, some of it urgent'. They say that local authority social workers are unlikely to see more than a small proportion of those who might have a claim to their attention and are able to give comparatively little time to most of those they do see.

2   *Residential and day-care* provision are described as the 'Cinderella services of social work' (Barclay Report). This is due partly to the stigma arising from their Poor Law antecedents and partly because of recent moves to integrate some establishments with those for offenders (see page 377). Thus many social workers see residential institutions only as a last resort, whereas for some people it might be appropriate at an early stage. Undoubtedly, with some there are avoidable defects such as rigidly hierarchical and impersonal regimes (children in care using official order books for their personal shopping is a prominent example). Where Social Service Departments (SSDs) have decentralised field social workers, so that they operate from homes and other establishments there is the likelihood of greater understanding and flexibility.

3   *Too big and bureaucratic* is a common criticism. Professor Davies in *The Essential Social Worker*, says that, 'Social workers bring a humanising face, a caring component into the increasingly large-scale welfare setting . . . which . . . can so easily slide into heart-lessness and become alienated from the compassionate thought that fired its orginators.' But social workers themselves may be equally guilty since they work in (post-Seebohm) large LASS departments, and decision-making may be slowed down as there is a need to refer things up the line; and the problem may be exacerbated by poor communications or hostile relations with other agencies (DOH, DOSS, housing departments, voluntary organisations).

4   *Difficult choices* and decisions continuously face social workers, such as taking a child into care, allowing him home on trial, or seeking a client's compulsory admission to psychiatric hospital or removal from his insanitary dwelling. They also play an uncomfortable 'social policing' role, as when they have to investigate, e.g. suspected cases of child or granny battering. Some ask whether control (e.g. probation) is compatible with the caring role. Social workers also have to protect and husband scarce resources and must therefore ration them, decide priorities and ultimately say 'no' to many demanding clients who will then feel resentful.

5   *Sustaining an unjust society* is how some critics describe the social workers' role insofar as they aim to get people to adjust to their problem. The 'radical' social worker seeks to change the system by engaging in struggle (including strikes) for more resources for client services, and he accuses others of covering over the failures of social policy by taking a 'social pathology' view of social problems – which blames the clients for their problems rather than the unfair social order.

6   *Demoralisation and stress* among social workers may be a product of this radical critique. But there are other contributory factors

including expenditure cuts, trade union dissention and public and media criticism (especially in relation to child abuse cases, where social workers often seem to be in a Catch-22 or no-win situation over interfering in families too much or too little). There is also the growing concern over social workers' vulnerability and exposure to violence.

7   *Appropriate training and specialisation* is a continuing problem in any profession. It has never been easy to decide what is appropriate input for social work courses in terms of the relevant core of knowledge and the requisite skills and competencies and their proper combination or balance (in relation to their role in family violence, mental disorder, child abuse, the social consequences of AIDS and the aftermath of tregedies such as Hungerford, Hillsborough and Bradford, the Manchester and M1 aircraft, *The Marchioness*, King's Cross and Clapham. The CQSW appears to be broadly accepted but there are criticisms that it is too academic and irrelevant. And the newer CSS has taken some time to have its credibility confirmed. Recent training reform proposals (which involved merging the two qualifications) were rejected by the Government (see page 401) and created considerable uncertainty. But in 1989 CCETSW launched the new two-year Diploma in Social Work.

But the greater problem is that of reconciling the (generic) family-based approach in social work with the undoubted need for some specialisation. One of the public criticisms revealed by the Barclay Committee came from parents of handicapped children who thought social workers generally to be inadequately expert in that area. Similar doubt in the service provision and compulsory hospitalisation of the mentally disordered has led to legislation requiring the special training of some social workers (see page 164). In practice a balanced generic–specialist approach has often been developed by the setting up of generic social work *teams* containing a mixture of general and specialist social workers (which is rather similar to some doctors in health centres). And the Barclay Committee's research does suggest a general satisfaction about field social workers by clients to the extent of some 66 per cent of those questioned. It was in fact largely because of these widespread uncertainties about the proper role of social work, which these points reveal, that the Government helped to set up the working party inquiry (the Barclay Committee) in 1980.

Social work tomorrow?

The Barclay Report. It is important to realise that the bulk of social care is provided not by the formal statutory or voluntary social services, but by ordinary people acting individually or as members of spontaneously formed local groups. Indeed the Barclay Report, *Social Workers: their role and tasks* (April, 1982), declares that, 'It is difficult to overestimate the importance of the social care that members of communities give each other.'

Because they are so important, the Report recommends that there should be greater support of these informal networks – 'care for the carers' – and that social work should develop a much more **community-oriented** service. 'Social workers . . . need to find ways of developing partnerships between informal carers (including self-help groups), statutory services and voluntary agencies, in which each partner is regarded as a partner whatever the level of resources each brings to their collaborative efforts . . . This partnership is the essence of what we mean by community social work.' It also implies greater de-centralisation and delegation of services, down to area offices and from them down to social workers themselves: see page 402.

Problems and dissent. Such a development in social work has a number of merits: it could lower financial costs; it would bring social services back closer to the community whose problems they serve to meet; and they would fit in with similar developments in other areas (such as community politics and community policing).

Equally it would have to face a number of difficulties including the crumbling of communities through slum clearance, inadequate transport or loss of jobs. There is also the danger that such an approach will increase the disparities in level for different parts of each local authority area or among different client groups, particularly since some communities have very little community identity or network, and other communities can be very hostile or ungenerous to certain individuals and groups in their midst. Difficulties may also arise from allowing greater participation by the community in decisions on the allocation of resources. Finally, it might increase the burden on social workers themselves as they find their loyalties being stretched in various directions.

The Barclay Report also contained two notes of dissent. On one side, Professor Pinker disagrees with the move to greater community social work, believing that the client-centred, casework approach is basically the right one for social work. In some ways he sees the suggested more local system of social services as a return to the Poor Law (see page 5) with the stigma arising from being known to be 'in trouble' by your neighbours.

Conversely, Professor Hadley feels that the Report does not go far enough in advocating the community approach. He argues strongly for a 'patch system' of social work. This comprises very local social service offices (at neighbourhood, street or village level) with the teams of local social workers integrating far more closely with other social service agencies (e.g. primary health care and local voluntary organisations) and with the informal caring networks (friends, relatives and neighbours).

However, the Barclay Report was not seeking to provide a blueprint or uniform pattern for social work. It aimed at producing ideas and indicating possibilities: unlike Seebohm, there is no intention to legislate on this. Clearly it is up to individual LASS departments and social work teams to alter their patterns of work or not as they feel appropriate in the interest of the service to clients.

Volunteers and voluntary organisations

The Voluntary Sector

Outside the State or statutory sector social services may be provided by (i) the informal network of carers (family, etc, including those many young children who look after their disabled parent(s)), (ii) self-help groups who organise (formally or not) to protect or promote the interest of members (e.g. tenants' groups, mother-and-toddler groups), (iii) formally organised voluntary bodies and charities whose object is essentially to help others (e.g. Relate/Marriage Guidance, Samaritans, Mencap, Dr Barnardo's, Spastics Society); in 1988 there were 154,000 charities registered with the Charities Commission – claimed to be the largest number for any nation, and most belonging to the National Council of Voluntary Organisations, (iv) commercial provision (e.g. private nurseries, private schools, nursing homes, hospitals, private social workers, etc.). But in contrast to professional social work most people in the voluntary sector of social care are untrained and unpaid i.e. they are volunteer amateurs (though some larger voluntary organisations do have salaried staffs and rigorous professional training, e.g NSPCC, MG, Shelter).

A day in the life of a social worker

Into the office: consult desk diary for day's commitments; query from secretary typing my (yesterday's) case notes.
Some mail: letter of reply from DOSS *re* case of Mrs A; 2 letters from clients (about housing and finance).
Query from colleague *re* her new client: we discuss what I know about the client from previous experience.
Team meeting: mainly concerned with allocation (of new cases) but team leader (senior social worker) also (a) outlines new arrangement for juvenile police liaison; (b) indicates imminent

staff changes, (c) invites volunteers to help with proposed summer play scheme; (d) explains progress on new community centre for young mentally handicapped (joint venture with Health Authority). Some discussion on these; also on a particular long-term case involving local family. Questions *re* impact of forthcoming mental health legislation; some discussion on recently installed filing system. Student/trainee introduced to team.

Write up some case notes from yesterday's visits and office calls.

Several phone calls in and out – one is urgent: have to leave office for possible 'section' case (for compulsory mental hospital admission); meet doctor at house of client (depressed following wife's death, acting irrationally and danger to himself)? Calms down: we decide against section.

Go straight to (late) appointment with client: not at home.

To another: Les (unemployed) and Jen (slow and not very capable), daughter age 3; problems with money and generally coping; some risk of non-accidental injury (NAI)? Discuss possible stay in Family Rehabilitation Centre; encourage continuation of debt repayments.

Back to office after quick, late lunch: write up notes; letters (*re* Family Centre, etc.) and phone calls.

(Social workers also have a 'duty day' when they deal with new (intake) 'walk in' cases involving such problems as unsatisfactory housing, family argument, advice on care for granny, accommodation for teenage mum, etc. Periodically they may be on call after normal office hours.)

With the rise of state social services, it is easy to overlook the important role still played by the voluntary sector. Yet as the Prime Minister said:

The Government recognise that there are very real limits to what the Government – to what any Government – can do through expenditure on social services. On many problems – juvenile delinquency perhaps and certainly loneliness in old age – there is a limit to what Government can do directly to tackle the root problem. In the latter case the role of voluntary organisations is not just a useful adjunct to Government services but it is fundamental and irreplaceable. This is not just a ritual acknowledgement of the work of voluntary organisations. Nor is it a plea for unpaid assistance in hard-pressed public services. It is a recognition of the distinct, indispensable and socially invaluable role that the voluntary organisations now play in tackling social problems and creating a better society. Nor is the role of voluntary organisations simply at the local community level.

There is also a central role in the formulation of social policy at national level. (Harold Wilson, 1975).

He said that although the State can do a great deal to meet basic requirements, voluntary groups can offer a form of service which the State is ill-fitted to provide – namely, in the area of personal social services. That is what voluntary organisations – in addition to their legitimate work as pressure groups – are best fitted, perhaps uniquely so, to provide. The answer therefore is a *partnership* (sometimes called 'welfare pluralism' or 'mixed economy') between the organised community and voluntary effort.

The Government, in making decisions on priorities – decisions which are far from easy or pleasant – must never lose sight of the objectives of social policy. In simple terms, priority must be given to enabling everyone to have a full share in our society. That is why adult literacy is so important, or hostels in the community for the mentally handicapped. Poverty is degrading. This is true where poverty brings material deprivation and, as in so many countries, hunger and starvation. But it is also true where poverty separates a person from the normal life of the society. In deciding on priorities in social policy we must never lose sight of how policies will affect the place of the individual and family in society.

Mr Wilson also drew attention to a report of the Central Policy Review Staff (the 'think-tank' or advisers of the Cabinet, abolished 1983) entitled 'A Joint Framework for Social Policies' (HMSO), which had implications for policy for all the voluntary organisations. The Home Office has a Voluntary Services Unit to promote and monitor voluntary provision.

What is a good volunteer?

Would-be volunteers should first make contact with the local Council of Social (or Voluntary) Service, Social Services Bureau or Volunteer Centre, or the CAB. These should know where there is immediate need and should ascertain what particular interest or skill the would-be volunteer has.

The volunteer should be informed of the nature of the work he will undertake, the need for regularity and the prospect of training in some cases. Certain services demand training, e.g. Red Cross, St John Ambulance Brigade, Relate/Marriage Guidance. Others may require little more than visiting the old or bedfast. It is impossible here to cover the whole of the volunteer spectrum.

The rewards of voluntary service are spiritual, in the main, though active elderly folk who volunteer are less likely to become geriatric cases themselves, and the fulfilled middle-aged woman who is actively involved in helping others is less likely to haunt doctors' surgeries for tranquillisers or to make her children's lives a misery by her own complaints. A healthy outgoing activity is an insurance against what has been described as 'well-heeled boredom and self-absorption'.

A good volunteer falls into no particular class, belongs to no particular profession or age-group, and may be motivated by religious duty or merely a desire to do some good to his fellow human. The main challenge is to ensure that intelligent, well-informed and useful volunters cooperate with others in the professional paid services so that good relations are maintained between the two sectors.

Advantages of voluntary organisations and volunteers are:

1   Freedom from central or local government control and 'red tape'.
2   Experimental, pioneering and initiating persons or groups who devise new forms of aid (especially for unfavoured minority groups, e.g. 'gays', unmarried mothers, gamblers, HIV or AIDS sufferers etc.). The hospice movement is a prominent illustration; see page 116.
3   Flexible and can act quickly to help those in immediate need.
4   Useful in 'neighbourhood care' in providing both *self-help* and *mutual help*, e.g. where A and B are both disabled, A does for B what B cannot do for himself, and B does for A what A cannot do for himself.
5   Useful in breaking down barriers between institutions and the community, e.g where an inmate of an institution is helped to re-establish himself by a volunteer who befriends him (takes him for a drink, or to a club, meeting, match etc.) – known as 'building bridges'.
6   Outlets for religious feeling, social care, goodwill and generosity.
7   Cheaper at a time when social services are becoming more costly. Thus a number of SSDs (e.g. Kent, Gateshead) are contracting out some of their services with local voluntary organisations so that services can be provided on a domiciliary basis rather than having to place clients (such as the frail elderly) in the more expensive residential care. (See also 10 below.)
8   Useful as pressure group for reform; critical of service shortcomings, alerting authorities to gaps. They may press for reform (e.g. Welfare of Children in Hospital Association, a group of mothers fighting to improve hospital care for children and parental rights of access during treatment) or may seek to make their own provision to fill official gap (e.g. Women's Aid, providing shelters for battered wives).

Table 13 Selected advisory and counselling services

United Kingdom	Branches/centres (numbers)			Numbers and thousands — Clients (thousands)		
	1971	1981	1986	1971	1981	1986
Al-Anon Family Groups	135	612	892	1.2	7.3	10.7
Alcoholics Anonymous	420	1,550	2,200	6.3	30.0	35.5
Catholic Marriage Advisory Council	63	68	81	2.5	3.3	9.9
Citizens Advice Bureaux	512	914	1,123	1,500.0	4,514.6	7,277.2
Cruse	13	73	122	5.0	9.1	12.3
Disablement Information and Advice Services		44	82		40.0	250.0
Law Centres	1	41	54	1.0	155.0	160.0
Leukaemia Care Society	1	21	27	0.2	1.7	4.0
National Marriage Guidance Council	141	178	166	21.6	38.3	45.2
Samaritans	127	170	182	87.0	303.8	393.0
Young People's Counselling and Advisory Services		55	88		30.0	47.0

Note: (Some figures are for Britain, proximate years, or may refer to cases/inquiries rather than clients.)
Source: Social Trends, 1988

9   Provides interest and work for those who are otherwise out of work.
10   Provides clients with a choice of service ('Welfare pluralism').
11   Ex-clients may provide a source of volunteers.
12   Can specialise with particular client groups (e.g. by age or problem/symptom) compared with generic LASS social worker.

Some of the *disadvantages* of volunteers and voluntary organisations are:

1   Their methods of work may be out of date.
2   Usually lack training and may be inefficient, lack time, resources, urgency.
3   Frequently duplicating the services already supplied officially.
4   May be unreliable and inconsistent, and create unjustified variations in standards of provision (whereas a statutory framework of provision can ensure equitable distribution).
5   Volunteers may cause industrial unrest among the paid professional social workers, e.g. where redundancies of paid staff are threatened by the increasing use of unpaid volunteers.
6   Usually available only in evenings and at week-ends. Social work continues throughout the 24 hours of each day.
7   Lack of public accountability.
8   May ameliorate problems and so unwittingly conceal them.

These are generalisations only. There are wide differences among voluntary organisations: some are generously supported financially, well-informed and trained (e.g. through the Institute of Welfare Officers), professionally staffed, energetic and pioneering. Such make a unique contribution in the field of social welfare and care.

The future

The Wolfenden Report, (*The Future of Voluntary Organisations*, 1977), urged public authorities to provide more support for voluntary organisations and help them to expand, partly because demand for welfare help of all kinds shows no sign of diminishing and statutory services cannot go on expanding. It was pointed out that the voluntary contribution in total amounted to about 16 million hours of work each week, which was equivalent in terms of man-hours to that of all paid staff in local authority personal social services departments. A survey 1981 showed that nearly a quarter of those over 16 undertook some voluntary work in the community (*Social Trends*, 1984). An estimate for 1986 suggested that 18 million did some voluntary work in that year. And in a survey in 1988 some 27 per cent of people claimed to do some voluntary work at least once a month (though this would include work with animal charities, private schools etc.).

The Report points out that while some consider that the family and the community are in decline, there is plenty of evidence that informal systems of caring survive and remain extremely important. A relatively small amount of assistance can have dramatic effects in enabling initiatives to get going and at a fraction of the cost of providing comparable service publicly. The Government's (1976) 'Good Neighbour' scheme (not to be confused with the 'Neighbour-hood Watch' scheme: see page 393) is a good example in seeking to promote and reinforce informal caring. But the Report suggests that more ambitious developments should include funding local social development through the medium of 'animateurs' whose task is to spark off new organisations and back up existing ones. The Report recommended the Government to devote an extra £2.5 million a year to 'intermediary bodies' such as local councils of voluntary service, rural community councils and other bodies able to help and support local groups.

In recent years, **charities** have developed a much higher profile e.g. the telethon for 'Children in Need' and the huge rock concerts, Live Aid, Food Aid, Sport Aid, Comic Relief etc. for international appeals for aid for Ethiopian famine or the Armenian earthquake.

There is much more sponsored fund-raising both by individuals and by businesses. Businesses also contribute through donations (e.g. Marks & Spencer £3 million, BP £2.5 million, ICI £1.4 million, Natwest £1.3 million in 1986) or by establishing foundations (such as those promoting research including such renowned ones as Nuffield, Woolfson, Wellcome, Leverhulme). And there are regular business contributions through schemes such as the Council for Charitable Support, the Per Cent Club (i.e. a percentage of profit) and Business in the Community (BiC). Altogether charities raise over £12,500 million a year, and according to the Charity Aid Foundation's publication *Charity Trends* net income to charities has risen by 90 per cent in real terms between 1976–86 (during which time the number of charities has risen by 27 per cent – and for both of these figures, 'charities' includes private schools, housing associations etc.).

The Government itself contributes a great deal – over £3 billion in tax foregone (as charitable status confers exemption from taxation) and further encouragement has been given recently in the 'Give as you Earn' or payroll giving scheme, where contributions (of up to £240 a year) enjoy tax relief (and this latter sum also goes to the charity).

Overall, however, the increased sums reflect generally rising incomes rather than increased generosity. Business donations have remained at 0.2 per cent of pre-tax profits since 1982. And while the figures mean that the average household makes donations of £70 a year, the true figure (which ignores the few big donors) amounts to just 0.25 per cent of gross income, which compares to over 2 per cent in the USA.

Charities themselves have become much more business-like in their general management and fund-raising. Indeed many are appointing full-time, professional fund-raisers. As a result they may begin to lose some of their advantages as they become big, more bureaucratic and inflexible and perhaps less approachable. There is mounting concern, too, at the accountability and openness of many charities; at the way they secure their funds and the ways they dispose of them, both in terms of efficiency, compared to waste, and effectiveness, in directing their resources at their primary goal – the clients. There is the added risk of accepting Government aid and of becoming political e.g. as with housing associations taking over council housing (see page 282).

The role of the voluntary sector is certain to increase (though some have been badly hit by the ending of the Community Programme: see page 332). Not only are there more potential willing hands as more people retire, but there is more encouragement from the Government for the 'active citizen' (through urban programmes, crime prevention, 'crime stoppers' etc.). But some people are uneasy about this for they see the proper role of voluntary organisations as filling the gaps left in State welfare, whereas they are now beginning to be used as substitutes for State provision (e.g. the replacement of council houses by housing associations or the administration of the Social Fund (see page 56) where officials are required to refer claimants to local trusts and charities).

In short the impulse to social service is still powerful in our society as witnessed by the number of applicants to the caring professions and it is practical common sense to encourage volunteers and their organisations to continue and flourish and to work alongside their official and salaried counterparts as efficiently as possible.

Government response to Griffiths Report on community care (1988)

In 1989 the Government announced its broad acceptance of the Griffiths proposals (see pages 138, 140, 153 and 163) with a view to implementation in 1991. Local authorities are to be given the key role in planning and developing community care; they are also to secure its provision either directly or, especially, by enabling others (voluntary, private etc.) to provide. Money will be transferred from social security spending on private residential care (see page 135) to local authorities who will use it to assess needs and decide appropriate packages of care (private, voluntary, LA homes or – ideally – domiciliary), and there will be a specific grant disbursed by health authorities for local councils to develop social care for the mentally ill. Local authority homes are to be subject to inspection. (See the White Paper, HMSO, October 1989.)

Questions

1 Briefly explain the origins of social work.
2 There are various kinds of social workers. Name the more important.
3 Trace the history and describe the present-day organisation of training and qualifications for social work.
4 Enumerate the qualities needed for successful social work, and indicate how far these qualities may be evoked or improved by training.
5 What is the Central Council for Education and Training in Social Work?
6 What are the advantages and disadvantages of voluntary organisations?
7 Indicators of success in local government may be (a) convenience and (b) efficiency. How would you establish whether a PSS department is successful?
8 Discuss the suggestion of giving greater priority to community social work.
9 Find out how many voluntary organisations there are in your area. Choose one and examine it closely. Compare your study with someone else's.
10 Six major strategies or methods for social work intervention are: (a) counselling, (b) behaviour modification, (c) task-centred case work, (d) group work, (e) life skills training, (f) welfare rights/financial counselling. Find out what each involves and discuss their relative merits.

15
Finance and the social services

A popular joke among comedians is the one about the photograph which shows the drain down which the Government pours all our money. In this section we shall be examining this 'drain' in some detail, paying particular attention to that part of it which affects the social services.

The National Income of any country is the value of what that nation produces in a year. It is the equivalent of what everyone receives in income from wages, profits, rent or interest over the 12-month period. The figures in Table 14 show that in recent years about half of this National Income passes through the hands of the State, by way of taxation, licence fees, fines, charges or loans. Some is spent on goods and services, such as buying tanks or paying the wages of civil servants, soldiers and local government staff. The rest, over 40 per cent, is simply transferred to people (through pensions, employment subsidies, capital investment grants, etc.) for them to spend.

What is significant is that half of all State expenditure goes on the social services: excluding employment and probation, this amounts to £86,400 million (1986) which is a quarter of the National Income (GDP). Table 14 shows that this figure has grown enormously since 1890. The Welfare State really is the creation of the twentieth century, despite the solid foundations of the nineteenth century. Yet when we look back at the growing commitment of the State to give everyone a free health and education service (among others), it is hardly surprising that the cost of it all should be so enormous.

Meeting the cost of the social services

This is the problem: how do we pay for it all? In some ways it is easier today than it was at the beginning of the century. In earlier decades many people questioned the desirability of, and objected to, the expenditure itself, not just to the taxation to pay for it. These days we all, more or less, accept the validity of the social services though we may quibble about particular expenditures. The social services have become part of our way of life, and many people cherish the 'social

Table 14 The social services and their cost

Year	Public (State) Expenditure		Expenditure on Social Services		
	£m	Percentage of GDP	£m	Percentage of Public Expenditure	Percentage of GDP
1890	130	9	27	21	1.9
1900	270	15	50	18	2.6
1928	1,000	25	435	40	9.6
1955	6,000	37	2,740	45	16.3
1968	18,000	49	8,700	48	24.3
1975	54,465	58	28,277	52	30.0
1977	61,900	50	32,056	52	26.0
1980	103,700	45	59,200	57	26.0
1983	116,000	50	71,500	61	31.0
1986	164,600	51	86,500	54	27.0

Source: Peacock and Wiseman. *The Growth of Public Expenditure, Annual Abstract of Statistics,* and *Economic Trends,* HMSO.

Table 15   Expenditure on main social services

Service	£m 1986	(1976)	Percentage 1986	(1976)
Education	17,500	(7,423)	20	(23)
Health	17,500	(6,234)	20	(20)
Housing and environment	4,300	(5,195)	5	(16)
Personal social services	3,500	(1,208)	4	(4)
Social security	47,800	(11,527)	51	(36)
Total (rounded)	86,500	(32,056)	100	(100)

Source: *National Income and Expenditure, Annual Abstract of Statistics, Social Trends*, HMSO.

wage', i.e. benefits derived from public social expenditure. Our problem is meeting the huge and growing bill. At present the cost of the social services generally is met in the following ways:

> 70 per cent from **taxes** and rates
> 20 per cent from **insurance contributions**
> 10 per cent from **charges**

These figures are only approximate, and for any particular service the proportions may be quite different. For example, charges cover about 30 per cent of housing expenditure (in the form of rents), whereas they only bring in about 5 per cent of the money needed for the NHS, and in social security contributions finance about 60 per cent of expenditure.

Can we afford the social services?

Before we answer this question we might first ask: can we afford to be *without* the social services? What would happen if we were to abolish State education or the NHS and personal social services? If taxes were correspondingly cut, no doubt people could afford to buy similar services from private sources, but low-income groups would suffer and other groups simply may not spend their incomes on such services sufficiently. In many ways the whole purpose of the social services is to maintain the welfare of the nation, especially where individual people would not do this themselves: for example, those who do not save adequately for their old age may be forced to do so through a State superannuation scheme. Similarly, there is an element of national self-interest in compulsory schooling. This raises moral and philosophical questions about such issues as self-reliance and freedom (echoing the arguments of J. S. Mill and T. H. Green at the end of the nineteenth century). Modern discussion is to be found in the works of Hayek, Popper, Friedman, Titmuss and Rawls, but space forbids that we delve into this here.

Briefly we must say that there are three views on social services:

1 The first sees the social services as the expensive product of a wealthy society: it sees them as perhaps desirable but not essential. At most, this views the social services as a **residual** element in society, i.e. providing a 'safety net' or guaranteed minimum, especially by focusing on the weaker members of the community. This is often expressed as 'selectivity'.

2 The second point of view may be called the **insitutional** view, for it sees the social services as an essential part of the fabric of any modern society with the services aiming to provide a national optimum standard rather than just a minimum. Exponents of this view often hold what is called the 'universalist' view, whereby benefits are available to everyone irrespective of their circumstances. They dislike the more selective approach because it is divisive: claimants become identified, labelled and humiliated. They see the social services as a means of achieving a more egalitarian society through the redistribution of the nation's resources to the less well off, be it in money, health or intellect.

3 These two points of view, drastically summarised here, really reflect different approaches to the issue of what kind of society we want. The third view is much more down to earth. It sees the social services quite simply as something we are 'stuck with' regardless of their desirability. This view is rather shallow and cynical but probably realistic. After all, what politician is going to risk unpopularity by advocating the dismantling of the Welfare State? (as did the government's 'Think Tank' report in 1982).

The growing demand

It is easy for people to say 'cut expenditure', but not so easy for them to say precisely where the cuts should fall. In fact, many of these same people will, in the next breath, be asking for more spending on a particular project such as a local hospital or school. Indeed, there is an endless list of justifiable calls for increased expenditure: smaller classes in schools, help for single-parent families, homes for the elderly, or closer supervision of children at risk.

There are, in fact, certain factors which are bound to raise costs or create further demands on the social services. These are:

1 The **growth in population.** By 2001 it is estimated that Britain will contain another 2 million people, of which about ½ million will be

people aged 65 and over. Indeed, those aged over 75 will increase by nearly one third; and the average person aged 75 or over costs the health and personal social services seven times the cost of a person of working age.

2 **Rising expectations.** As we have seen, people are not content with present standards of housing or education. Indeed, every new advance in, say, medical technology raises people's expectations, and perhaps has to be introduced despite its great cost (e.g. organ transplanting). In 1948 it was claimed that as people became healthier under its aegis so the NHS would 'wither away'. We have now discovered that the demand for health is in fact unending.

3 **Discovering new needs.** The discovery of further unmet needs continues. For example, in the later nineteenth century compulsory education led teachers to discover serious deprivation among children; today, Probation and After Care uncovers housing and family problems among its clients. In recent years the Government has deliberately sought to locate unmet needs through surveys – for example, under the *Chronically Sick and Disabled Persons Act, 1970* – or through greater publicity of the services available. Similarly, there are many housing and welfare rights groups springing up across the country, and some social security claimants have formed influential 'unions'.

4 **Unemployment.** Today we have high levels of post-war unemployment, at over 2 million. This immediately increased social security claims, with each unemployed person costing between £4,000 and £5,000 a year in benefits and lost taxes (i.e. over £12 billion p.a. in all). But it has longer term effects, such as increasing ill health or creating family stress (see page 112). But perhaps above all is the effect it will have on unemployed young people (20 per cent of the 16–24 age group are out of work). If unemployed school-leavers develop a cynical and jaundiced view of society, this may lead to many social problems, of which perhaps the inner city violence of 1980 and 1981 (in Bristol, Brixton and Liverpool and the miners' strike against pit closures in 1984) were but an indication.

5 **Family patterns.** There have been a number of significant developments in our population and family structures in recent years. As we have seen (page 126) more people are surviving into old age and those (more dependent) over 75 are increasing rapidly. Secondly, young people are becoming independent of their families at earlier ages and living apart from them. Up to 1985, we were also experiencing a bulge or peak in the 18-plus population – and this implies more marriage and increased household formation. Finally, there is the well-publicised but no less real increase in divorce (at 150,000 p.a.) and family breakdown, so that 1 in 8 families are now headed by a single parent (of which

100,000 are men). These developments increase need and thus calls on all the major social services (housing, PSS, benefits).

6 **Inflation.** We are all adversely affected by rising prices, but it may be that the social services are affected more than average because (i) low-income groups tend to fall behind, at least in the short run, in the 'incomes scramble', and so have a justifiably bigger call on the social services, and (ii) the social services tend to be labour-intensive and with the rise in the wages bill in recent years find their costs tend to rise faster than average. To deal with inflation we are obliged (at least on 'monetarist' principles) to reduce public expenditure. This will reduce State borrowing (PSBR) which should cut the money supply and inflation. It will also cut taxation and what many feel as the tax burden on incentives to work, innovate and re-structure industry. Finally, less State spending should release resources for productive private invest-ment. Since social services are such a large part of public expendi-ture, they too must be cut. It should be noted that such '**cuts**' may mean any one of three things. First it can mean a reduction in *planned* increases which aimed to improve the standard of service (e.g. more psychiatric hostel places or more class-contact hours for GCSE students). Secondly it may mean real cuts in the sense that an increase in need is allowed to occur unmatched by an expansion in services to meet it (e.g. residential places or home visits to the growing number of over-75s). Thirdly there may be a positive cut in expenditure on services for a growing or stable need (e.g. university places or house building/renovation).

However, it can be argued that spending on social services is itself a **productive** investment e.g. health care or education provision in-creases the productivity of the labour force; good housing improves health and morale; and social security arrangements can help pen-sions funds provide a useful form of saving; and social security payments can help support or stabilise the economy in times of recession. In addition it can be shown that overall tax and State expenditure levels as a percentage of National Income in Britain are only about average for industrial countries generally, and indeed our social expenditure is significantly lower than some.

Alternative sources of finance

Finding the money for the social services is a big problem. Here we can only indicate some of the possible strategies which may be used:

1 **Taxation.** This is the biggest source of revenue (see pages 420 and 471) and has the merit of spreading the burden over society as a

whole. Income tax is also equitable in that it is progressive, taking more from the better off. But it is said that income tax (and rates) have reached the limit of what people are prepared to pay. If this is so the Government could perhaps shift the emphasis to indirect taxes (e.g. VAT), though this might be inflationary and less equitable. If, however, incomes continue to rise through inflation, the Government may take no action, but rely instead on the extra revenue which results from 'fiscal drag' (i.e. as incomes rise so more people become liable to tax as they cross the tax 'threshold'. Thus there is more tax revenue even though rates of tax remain unchanged). In 1977 tax allowances were 'indexed' to the rate of inflation; but this ceased in 1981 and consequently even the low paid become subject to tax and feel the impact of the cost of social services, especially with the introduction of the community charge (or poll tax) in 1988–90.

2   **Contributions.** The National Insurance contribution is revenue which is earmarked by the Government for expenditure in a particular service (social security and the NHS). It may be that such contributions are regarded with somewhat less hostility than taxes. If this is so, there may be scope to increase contribution rates. Yet many people see them as just another tax, and these rates have already increased significantly in recent years (from 6.5 to 9 per cent 1978–84) so that any further increase may just lead to bigger wage demands. Employers too are already paying a heavy rate of 11.45 per cent on each employee's earnings, and although they might acquiesce in a further increase this could lead to further redundancies or their simply passing on the increase to consumers through price increases.

3   **Charges.** These provide such a small source of revenue that any more would have to be enormous to be worthwhile. If the range of charges was extended (e.g. to include visits to the doctor) this would hit the lower paid and raise the issue of 'selectivity' in the social services (see page 453). On the other hand, some nominal charges might diminish the abuse which is alleged to occur in some services. In recent years charges have been increased for school meals, rents, leisure, library and health services.

4   **Voluntary services.** These could perhaps be encouraged to expand and thus replace and supplement some aspects of public social services. This is indeed already happening in many fields – e.g. friendly visiting, adult literacy. But the scope here must be limited because voluntary services and charities are also squeezed by rising costs of inflation and the diminished resources of former volunteers, some of whom are now unemployed. There have also been cuts in local authority grants.

5   **Reappraisal of priorities.** This can refer to (i) public expenditure generally: is there e.g. scope for reducing still further expenditure

on defence or roads to pay for, say, health and housing? (ii) Within the social services sector is there any way we can assess whether we are spending too much on, say, health to the detriment of housing or education? (iii) Within a social service, have we got the right balance between expenditure on, say, the universities and the nursery schools, or welfare services for the elderly compared to the handicapped?

6 **Private provision.** An alternative to raising charges is to 'hive off' or 'privatise' some statutory social services to private enterprise in the form of private schooling, private hospitals, private insurance, etc. This raises similar issues to those in 4 above, and the suggestion that the services may be run more efficiently in private hands opens up the whole question of efficiency. Another approach is commercial **sponsoring** e.g. a firm's financing a student through university or providing a school with a 'lollipop' road crossing patrol.

7 **Savings and efficiency.** Without the margin of 'fat' created by economic growth, all social services must be constantly cost-conscious. This does not just refer to savings on post, telephones or fuel: it implies an examination of working methods, work schedules and machinery for coordination to avoid overlap between, say, social workers and probation officers. It may imply spending now to save in the future, as with the policy of discharging people from institutions into community care service, or the provision of family planning or preventive medicine. Or it may entail attempts to substitute capital for expensive labour, as with automated hospital equipment or factory-built housing components. However, with any service it is never easy to assess or measure efficiency. How does a senior officer, or indeed the client himself, know whether his social worker is efficient or not? Is it really efficiency when hospital costs are decreased by discharging patients early if the hidden cost then falls on the household who provide the after care? What is the effect on a village when its small school is closed or on a secondary school when it loses its sixth form to a college?

Yet there are some areas where real savings may be made. In the field of health for example, there are unexplained variations between say bed-stays for the same operation (e.g. 9½ days in Leeds, 6½ in Nottingham). Oxford Health Authority plans to save £16 million 1983–93 by shifting health care from hospital to community provision, with more day-care surgery and shorter admissions for maternity patients. Above all, so much ill-health and its costs are avoidable, e.g. excess consumption of alcohol or smoking (described by the Minister as 'the single most preventable cause of death and disease'). Recent reports on heart disease and cancer have drawn attention to the widespread lack of exercise and bad eating habits (with our diet comprising an excess of fats, sugar and processed foods).

It is claimed that 90 per cent of health is a product of social, political and economic forces rather than medicine. (e.g. See the *Black Report*, DHSS, 1980). But managing those forces in the interests of better health involves political action – and many of the affected interests wield considerable political influence.

In times of recession, it is argued that social welfare must take a 'back seat'; that we cannot afford the same level of social services, since they are dependent on the state of the economy. This seems commonsense. And yet, social services may be seen as a factor of production, i.e. as a contributor to economic growth: they not only help to produce fit or educated workers, but also, perhaps a body of citizens who share a sense of fairness, community and security (though some may question the sense of community derived from large welfare bureaucracies, e.g. DHSS). In this sense, adequate social provision may be regarded as a pre-condition of the thriving economy.

This section has raised more questions than answers. In the end choices will have to be made. They will probably reflect a mixture of internal pressures (Cabinet 'wets and dries' i.e. spenders and cutters), public outcry (remember Kimberley Carlile, Maria Colwell or 'Cathy Come Home'?), administrative techniques (e.g. programme budgeting, performance indicators, zero-based budgeting, cost-benefit analysis), politics (party and non-party), sheer inertia and arbitrary cuts in spending and service provision.

Questions

1 How much do we spend on the social services? Approximately what proportion goes on each service?
2 Why is there increasing demand for resources for the social services?
3 Name and briefly explain two differing views of the role of the social services.
4 In what ways do we pay for the social services?
5 Suggest three ways of raising additional finance for the social services.
6 If you had to reduce expenditure on the social services, state which (a) service or which (b) part of that service you would choose. Give reasons.
7 Find out what your local authority spends (i) on each major service, (ii) on particular social services. Has the pattern changed in the last 10 years, and why?
8 Conduct a small survey asking people if they would prefer cuts in taxes and rates or cuts in services.

16
Complaints: how to make them

General

In the best of all possible worlds there would be no need for complaints. Everyone would be happy, kind and considerate, and the system of government (if one were needed) would ensure that all stayed that way. Alas, poverty and injustice exist in the real world. The system fails to offer the remedies, it creaks and breaks down, the 'shoe pinches' and people start to complain.

In this book we deal with *services* which are provided by the central Government, local authorities and other bodies, all staffed by human beings who are expected to work efficiently and well. We do not deal with the provision of goods by private industry or shopkeepers. In general, complaints about goods are settled by the buyer complaining to the retailer directly. If he does not provide suitable goods the consumers can take their custom elsewhere. The shopkeeper's business suffers and he may eventually go bankrupt. No such fate awaits the Government or local authorities in normal circumstances. The customer has no choice; he cannot take his custom elsewhere (unless he can afford to 'go private').

Complaints about Government or local authority services or the public corporations (British Rail, Post Office, NHS and others) tend to increase as these bodies proliferate. If a service is bad we can moan about it with a friend or neighbour. If it is very bad we can complain effectively by approaching someone who has it in his power to alter the system for the better – for example, our MP, local councillor, the chairman of a public board, a consumer council or the Post Office Users' National Council, to get matters put right. If you do not know how to complain, visit the Citizens Advice Bureaux to find out the best approach, and write.

Complaints are so varied and numerous that it is impossible to categorise them into neat classes. Many social services have special provision for dealing with clients' complaints. These are called **tribunals**, panels or committees and they take the form of comparatively informal hearings before a small group of neutral people. Thus, it may be possible to appeal in this way on matters of social security payments, disablement assessment, mental hospitalisation, dismissal from employment, denial of the school of your choice, wrongful tax or rateable value assessment, rent or children in care. There are others, but services and possible complaints are so varied that it is impossible to cover them all or indeed to categorise them into neat classes. In any particular case, a local authority officer or councillor or the CAB can advise. Otherwise we may say that broadly there are: (1) minor complaints; (2) complaints of maladministration; and (3) legal complaints.

Minor complaints

Generally these complaints arise where we have suffered no real injury or loss. They range from uncleanliness in offices, discourtesy, off-handedness by staff, delay in handling requests from the public and so on.

We all forget that it is the small things in life which create happiness and make life much more agreeable. A smile, a gesture, a friendly helping hand can work wonders. Equally, a discourtesy from a bombastic civil servant or local government official who cannot be bothered with a young student or an old-age pensioner can cause unpleasantness far beyond what he imagined. 'Civility costs nothing, and buys everything.' (Lady Montagu). 'Manner is *something* with everyone, and *everything* with some.' How a service is rendered is mightily important.

How you deal with small complaints depends on you. You may complain to the individual's superior officer there and then, and confront him with the situation. You can go home and write a letter to the local authority or Government department. If you are going to complain, deal with the matter early. Do not wait a week or a month.

That is one way. You can, of course, just forgive and forget it. Why waste time? Life is short and there is no need to dwell on trivialities, however incensed you may be; and you may feel better about the incident after you have slept on it. If it is a small matter do not use a sledgehammer to crack a nut. Small complaints, therefore, need not detain us. One word of caution – if you are complaining about a person or his manner officially do not over-state your case. Give the facts and leave them to speak for themselves.

Complaints of maladministration

Maladministration refers to *the way* in which a Government department's or a local authority's decision has been taken. Maladministration may be taken to cover administrative action (or inaction) based on or influenced by improper considerations or conduct. Arbitrariness, malice or bias, including unfair discrimination, are examples of improper considerations. Neglect, unjustifiable delay, incompetence, failure to observe relevant rules or procedures, failure to take relevant considerations into account, failure to establish or review procedures where there is a duty or obligation on a body to do so or the use of faulty systems are examples of improper conduct. As regards local authorities, the Local Government Commissioner has no power to question the merits of a decision taken without maladministration.

The Parliamentary Commissioner for Administration

In Scandinavian countries this official is known as the **Ombudsman**. Following the White Paper 'The Parliamentary Commissioner for Administration' (Cmnd. 2767), published in October, 1965, Parliament passed the *Parliamentary Commissioner Act, 1967*, which created the post of Ombudsman.

The Act provided for the appointment of the Commissioner by Letters Patent. The Act provided that he shall not be a member of the House of Commons or of the Senate or House of Commons of Northern Ireland; that his salary (£62,000 per annum) and pension shall be paid out of the Consolidated Fund; and that he may only be removed from office by an Address from both Houses of Parliament. The retirement age is 65.

Areas covered. A schedule to the Act lists the departments and authorities subject to investigation. Broadly these include all the Government departments and other 'authorities' which include the Public Trustee, the Public Records Office, Registry of Friendly Societies, the Royal Mint and bodies ancilliary to or under the supervision of a Government department or minister. The departments and bodies subject to investigation must exercise functions 'on behalf of the Crown'.

How may a complaint be made?

A has a complaint of maladministration in respect of some act or omission by the Department of Health and Social Security. *A* now wishes to complain to the Parliamentary Commissioner for Administration.

(a)   *A* makes a **written** complaint to an MP.
(b)   The complaint must amount to **maladministration**.
(c)   *A* **consents** to the reference to the Commissioner.
(d)   The MP **refers complaint** to the Commissioner.
(e)   MP **requests investigation** into the complaint.

Matters not Subject to Investigation

The Commission will not investigate any matter where *A*, the aggrieved person, has a right of appeal or review before a statutory tribunal (e.g. National Insurance Tribunal), or where *A* has a remedy in a court, unless in the latter case *A* has a reasonable excuse for not taking proceedings.

The following matters are specifically excluded:

(a) **Foreign relations.** Dealings between governments or international organisations.

(b) **Ambassadors, consuls.** Action by, outside the UK.

(c) **HM dominions.** Action by Dominion Governments outside the United Kingdom.

(d) **Extradition and fugitive offenders.** Action taken to retrieve offenders who escape from the United Kingdom to other countries.

(e) **Criminal investigation.** Action taken by the Home Secretary for the security of the State, and respecting passports.

(f) **Legal proceedings.** Commencement or conduct of civil or criminal proceedings before the courts of the Navy, Army or Air Force tribunals (Military Tribunals).

(g) **Prerogative of mercy.** Action taken by the Home Secretary respecting the prerogative of mercy.

(h) **Contracts and commercial transactions.** Action taken in contracts, etc., made in the United Kingdom or elsewhere by a Government department or authority to which the act applies. In this category, however, the following are **within the jurisdiction of** the Commissioner:

   (i) Transactions for or relating to the acquistion of land compulsorily or in circumstances in which it could be acquired compulsorily.

   (ii) The disposal of surplus land acquired compulsorily or in such circumstances as described at (i) above.

(i) **Personnel matters re armed forces, crown servants.** Action taken in respect of appointments, removals, pay, discipline, superannuation or other personnel matters in relation to (a) Armed Forces and their auxiliary forces; (b) civil servants.

(j) **Honours.** The grant of honours, awards or privileges within the gift of the Crown, including the grant of Royal Charters.

Time limit for complaints

The broad rule is that a complaint must be sent to an MP within one year of the time when the aggrieved party had notice of the matters alleged in the complaint. Where special circumstances apply the Commissioner may extend the period.

A complaint shall not be entertained unless the aggrieved person is resident in the United Kingdom or the complaint relates to action taken in relation to him while he was present in the United Kingdom.

Procedure in respect of investigations

The main points to be observed in regard to procedure are the following:

(a) **Audi alteram partem** ('Hear the other side'). The Commissioner will hear views expressed by the Government department against whom complaint is made.

(b) **Privacy.** Proceedings may be conducted in private. The Commissioner has a discretion to order otherwise.

(c) **Legal representation.** The Commissioner decides whether any person may be represented by a lawyer.

(d) **Information.** The Commissioner may obtain information from such persons, in such manner and may make such inquiries as he thinks fit.

(e) **Expenses.** The Commissioner may pay reasonable expenses to persons who attend or furnish information for investigation, and may make compensation for loss of time.

(f) **Evidence.** The Commissioner may require any Minister, officer or member of the department or authority concerned, or any person who is able to furnish information or produce documents relevant to the investigation to furnish any such information or produce such document.

(g) **Attendance of witnesses.** Witnesses may be compelled to attend and/or to produce documents. The Commissioner has virtually the same powers as a court of law in this respect.

(h) **Secrecy of Claim of Privilege.** In effect this means that witness (e.g. a member of a Government department) may not claim that his information is secret. Nor may such person claim 'privilege' and refuse to disclose information. The broad rule here is that the same procedure applies as that followed in a court of law.

(i) **Cabinet proceedings.** Information concerning Cabinet matters are secret and may not be disclosed.

(j) **Obstruction and contempt.** Obstruction of the Commissioner or a member of his staff in the execution of their duties amounts to contempt. Where the Commissioner certifies that an offence has been committed the matter is referred to a court of law which will deal with the matter.

Reports

The first duty is to notify the MP who forwarded the complaint whether the Commissioner has decided to investigate the complaint or not. Many complaints are received which do not warrant any action at all. If the Commissioner conducts an inquiry he notifies the result to the MP sending the complaint; where he makes no inquiry the Commissioner states his reasons for not proceedings.

Annual Report. The Commissioner shall annually lay before the House of Commons a general report on the performance of his functions under the Act.

Special Reports. The Commissioner may lay a special report before the House of Commons where the Commissioner believes that an injustice has not been, or will not be, remedied.

The reports are specially protected from action for defamation, and they are protected by the rule of absolute privilege.

Special provision is made in regard to the disclosure by a Minister of documents which would be prejudicial to the safety of the State or contrary to the public interest. In these cases the Commissioner is not authorised to communicate to any person the contents of the document or the information referred to.

The Health Service Commissioners

The *National Health Service (Reorganisation) Act, 1973,* established the posts of Health Service Commissioners for (1) England, (2) Wales and (3) Scotland. All three offices are at the moment held by the Parliamentary Commissioner for Administration. The duty of the Health Service Commissioners is to investigate maladministration in the National Health Service (see page 122).

The address of the office of the Parliamentary Commissioner and Health Service Commissioners is:

Church House,
Great Smith Street,
London, SW1P 3BW

The Local Commissioners for Administration

Two Commissions for Local Administration – one for England and one for Wales – were established under the *Local Government Act, 1974.* In addition to all principal local authorities, the authorities covered by these officials include: regional water authorities, Joint boards of local authorities (including the National Parks) and police authorities (other than the Home Office where the Home Secretary has responsibility for the London Metropolitan police).

There are three persons appointed to investigate complaints in England, and one responsible for Wales.

The address of the English Local Commissioner is:

> The Local Commissioner for Administration in England,
> 21 Queen Anne's Gate,
> London, SW1H 9BU

The address of the Welsh Local Commissioner is:

> The Local Commissioner for Administration in Wales,
> Portland House,
> 22 Newport Road,
> Cardiff, CF21 DB

The address of the Local Commissioner for Administration in Scotland is:

> 125 Princes Street,
> Edinburgh

Form of complaint

We will deal with a complaint of maladministration against a local authority. Let us say that the district council surveyor has come one morning and directed his men to cut off part of your lawn to widen the road and ensure better traffic conditions. Local authorities do not usually make such mistakes, but it is possible for the servants or agents of the local authority, i.e. the contractors, to be given the wrong house number and yours happens to be the one affected.

Let us assume that you have taken advice, approached your local councillor (as required by the *Local Government Act, 1974*), but have received no compensation for damage done or any letter of apology for the inefficiency. You therefore decide to approach the Local Commissioner (Ombudsman for the local authorities).

The following details are extracted from a booklet *Your Local Ombudsman*, published for the information of any person wishing to pursue this form of remedy for an alleged injustice.

Details required by the Local Commissioner

1 Your name and address.
2 Name of authority complained against.
3 Details of your complaint of injustice, stating the action which you consider to be maladministration.

4   An account of the way in which you have previously brought your complaint to the attention of the authority.

5   Particulars of any evidence which you wish to submit in support of your complaint.

6   Date on which action complained of took place.

7   Date on which you first heard of the action complained of.

8   Name (or title) of any individual employee, officer or member of the authority about whom you wish to complain (see notes (c) and (d) below).

9   Your reasons for complaining about any individual at 8 above (see note (d) below).

10   I want a member of the authority to refer my complaint to the Local Commissioner.

> Signed (by aggrieved person)
>
> Date

Notes:

(a)   Any letters which you have from the authority concerned or other relevant documents should be referred to here and should be sent to the Commissioner with this form: he will return them to you.

(b)   If the date on which you make your complaint is more than 12 months after the date on which you first heard of the action you should explain, on a separate sheet, why you have not complained earlier. The Commissioner may not consider your complaint unless he is satisfied with the reason for this delay.

(c)   If you give the name (or title) of any individual the Commissioner must inform him and give him the opportunity to comment on your complaint.

(d)   As to 8 and 9 above the booklet states: 'Do not complete these sections unless you want to.'

The Local Commissioner will not investigate any complaint until it has been brought to the attention of the authority complained against, either by the person aggrieved (or his personal representative) or by a member of the authority on behalf of that person, and until the authority has had a reasonable time in which to reply to the complaint.

A complaint intended for reference to a Local Commissioner should be made **in writing** to a member of the authority (i.e. a councillor) complained against with a request that it should be sent to the Local Commissioner. It should state the action which it is alleged constitutes maladministration. If the member does not refer the complaint to the Local Commissioner, the person aggrieved may ask the Commissioner to accept his complaint direct. Note that under the 1974 Act, complaints could not be addressed to the Local Commissioner directly. Under the *Local Government Act, 1988* this is now permitted, though one should still contact the council department in the first instance and it is probably advisable to contact a local councillor.

Complaints must normally be made to a member within **12 months** of the day when the matters complained of came to the notice of the aggrieved person. If there are special circumstances the Local Commissioner may waive this rule.

How the investigation is conducted by the Local Commissioner

The complaint will be examined to decide whether it is within the Commissioner's scope. He will not deal with (a) the commencement or conduct of civil or criminal proceedings before any court of law; (b) the investigation or prevention of crime, including all action taken by police forces or officers (for which there is a separate complaints machinery); (c) personnel matters including appointments, dismissals, pay, superannuation and discipline; (d) certain education matters, including giving of instruction and the internal organisation of schools and colleges.

If the complaint is outside the Commissioner's scope, a letter of explanation will be sent to the complainant and to the member who referred the complaint.

If a complaint is received directly from a member of the public, or if further information about the complaint is needed, the matter will be taken up in correspondence. Before beginning to investigate a complaint, the Commissioner will tell the complainant and the member that he has accepted it for investigation. He will also notify the authority and any person named in the complaint as having taken or authorised the action complained of, giving them an opportunity to comment on any allegations contained in the complaint.

If at any stage in the investigation the Local Commissioner decides that the action complained of also concerns a Government department or part of the NHS (e.g. a hospital), he will consult the Parliamentary Commissioner or the Health Service Commissioner as the case may be. If he thinks it is advisable that the complainant should ask for an investigation by either of those other Commissioners he may inform him of the steps necessary to do so.

When the investigation is completed a report giving the Local Commissioner's findings will be sent to the complainant, the member, the authority or authorities concerned and any person complained against. A report will not normally give the name or other identifying details of the complainant or of any person involved in the matter.

Reports. An authority which has been investigated must make the Local Commisioner's report freely available to the public and press for at least three weeks and publicly announce when and where copies of the report may be seen. Where a report finds that injustice has been caused to the complainant by maladministration, the authority must consider the report and inform the Local Commissioner what action it proposes to take. In certain circumstances a further report may be made.

Privacy. The Act requires that all investigations shall be conducted in private. There are limitations on the information which a Local Commissioner may divulge.

Evidence. A Local Commissioner has power to examine an authority's internal papers and to take written and oral evidence from anyone who in his view can provide relevant information.

It may prove necessary during the course of an investigation to obtain further information from the complainant or from other people. For this purpose the Commissioner's officers may visit the person concerned or ask him or her to attend for interview, if it is felt that this would be more useful than seeking information by letter.

Expenses. If a Local Commissoner requires someone concerned in an investigation to incur expenses (for example, by asking him to attend for interview), he may reimburse the expenses and pay compensation for loss of time within certain prescribed limits.

It is for the Local Commissioner to decide whether anyone involved in an investigation may be represented by counsel or solicitor or otherwise. This will not usually be necessary and investigations will be kept as informal as possible. If the Commissioner does decide that formal legal representation is called for, he may consider a payment towards legal costs.

The procedure for complaints of maladministration can therefore be summarised as follows:

For Complaints about	*Go to*
Central Government Ministries	Parliamentary Commissioner for Administration (page 429)
NHS	Health Service Commissioner (page 432)
Local authorities	Local Commissioner (page 432)

Summary of practical points

The above represents the official information and shows the procedure adopted in regard to complaints of injustice. We may now summarise certain points which should be borne in mind:

1 Discuss the matter first with an informed friend, local MP, a local councillor or a solicitor, if need be.
2 *Get the facts first*, i.e. persons you have seen, the time and date of the incident complained of, and the steps you have taken to remedy the matter. Avoid opinions, hearsay, rumour and irrelevant matter.
3 If there are witnesses, obtain their names and addresses.
4 Any official communications you make should be put in evidence. So keep copies of letters received and sent. Hence, type or photocopy whenever possible, and be firm and reasonable in your statements and, at the same time, be clear and courteous.
5 If you attend an official tribunal or inquiry, remember the aim is to make it as informal as possible, somewhat different from a court of law. State the facts in chronological order from what you know. Avoid exaggeration and, however incensed you may feel, keep cool and relate the facts and evidence in a calm and reasonable manner. If you are asked questions, reply courteously. You will create a better impression by so doing, and the Local Commissioner (or any other person at an inquiry) will be more impressed by what you have to say.
6 Be prepared for a public authority to try to justify its action or inaction. That also applies to a person about whom a complaint may be made. Senior officers will be tempted to protect their staff and they owe a certain loyalty to subordinates. Moreover, most local authority servants (and civil servants) know the system, are continually handling files and complaints and will usually be more experienced in contests of this kind than the average person. However, if you, the complainant, have the correct facts, no amount of shifting and covering up can hide the truth. And even if you imagine that your opponents are more educated or skilled, the inquiry is concerned only with establishing what happened (i.e. the facts), what the authority did or did not do about the matter and whether the local authority officers acted in accordance with accepted practice and with sensitivity to a member of the public or the public generally.
7 Be respectful to the person who is to decide the question at issue. It is not an easy task to decide whether maladministration has occurred. Of course he or she must hear both sides of the case, establish the evidence, and then decide fairly, whether there is or is not fault. The chairman is appointed because of special experience in public affairs and an ability to form fair and reasonable judgements. Any such person deserves respect, and you will enhance your case if you observe the normal courtesies of civilised behaviour.

Forming a pressure group

It may well be that you have approached your local Councillor and MP and you have sent your petition to the Local Commissioner. You may have achieved no success. What then do you do now? One way is to form a pressure group of persons who have suffered in the same way as yourself. It may be a group of parents who want to complain about lack of travel facilities for their children or who want a pedestrian crossing in their area. One complainant will be unlikely to move the authorities, but where there is a group of people who are affected it is quite sensible to petition in writing, or *en bloc* at the office of the chief education officer or the chief executive of a local authority, or the chairman of the committee responsible for the particular matter agitating the minds of the protesters. A note to the press or the BBC or IBA will usually focus public attention on the grievance or protest. A note to the police will also help if you propose to hold a procession. Providing the complaint is reasonable and the petition, in whatever form, is presented in reasonable terms one can be assured of public support.

Once public opinion is aroused it is surprising how readily local councillors or those holding power will respond.

Legal complaints

If you have a legal cause of action against a Government Ministry, a local authority, the NHS or any other public body, or any servant or agent of any of the above, here are some suggestions which you may note.

Take some simple examples: *A* is run down on the highway by a vehicle owned by the local authority and driven by an employee. *A* suffers injury and damage. *B* is operated on by a surgeon negligently at a hospital. *C* is assaulted by a nurse in a ward of a mental hospital. Many incidents arise as a reading of any newspaper will show, and many rise to potential legal action.

1   **Facts first.** Get the facts first, i.e. what actually happened. In other words, obtain the evidence. Half the problems of courts of law is to establish the facts. They may be denied by the other side, of course, so that it is imperative that reliable evidence be obtained if at all possible.

2   **Civil or criminal matter.** If it is a criminal matter the police should be informed. If it is a civil matter it is up to you to pursue your remedies, so see a solicitor as soon as possible. He needs to know the facts first before he himself decides whether you have a cause of action or not. So act quickly whether you inform the

police or a solicitor. The reason for this is obvious: the police cannot act in your interest if you delay because the offender may well have absconded. If you delay informing your solicitor in a civil claim you will be deemed to have acquiesced in the matter and it will make things difficult for yourself in terms of proof. Your witnesses, if any, will have forgotten the incident so their testimony will be weaker, and you may have to explain why you delayed in making your claim. If you wait too long the law may offer you no remedy at all.

3 **Preserve evidence.** Preserve any written evidence, photographs or articles which show in some measure what actually happened. 'This is a copy of a letter I wrote,' or 'This is the bottle he hit me with.' Statements like these in court compel attention. The letter and bottle are exhibits.

4 **Legal aid.** If you are unemployed or receiving benefits you may make use of legal aid (see page 445). If you have a modest income you may in any case be assisted so that you do not have to pay the whole cost of proceedings. So explore what help you may obtain here. A 'means test' is applied. The making of a legal claim is a technical matter, and proper procedures must be followed. The solicitor will advise you on the evidence he needs and how he proposed to obtain it, e.g. medical reports, statements, affidavits (sworn statements). Moreover, when a solicitor writes to your opponent a letter from him carries weight, so the local authority or person will be warned that legal action is, or may be, contemplated.

5 **Know your opponent.** The defendants, e.g. the local authority or other body, will make their own inquiries, obtain their own evidence, to establish whether there is or is not a legal defence which they may successfully offer to combat the allegation which you, the complainant or plaintiff, put forward. The two sides prepare files, and the issue to be determined is narrowed down.

6 **Settling out of Court.** If the claim is admitted, your opponents may well settle out of court. That can happen right up to the day when the hearing is due to take place. As to that you should take the advice of your solicitor, or counsel (barrister) should the case be one for trial at a High Court. Suppose no settlement is reached. The case is set down for trial, and you will have to give evidence in support of your case.

7 **Giving evidence.** It is wise, therefore, to go over your evidence to ensure that what you allege is true. So make sure of that. In court state the facts in clear and plain language, avoiding exaggerated statements and, above all, untrue matters. It is impossible to administer justice if untruths are told. Most witnesses are nervous in court, and judges are sympathetic to those under stress. If you are cross-examined by an opposing counsel or solicitor answer the

questions asked – again clearly and politely. No amount of tough cross-examination will avail if what you say is true. Often the more you are cross-examined the more you strengthen your case, if you speak to what you know and act with reason and calm. The outcome of a case in court may go one way or the other: it is impossible to predict. So often what looks like a 'cast-iron' case falls to the ground because some fact was not elicited in the first place or some fact was suppressed by you or the other side.

8   **Appeal.** If the judgement is clearly against the evidence or wrong in law your counsel may advise an appeal. Legal aid is also available for appeals (see page 445).

Conclusion

This chapter on the making of complaints has been included as a guide for those with a genuine cause or grievance which ought to be pursued speedily and at once. It is designed to be helpful to those who want some information on the approach, and not to encourage the making of frivolous complaints which can only serve to harass or embarrass those who are responsible for administering public or social services. Moreover, when allegations are made which are untrue or deliberately false only mischief and harm will be done. Where you make a complaint concerning an individual which turns out to be defamatory there is always the risk that the person so defamed will himself sue you; and if you commit perjury in a court of law by making a false statement which is material to the proceedings the court can, of course, award its own punishment for the offence (*Perjury Act, 1911*).

Use the *proper channels* open to you: through an MP, a councillor or other person, such as a solicitor. Each of these, experienced in public affairs, will be able to judge for himself whether your statement should be pursued and the matter investigated.

You can expect little help if you are raising trifling matters or mischief from which little good can come. On the other hand, if you are reasonable in your allegation and are trustworthy and credible you can – and should – expect the help of those who have it in their power to ensure that injustice or maladministration is remedied. That, indeed, is what democracy is about, for here the individual does count, whereas in a totalitarian regime a somewhat different fate awaits those who raise openly matters which those holding the reins of government want to hide.

Questions

1 Compare and contrast the roles of the Parliamentary Commissioner for Administration, the Health Service Commissioner and the Local Government Commissioners.
2 What is a pressure group? How does it operate to achieve its objective?
3 Should local authorities give grant-aid to welfare rights and other community organisations which may criticise or campaign against certain policies of local authorities?

17
Information, advice and legal aid

Citizens Advice Bureaux

Citizens Advice Bureaux (CAB) were established as voluntary bodies in 1939 on the initiative of the National Council of Social Service (NCSS):

1 To make available to the individual accurate information and skilled advice on many of the personal problems that arise in daily life;
2 To explain legislation;
3 To help the citizen to benefit from and to use wisely the services provided for him by the State; and
4 In general to provide counsel to men and women in the many difficulties which beset them in an increasingly complex world.

The Government made use of CABs during the war to disseminate information, interpret new legislation and war-time regulations. The CABs were staffed by volunteers, men and women, who wanted to help others in difficulties. So useful were these Bureaux that they were continued after the war, and under the *Local Government Act, 1948*, s. 134, local authorities were empowered to make a grant to ensure their continuance.

The points 1 to 4 above apply today and their need is greater now as life becomes more and more complex and more and more legislation is passed to regulate affairs.

Administration

The National Association of Citizens Advice Bureaux, 110 Drury Lane, London WC2B 5SW, coordinates the CABs nationally and supplies information about social services, legislation, etc. The very informative Citizens' Advice Notes Service (CANS) are distributed by the NCSS.

In 1966 there were 473 bureaux; by 1988, this number had increased to 1,210, operating throughout the UK. Most of them are in the cities and towns where there is most need. During 1988 CABs dealt with 7.5 million inquiries (1.2 million in 1966). We may say, therefore, that one in 16 of the total UK population over the age of 14 made use of a Bureau (see Table 16). The cost of handling each inquiry is about £3. This figure includes the cost of the central support services (NCSS and CANS) and the running costs of the local bureaux. CABs received an annual Government grant of £9 million, for 1987–8.

Staff

The work force comprises some 10,000 trained volunteers who have worked over the years in a spontaneous response to local needs. Bureaux have expanded, improved and extended their general advice and information-giving service, and are continually providing specialist sessions at Bureaux engaging the help of experts in legal, financial, welfare rights, consumer and housing advice.

The inquiry statistics are a barometer of the needs and changes in society. In recent years there have been large increases in social security inquiries and those concerning employment, both of which directly reflect the growing scale of unemployment. There has also been an increase in inquiries concerning taxes and duties which reinforces the overall picture of a marked growth in monetary problems, which may themselves be further reflected in the substantial proportion of family and personal problems shown. Inquiries about the administration of justice reflect a new public awareness of the availability of legal aid, and the increase in laws to protect the consumer are revealed in the figures.

Table 16 Inquiries received at CABs in the UK

	1975–76		1984–85
	(000s)	*(% of total)*	*(% of total)*
Family and personal	546	20	12
Housing, property and land	517	19	15
Consumer, trade and business	463	17	17
Administration of justice	214	8	8
Employment	195	7	11
Social security	167	6	15
Health	113	4	4
Travel, transport and holidays	167	6	5
Other (including education, taxes, immigration)	313	12	15
	2,695 =	100	100 = 5.8 million

Specialist services

The Annual Reports of the CAB refer to 'specialist services' where lawyers, accountants and other specialists attend and give advice. 'New areas of need have been identified and taken up, but the specialist services are still legal and consumer advice, now developed in every city and the majority of towns throughout the country.'

The number of Bureaux with solicitors' rota schemes has increased to about 160 with the legal profession's recognition that liaison with CAB provides the opportunity to reach a broad section of the community. The solicitors give advice in the Bureaux free of charge and, with waiver arrangements from the Law Society, can, if requested, take cases back to their practice when they cannot be resolved 'in bureau'.

Some five Bureaux (Birmingham, Nottingham and the London Boroughs of Lewisham, Kensington and Waltham Forest) now employ full-time solicitors, known as resource solicitors. In all more than 300 Bureaux can offer legal advice from a solicitor on the Bureaux' premises.

Some 34 Bureaux have now started running financial advice sessions, often giving advice to men and women facing bankruptcy or redundancy and perhaps in the dole queue for the first time in their lives. These sessions have been set up through local initiatives with the cooperation of local associations of chartered accountants whose members offer their services to Bureaux' clients in ways similar to those developed with solicitors. Such guidance and advice is clearly necessary in view of the mass of published official information (amounting to 2,000 million forms or leaflets each year; over 100 different ones for social security alone).

One or two Bureaux have building advice sessions attended on a rota basis by local surveyors, and several others run housing and welfare rights sessions. Some Bureaux are increasing their welfare rights expertise and providing assistance to appellants at appeals tribunals, providing an invaluable service to many since legal aid is not available here (see page 445). This area of their work will be extended through the experience of a tribunal representation project, based in Wolverhampton, which was set up in 1977 under the auspices of the EEC's Anti-Poverty programme.

Apart from CABs, there are developing throughout the country **voluntary agencies** giving advice on specialist matters. These include Housing Advice Centres, Law Centres, Welfare Rights' Centres, Money Advice Centres and Education Advice Centres (often grant-aided by local authorities, some of which provide their own such services).

Conclusion

Altogether the CABs have proved most successful, but there are problems. The staff is composed of volunteers who save the State much money. In the London Borough of Camden alone, it has been estimated that the voluntary workers in the six Bureaux save ratepayers a bill of over £25,000. This is the extra cost of an equivalent fully paid service, calculated on the number of hours worked by the 64 trained volunteers, including those who speak languages of the immigrant populations, and by solicitors, accountants and surveyors who attended specialist sessions. As family, personal and the many other problems rise there is inevitably a growing demand on the service. Increasing and complex legislation (some 60 or so public Acts become law each year, plus over 1,500 Statutory Instruments) will make heavier demands on those who undertake this form of voluntary service.

Legal aid and advice

History

Free legal assistance to persons of limited means has existed in a few courts since the thirteenth century. Such schemes were run by unofficial voluntary organisations known as Poor Man's Lawyers. Apart from such schemes, the general situation before 1949 was that legal aid and advice were available only to those who had the money to pay for them.

The *Legal Aid and Advice Act, 1949*, revised existing schemes and expanded them into a service covering the full range of needs and providing (i) free, or assisted, representation for all who require it, and (ii) virtually free legal advice on matters unconnected with court proceedings (known as non-litigious matters), e.g. making a will. The term 'representation' means representing another in court, by a solicitor or barrister.

Since 1949 amendments have been made following experience in the working of the Act, and the present law is contained in the *Legal Aid Act, 1974* and the *Legal Aid Act, 1988*. It is now a comprehensive service covering (1) civil proceedings and (2) criminal proceedings.

(1) Legal aid in *civil* proceedings

Civil proceedings include those proceedings such as actions for debt, breaches of contract, torts and matrimonial and affiliation proceedings (commonly known as 'domestic proceedings' and which account for a large part – 67 per cent – of the cost of civil legal aid). Criminal proceedings before Magistrates' and Crown Courts are dealt with later.

How administered. The Legal Aid Scheme is run by the Legal Aid Board under the general guidance of the Lord Chancellor. There are 15 area committees and a network of local committees composed of barristers and solicitors (who may be paid a fee) with a salaried staff. The cost of operating the scheme is met by (i) contributions from assisted persons; (ii) costs recovered from opposite parties in litigation; (iii) grants from the Treasury.

Eligibility for legal aid in civil proceedings depends on an applicant's 'disposable income' and 'disposable capital'. The figures are adjusted by regulation to accord with rising prices.

(a) **Free** legal aid is available to those with a disposable income not exceeding £49 p.w. and whose disposable capital is £3,000 or less.
(b) **Contributory** legal aid is available to those with a disposable income which does not exceed £115 p.w. and whose disposable capital is less than £5,000 (1988 figures). The figures are adjusted by regulation from time to time to accord with rising prices.

Procedure. An applicant for legal aid should first approach any solicitor or solicitors' firm which takes part in the Legal Aid Scheme. The emblem is usually affixed to the outside of a solicitor's office or in the window.

Note that a 'means' test is applied, so an applicant will be required to complete a form showing details of his capital and income. The statement is assessed by the Department of Social Security (DOSS) in accordance with regulations, taking into account any maintenance expense of dependants, interests on loans, income tax, rent, etc., as well as the value of an applicant's house, furniture and household effects.

The form of application is sent to the local committee, who will examine it, and if the applicant has reasonable grounds for his claim he will be informed. The solicitor selected by the applicant may proceed with the legal matter for which aid or advice is sought. If necessary, the solicitor may instruct that the claim or petition be dealt with by a barrister who operates under the Legal Aid Scheme. Certain matters may be dealt with in a County Court and certain actions are triable in the High Court where the services of a barrister (counsel) will be required if representation is requested.

Small matters may need only one letter to be despatched, but other matters may be involved, demanding much work.

Legal advice and assistance (or Green Form Scheme), Under this scheme (introduced in 1972) a solicitor may perform work under the Legal Aid Scheme – e.g. giving advice, writing letters, helping with problems of hire purchase or a will, etc. up to a cost limit of £40 (£75 in divorce cases in England and Wales) without the need for prior approval by the local committee. The work does not extend to representation, i.e. the solicitor will not appear in court (except, since 1980, in domestic proceedings in Magistrates' Courts). His function here is to give **advice and assistance**.

There is a means test and legal advice and assistance is *free* only to those on low incomes; if your income exceeds £58 p.w. the applicant must pay a *contribution*, perhaps (where income is £122 or more) the full cost, up to £40. If the work exceeds this figure, it must be approved by the local committee. And where representation in court is required, an application must be made for legal aid.

Fixed fee interview. Although not strictly part of legal aid, this scheme (introduced in 1977) is operated by some 7,000 solicitors' offices undertaking legal aid. A solicitor will charge not more than £5 (inclusive of VAT) for an initial interview of up to half an hour. Again a 'means' test is applied; poor people will pay nothing but others pay according to their means. The client should make sure that the solicitor knows that he (the client) is asking for a 'fixed fee interview' when making an appointment. The major benefit of this scheme is to clients who do not qualify for the Green Form Scheme. Thus solicitors may in the short space of half an hour allay the fears or give practical advice to the applicant which may clear up the matter.

(2) Legal Aid in *criminal* proceedings

Anyone, child or adult, charged with a crime can apply for legal aid. Most adult criminal cases – theft, burglary and similar offences – are legally aided. Trivial offences – for example, simple drunkenness, riding a pedal cycle without a light or speeding offences – do not qualify. The court *must* make an order in cases where a person of limited means is committed for trial in a Magistrates' Court on a charge of murder, which will be heard in a Crown Court. The court will, however, not make an order in other cases unless it is satisfied that the person's means are such that he requires assistance in meeting the cost of the proceedings in question. If disposable income is under £50 p.w. no contributions are payable. Above that they are based on income e.g. £55–£60 £2 is payable; £60–£64 £3 etc.

Application for legal aid should be made to the appropriate court where proceedings are to take place. The applicant has to give the court a written statement of his means. Where there is any doubt about whether legal aid should be granted, the decision must be in the applicant's favour.

As a general rule, legal aid in criminal cases includes representation by solicitor and counsel in Crown Court cases, while in proceedings before a Magistrates' Court representation will be by a solicitor alone unless the offence is serious. Even where the person concerned pleads 'Guilty' legal aid may be granted if the court needs to know more about the case and it is reasonable in the circumstances.

Legal aid may also be granted in connection with appeal proceedings: for example, on appeal to the Court of Appeal (Criminal Division) and, if need be, to the House of Lords. These cases are rare. In 1984 the Government extended legal aid to prisoners facing serious disciplinary charges (e.g. riot, assault, attempted escape) before boards of prison visitors.

The Home Office has overall responsibility for criminal legal aid, but in practice it is up to each court to consider applications and make the awards. It is generally accepted that legal aid should be available *as of right* to a defendant who may be in danger of losing his liberty.

Table 17 Legal aid and legal advice and assistance: by type of case (England and Wales)

	1976– 77	1981– 82	1985– 86
Civil legal aid: certificates issued (thousands)			
Matrimonial proceedings – issued to men	32	30	37
issued to women	123	82	87
Other cases	56	65	108
Total	211	177	232
Criminal legal aid: applications granted Total, all criminal proceedings and appeals (thousands)	362	451	571
Legal advice and assistance *Type of case (percentages)*			
Matrimonial and family	56	50	41
Criminal	15	23	26
Other	29	27	33
Solicitors' claim paid (thousands)	292	649	1,039

Source: Social Trends, 1988

Information about legal aid for criminal cases is available at courts, police stations and CABs.

Criticisms. Criticisms have been made that there is insufficient control of the legal aid scheme (especially for criminal cases). In the five years up to 1984 the **cost** doubled, to £300 million; in 1988 it had risen to £500 million, and the Lord Chancellor has described the scheme as 'cascading out of control.' Unless tight control is maintained now there will be public reaction against paying the increasing costs, and Parliament may be forced to consider putting a limit to the detriment of all. There are gross **inequalities** in the way in which Magistrates' Courts grant legal aid (e.g. a 28 times greater likelihood of refusal as between Slough and Reading existed in 1982). The Lord Chancellor has conceded that the discrepancies in granting legal aid were 'a very real problem' and he is considering the possibility of allowing the right of appeal against refusal of legal aid.

Generally we may say that there is greater public awareness of the availability of legal aid. But there is still a large **unmet need** due to failure to recognise that a solicitor can help; the problem is not within the scope of a particular solicitor's practice; legal aid is not available or the legal aid financial limits are too low. With inflation, there is always the problem of adjusting income limits: thus in 1950 an estimated 80 per cent of the population was eligible for help but by 1987 the figure was only 50 per cent. The limits have been revised but the problem remains. Under the *Legal Aid Act, 1982* more people will be expected to contribute to costs. Thus of the 451,000 who received criminal legal aid in 1981, 32,000 made some contribution; subsequently this doubled to 67,000 (equal to 15 per cent).

The Scheme is also criticised for being restricted to the poor: since the wealthy can afford to take action through the courts, it remains the middle-income groups who are deterred from taking legal action because of the costs involved. Clearly any extension here would raise costs. And, on the other hand, it is also alleged that clients on legal aid get an **inferior standard** of service (partly because much legal aid work is unprofitable to solicitors and may be loss making).

Claimants who are represented are more likely to be successful (Lord Chancellor's Department 1989) yet legal aid is not generally available for representation in **administrative tribunals**, e.g. claims for industrial injuries benefit or pensions appeal tribunals (though advice on how to proceed is). The exceptions are the Lands and Employment Appeals tribunals. However, trade unions often step in to assist their members in presenting claims and may represent the claimant at a tribunal. Other voluntary organisations may do the same, e.g. MIND or the Child Poverty Action Group. Administrative tribunals tend to increase, and they are found particularly in all the areas of social services – education, housing, NHS, employment, social security. The more a government legislates to control or transform society the more frequently we find that there are clashes between the individual and the central or local government or its agencies.

In 1974 the Lord Chancellor suggested tackling the problem by extending legal services (particularly law centres) by encouraging the development by the legal profession of expertise in fields of welfare law and by increasing the public's knowledge of the legal services available to them. In fact both the Law Society and the Bar Council are alive to the challenge and have *ad hoc* committees dealing with welfare rights and legal aid.

Since 1987, stricter control has been exercised over legal aid fees for lawyers. But it is alleged that one consequence is a lower standard of work and many solicitors have decided to opt out of the scheme, and there are long delays in dealing with applications.

Law centres

These are local centres, with solicitors, which will handle cases from beginning to end, including representation in court or at a tribunal, if need be. There are 54 such centres (with some 200,000 clients in 1984) located in the larger towns. The first began in 1971. They are financed by central and local authorities (some under the Urban Aid Programme – see page 302) and are joined in a Federation of Law Centres.

Legal advice centres

These are basically for giving legal advice, as the name suggests. If an applicant needs further help he will be advised where to go – e.g. to another solicitor locally – and whether he may have the advantage of free or contributory help under the Legal Aid Scheme. There are about 50 legal advice centres outside London, and about 40 in London (addresses obtainable at CAB).

Many of these centres – and indeed many other social services – are threatened by 'rate-capping', whereby the central government places an upper limit on certain local authorities' rates (i.e. local property taxes). Since the *Rates Act, 1984* approximately 15–20 councils a year have been so 'capped'. The same system is applicable, if necessary, under the **community charge** (or poll tax) which replaces domestic rates in Scotland (1989) and England and Wales (1990).

Other organisations

Trade unions and other representative organisations of employees or employers have schemes to assist members who are sued or prosecuted or who wish to pursue claims, particularly in matters arising out of employment, such as redundancy payments, industrial injuries and so on. These organisations protect the interests of the member and usually build up an expertise and knowledge in the particular field, e.g. in making pension claims.

Motoring organisations like the AA and RAC also provide legal aid to members. Leaflets provide the extent of the services available to the membership, e.g. legal advice and representation in cases of road traffic offences or civil claims arising out of road collisions.

Questions

1   What services are available to obtain information and advice on the social services? Evaluate the importance of Citizens Advice Bureaux.
2   Visit your local Citizens Advice Bureau, obtain a copy of its annual report and compare the statistics of inquiries received locally and nationally. How do you account for the differences in the kinds of inquiries made locally and those made nationally?
3   Give an account of the system of legal aid and advice available in this country. What improvements might be made to the arrangements?

18
The Welfare State: success or failure?

The aim of this concluding chapter is to make an assessment of the impact of State social provision. What are the aims and the achievements of the social services? And who benefits from their provision?

The aims of the social services

Individual social services will have their own particular objectives – to improve health, to reduce poverty, to increase the quality and quantity of housing, etc. But what do the social services seek collectively? What does society, through the State, expect of its social policy?

It is not always easy to discover this since 'the State' and 'society' are collections of indivduals, groups and institutions, and there is no one voice speaking for them. Equally 'social policy' is an amalgam of the various social services, together with other State actions (such as taxation and monetary policy or subsidies for transport, sport and the arts) which may have an impact on society's welfare.

We can get some idea of the aims of social policy from the speeches, debates or memoirs of politicians or officials; by reading government statements in White Papers and government reports together with the reports of Royal Commissions and other influential committees (e.g. Beveridge); by examining the declarations of political parties and pressure groups; or from the writings and historians and social scientists, and the commentaries of the media.

All this requires time, effort and patience. But it is necessary because social policy is not always (perhaps is seldom) explicit and rational in its aims. Policies may be based on blind faith rather than sound information. Parties may adopt policies in hasty reaction to their opponents' moves or out of sentimental attachment to out-dated ideology or principles. Policies may be adopted because they have (short-term) popular (electoral) appeal (e.g. in response to media coverage of a dramatic social or family incident). Consequently some policies are inconsistent, even contradictory or have awkward and unintended effects (e.g. planning blight, the poverty trap, dependency – sometimes known as 'dysfunction').

So, social policy is not necessarily logical or rational in its aims. But is it possible to detect or infer any general objectives underlying the varied form of State social provision?

The answer is yes: we can say that **the general aim of social policy is to improve the condition of the least fortunate in society i.e. it gives social protection.** Such people are fairly obvious – the poor, handicapped, homeless, etc. But anyone can be faced at some time by overwhelming problems (sickness, unemployment, bereavement) and consequently State provision is made widely available rather than confined to particular groups.

Perspectives on the Welfare State

We may now go beyond the first question posed above and ask *why* does the State seek to improve the lot of the unfortunate? Again the answer is not clear or simple. Here we shall examine three different views:

1 The first view, which we call **Liberal–Conservative**, is based broadly on social conscience since it aims to compensate and 'pick up the pieces' left by modern industrial society (unstable families, broken communities, etc.) by providing help in the form of a safety net. Such help is seen as residual or secondary to that provided by others – the family, voluntary organisations, self-help, the market or commercial provision; it only becomes necessary (and valid) when these other agencies have failed to make adequate provision. The aim is to especially help the weakest, by selectively concentrating resources on them alone; thus there is a general preference that those who can afford it should provide for themselves, leaving State provision for the rest. It is also intended that State provision is financed as far as possible from growth in the economy (which automatically and 'painlessly' raises tax revenues) and does not interfere with pay differentials and incentives as high tax rates might (e.g. the average taxpayer contributes £40 p.w. to social security outpayments). Talent is a scarce resource and not to be wasted: consequently equality of opportunity is recognised but not equality as such.

2 The second view, which we call **Labour-Socialist**, sees the social services as an integral part of the modern State – not just 'playing second fiddle' or filling the gaps left by other providers of welfare. Thus the State has as much right to make provision as anyone else. Indeed, if problems are created in and by society, then it is

not enough for society to provide assistance or first aid: rather, society itself should be changed. The underlying aim here is equality through the reform of society and the redistribution of resources from the better-off to the less-well off.

These first two views are theoretical perspectives; each is a summary or brief statement of what are really two clusters of views (like an average of a varied collection). Furthermore in practice the differences between them tend to be eroded or diminished in the course of implementing or operating the social services. Thus in practice Labour (Socialist) governments (in power 1945–51, 1964–70, 1974–9) have not been as radically reformist of society as their principles, ideals or spokesmen would suggest. Equally, Tory (Conservative) governments (in power 1951–64, 1970–74, 1979–) have not (perhaps until recently) sought to dismantle the NHS, State education or social security: indeed owing to unemployment and the growth in the elderly population, social security, training and employment (DE) schemes are being expanded. In fact, the post-war period had been characterised as the years of 'consensus government', and the more committed (or 'extremist') of each party has criticised their party leadership for being too moderate, for compromising and pursuing policies not dissimilar to their opponents'.

3 The third view, the **Marxist view**, holds that true social welfare cannot really be achieved in a capitalist society. This view despises the Welfare State as a capitalist device or ploy to weaken or distract the working class (or 'proletariat') from their real plight or condition. State social provision fools the workers into thinking that they are truly better off, that they have a real place in society, that they can be satisfied with their life and status. By thus removing old class tensions, the social services divert or 'buy off' the workers from what Karl Marx (1818–83) saw as their historic role: to lead the revolution and inaugurate the communist society. Indeed, in some ways it is held that the social services help sustain capitalism by providing well educated and healthy workers (e.g. the NHS has been called a 'repair service for capitalism'). Thus despite its cost in taxation and insurance contributions, State social provision is really a bargain to the capitalists because it allows the fundamental inequalities of wealth and of social and economic power to continue. The Welfare State is thus seen as an instrument of **social control**.

If the Welfare State is in fact a device to sap the insurrectionary spirit of the working class, it seems to be highly successful: there is little evidence of a workers' revolution in modern Britain. Indeed, in the 1960s there was much talk of the 'embourgeoisement' – that is, of the workers becoming affluent and turning middle class. The British

Communist Party has only some 20,000 members and only collects about the same number of votes in general elections. We cannot be sure how many people belong to other 'hard' Left political groups (Militant, Socialist Workers Party, etc.) but they are relatively few and are probably matched by the support given to movements on the political Right (the National Front, British Movement, etc.). At the same time there is evidence of widespread satisfaction with life in Britain and with the social services generally: some 80 per cent believe Britain is a reasonably good place to live in and that they get fair treatment from government administration (*New Society*, 29 November, 1979).

So, perhaps the Marxists are right: that State social provision in a capitalist society neutralises the workers' discontents and their quest for radical change through revolution. Equally, though, their torpor may be due to other factors, such as genuine satisfaction with better levels of pay or greater political power (e.g. through trade unions). Or, thirdly, it may be simply that Marx was wrong and that the workers are just not a revolutionary class.

Social services and equality

It is widely believed and frequently stated (both officially and elsewhere) that an important aim of social policy is to increase equality in society. Furthermore, it would seem that a combination of progressive tax (which is tougher on the rich) and freely provided social services must automatically transfer resources and re-distribute incomes and wealth in favour of the less-well-off. In the remainder of this final chapter we shall examine to what extent this has occurred.

It seems fairly obvious that the Welfare State has reduced inequalities in Britain since the Second World War (1939–45) if not since the First World War (1914–18). In 1948 the NHS made health services freely available (i.e. without charges or insurance conditions) and brought great relief to millions of ordinary people who were previously denied medical services because of the fees. Similarly, secondary education became universally free and grants widened the 'ladder of opportunity' to further and higher education. In the field of housing, the pre-war years (the 1930s) saw the building of millions of low-cost houses (private and public sector) and the war was followed by years of frozen (controlled) private rents and substantial local authority housing subsidies. And in the field of social security, funds are transferred to the low income receivers, e.g. those on low- or nil-earnings such as the sick, unemployed, retired or widowed.

Thus it has been calculated (in S. Pollard and D. Crossley, *The Wealth of Britain*, 1968) that redistribution in the first half of this century was as follows:

1913 the working class paid	20% *more* in taxes than received in social benefits
1925 the working class paid	15% *less* in taxes than received in social benefits
1937 the working class paid	£386m *less* in taxes than received in social benefits
1949 the working class paid	£1,260m *less* in taxes than received in social benefits

A comparison of taxes and welfare benefits for the year 1950–51 by Professor A. Peacock showed 'a very marked vertical redistribution' to the lower income groups (*Income Redistribution and Social Policy*, 1954). And in the same year Seebohm Rowntree (see pages 35 and 80) conducted his third social survey of York; it showed that poverty among the working class had fallen to 3 per cent (compared to 31 per cent in his survey of 1936). He also estimated that *without* the Welfare State services, the figure for working-class poverty in 1950 would have been over 22 per cent.

This immediate post-war period enjoyed the new experience of full employment and it was followed by a rising trend in the employment of married women, i.e. doubling family incomes (which was reflected in increased working-class expenditure on consumer goods, which suggested 'embourgeoisement' – see page 454). Consequently incomes tended to become more equal both before and (especially) after tax – see Table 18.

When account is taken of the distribution of welfare benefits, the equalisation effect is much more evident. Table 19 shows clearly that the lower income groups receive vastly more in benefits (money and services) than they pay in taxes or national insurance contributions, with the lowest 10 per cent of households gaining some £3,840. Conversely, the upper income groups substantially lose on balance, with the highest 20 per cent handing over £7,000 in the year 1985. (See Table 19 page 458.)

Consequently, it is not surprising that current government (monetarist) policy has been condemned as 'an attack on the working class'; for it is based on the principle of cutting public (State) spending, and this has resulted in the closure of residential homes and hospital

Table 18   Percentage distribution of total incomes

Share of total income received by:	1938	1949	1957	1970
top 1 per cent (pre-tax)	17.0	11.2	8.2	8.0
top 10 per cent (pre-tax)	40.0	33.2	28.1	28.2
top 1 per cent (after tax)	12.0	6.4	5.0	5.1
top 10 per cent (after tax)	34.0	27.1	24.0	22.0

(*Source:* R. J. Nicholson, *The Distribution of Personal Incomes*, Lloyds Bank Review, January, 1967; *Economist* April 5, 1975; J. Pen, *Income Distribution*, 1971.)

wards, reductions in social work and home help services, a virtual cessation of council house building, cuts in school books and equipment, grants to students and places at universities, together with the abolition of earnings-related benefits and delays in the up-rating of benefit levels to match inflation, and above all, reductions in the level of entitlement to benefits (especially housing benefit following the *Social Security Act, 1986*).

However, there is evidence to suggest that it is not just the working class who may suffer from such reductions in provision: that to a large extent it is the middle class who gain much, if not most, from State social expenditure. We turn to this in the next section.

Inequality in the Welfare State

In the 1950s and 1960s – the 'age of affluence' – doubts were already being raised by some about the equalising effect of the social services. Books were written about the 'casualities of the Welfare State', as it was discovered that there were not just local 'pockets' but substantial layers of poverty. This poverty took the form not so much of absolute deprivation (subsistence) – though that was found to exist – but rather of large numbers (amounting to millions of people) living at a standard so low that it excluded them from many of the activities that were widely taken for granted in society (i.e. not just adequate clothing, diet or housing but being able to travel to visit friends and relatives, able to buy gifts or hold a children's party, able to afford membership of a trade union or to buy newspapers, etc.). In other words, it was a matter not of inequality as such (this is likely in any society) but of **substantial or serious inequalities**.

Recent figures for income and wealth distribution show considerable differences, even after tax. Table 22 shows that even after taxation, the top 10 per cent of income receivers have nearly eight-to-ten times the income of the lowest tenth of the population. This is partly due to inheritance of unearned income and to substantial difference in earnings which governments are reluctant to hit with heavy taxes for fear of its effects on work incentives and emigration (the 'brain drain'). But it is also due to the existence of substantial (legal) tax arrangements to avoid tax (e.g. before its abolition in 1974, death duty – an inheritance tax – could be avoided easily by distributing one's property to relatives well in advance of anticipated death in old age. Another device is to claim large business 'expenses'.) Some people are paid in a form which may not be so subject to tax, such as a company pension scheme, a company car, company shares, subsidised meals, loans, accommodation or clothing. In addition many people benefit from reduced taxation as a result of tax allowances, which they receive for paying into a private pension or

Table 19　Summary of the effects of taxes and benefits, 1985

	Quintile groups of households ranked by original income					Average over all households
	Bottom fifth	2nd fifth	3rd fifth	4th fifth	Top fifth	
Average per household (£ per year)						
Original income .. ：　.. ：　..	120	2,720	7,780	12,390	22,330	9,070
plus cash benefits ：　.. ：　..	3,260	2,570	1,200	790	670	1,700
Gross income ：　.. ：　..	3,380	5,300	8,980	13,170	23,000	10,770
less income tax and employees' NIC ：..	−10	360	1,460	2,560	5,300	1,930
Disposable income ：　.. ：　..	3,390	4,940	7,530	10,610	17,700	8,830
less indirect taxes ：　.. ：　..	790	1,420	2,050	2,640	3,840	2,150
Income after cash benefits and all taxes ：..	2,590	3,520	5,480	7,970	13,860	6,680
plus benefits in kind ：　.. ：　..	1,370	1,400	1,440	1,490	1,590	1,460
Final income ：　.. ：　..	3,960	4,920	6,920	9,460	15,450	8,140
Net gain(+) or loss(−) ：　.. ：　..	3,840	2,200	−860	−2,930	−6,880	

Source: Economic Trends, July 1988. HMSO (minor discrepancies probably due to rounding of figures).

Table 20 Distribution of original, disposable and final household income

	Quintile groups of households					
	Bottom fifth	Next fifth	Middle fifth	Next fifth	Top fifth	Total
Original Income						
1976	0.8	9.4	18.8	26.6	44.4	100
1981	0.6	8.1	18.0	26.9	46.4	100
1983	0.3	6.7	17.7	27.2	48.0	100
1985	0.3	6.0	17.2	27.3	49.2	100
Disposable Income						
1976	7.0	12.6	18.2	24.1	38.1	100
1981	6.7	12.1	17.7	24.1	39.4	100
1983	6.9	11.9	17.6	24.0	39.6	100
1985	6.5	11.3	17.3	24.3	40.6	100
Final Income						
1976	7.4	12.7	18.0	24.0	37.9	100
1981	7.1	12.4	17.9	24.0	38.6	100
1983	6.9	12.2	17.6	24.0	39.3	100
1985	6.7	11.8	17.4	24.0	40.2	100

Source: Economic Trends, November 1988, HMSO.

paying interest on housing mortgage. (Some people use the latter facility unofficially to spend on non-housing expenditures such as a holiday or car.)

Attention was drawn to these distortions by Professor Titmuss in his book *Income Distribution and Social Change*, 1962, where he concluded that, contrary to popular opinion 'there is more than a hint . . . that income inequality has been increasing since 1949 . . . while the ownership of wealth . . . has probably become still more unequal'.

As with the calculation of incomes, the information on wealth is fraught with problems (e.g. should we include peoples' State and private pension rights? Do we count household units or indivduals, including property-less children? Etc.). The Royal Commission on the Distribution of Income and Wealth gave the following data for the distribution of wealth (defined as 'marketable assets') for the year 1976:

Table 21 Percentage of the population owning wealth

Top 1 per cent of the population own 25 per cent wealth (cf 60 per cent in 1923)
Top 5 per cent of the population own 46 per cent wealth
Top 10 per cent of the population own 60 per cent wealth (cf 90 per cent in 1923)
Top 20 per cent of the population own 77 per cent wealth

Table 22   Percentage distribution of total incomes 1976–77

	Pre-tax	After tax	
Highest 10 per cent of income groups received	26.2	23.2	(25.6)
Highest 20 per cent of income groups received	42.4	39.2	
Highest 50 per cent of income groups received	75.9	73.1	
Lowest 10 per cent of income groups received	2.5	3.0	(2.4)
Lowest 20 per cent of income groups received	7.2	7.5	
Lowest 50 per cent of income groups received	24.1	26.9	

(*Source: An A to Z of Income and Wealth*, Royal Commission on the Distribution of Income and Wealth, HMSO, 1980) Figures in brackets refer to 1981.

This means that 80 per cent of the population own only 23 per cent of the nation's wealth, though if occupational and State pension rights are added, the figure rises to 45 per cent. And the recent increase in sale of council houses may have altered the pattern further towards equality. Indeed, the figures for 1986 show that the top 1, 5 and 10 per cent groups now own 20, 40 and 54 per cent respectively, so that there has been further equalisation up to that date. Nevertheless, the overall pattern of wealth ownership today remains very uneven (and greater than in the USA). Furthermore, income distribution has actually become more unequal (see Table 20).

Whose Welfare State?

Professor Abel-Smith asked the question: 'Whose Welfare State?' (in N.McKenzie, *Conviction*, 1958) and answered by saying: 'The middle class get the lion's share of the public social services, the elephant's share of occupational welfare privileges and in addition can claim generous allowances to reduce their tax liability.' He showed, for example, that it was the middle class who largely benefited from the post-war abolition of fees for health and secondary education, and that taxation (taken as a whole and including national insurance) was not only not progressive (i.e. hitting the rich) but was often regressive (i.e. hitting the poor). 'For the rich, Britain has become a fiscal paradise.' J. Bellini, *Listener*, 5 March 1984.

This latter tendency in **taxation** has been confirmed more recently by Frank Field (*Inequality in Britain*, 1981, and in *The Wealth Report* 2, 1983), who shows that in terms of direct taxes (e.g. income tax), national insurance and indirect taxes (e.g. VAT), the Welfare State is being paid for substantially and increasingly by the working people themselves. For example, whereas in 1949–50 the bottom 50 per cent of income groups contributed only 5 per cent of the income tax fund (of £1,101 million) in 1978–9 the figure was almost 20 per cent (of £20,400 million).

In relation to the **social services**, Professor Titmuss has argued that although free provision means universal access, 'equal opportunity of access by right of citizenship to education, medical care and social insurance is not the same thing as equality of outcome' since in practice 'the major beneficiaries of the high cost sectors of social welfare are the middle and upper income groups . . . In short, we can now say that the advent of "the Welfare State" in Britain . . . has not led to any significant redistribution of income and wealth in favour of the poorer classes.' ('Goals of Today's Welfare State', in *Towards Socialism*, 1965, and V. George and P. Wilding, *The Impact of Social Policy*, 1984.)

All of this appears to conflict with the data in Table 16. But unfortunately that data is incomplete (e.g. it does not include road expenditure) and there are problems involved in its accurate allocation of tax burdens and service benefits among groups in the population. On the other hand, recent specialist studies provide further evidence of substantial upper-income or middle-class gains from State social service provision:

Health. In 1980, the Black Report *Inequalities in Health* (DHSS) and the Health Education Authority's *The Health Divide* (1986) showed that the death rate for unskilled working men was almost double that for those in professional occupations. Such differences in specific death rates (e.g. from cancer, or bronchitis and infant mortality) have not changed since pre-NHS days. And in terms of illness ('morbidity') the Report indicates that in relation to their need for medical treatment, the working class make less use of the health services than do the middle class. The evidence of Julian Le Grand (*Strategy for Equality*, 1982) suggests that 'the top socio-economic groups receive 40 per cent more NHS expenditure per person reporting illness than the bottom one'.

Housing. Until recently council house subsidies have amounted to some £1,800 million p.a. This largely benefits the lower income groups (augmented by rent and rate rebates). But such sums are at least or more than matched by tax allowances to those buying houses with loans or mortgages – and the higher the income, the more valuable the tax relief (though there is a limit on the size of the actual mortgage eligible for such relief: see page 267). Overall, and taking account of 'expenditure' in the form of tax revenues lost through reliefs and allowances, Le Grand estimates that housing expenditure favours the better off twice as much as the less well off.

Housing subsidies in England and Wales had fallen to £1,090 million by 1986.

Education. Le Grand shows that up to school leaving age there is no obvious class differential in benefit from State expenditure. But beyond 16 and especially over 18, the high income groups gain most from such expenditure on education (with the possible exception of student grants). A Halsey (*Origins and Destinations*, 1980) shows that only a small proportion of the working class get to university or higher education (the highest cost sector of the education system). Little appears to have changed here in 50 years (see Robbins Report, page 250).

Transport. Again, Le Grand shows that the middle class gain most from State expenditure here, especially in regard to private transport (road provision and company car tax concessions) and rail subsidies.

Social security. It might be that expenditure on this service – by far the most costly (see page 420) – might compensate the working class for the apparent 'losses' in the other social services outlined above. And yet there is contrary evidence; for example, one study has concluded that 'for the average household with children . . . cash benefits (including indirect benefits such as housing and food subsidies) were small and substantially outweighed by taxes' (M. Nissel, *Taxes and Benefits*, Policy Studies Institute, 1978).

All this has been recently re-iterated and reinforced in B. Gooden *et al. Not Only the Poor* (1987).

Why unequal benefits?

Briefly it may be suggested that the middle class derive more than the working class from the Welfare State because:

(a)   they have better knowledge of the services available;
(b)   they have greater ability to pursue their social rights, (e.g. able to present their case, written or spoken, to officials, tribunals, etc.), i.e. they can 'handle' bureaucracy;
(c)   they encounter the same type of (professional) person as themselves providing the services (doctors, teachers, administrators, etc.);
(d)   they can 'afford' to make use of the social services (e.g. moving house near the better State school, extending full-time education beyond the school leaving age, taking time off work for medical attention, having telephones to make appointments and avoid long waiting times, etc.);
(e)   they have more 'positive' attitudes (e.g. to the value of good health and fitness, to education, etc.).

One study suggests that State welfare services are bound to favour the middle class because State provision depends for its *delivery* on the professions who can then use their position to bargain and modify the service to suit their own interests. Its author suggests that voluntary (non-statutory) provision would not be vulnerable to such pressures (see: D. Green, *The Welfare State: For Rich or for Poor?*, Institute of Economic Affairs (IEA), 1982).

What should be done?

The Welfare Stae is failing to achieve some of the major objectives* of its creaters and supporters in that (i) equality and re-distribution is not being achieved or is happening too slowly, or (ii) the needs of the poor and those in greatest need are not being met or are being fulfilled too slowly. In short the Welfare State is failing to meet need and prevent deprivation. Hence the recent spate of books which are highly critical of the operation and the achievements of the Welfare State, such as: *Housing, the Great British Failure; Social Security, Another British Failure; What's Wrong with Hospitals; On Our Conscience; Can Social Work Survive; Born to Fail; Trapped within Welfare; Social Welfare and the Failure of the State.*

All this has been most recently documented by the DHSS research study *Despite the Welfare State* (by M. Brown and N. Madge, 1982) in which Norman Fowler, the Secretary of State for the Social Services has written, '. . . deprivation and disadvantage . . . are a reality; and they persist despite changes in social policy which were intended to eliminate them and despite very broadly based improvements in the living standards of most people'.

A recent review of poverty schemes in the Common Market countries concluded that, 'The experience of the past 30 years demonstrates conclusively that economic growth does not, in itself, eliminate poverty and that the expanded social services have not had a major redistributive effect towards the poorest. Relative living standards and life chances, whether in health or education, do not appear to have narrowed. Indeed the reduced rate of economic growth since 1974 has added to the traditional poor a growing group of new poor deprived of the opportunity to participate in work. The burden of the economic crisis has fallen disproportionately on the young, the unskilled, immigrants and those with . . . handicaps . . . The gaps in the Welfare State are large and cavernous.

'Poverty . . . is not only multi-dimensional, it is also cumulative.

---

*This is not to suggest that the Welfare State may not have other aims which are being met, such as promoting economic efficiency, providing employment for welfare staff, providing a source of public spending and so economic management, providing a basic minimum or providing a form of social control.

Disadvantage is piled upon disadvantage. Each separately creates certain problems for the individual or family concerned. In combination, the effect may be serious and growing deprivation. Moreover, poor people, struggling to extricate themselves from the weight of these accumulated disadvantages, are least likely to be able to participate effectively in those organisations with the power and influence to improve social conditions or change the distribution of society's goods and services. Their interests are often the least regarded when they conflict with other more powerful groups'. (Commission of the EEC, 1982.)

In asking what can or should be done to alter this situation, there appear to be four broad options:

1   Reduce the scale of the Welfare State by concentrating help on those most in need (the 'selective' approach). This indeed appears to be the objective of the recent developments in the social security system (see page 56) and of rate-capping (see page 450). Additionally, or alternatively, the Welfare State could be dismantled by handing over responsibility to the **private** sector (see A. Seldon, *Wither the Welfare State*, IEA, 1981, and P. Minford, *State Expenditure: A Study in Waste*, IEA, 1984) or to the **voluntary** sector (see S. Hatch, *Outside the State*, 1980 and National Council Voluntary Organisations, *Beyond The Welfare State*, 1980; see R. Sugden, *Who Cares?* IEA, 1983) or to **individuals** themselves (see C. Murray, *Losing Ground*, 1984 and G. Wilder, *Wealth and Poverty*, 1981).

2   Continue with the Welfare State, but one which is reformed and improved – more committed, more responsive and more effective. We have observed a number of the deficiencies in particular services. One of the most crucial is social security; yet a 1983 report shows how far it is failing to cope with the increased demand arising from the growth in pensioner households (up 18 per cent 1971–81) and in one-parent families (up 70 per cent 1971–81, and comprising a third of households in some areas) – both developments helping to increase Supplementary Benefit claimants up to 50 per cent (1966–81, excluding the doubling of unemployed claimants 1981–82). Thus 'the original Beveridge scheme is being washed away, and more . . . poor people are having to go through the means test with all the stresses that implies for themselves and for those who run the system'. (*Pressure Points*, NCC.)

3   Reform the socio-economic structure of society. Since deprivation is rooted in society (see P. Townsend, *Poverty in the United Kingdom*, Penguin, 1979, and the Black Report, *Inequalities in the National Health Service*, DHSS, 1980) then it requires a radical and fundamental change in the social structure to eliminate it. This would require Parliament to will the means.

4 Mass insurrection and revolution. This would provide a non-peaceful route to the third option above. And indeed there has been some recent talk of 'extra-Parliamentary action'. Yet this seems unlikely as we have seen above (page 454). Besides most people seem content and unaware of the existence of deprivation (especially in so far as 'comfortable Britain' moves away from the estates and inner city areas) – or they actually blame many of the poor themselves for their plight (see below; also P. Golding, *Images of Welfare*, and *New Society* 1 April, 1982).

Even the unemployed 'are not growing angrier with the Thatcher government; they are merely relapsing into more television watching and much apathetic despair' (survey in *The Economist*, 4 December, 1982). Indeed the latter survey revealed that only 1 per cent of the unemployed put the chief blame for unemployment on the employers. So, as in the 1930s depression, there is not likely to be an anti-capitalist revolution (especially with the cushion given to some by substantial redundancy payments, amounting to a estimated £6,000 million in 1984).

Neither the second nor third options (above) seems likely in the foreseeable future, since as Professor Donnison (in *Housing Policy*, 1982) has said, 'for the first time since the war Britain has a government for which reducing unemployment, improving the living standards of families with children, getting people off means-tested benefits and helping the worst-housed to get decent homes are not urgent priorities'. The present Government came into office (in 1979) with plans to increase individual choice, freedom, independence and wealth creation. Its actions have progressed through three phases: (i) dealing with the economy by reducing State expenditure, taxes and inflation, (ii) dealing with trade unions and local government and (iii) dealing with social welfare – the current phase (though all three overlap and are continuing, as with the present *Employment Bill* which seeks to deregulate the employment of young people, just as in 1987 they were taken out of the wages councils' minimum wages conditions).

In general, the Government has sought to encourage the 'enterprise culture' to which end it has instituted a policy of reducing taxation, restructuring social security, redirecting education programmes and generally promoting a wholesale public orientation to enterprise. Equally, it has attacked the 'dependency culture' and the 'treacle-well' effect of the welfare state. 'Under the guise of compassion people's confidence and will to help themselves was undermined' (John Moore, Secretary of State for Social Security, 1987). Consequently, the role of the State is being reduced and/or altered to one of facilitating (or enabling) rather than directly providing, both at central and local government level (see T. Byrne, *Local Government in Britain*, Penguin, 1990). The concept and practice of 'Workfare' is beginning to appear (e.g. where the unemployed are required to work – even at low rates of pay – or undertake training as a condition of benefit payment). And people are being encouraged or urged to provide for themselves (through private pensions, home ownership or private health care) or for one another (through charity and self-help). Government ministers are promoting the ideal of 'active citizens' i.e. those who voluntarily contribute to the community through general participation and the donation of money, skill or time (such as JPs, blood donors, school governors, and members of voluntary organisations).

Yet it could be argued (a) that the Government has itself increased dependency by increasing the number of unemployed and those dependent on social security, (b) that the Government is only trans-fering dependency, from the State to private provision e.g. while the number of places in private residential homes has doubled 1981–8 (and the subsidy has increased five-fold to £500 million) places in local authority homes have fallen by 30 per cent, and (c) we are all dependent in some way or stage of our lives – on farmers for food, on businesses for employment, on families for care, on neighbours for status or place etc. There is no evidence of an overwhelming desire for dependence on the State for these things e.g. only 2 per cent of the elderly live in State residential care. Further, it may be asked whether State provision is such a bad thing. The religious writer for *The Times* has stated that 'the institutionalisation of welfare through the welfare state has dehumanised compassion itself'. Yet revelations about the abuse of children, the handicapped or the elderly within families or in private institutions may suggest otherwise. And dependency within families can cause stress. The alternatives are dependency on charity and voluntary organisations, which can be not only patronising but capricious and unreliable (and 'cheap'), or on money lenders and loan sharks.

In effect the Government has argued that the goal of welfare should be subservient to the goal of economic growth; that wealth is a pre-condition of welfare; that economic growth creates social growth, on the basis of the 'trickle-down effect'. Yet in practice the share of the poor has fallen in relation to that of the rich; the final incomes (net of taxes and benefits) of the bottom fifth has fallen by 9 per cent since 1979 while the share of the richest fifth has increased by 6 per cent (see Table 20). This is the result of the combination of tax cuts benefitting the higher paid and reductions in social security and housing expenditures. According to the Labour party's *File on Fairness* (1989) the poorest four million households are 6 per cent worse off since 1979 having lost an average of £2.30 a week through higher unemployment, price and VAT rises, benefit changes and low wages – which demonstrates that not all groups benefit from overall growth.

Recent policies have also exacerbated, if not recreated, the North-

South divide or the 'two nations' of Britain. Indeed, the whole quest for personal achievement, reward and meritocracy (or individualism) has been condemned as divisive and of creating resentment. Conversely, one particularly striking consequence has been the emergence of an underclass (estimated at 5–7 per cent of the population) comprising the long-term unemployed young, who are losing traditional links with the community because they feel that they have no stake in society and no commitment to its values of work, family, home etc. See also F. Field, *Losing Out* (Blackwell, 1989).

Current evidence points to another victory for the Conservative party in the next election (see *British Constitution Made Simple,* Heinemann, 1987). Meanwhile, Mrs Thatcher has declared that : 'There is no such thing as society, only families and individuals.' Consequently, the outlook for the Welfare State is not bright, and the first option above seems to be the most likely development for the immediate future and perhaps beyond.

Appendix 1
Poverty in Britain: a social measurement

In 1983 London Weekend TV commissioned the organisation MORI (Market Opinion and Research International) to undertake a survey of public opinion. A cross-section of the population were asked what they thought was meant by 'poverty'. They were asked their views on what constitutes an unacceptable low standard of living today by nominating (from a list including heating, diet, clothing, household goods, social activities) those items of everyday life which they thought were necessary and *which all people should be able to afford*, i.e. which no one should have to do without. The results showed that:

66% defined necessities as:

heating
an indoor toilet
a damp-free home
a bath (not shared)
enough money for public transport
a warm waterproof coat
three meals a day for children
self-contained accommodation
two pairs of all-weather shoes
no overcrowding, with enough bed-
  rooms for children
a refrigerator
toys for children
carpets
celebrations for special occasions such
  as Christmas
a roast joint or its equivalent once a
  week
a washing machine

50–65% defined necessities as also:

new, not second-hand, clothes
a hobby or leisure activity
two hot meals a day (for adults)
meat or fish every other day
presents for friends or family once a
  year
holiday away from home for one week
  a year
leisure equipment for children
a television

Thus we have a minimum standard of living as laid down by society. It provides what might be called a **social measure of poverty** today. It is not an official definition; it is not the theory of experts; it is not based on DOSS benefit scales. In short it is what we in Britain broadly regard as the basic minimum required to avoid poverty.

The extent of poverty

The survey investigated which items people did not possess because they could not afford them. The results, applied to the nation as a whole, showed:

(a) 3 million people cannot afford to heat the living areas of their homes;
(b) 6 million go without some essential item of clothing because of lack of money;
(c) 1½ million children go without toys or leisure and sports equipment;
(d) 3½ million people do not have household goods (e.g. carpets, fridge, washing machine);
(e) 5½ million regularly go without some essential food items, (e.g. failing to achieve even two hot meals a week);
(f) 3 million cannot afford celebrations at Christmas or presents for family once a year;
(g) ½ million children do not have three meals a day;
(h) 4 million live in damp housing.

This means that **overall 7½ million people in Britain are poor** in the sense of being unable to afford three or more items classed as essential; 5½ million cannot afford five items or more ('a level of deprivation that affects their whole way of life').

Attitudes to the poor

The survey asked for explanations of *why* people lived in poverty. The respondents (100 per cent) gave the following reasons:

Too much injustice	33 per cent
It is an inevitable part of modern progress	26 per cent
Laziness and lack of willpower	23 per cent
They were unlucky	13 per cent

In 1976, when the same questions were asked, 46 per cent said laziness and lack of will were the main reasons. Clearly people's attitudes have changed and show greater sympathy. This may be due to better understanding and knowledge – but equally it may be that so many more people are now on the margins of poverty or at risk themselves.

Finally it may be noted that 74 per cent of respondents thought that the gap between rich and poor is too wide; 57 per cent thought that the present Government was doing too little to help these poor; and 74 per cent said they were willing to pay an extra penny in the pound income tax to enable others to get the necessities, (it would raise about £1,000 million).

Appendix 2
How public spending is paid for

Table A Sources of state income, 1986–7, £ million

Income tax	39,000
National Insurance etc. contributions	26,000
Value added tax	21,000
Corporation tax	10,000
Local government rates	16,000
Road fuel, alcohol, tobacco duties	16,000
North Sea oil revenues	7,500
Interest, dividends	7,500
Borrowing (PSBR)	8,000
Other	13,000
	164,000

Source: Economic Progress Report, March 1986, HM Treasury (adjusted).

Table B The international tax league

	% Married 2 children	% Single person
Netherlands	33	42
Sweden	25	35
Germany	24	37
UK	20	32
Italy	19	24
Japan	17	22
USA	16	24
France	6	43

Source: Inland Revenue, October 1983.

Table B shows the proportion of income taken in income tax and National Insurance contributions from a person on average earnings in eight countries in 1982–3.

Appendix 3
Population projections, Great Britain 1985–2025 (000s)

Age	1985	2025	Change 1985–2025
0–4	3,475	3,671	+ 196
5–9	3,270	3,633	+ 363
10–14	3,752	3,494	− 258
15–19	4,396	3,415	− 981
20–24	4,612	3,559	− 1,053
25–29	3,989	3,846	− 143
30–34	3,671	3,918	+ 247
35–39	4,047	3,640	− 407
40–44	3,334	3,378	+ 44
45–49	3,092	3,140	+ 48
50–54	2,967	3,532	+ 565
55–59	3,006	4,016	+1,010
60–64	3,075	4,004	+ 929
65–69	2,481	3,210	+ 729
70–74	2,346	2,626	+ 280
75–79	1,787	2,389	+ 602
80–84	1,086	1,457	+ 371
85–89	478	818	+ 340
90+	193	513	+ 320
All ages	55,057	58,259	+3,202

Source: *Population Projections 1985–2025*, OPCS HMSO, 1987.

Appendix 4
Selected social and economic needs of population groups: by age

People aged:	Population index							Social and economic needs of different age groups of the population
	1971	1981	1986	1991	2001	2011	2025	
Under 1	120	97	100	109	101	95	101	Maternity services, health visiting, preventive medicine
1–4	127	94	100	108	110	98	105	Day care, nursery education
5–15	121	113	100	97	110	104	101	Compulsory education
16–19	85	105	100	84	80	92	78	Further and higher education, training, employment
15–44 (Females)	86	95	100	100	95	91	89	Maternity services
20–49	90	94	100	105	101	99	94	Employment, housing, transport
50–59/64	109	104	100	98	115	123	130	Pre-retirement training, early retirement
60/65–74	98	102	100	99	94	107	122	Retirement pensions
75–84	73	90	100	105	109	106	132	Retirement pension, health care, home helps, sheltered housing, retirement homes
85 or over	68	84	100	124	164	186	191	

Source: Social Trends, 1988.

Appendix 5
Local authority personal social services: current expenditure, England 1987

Services	£m
Personal social services: Total	644,455
Field work	
Social work – staff and related expenses	68,554
Administration	25,701
Residential care	
Community homes for children	83,834
Other children's accommodation	7,518
Accommodation for the elderly	173,041
Accommodation for the younger physically handicapped, blind and deaf	8,909
Accommodation for the mentally handicapped –	
(i) children	4,031
(ii) adults	12,205
Accommodation for the mentally ill	4,053
Temporary accommodation	5,032
Other accommodation	1,000
Administration – residential care	33,368
Support services	
Day care	
Day care centres for children	574
Intermediate treatment for children	559
Day nurseries	19,944
Pre-school playgroups	1,480
Child minding	–
Day centres and clubs for the elderly (other than meals)	5,233
Meals	3,835
Day centres, occupational centres and clubs – other	12,745
Adult training centres	22,692

Community care
Home helps	73,258
Laundry	229
Boarded out children in foster homes	11,176
Boarded out – others	64
Preventive and supportive services (families)	3,476
Meals in the home	8,438
Adaptations to homes	2,767
Aids	1,829
Telephones	2,468
Contributions to Wardens' salaries	1,539
Holidays	2,940
Other community care	6,568
Approved adoption allowances	–
Miscellaneous support services	3,307
Administration – support services	28,361
Training	–
Research and development	3,127

Note: Charges (in 1985) brought in over £300 m. of which:

£230m was from accommodation for the elderly
  22m from accommodation for mentally ill/handicapped
  20m from home helps
13½m from meals on wheels
  3m from adult training centres
2½m from day nurseries
  2m from day centres
  2m from holiday provision

Source: Health and Personal Social Services Statistics, 1987, HMSO.

Appendix 6
What is QALY?

The quality-adjusted life-year, or QALY, has been developed in order to include the factor of quality of life in health care assessment. The QALY is therefore a measure of outcome in which a patient's expected survival has been adjusted to allow for expected quality of life.

For example, in the case of a patient who is expected to live in perfect health for 10 more years following a heart transplant, the QALYs gained from that procedure are calculated by multiplying 10 years by a factor of 1.0, yielding 10.0 QALYs. The factor of 1.0 represents the difference between perfect health and expected death.

A patient who undergoes treatment for leukaemia may also live for 10 more years, but he may feel that because of limitations in his social life and general well-being, due to the illness and to frequent hospital treatments, his quality of life is only half as good as it would be if he were in perfect health.

The adjustment factor would therefore be 0.5, and the QALYs gained by providing this form of treatment would be 10 years × 0.5, i.e. 5.0 QALYs. Thus the QALY gain for the patient with leukaemia is only half that for the transplant patient.

If the third factor of cost is then considered, we can see that outcomes for procedures in totally different areas of health care can be compared.

For instance, if £100,000 is available to be used for either heart transplants or for treating leukaemia, and this sum would allow one patient to be given a heart transplant or five patients to receive chemotherapy for leukaemia, the cost per QALY can be simply calculated.

For the heart transplant (one patient), £100,000 will yield 10 QALYs, i.e. the cost/benefit is £10,000 per QALY. For leukaemia treatment (five patients), the same sum produces 25 QALYs (5 × 5), i.e. £4,000 per QALY.

On this basis the leukaemia programme would appear to be a better choice in terms of maximising the benefit to patients. For the same amount of resources – represented here in financial terms – the leukaemia programme would appear to generate two and a half times more 'benefit'.

Table of statutes

Index